ISBN 978-1-330-46511-0
PIBN 10052275

COLONIAL AND REVOLUTIONARY

HISTORY

OF

UPPER SOUTH CAROLINA,

EMBRACING FOR THE MOST PART THE PRIMITIVE AND COLONIAL HISTORY OF THE TERRITORY COMPRISING THE ORIGINAL COUNTY OF SPARTANBURG WITH A GENERAL REVIEW OF THE ENTIRE MILITARY OPERATIONS IN THE UPPER PORTION OF SOUTH CAROLINA AND PORTIONS OF NORTH CAROLINA.

BY

DR. J. B. O. LANDRUM.

1897:

SHANNON & CO., PRINTERS AND BINDERS,

Greenville, S. C.

E263
.S7L2
Copy 2

TO MY WIFE,

Caroline Millie Landrum,

THE DEVOTED COMPANION OF TWENTY-SEVEN YEARS,
AND THE DESCENDANT OF REVOLUTIONARY ANCESTRY
WHO ADVOCATED THE PRINCIPLES OF FREEDOM OF
SPEECH, LIBERTY OF CONSCIENCE,
AND RIGHT OF SELF-GOVERNMENT,
AND WHOSE HEROIC DEEDS IN BATTLING FOR AND MAINTAINING
THE SAME IN OUR COUNTRY'S GREATEST PERIL,
ARE IMMORTALIZED AND WILL BE
PERPETUATED BY GENERATIONS YET UNBORN,
THIS VOLUME IS
SACREDLY INSCBIBED BY THE
AUTHOR.

INDEX.

PREFACE

IN presenting this volume to the public, the author would state that, in the collection of material, it was his first intention to write merely a series of articles for the *Carolina Spartan*, devoted mainly to those important historical events which occurred within the limits of the original County of Spartanburg. But he soon found that, to give a proper chain of connection, more extensive lines would have to be drawn, and upon subsequent suggestions, he decided to present the articles in book form, based upon the proposition that a record of events and traditions would be more acceptable to the public in general and remain, for the future, in a better state of preservation.

As research continued and data gathering progressed, it became more and more evident that a comprehensive history of Spartanburg County, would necessarily include an extensive review of all of upper South Carolina and much of North Carolina, thus requiring more space than could be crowded into one volume, and a two-volume plan was therefore adopted; the first, devoted in general to the Colonial and Revolutionary History of the upper portion of South Carolina, but principally, to Spartanburg County, and the second, to a history of Spartanburg County proper, from its organization in 1785, to the present time.

This change necessitated a revision of the original manuscript, which has been done with as much pains as time, largely consumed by public duties, would permit.

Much of our most interesting past being now scattered in books long since gone out of publication, the author feels the force of suggestions made to him, that the time has come when that part deserving preservation and perpetuation should be made of convenient and lasting record. In no one work examined has he found a complete list of battles and skirmishes occurring in our immediate vicinity during the Revolutionary war. No record of this period tells of both the battles of Blackstock's and Musgroves, and yet they were fought within nine months of the same date, as well as within ten or twelve miles of the same point.

It is the author's purpose to present only such statements as he firmly believes to be wholly true, eliminating all matters of doubtful authenticity. The traditions herein published for the first time, have been gathered from trustworthy sources and can be relied upon as, in the main, correct.

Without copying surreptitiously from other books, the general lines of old history have been followed, along with quotations from authors long since silent, both of voice and type. The object, therefore, has been not only to bring together, but to renew chronicles of the past, reviving deserving names, characters and traditions that had once been the hearthstone talk of generations long since passed away.

Should his humble efforts meet with the approbation of those in quest of reliable and interesting historic reference, his purpose shall have been attained and his ambition for this volume and the one to follow realized. Especially, is the author hopeful of attracting, entertaining and enlightening the youth of the present day, who are seeking familiarity with the glory and achievement of that territory and time touched upon in these pages.

The author cannot find words to express his thanks to the Hon. John B. Cleveland, Capt. John H. Montgomery and Dr. Jesse F. Cleveland, all of Spartanburg, for their generous aid in advancing a sum sufficient to defray the expense of publication, thereby enabling him to place this volume before the public. Already high in esteem of their fellow countrymen, these gentlemen, not knowing selfish consideration, were actuated bv that higher magnaminity and patriotism which sought to place before the public a work that had convinced them of its real value.

The author also acknowledges his indebtedness to others for encouragement and kind assistance, and especially to Dr. James H. Carlisle, President of Wofford College, through whom he, at all times, had access to the Kennedy Library. Thanks are also due to the Honorables John Earle Bomar, Charles Petty, of Spartanburg, Hon. Thomas J. Moore, of Moore, the late Hon. O. P Earle, of Earlesviile, Prof. Wm. S. Morrison, of Clemson College, and Mr. Frank Morrell, Jr., of Wellford, for the loan of books and material and for information which proved valuable in the preparation of this volume.

The author would acknowledge the services of Mr. T. B. Thackston, Secretary of the Young Men's Business League, Spartanburg, and to Mr. Jesse Cleveland, for conducting a correspondence with various publishing houses and the solicitude manifested by them for the success of this enterprise. His thanks are also due to Rev. and Mrs. E. E. Bomar, of Aiken, S. C., for valuable services rendered in reading and correcting proofs, a task of no small magnitude.

In conclusion, the information gathered and herein recorded, has been handled under very trying circumstances. But while it has required much time, energy and patient investigation, it has, notwithstanding, been to him a labor of love, although performed for the most in the midst of a busy country practice of medicine for a quarter of a century, followed by four years of arduous service connected with the General Land Office of the United States, in the territory of Oklahoma.

During the latter period while separated from home, family and former associations, the additional disadvantage of being remote from public libraries presented itself. These inconveniences are mentioned by way of apology for the apparent shortcomings in the preparation of this volume. But whatever degree of favor it may meet with will encourage him in the preparation and completion of a second volume, to which he earnestly invites the aid and encouragement of a generous public.

Guthrie, O. T., June, 1897. J. B. O. L.

CHAPTER I

OUR COUNTRY AS IT WAS.—ITS NATURAL CHARACTERISTICS. ITS BEAUTY OF SCENERY.—ITS ABUNDANCE OF GAME, ETC.

IF we accept the testimony of able and truthful writers, we may readily conclude that the sun never shone upon a country more beautiful and attractive than this of ours as it appeared in primitive times. It was with enthusiasm that the ancient hunters spoke of it. James Adair, an old trader, in describing the Blue Ridge of Carolina, which at that time embraced the present States of North and South Carolina, said: "From the historical description of the Alps and a personal view of the Cherokee Mountains I conclude that the Alps are much inferior to several of those mountains in height and rockiness."

James Glen, one of the most intelligent of the early Governors of South Carolina, in an expedition to the Cherokee Nation in 1755 (of which an account will be given in a future chapter), wrote a description of the upper portion of Carolina, in which he says that it was the most delightful. as well as the most fertile, in the world, abounding in large and extensive plains and savannas, swarming with deer and buffalo. "I should," says the writer, "be afraid to indulge the liberty of copying lest I should be thought drawing a picture or printing a landscape"

In the "History of Upper Carolina," by that able and fluent writer, John H. Logan, we find the following words, which confirm the statements already expressed: "At this day (1855) the upper country of South Carolina presents a very different aspect from that of the same territory in the middle of the eighteenth century. It was then new and beautiful and as remarkable for the luxuriant richness of its landscape as it is still for the striking features of its rolling hills and its towering mountains, but under the iron tread of what is called a progressive civilization, its ancient glories of forest and flora and fertile soil have been well nigh washed and ruined."

It is said that the face of our country was a region of romance interspersed here and there with forests, prairies and great canebrakes, which lined not only the valleys and streams, but stretched over the evergreen surface of the country for miles, which Logan says "was not surpassed in picturesque beauty and grandeur by the best portions of Texas of the present day; and its virgin soil was not inferior to that of the same boasted State."

Up to the breaking out of the Revolutionary war, the woodlands in the upper portion of South Carolina were carpeted with grass, and the wild pea vine grew, it is said, as high as a horse's back, while flowers of every description were seen growing all around. The forests were imposing, the trees were large and stood so wide apart that a deer or buffalo could be seen at a long distance; the grasses and the pea vines occupied the place of the young, scrubby growth of the present day. The name *Fair-field* was given by Pearson, in his description of the primitive region of the county which now bears that name, and the name *Fair-forest* originated from an expression made by Lord Cornwallis, who, in his admiration of the forests and rivers, rolling hills and undulating plains, exclaimed: "Oh! what a *fair forest.*"

It is a fact well authenticated, that in the early history of the upper country there were numerous prairies covered only with the grasses and the pea vine, but which have since been covered with pine, oak, and other growth. These physical changes, which time has brought about spring an interesting question in science as to their causes.

The oldest and most interesting history of our country in early times is found in Carrol's "Historical Collections of South Carolina," beginning with data as early as 1680, and although these interesting pamphlets refer to the entire province of Carolina, not specially to our up-country, yet we beg the indulgence of the reader while we make some quotations, as they have a bearing upon what has already been stated.

The record shows that the writer entertained magnified ideas as to the extent of Carolina, which is apparent in the following words:

"Carolina is the Northermost part of the Spacious and Pleasant Province of Florida. It lies in the North Temperate Zone between the Latitude of Twenty-nine and Thirty-six Degrees. It is bounded on the East by the Atlantic or Northern Ocean, on the West by the Pacific or Southern Ocean, on the North with Virginia and on the South with the remaining part of Florida. It derives its name from our present Illustrious Monarch (King Charles II) under whose glorious auspices it was first Establish'd an English Colony One Thousand Six Hundred and Seventy * * * * This country hath Oak, Ash, Elm, Beach, and all sorts of useful timber that England hath not, as Cedar, Red and White Locust, Laurel &c. * * * The Sassafras is a Medicinal tree whose bark and leaves yield a pleasing smell; it profits in all Diseases of the Blood and Liver * * * the Black Walnut for its grain is most esteem'd. The Wild Walnut or Hiquery Tree gives the Indians by Boyling its Kernal, a wholesome Oyl, from whom the English supply themselves for their Kitchen uses * * * * * the Chincopin bears a nut, unlike the Hazel, the shell is softer, of the Kernal is made chocolate not inferior to that made of Cocoa * * * *. Vines of divers sorts bearing both Black and Gray Grapes, grow, climbing their highest trees, running and overspreading their lower Bushes * * *. Carolina will in a little time, prove a Magazine and Staple for Wines to the whole West Indies * * * * the woods are stored with Deer and Wild Turkeys of great Magnitude, weighing many times above fifty pounds apiece and of a more pleasant taste than in England, being in their proper climate * * * * Deer of which there are such infinite Herds, that the whole Country seems but one continned Park, insomuch that I have often heard Capt. Matthews, agent to Sir Peter Colleton for his affairs in Carolina (say) that one hunting Indian had yearly killed and brought to his Plantation more than one hundred and sometimes two hundred head of Deer. Bears there are in great numbers, of whose fat they make Oyl, which is of great Vertue and efficacy in causing the Hair to grow, which I have heard the Indians daily used, by which means they not only keep their Hair clear and preserved from Vermine, but by the nourishing faculty of the Oyl it usually extended in length, &c. * * * There are Beavers, Otters, Foxes, Raccoons, Possums, Musquasses, Hares, Coneys, Squirrels of five kinds, the Flying Squirrel whose delicate skin is comforting, if applied to a cold Stomack * * * *, for prey the Pelican Hawk and Eagle, for pleasure, the Mocking-bird * * the Humming bird * * They are a deep Green * sleep the whole Winter. At Barbadoes the Jews curiously skin these little Birds, filling them with Sand and perfuming their Feathers. They are sent into Europe as pretty Delicacies for Ladies who hang them at their Breasts or Girdles * * * There are in Carolina great numbers of Fire Flies who carry their Lanthorns in their Tails in dark nights enlightening it with their Golden Spangles * * * Birds for Food and pleasure of Game and the Swan, Goose, Duck, Mallard Widgeon, Teal, Curlew, Plover, Partridge, &c. * * * As the Earth and Air are enriched and replenished with the Blessings of the Most High, the Seas and Rivers of the same bounty equally participate in the Vanity of excellent and wholsome fish. Sturgeon, Mullet, Whale, Salmon, Trouts, Bass, Drum, Cat-fish whose head and glowing eyes resemble a cat * * * the tortoise * * * Green and Logger-head Turtle." *

We have quoted from this old volume to show that in the early discovery and settlement of Carolina, there was a uniformity over the entire region of country with regard to beauty of scenery, game, etc.

But returning to the description of Upper Carolina, Logan says (see Logan's History of Upper Carolina, page 22) that in the ancient territory of the Cherokees "deer were so numerous at this period in the upper country, that large herds of them were scarcely ever out of sight of the pioneer, even while standing in his own cabin door * * * * it was no uncommon thing to meet with deer, sixty or seventy head."

Anthony Park, who settled on lands now embraced in the county of Newberry, asserted that "a man could at that time stand in his door and kill more game than would be sufficient for the support of two families." John Duncan of the same region, relates the following: "Sitting one evening at dusk in his door with his foot against the frame, a bear slyly approached the house and threw him for a moment into a great fright, by springing suddenly over his leg into the cabin; recovering himself, he seized his gun and before the bold intruder could effect his escape, shot him dead upon the hearth."

The large numbers of deer and other animals in our country, which existed at its earliest settlement, can be better appreciated by reference to the Commercial Report of Charlestown for 1731 (see Carrol's Historical Collections of South Carolina, Vol. 11, page 129) in which it is shown that three hundred casks of deer skins, containing eight or nine hundred each, were exported; and further, by reference to the report of 1747, we find that two hundred pounds of beaver, and seven hundred and twenty hogsheads of deer hides were exported. Logan says that deer were so abundant in the woods around Old Ninety-six that the carcass of a buck brought no more than a half a dollar in the streets of Cambridge.

It will doubtless appear difficult for many of our readers to appreciate the fact that the buffalo, an animal destined 'ere long to become extinct on this Continent, roamed at one time in great herds in our country. Logan says: "At the earliest period of emigration into the upper country, an old pioneer from Virginia, often counted a hundred buffaloes grazing on a single acre of ground in the present territory of Abbeville and Edgefield." What was true with reference to that section would also naturally apply to the territory embraced in the counties of Union, Spartanburg and the entire up-country. Great numbers of buffalo were killed by the old hunters. They were hunted only for their skins and tongues, since deer, turkey and other game, which were so abundant, were far preferable for their flesh. Logan says that they were the first of all the original game of Carolina, except the timid elk, to disappear. Attacked on all sides in a wooded country by hunters, who were armed with the deadly rifle, they were quickly exterminated or driven away into the deeper wilds of the west. Long after their departure, their moss-covered bones and deep-worn trails, leading to favorite ranges and licks, were seen marking the country in every direction.

To confirm all that has been said in reference to the natural characteristics, game &c., of Upper

Carolina, the writer begs leave to close this chapter by presenting a quotation, from that eminent historian and patriot, Dr. David Ramsey. In "a general view of the up country (see Ramsey's History of S. C., appendix, page 305) the writer says:

"In the year 1750, when the settlement of the upper country began, there were so many buffalos, which have long since disappeared, that three or four men, with their dogs, could easily kill four or five a day. A common hunter could kill, in the autumnal season, as many bears as would make two or three thousand weight of bear bacon. The waters abounded with beavers, otters and muskrats. Twenty beavers have been caught in one season, by one man, on the waters of Fair-forest. The country was also overrun with wolves, panthers and wild-cats. There was a great facility of raising stock, from the profusion of native grasses and canes. When the whole country was within the grasp of a few settlers, the preference of one spot over another was generally decided by a comparative plenty of canes. Though provisions were easily raised, the labor of raising them for sale was but indifferently rewarded, for there was no market for any crop nearer than one hundred miles. The skins of wild beasts were the most profitable remittance to Charlestown; next to them was butter and tallow; afterwards, flour and hemp. In a few years indigo began to be an object of industry. Tobacco and other heavy articles would frequently do little more than bear the expense of bringing them to market. Since the year 1790, the general cultivation of cotton has matterially altered the state of the country."

CHAPTER II.

THE FIRST PEOPLE OF OUR COUNTRY.—THE CHEROKEE INDIAN.—HIS HABITS, CHARACTERISTICS, ETC.

IN the territorial distribution of the different tribes of Indians, the upper or north-western portion of South Carolina, belonged to the Cherokees. The early history of our up-country would be incomplete without giving them their proper place.

The earliest and most reliable record we have of their habits and cheracteristics is found in "Carrol's Historical Collections of South Carolina." In Volume II, page 80, we find the following paragraph, which we quote, in a chapter on the "Complete Discovery of the State of Carolina," written in 1682:

"The Natives of the Country are from time immemorial ab Origine Indians of a deep Chestnut color, their Hair black and straight, tied various ways, Sometimes oyled and painted, stuck through with Feathers for Ornament or Gallantry; their Eyes black and sparkling, little or no Hair on their chins, limb'd and feathered, painting their Faces with different Figures of a red Sanguine color, whether for beauty or to render themselves formidable to their enemies I could not learn. They are excellent Hunters, their Weapons, the Bow and Arrow, made of a Read, pointed with sharp stones, or Fish Bones; their cloathing, Skins of the Bear or Deer, the Skin drest after their Country Fashion."

From the description given of them by other writers, we find, that in stature, they were medium sized, and, to all appearances, strong and well made. Deformities in nature were few among them. Being of a brown color, their skin glistened, being generally varnished with bear's fat or paint. In ancient times, the men of this and other tribes of Indians, had little or no beard and no hair on their heads, except a round tuft on top. This defect was not natural, but the effect of art, which brought the hair out by the root. They generally went half naked in warm seasons. The huts in which they lived were foul, mean and offensive. Their manner of life was poor, unclean and disgustful. During their hunting season, the men were eager and indefatigable in pursuit of their game. When this was over, they would fall into a kind of brutal slumber, and a state of indolence and ease. In their hunting seasons they endured hunger long, and carried but little with them for subsistance, but when this was over, and they were in their days of plenty, they were as voracious as vultures. In domestic life, they had but few habits of industry. Says a writer in Carrol's collections: "Manufactures or Arts amongst them, I have heard of none, only little Baskets made of Painted Reeds, and Leather, Drest sometimes with black and red Chequers colored." Agriculture, they left to their women, being considered an employment entirely unworthy of men. Devoid of tender passions, they treated their women like slaves, or inferior beings. Scolding, insults, quarrels and complaints were seldom heard among them. They were open and merry at feasts and entertainments, but on solemn occasions they were thoughtful, serious and grave. Except in liquor, sudden anger was looked upon as ignominious and unbecoming. They seldom differed from their neighbors, or did them any harm or injury.

They had no riches and coveted none. While they had plenty of provisions, they allowed none to suffer through want. "If they were successful," says a writer, "in hunting, all their unfortunate and distressed friends shared with them in the common blessings of life."

It is said, that while in some particular things the separate tribes of indians differed from each other, yet in their general principles and mode of government, they were very similar. They had general rules with respect to other independent tribes around them, which they were careful to observe. The great questions of peace or war were canvassed in assemblies by deputies from all the different towns. When injuries were committed and Indians of one tribe happened to be killed by Indians of another, then such assemblies were called. If no person appeared on the side of the aggressors, the injured nation deputed one of their warriors to go to them and demand satisfaction. If this was refused, and they thought themselves too weak to go to war against the aggressive tribe, then a number of warriors, generally the friends of the deceased, would take the field for revenge, and looked upon it as a point of honor, never to leave the field until they had slain a number of the enemy corresponding to that of their slain kinsmen. Having done this, they would return to their homes, carrying their scalps with them, and, by some sign or token, would let the enemy know that they were satisfied. Scalp for scalp, blood for blood, death for death, was a fixed principle with the Indian.

It is said, that sometimes the nation to whom the aggressors belonged, would be disposed to peace, and would search for the murderers who were capitally punished, by general judgment of the nation, and even by near relatives, to prevent others from becoming involved in the quarrel. The criminal never knew of his condemnation until the moment the sentence was to be put into execution, which sometimes happened while he was in the war dance, or bragging to his friends of the verv exploit, for which he was condemned to die.

In the selection of chiefs, they had reference to personal wisdom and courage. The warrior who excelled in these qualifications was entrusted with leadership. Having this honor and distinction conferred upon him, he had to be very circumspect in his conduct and gentle in the exercise of his power.

The Indians, like all ignorant and rude nations, were very superstitious. Besides their chief, they had judges, conjurers and medicine men. They believed in a superior being, and in all hazardous undertakings, invoked the protection of good and evil spirits. Each tribe had their conjurers and magicians. They called them the *beloved men*, and placed great confidence in their prophetic declarations. They were fond of inquiring into future events, and laid great stress on omens and dreams. They looked upon fire as sacred, and at the time of the full moon they would observe feasts and ceremonies, claiming for them some religious origin. Their warlike enterprises to procure subsistence, were always preceded by certain observances and ceremonies. They offered in sacrifice the first deer or bear they killed. When taken sick, they were particularly prone to superstition. Their physicians or medicine men, administered their simple and secret cures, with a variety of strange ceremonies and magic arts, which gave the patients courage and confidence, and sometimes the treatment was attended with good results. Adair asserts that he never knew an Indian to die from the bite of the rattle-snake or of any other of the venomous reptiles which were numerous in this country in his day. When going into the woods or upon an expedition, every Indian provided himself with a pouch of the best snake root, such as the seneka (*Senega polygala*) or fern snake root.

It is not strange that Indians, in the early discovery and settlement of our country, should have been jealous of the encroachments of strangers upon a soil which had belonged to them from time immemorial. They were happy and contented. The country, as we said in a former chapter, abounded plentifully in game, and they had enough to subsist on. Civilization and agriculture were distasteful to their whole nature and circumstances. To win them over, therefore, and bring about links of friendship between the two races was the careful and patient study of the first pale-faced adventurers.

Says an able writer: "The first bond of union and friendship between Europeans and Americans was conveniency." By his own ingenuity, the Indian had constructed such rude instruments of wood and stone as to meet a few simple requirements. To him, therefore, a knife, hatchet, axe, hoe and tomahawk, to say nothing of guns and ammunition, which fell into his hands later, were priceless acquisitions to his ease and comfort. He admired the skill and facility with which the strangers met their wants and requirements, and being a lover of ease by nature, he would rather give the profits of a whole year's hunting, than to be deprived of these instruments of comfort. What was at first esteemed a convenience now became, as his wants increased, a necessity. His dependence upon the skill of the white man, soon wrought a strong cord of friendship between the two races. A channel of commerce was soon opened up and the Indian found that he was not only treated with friendship and civility, but that the white men were equally as fond of his skins, furs and land, as he was of their trinkets and various articles of necessity It was this that induced the Indians to admit the white people, to live among or near them and to allow them to clear and cultivate their lands. In this way, a better opportunity was offered to study their character, nature and disposition.

Of the peculiar history of the Cherokees, who were once numerous in all the upper portion of South Carolina, em bracing, says Logan, the present counties of Abbeville Anderson, Edgefield, Greenville, Pickens, Oconee, Newberry, Laurens, Union, Spartanburg, Fairfield, Chester, Lancaster, York and Richland, the reader is respectfully referred to that work, "Logan's History of Upper South Carolina," which presents so ably the scenes connected with this ancient territory of the Cherokees. In many respects they had noble traits of character. Being savage by nature and entirely ignorant of everything pertaining to a progressive civilization, they used to the full extent of their capabilities, the talents committed to their care. The sin of abusing them can never be placed at their feet. "He never," says Logan, "wantonly took the life even of the least useful of the animals of the forest. His lauded patrimony was given him from the hands of God, a magnificent country; still he yielded it up to a more vigorous race which supplanted him." As civilization widened, his territory became naturally more circumscribed, and of course his chances of subsistence on game, became proportionatelv less. In the future chapters of this work, we will endeavor to show the facts and circumstances which drove, step by step, this noble tribe of Indians to the regions of the Great West. During the Revolutionary war, the Cherokees sided with the English. In the conquest of 1776–'7, they ceded to South Carolina their lands east of the Unakaye Mountains, reserving to themselves the territory which now comprises, for the most part, the present county of Oconee. The last remnant of this tribe crossed over the mountains into Western North Carolina some years after the Revolutionary war, having sold their possessions to South Carolina. Before the Revolution in South Carolina, in 1719, Governor Johnson furnished to the Lords-Proprietors a report of the number of Cherokee inhabitants, which then amounted to more than eight and twenty thousand souls. Their numbers, as time rolled on, gradually diminished. A small remnant of this tribe still reside in Western North Carolina. They are peaceable and law abiding. They have churches and schools. The writer knows but little of the present condition of the Cherokee family in the west.

The principal towns and settlements of the Cherokees were in the north western part of our state, along the Savannah, Tugaloo, Seneca, Keowee and Flint rivers, but we have unmistakable evidence of their having had their abode, at one time, in Spartanburg and other counties. The traditions of the writer's own neighborhood bear testimony to the fact. Signs and traces of them are yet to be found at different places, particularly along the larger water courses where the swamps on either side afforded good hiding places and ample game. In our rambles here and there, we have found pieces of broken soap-stone vessels, stone axes, tomahawks of the hardest flint, war clubs, clay pipes, arrow heads, and other interesting and curious articles. Several years ago the writer presented a collection of these to the Museum of Wofford College, and later, another collection to the museum of Charleston College. Among the latter was an unbroken soap stone bowl, plowed up in the low grounds of North Pacolet (near Earlesville) bv Richard Ballenger, (*) a nephew of the writer.

Although much has been written of the cruelties, barbarities and treachery of the Cherokee and other tribes, yet it is unfair that the mind of the reader should be prejudiced against them. It is due to them to say, that on account of friendly alliances which men made with them at different times, they rendered much valuable assistance to the Governor of the colony of South Carolina, particularly during the time of the war between the English and French.

The writer has dwelt at length on their history and characteristics, in order to give to this noble tribe, the place they justly deserve to occupy.

Of the existence of a race of people in this and other states, in prehistoric times called the *Mound Builders*, there can be no doubt. Mounds are to-day seen in different sections of our country well formed and symmetrical, showing that they were constructed by artificial means. Logan, in his work, speaks of several of these in Abbeville, Laurens and other sections of our country, and of some in Spartanburg County. He speaks of an interesting one opposite the battlefield of Blackstocks, on lands which formerly belonged to Dr. Winsmith. He speaks of others in the romantic top of Gilkey's Knob, near Limestone Springs.

Several years ago, in a series of articles in one of our county papers, the writer called attention to a mound on the plantation of Mr. O. P. Earle, on North Pacolet, covering about one acre of land. It is situated near, and on the north side of the river, where the bottoms widen for a mile or more. Its top is not more than fifteen feet above the level of the lands surrounding, and while the latter is of the richest soil, the surface of this mound is of the poorest red clay, covered with a scrubby growth. Mr.

* Now deceased.

Henry M. Earle, now deceased informed the writer that he was written to some fifty vears ago concerning this, by a professor in the South Carolina College. There are others of a similar character, up and down the same stream, which may, in the future, prove an interesting study, and throw more light upon a dark and mysterious past.

Since this chapter was written the County of Cherokee has been formed out of portions of Spartanburg, Union, and York counties, and was named in honor of the Cherokee Indians, the first inhabitants of that region.

CHAPTER III.

CHANGE FROM PROPRIETARY TO ROYAL AUTHORITY. TREATY OF SIR ALEXANDER CUMMING WITH THE CHEROKEE INDIANS.—THE FORERUNNERS OF CIVILIZATION.—THE STOCKMEN.—COW-PENS MEN.—INDIAN TRADERS, ETC.

THE upper portion of the province of South Carolina, particularly the Northwestern, was territory that belonged to the Cherokee Indians until the treaty of Governor Glen in 1756.

During the year 1730, however, great political changes were brought about, among which was the overthrow of what was called the *Proprietary* government, under the administration of Governor Robert Johnson. Up to this time, the province was under the control and influence of Lords-Proprietors, who, under the authority of Great Britian. held titles to large tracts or territories of land called, at that time, *plantations.*

It would consume too much time to explain the grievauces of which the people complained, and the circumstances which terminated in a great political revolution and, which very soon, brought about a division of Carolina into two provinces—North and South Carolina. One of the chief causes of complaint, doubtless, resulted from the discordant elements of society. Those who were known as Dissenters had an aversion to everything connected with the Established Church of England, and particularly to the High Courts or Commission for the trial of ecclesiastical causes. That class known as the farmers or planters complained of the reduction of paper money circulating in the province. They stood, as many do now, indebted to the merchants. They claimed that the pro vincial currency was not only necessary to meet the exi gencies of the government, but was also useful and convenient in the payment private debts. Gold and silver were foreign coin and the different assemblies of the different colonies fixed their value by laws to suit their convenience. There were still other grievances complained of, such as having to submit to a heavy taxation to build forts and the maintenance of garrisons to occupy them. The seat of government (Charlestown) was remote from the people, the public credit was at a low ebb,—so low in fact, that no man of means would risk his money in the public treasury.

But a change having been happily brought about—a change from proprietary to royal authority (the government of the province being directly under the control of the Crown), a new order of things was introducd, Up to this time the up country of South Carolina was uninhabited by the white man. Being a part of the territory of the Cherokee Indians, no one had dared to infringe upon their possessions, and before this could be done, it was necessary to form a new treaty of alliance with these people. For this purpose, Sir Alexander Cumming was sent out in 1730, by Governor Moore (successor to Governor Johnson) to conclude a treaty with them. The Cherokees had, at that time, the reputation of being a warlike and formidable nation of savages. The main body of them occupied lands about the head waters of the Savannah River, (the Tugaloo and Seneca, while some of their towns were settled along the base of the mountains. They numbered in population more than twenty thousand, with six thousand warriors, ready at any time to take the field. The country which they claimed as their hunting ground, embraced at least, the upper half of the present territory of South Carolina.

Sir Alexander Cumming explored the Indian country some three hundred miles from Charlestown. He took with him as his guides some Indian traders, who were acquainted with the streams, woods, and trails, and an interpreter, who understood the Indian language, to assist him in his negotiations. He dispatched messengers beforehand to announce his coming. He met the chiefs in the town of Keowee, who received him with marked friendship and esteem. After the different ceremonies of the Indians were over, Sir Alexander made a speech to them, acquainting them with the fact, that he was clothed with authority from the Great King George, who loved them, and that he had come a great way to demand of Moy Toy (the Chief of the Cherokees), and all the Chieftians of the nation, to recognize the authority of the King and become his subjects. The Chiefs, falling upon their knees, promised fidelity and obedience, calling upon all that was terrible to fall upon them, should they, in any instance, violate a single promise made. Stipulated articles of agreement were drawn up in language as similar as possible to that of the Indians and signed by Alured Popple, Secretary to the Lords Commission of trade and plantations on one side, and by the marks of the six chiefs on the other. Every article, as it was signed, was accompanied with presents of different kinds, such as cloth, guns, shot, vermillion, flints, hatchets, knives, &c.

In one of the articles agreed upon, it was provided, that, with the consent of the whole nation of Cherokees, six chiefs were to be deputed by Moy Toy, their chief warrior, to accompany Sir Alexander Cumming to Great Britain, where they were to be presented to the great King George. The six who were clothed with this honor, upon their arrival in England, met with kind and generous treatment. By authority of Moy Toy, they placed at the feet of King George the crown of their nation, the scalps of their enemies and their feathers of glory. The crown referred to was brought from Tanessee, their chief town, and consisted of five eagles' tails and four scalps of their enemies. They returned home next year (1731) with Robert Johnson,* who was last Governor of South Carolina under proprietary rule, and who had been re-

*The remains of Governor Robert Johnson were interred in St. Philips Church Cemetery, Charleston, S. C.

invested by the King with the same office and authority as had been held by his predecessor Moore.

We have been particular in giving the details of this treaty of Sir Alexander Cumming with the Cherokees, because it was the first step looking to the introduction of the white man into the up country of South Carolina. It was simply a general treaty of friendship. (See original Articles of Treaty, Ramsey's History of S. C., page 57.) "A chain of friendship" so expressed, which "was now like the sun which shines both in Britain and also upon the great mountains where they live, and equally warms the hearts of Indians and Englishmen; that as there are no spots or blackness in the sun, so neither is there any rust or foulness in this chain." In this treaty no lands were ceded by the Cherokees and no boundaries whatever were expressed. The object was simply to establish peaceable and friendly relations, and to open up business and commercial intercourse, as is shown by the following clause in one of the articles:

> "The Great King and the Cherokees, being thus fastened together by a chain of friendship, he has ordered, and it is agreed; that his children in Carolina do trade with the Indians, and furnish them with all manner of goods they want and to make haste to build houses and to plant corn from Charlestown towards the towns of the Cherokees * * * ; that he desires that Indians and Euglish may live together as one family; that the Cherokees be always ready to fight against any nation, whether white man or Indian, who shall dare molest or hurt the English; that the nation of Cherokees, shall on their part, take care, to keep the trading path clear; that there shall be no blood on the path where the English tread * * * ; that the Cherokees shall not suffer their people to trade with white men of any other nation but the English."

This treaty was so strong that for many years, perhaps twenty or more, the Cherokees remained in a perfect state of friendship and peace with the white settlers and the traders, who followed their vocations without the least seeming dread, terror or molestation.

A new order of things, viz: a new government and new treaties, having been brought about, new life and

and energy was infused into the people of the province. Up to this time, the colonists who lived in the low country were said to have been an indolent set of people, with no apparent interest in agriculture, education or progressive civilization. The country appeared like a desert with little places cleared here and there, scarcely perceivable in the midst of a vast and almost unbroken forest. The houses were miserable and clumsy huts. Thev had no vehicles or wagons of any kind. Traveling was done either on horseback or in boats along the streams. Even Charlestown, at this time, did not possess more than five or six hundred houses, constructed mostly of wood. They were not comfortable and indicated wretchedness among the people.

But, as we have said, the time had come for the people to be inspired with new spirit and vitalitv. The produce of the province was doubled in a few years, and the exports of rice, deer skins, furs, naval stores, kept pace with the imports, and credit in England was secured. The march of civilization, however, was slow and cautious and did not, as we will presently show, reach the up country of South Carolina, much before the treaty of Governor Glen in 1755, an account of which we will give in another place.

In advance of the regular settlers of the up country of South Carolina were two classes of persons. The first were the stock or cowpens men, who were the owners of ranches, or as they were then called *cowpens*, where cattle were cared for. In a previous chapter we have shown that at that time the country was covered with canes, wild pea-vines, and grasses, and possessed natural advantages for raising stock.

These stock or cowpens men, generally went where there no settlements; central spots were selected in front of the settlements, where cattle could be rallied and domesticated, and were called, as we have said, *cowpens*. As they did not interfere with the hunting and sporting of the Indians, they seldom gave offense, though sometimes they were observed with jealousy as the precursors of approaching civilization.

The second class were the Indian merchants or traders. Indian trading posts were established at different points in the nation, where the traders would go and give in exchange for furs, skins, buck horns, &c., such articles as guns and ammunition, fanev trinkets, &c. On account of the genuineness of the peace which had been established by Sir Alexander Cumming with the Cherokees, these traders advanced without ceremony into the hearts of their settlements. Says Ramsey: "Speculative men have drawn comparisons between savage and civilized life, highly colored in favor of the former. Their theories have been acted upon ever since the discovery of America by individuals, who, turning upon civilized society, have voluntary chosen a residence among the Indians. Of this description, there were several who, at an early day, settled among the Indians at a great distance from the white people."

Anthony Park, who, it is said, was one of the first settlers of Newberry district, traveled several hundred miles through the Indian nation in 1758. Going west of the Alleghany mountains, he found several white men, chiefly Scotch or Irish, who said that they had lived among the Indians, as traders, for more than twenty years. He found a few who said that they had been among them forty and fifty years, and one, whose abode there had been for sixty years. One of these said he had at least seventy children and grand-children in the nation. It is possible, says a writer, that if these accounts are correct, the oldest of the traders must have taken up their abode among the Indians before the close of the seventeenth century, when civilization, in our state, had not extended more than twenty miles from the sea coast, which observation is corroborated by other records before us.

CHAPTER IV.

TREATY OF GOVERNOR GLEN WITH THE CHEROKEE INDIANS.—THE FIRST SETTLERS OF UPPER CAROLINA.

AS we have said in the preceding chapter, the march of civilization westward from Charlestown was slow and cautious, so much so indeed, that in 1736 it had only advanced from the sea coast about ninety miles. Later, between 1750 and 1760, other germs of settlements were planted two hundred miles from Charlestown by emigrants from Virginia, Pennsylvania and other colonies, which had advanced from north to south and in front of the eastern settlers. This left in the undisturbed possession of the aborigines, a considerable tract of country between what is understood to be the eastern and western settlements. This fact gave rise to the early distinction of *Upper* and *Lower* Carolina.

Among those who were classed as the early settlers of the Upper or Northwestern portion of South Carolina, was Colonel Elijah Clark, who, afterwards became noted as a revolutionary soldier and an officer of distinction, whose daring and noble deeds will receive further notice in this work. Ramsey records the fact that he settled on Pacolet. Being the first settler he might be truly styled, the "Daniel Boone" of the present progressive County of Spartanburg. In the course of six years, he was joined by eight or ten families from Pennsylvania, doubtless Scotch-Irish, who settled on the three forks (north, middle and south) of Tyger River. These constituted the whole white population in the territory of the present County of Spartanburg, prior to 1755. Settlements in other localities took place about the same time. The settlements on the Long Cane, in Abbeville County, were made by Patrick Calhoun and other families. Previous to the Revolution, Richard Paris, an English Indian trader, boldly advanced into what was then the Cherokee Indian Nation and settled at or near the present city of Greenville. Paris Mountain was named in honor of him. Tradition, which the writer has also investigated, shows that a settlement was made, of excellent material, in the present northeastern (dark corner) portion of Greenville County, near Hog-back Mountain, before the acquisition of that section by the treaty of Colonel Williamson in 1776.

These miniature settlements were not permitted very long to enjoy their peace and quietude, so much to be desired and so absolutely necessary to the prosperity of a new country. But a few years after the beginning of the first settlements westward, active hostilities commenced between the governments of Great Britain and France. We can only refer the reader to the pages of history to understand properly the differences which sprung up at this time between these two great countries. Suffice it to say here, that one of the principal causes of dispute, was as to the proper location of the boundary line between the possessions of each on the American Continent. In the midst of this dispute, acts of indignity were committed, perhaps on both sides, which only had a tendency to widen the breach between the two countries. One of these was the capture of William Henry Littleton by a French squadron. Littleton had been appointed by the British Government, Governor of South Carolina, and while on his way to this country, through the Bay of Biscay, was captured and taken to France, but was subsequently released after several months imprisonment, by order of the French Court. While negotiations were were pending for his release, and in retaliation for this outrage, the British Commanders were ordered to seize and bring into port, all French vessels they could find. This also tended to widen the breach between the two countries.

William Littleton, to whom we will again refer, and who figured so prominently in the affairs of South Carolina, was an Englishman by birth, and in his native country was known by the title of Lord Wescott.

All negotiations looking to a peaceable settlement between these two great powers being of no avail, war was publicly declared by Great Britain against the French on the 17th day of May, 1756. It ended in 1763.

Previous to the arrival of Governor Littleton, South Carolina had been governed from 1743 to 1756 by Governor James Glen, a gentleman of fine judgment and common sense, who, appreciating the importance of maintaining friendly relations with the Cherokee Indians during the approaching hostilities with France, met the Cherokee warriors, about five hundred in number, in their own country, from whom he purchased lands and with whom entered into a solemn treaty. The lands which were obtained by this treaty, form the present counties of Edgefield, Abbeville, Laurens, Newberry, Union, Spartanburg, York, Chester, Fairfield and Richland. The territory of Pendleton (which embraces the present counties of Anderson, Pickens and Oconee) and what is now Greenville County, was reserved by the Indians in this treaty, together with other territory in the States of Georgia and North Carolina. As already stated, the present line between the counties of Greenville and Spartanburg, was the boundary line between the province of South Carolina and the Cherokee Nation.

Governor Glen, on the occasion referred to, made a speech to the Cherokee warriors in the name of the Great King, representing his great power and goodness to them and reminded them of the happiness they had enjoyed

The spokesman of the warriors, Chuloch-Culla, by name, approached Governor Glen, and took a seat by him under a tree. Holding in one hand a bow, and a shaft of arrows in the other, he spoke as follows: "What I now speak the Great King should hear. We are brothers to the people of South Carolina, one house covers us all." Taking his boy by the hand, he presented him to the Governor and said further: "We, our wives, and children, are the children of the Great King George. I have brought this child that he may, when he grows up, remember our agreement on this day and tell it to the next generation that it may be known forever." Then opening a bag of earth and laying it at the Governor's feet, he said: "We freely surrender a part of our lands to the Great King. The French want our possessions, but we will defend them while our nation shall remain alive." Showing his bow and arrows he further said: "These are all the arms we can make for our defense. We hope the King will pity his children and send us guns and ammunition. We fear not the French, give us guns and we will go to war against the enemies of the Great King." Then delivering to the Governor a string of Wampum (a string of shells or beads representing the currency of the country) to confirm what he had said, he added, "My speech is at an end, it is the voice of the Cher okee Nation. I hope the Governor will send it to the King that it may be kept forever."

By this treaty the Cherokees relinquished what is one of the most attractive portions of South Carolina, a portion which now represents a part of the great Piedmont Belt, a country which, in a former chapter, has been described as having pure air and water, with lovely and attractive scenes, such as beautiful mountains, fertile valleys, extensive lowlands, beautiful streams, great water powers, and other attractions such as game, fish, and precious minerals yet unearthed. It was indeed, as it is now, a magnificent country, and we have only mentioned these facts to show that the Indians, in yielding it up, according tc the terms of treaty (or Congress as it was called, where deeds of conveyances were duly executed) conferred a princely and generous gift upon the *man white*, as he was called by them. A gift which, notwithstanding the many changes which have since taken place, should be remembered and appreciated by us, who first saw the light and now enjoy a happy peace and freedom in the country embraced in the terms of this great treaty, and which should also serve to perpetuate the memory of Governor Glen in the annals of South Carolina.

It is due to the memory of the Cherokee Indians to say, that notwithstanding they had been called savages and barbarians, on account of their many seeming uncalled for atrocities to the white settlers, yet, the spirit which prompted them to make this cession of lands to Governor Glen, was a noble and generous one, and no matter what transpired subsequently, this should always be placed to their honor and credit.

But to return to the settlement of the up country. The people coming in small colonies, formed *settlements* in in different localities in the hitherto unexplored forests. Each settlement generally took a name and the word *settlement* is in common usage today in the back country, as applied to neighborhoods.

According to Dr. Howe's "History of the Presbyterian Church of South Carolina," the settlements on the North and Middle Tyger did not take place earlier than 1755. This was the year of Governor Glen's treaty, and this statement is corroborated by Ramsey, who refers to the small colony as following Colonel Clark and settling in Spartanburg County, in 1755. (See Ramsey's History of S. C., page 118.) Among these settlers are found the present familiar family names of Moore, Barry, Jordan, Nesbitt, Vernon, Collins, Pedan, Nichols, Caldwell, Wakefield, Anderson, Snoddy, Miller and others. Of the early settlers in other localities in Spartanburg, Union and other counties, it is almost impossible now to ascertain. It is probable that when the tide of emigration was turned, that different sections were simultaneously occupied. Mills in his statistics says that "this section of the country was settled between 1750 and 1760, but from its exterior and exposed situation, it did not much increase in population until 1776. The first settlers were from Virginia, Pennsylvania and North Carolina."

By examination into the early court records of Spartanburg County, beginning in 1785, and of the United States census returns for 1790, which the writer has procured from the Census Office in Washington, we readily see that the early settlers of Spartanburg County were composed for the most part, of the following familiar family names, as Alexander, Allen, Arnold, Abbett, Austell, Byars, Bagwell, Bonner, Barnett, Bostick, Belcher, Burton, Bishop, Bobo, Berry, Brown, Brice, Bruton, Burnett, Bryant, Biter, Bostick, Blackstock, Bennell, Buffington, Ballard, Casselberry, Couch, Chesney, Childers, Casey, Cole Central, Crowder, Cannon, Cook, Camp, Crow, Cox, Crocker, Culberson, Cooper, Clayton, Davis, Dean, Dodd, Drummond, Dewberry, Davidson, Elder, Floyd, Edwards Evans, Foster, Fowler, Farrow, Ford, Finch, Fielder, Gentry, Goodlett, Golightly, Gaston, Garnett, Gibbs, Griffin, Griffith, Gilbert, Johnson, Hill, Harris, Hammett, Harrison, Henderson, Kelly, Kirby, Lewis, Lipscomb, Littlejohn, Lancaster, Lemaster, Landford, Lawrence, McAbee, Mason, Oats, O'Shields, Price, Pearson, Jackson, Pool, Rogers, Roebuck, Rhodes, Ross, Rainwaters, Roddy Ray, Smith, Sims, Surratt, Stone, Todd, Tinsley, Tolleson, Trimmier, Thomson, Tapp, Timmons, Turner, Thomas, Underwood, Varner, Wakefield, Ward, Waters Wells, Westmoreland, Watson, Waldrop, West, Wofford, Walker, Wilson, Wingo, White, Wilkens, Williams, Williamson, Vaughn, Young and very manv other family names, which it is impossible now to gather up. Among the early settlers on the waters of the North Tyger. in the vicinity of the present Mount Zion (Baptist) church and old Fort Prince, were the families Wood, Wingo, Prince and Ballenger. The families of Bomar, Chapman, Foster, Pollard and Richardson, were like their neighbors already mentioned, emigrants from Virginia and probably settled between the years 1795 and 1800.

Among the early settlers on South Pacolet were the families of McDowell, McMillen, McClure and Dickson, all Scotch-Irish ; and on North Pacolet, the families of Jackson, (Scotch-Irish,) Earle, Hannon. Page and other emigrants from Virginia.

These people coming as they did, for the most part, from North Ireland, Pennsylvania and Maryland, were of different make up from the early settlers which composed the eastern portion of the province of South Carolina. It is due to them to say, that they were a brave and noble set of pioneers, well worthy to be the entering wedges of civilization in the up country of South Carolina. They came to confront the Indian tomahawk and scalping knife, with a true heroism and patriotism, and a spirit of energy and progressiveness, which they transmitted to a noble prosperity. They braved all dangers and diffi culties, and their humble efforts to better their condition and to lay the foundation for the generations that succeeded them, have been crowned with brilliant success.

CHAPTER V.

UNEXPECTED OUTBREAK AND MASSACRES BY THE INDIANS ON THE BORDERS.

AFTER the treaty of Governor Glen with the nation of Cherokee Indians, the particulars of which have been given in the preceding chapter, it might have been a reasonable supposition that all danger of molestation or outbreak on the part of these people was at an end. It appeared, at that time, to be a lasting peace between the white adventurers and the red men of the forest. The peaceful relations between the two races, however, was of short duration, owing to an unexpected and unfortunate occurrence, which we will relate as briefly as possible.

In the beginning of the war between Great Britain and France, the Cherokees sided with the former, and many of them were enlisted as soldiers. Returning to their homes through Virginia, after the famous expedition against Fort Duquesne, they thought it right, as it had been a previous custom among the whites, to take horses wherever they could find them. The Virginians considered this robbery and resisted the same by violence. They killed a number of warriors and took quite a number of prisoners. As an act of retaliation, parties of young warriors rushed down upon the frontier settlements, and the massacre became general along the borders of South Carolina. When, however, the Chiefs of the Cherokees became aware of the fact, they sent a deputation to Charlestown, consisting of twenty-four men, to disarm the anger of the people and bring about a reconciliation. Governor Littleton, who had succeeded Governor Glen in office, and who was by far the inferior of the latter for judgment, discretion and sagacity, very imprudently and unjustly, treated these messengers of peace with indignity and caused them to be imprisoned. Burning all over doubtless for military glory, he had already resolved upon an expedition against the Cherokees, and for this purpose, had mustered fourteen hundred men upon the banks of the Congaree. The Cherokee messengers, in order to give further guarantees of their contined friendship, agreed that twenty-two of the twenty-four of their number, should be held as hostages, while the other two, should return to the Chiefs who were to secure the young warriors that had committed the murders upon the defenseless Carolinians. To this proposition Governor Littleton assented and caused the prisoners to be sent to Fort Prince George, on the waters of the Savannah River.* This fort was commanded by a Captain Cotymore, who was detested by the Indians. Occonostola, a chief of influence and an enemy to the Carolinians, took it upon himself to capture this fort and relieve the prisoners confined in it. He collected a strong force of Cherokees and surrounded it, but finding he could make no impression upon it or alarm its commander, he resorted to stratagem. Placing his savages in a dark thicket by the riverside, he sent an Indian woman to tell Cotymore that he had something of importance to tell him and wished him to meet him at the bank of the river. Cotymore consented, and, accompanied by his Lieutenants Bell and Foster, went to meet him. Occonostola said he wanted a guide to conduct him to

---

*Feeling an interest in knowing the precise location of Fort Prince George, and also the history of a gold ring a hundred years old, which had been found there, the writer, in answer to an inquiry received the following letter which explains itself:

CLERK'S OFFICE UNITED STATES CIRCUIT COURT,
DISTRICT OF SOUTH CAROLINA.
Pickens, S. C., Sept. 23, 1891.

Dr. J. B. O. Landrum, Landrum, S. C.:

Dear Sir:—Yours was received. Fort George was erected on Keowee River, in Pickens County. The land is now owned by Capt. Robt. E. Steele, and is in a large bottom of 50 acres near the river and there is a mound in the bottom plainly visible and cultivated by Capt. Steele. Fort George is 15 miles west of this place. The large, solid gold ring when found was just one hundred years old the day it was picked up in the bottom by a negro woman who was ploughing on the 26th June, 1858. I have seen the ring often. Gen. Jas W. Harrison had the ring on his watch guard. Will be glad to give you any information I can.

Yours very truly,
J. E. HAGOOD.

Charlestown, but while he was still parleying with Cotymore, he waved a bridle which he had in his hand, three times over his head and the savages appeared. They killed Cotymore and wounded his lieutenants. In consequence of this bloody deed the garrison proceeded at once to put the prisoners in irons. They resisted and stabbed three of the men who attempted to put manacles upon them. The garrison, exasperated to the highest degree, fell upon and killed the last one of them.

This unfortunate castrophe maddened the whole Cherokee nation. The pleasant relations which had been so recently formed with these people were at an end. It is said that in the murder of these hostages there was scarcely a family among the Cherokees that had not lost a friend or relative. The whole nation seized at once the hatchet, sang their war songs, and, burning for revenge, fell upon the frontier settlements of Carolina, and with merciless fury set to work murdering men, women and children. The settlements everywhere, alarmed and terrified, lost no time in setting to the work of building of forts and stockades. It is said that a line of these forts extended along the borders of the outer settlements from Virginia to Georgia.

Just what were the particulars of the murders committed upon the white people who settled the country now comprised within the territorial limits of Spartanburg and other counties, it is impossible now to know. Judge O'Neal in his "Annals of Newberry," says that after the killing of Cotymore and the wounding of Bell and Foster, the Indian savages rushed upon the defenseless settlements of Long Cane, Saluda and Little River, and committed their work of murder and devastation. We certainly know that it was during these troublesome times that old Fort Prince, Poole's Fort, near Wofford's Iron Works, now Glendale, Nichols' Fort at "Narrow Pass," near Capt. David Anderson's, Block House, Earle's and Thickety forts were built, an account of which, we shall give in the succeeding chapter.

CHAPTER VI.

FORT PRINCE AND OTHER FORTS.—BLACKSTOCK ROAD. CKEROKEE WAR CONTINUED.—ENDING OF THE SAME.—RENEWED PROSPERITY OF THE COUNTRY, &c.

OF the old forts or stockades mentioned in our last chapter, Fort Prince was the general rallying point in times of danger, when it was necessary for the people of the different settlements to concentrate their strength This old fort was constructed near the historic Black stock road, about three-fourths of a mile Southeast of Mount Zion Church, and about two and a half miles Northwest of the present village of Fair Forest. It was built near a stream now known as Grav's Creek, one of the branches of the North Tyger River. This stream is the only water crossing on the Blackstock road between Motlow's Creek, one of the prongs of the South Pacolet River, and Tyger River at Blackstock's Ford, a distauce of forty or forty-five miles. The fort was built circular in shape, and of heavy timbers from twelve to fifteen feet high. Surrounding this was a ditch, the dirt from which was thrown against the walls of parapet height. This was secured in front by an abatis of heavy timbers, making, when finished, a respectable place of defence against the assaults of the enemy. In the upright pieces, port holes were cut one and one-half by four inches in diameter for the riflemen inside. What we have said with regard to the construction of this fort will probably apply to the others already mentioned. It took its name by reason of the fact that it was built near the residence of a Mr. William Prince, grandfather of Mr. William Prince, who died on the North Pacolet River, (Polk County, N. C.,) in 1878, at the advanced age of ninety-five years, in the full vigor of his mind to the day of his death. To "Uncle Billy" Prince as he was called by his neighbors, and also to "Draper's King's Mountain," the writer is indebted for the history he has obtained with regard to this old place of refuge, built by the fathers more than one hundred and thirty years ago. During the perilous times just mentioned, it was here and at Fort Nichols, and perhaps other places, that the men, women and children—in other words, the ancestry of a large and respectable portion of the present population of Spartanburg County—were sheltered.

Just in front of the site of the old fort is a beautiful shoal on the creek, where stood a mill which did the grinding for the inmates of the fort. It was afterwards known as Gray's Mill and stood for some years after the close of the Revolution.

The writer having been born and reared in less than two miles of the site of old Fort Prince, and feeling an interest in knowing the precise spot where it stood, was accompanied, some thirty years ago to the place by an esteemed and venerable friend, Mr. Samuel Turner, who lived near by and on whose plantation it was to be seen. A circular depression in the ground on one side, was distinctly discerned, which gave an idea of the size of the fort. It was probably about one hundred and fifty feet in diameter. On the bank of the branch near by, Mr. Turner showed what appeared to be an ancient bank of ashes, which, he said, was the place where the washing was done by the inmates of the fort.

How long Fort Prince and the other forts were ocenpied, it is impossible now to know, but it is reasonable to suppose, until the troubles with the Cherokees were ended. In a future chapter, we will give more history in connection with Fort Prince. Before speaking of the particulars which brought about an end to the war with the Cherokees, let us again refer to the Blackstock road.

Several vears ago, the writer prepared a series of articles for one of our county papers, headed "Blackstock Road and Vicinity One Hundred Years Ago," in which he endeavored to present many scenes connected with this old road, and as he will have occasion to refer to them again, its location might here be given.

Running in a Northwest direction from Cambridge, or Ninety-Six, the Blackstock road crossed Tyger at Blackstock's Ford, near the battle ground of same name, and ran, as it does now, on a beautiful ridge, dividing the waters of the Tyger on one side, and the waters of Dutchman's Creek, head waters of Fair Forest and Lawson's Fork, on the other. Its course, in other words, lay by what is now known as the Ferguson old place. Walnut Grove, Becca, Fair Forest, old Fort Prince, Mt. Zion Church, to the Frank Bush place, near Shiloh Church. Up to this point the old road, as known in Revolutionary times, runs at present, for most part, over its original road bed. The remaining portion of the old road, except for a short distance at different places, has long since been abandoned. The continuation of its course in a Northwestward direction, ran by Gowen's old muster ground, Samuel Burns', Crawford Earle's—crossing South Pacolet at Guthrie's Ford—and thence by Fairview Church, Bird Mountain old camp ground, to the North Carolina line, at the Block House.

Besides Fort Prince there were two other forts located on the Blackstock road—one of these was Gowen's Fort, the site of which, is near Williams' Mill, on the waters of South Pacolet River. This old fort is mentioned in Governor Perry's articles, which appear, in Johnson's Tradi tions. The other referred to, is the Block House Fort which stood near the present residence of Ceburu Foster, on the present dividing line between the counties of Greenville and Spartanburg, and within a few steps of the North Carolina line. It was located, in other words, in the extreme Northwest corner of Spartanburg County.

The Blackstock Road is perhaps the oldest road in Spartanburg County and in the extreme up country. It was originally an Indian trail. Governor Perry, in some of his writings, informs us that the Block House was an

Indian trading post, and it was doubtless over the Blackstock Road that the merchants or Indian traders from Charleston, in times of peace, and prior to the first settlements in the up-country, traveled, to exchange with the Indians, guns, ammunition and other articles of convenience and comfort, for skins and furs which they carried with them on their return to Charleston, and which were exported to different parts of the world.*

In colonial times, public bridges were scarcely known. The public roads of the country were made with reference to the gaps in the mountains and the shoaly crossings on the streams.

But returning to the Cherokee war, let us relate briefly the circumstances which terminated the same. (See page 35). The Government of South Carolina was too feeble to put an end to the Indian insurrection. In Charleston the small-pox was prevailing to an alarming extent and no troops could be spared from that place. Virginia and North Carolina, however, came to the rescue, and together they sent seven troops of rangers. They united with a force of British regulars under Col. Montgomery, who assumed command of all. Montgomery, in 1760, chased the Cherokees for some distance, killed a number of their warriors, but did not humble them to submission. He was compelled to return to New York, from whence he had come, and the upper settlements of South Carolina

---

* See Commercial Reports of Charleston, 1831-'47. In 1831 three hundred casks, containing eight or nine hundred each of deer skins were exported from that place. The report of 1847 shows that two hundred beaver hides, and seven hundred and twenty hogsheads of deer hides were exported. (See Carrol's Commercial History of S. C., Vol. II, pages 129 and 237). Says Carrol, (page 128) "The trade in Carolina is now (1831) so considerable, that of late years there has sailed from thence annually, about two hundred ships laden with merchandise of of the growth of the country, besides three ships of war, which they commonly have for the security of the commerce, etc."

The trade with the Indians in the up-country of South Carolina was mostly by English merchants. Says Carrol, further, "They carry on great trade with the Indians, from whom they get great quantities of Deer Skins and those of other Wild Beasts, in exchange for which they give them only Lead, Powder, Coarse Cloth, Vermillion, Iron ware and some other goods, by which they have a very considerable profit."

were still in danger. A provincial regiment was raised, the command of which was given to Col. Middleton. Among the field officers of this regiment were Henry Laurens, William Moultrie, Francis Marion, Isaac Huger and Andrew Pickens. This regiment united with a force of British regulars under Col. Grant, which landed at Charleston earlv in **1761**, and together with some friendly Indians this force consisted of about twenty-six hundred men, the command of which was entrusted to Col. Grant. The Indians were pursued by Grant, who destroyed their graneries and corn fields, to their habitations in their own country. This expedition was known as the *Grant Indian war.* It brought to the Indians desolation and despair and caused them to sue for peace through an old friendly chief, Attakulla Kulla. Peace being declared, the forts were deserted. The people of the different settlements returned to their homes to pursue their domestic avocations. This was the true beginning of prosperity in the settlements of upper South Carolina. The colony began to flourish to a surprising degree; multitudes of emigrants came from all parts of Europe, Pennsylvania, Maryland and Virginia. It is said that in the space of a single year more than a thousand families, with their effects, horses, cattle and hogs, crossed the mountains and pitched their tents along the frontiers of South Carolina. As the white people began to increase, the danger from the savages was lessened. For several years the colony continued to flourish, the chief productions of which was flax, tobacco, furs and grain. The passage of the Stamp Act, however, by the British Parliament, soon after this awakened a jealousy in the bosoms of the people, and having a pride in their own strength, they resolved after several years of patient endurance, to throw off what has been properly called the *British Yoke.*

Having thus given an outline of the troubles and sacrifices of the early settlers of our country, let it be borne in mind, in conclusion, that their memories should not be forgotten. A great many, doubtless, think the greatest of their trials and sacrifices was during the Revolutionary war. This is a mistake. We think we have already presented facts to prove that their greatest hardships were before that period. Perhaps the only practical good that grew out of these difficulties, was to unite the people of the different settlements and nationalities and make them, as it were, *one people*, sooner perhaps than if they had been left undisturbed. It is true they were from different countries and had been, to some extent, educated with different ideas, but they all loved alike, God, liberty and their country, and transmitted the same spirit to their descendants, who, by their patriotism, valor and heroism, have given ample testimony to this fact, on many hard-fought battle fields, since their day and generation.

NOTE—Under date of April 19, 1897, the writer received a letter from A. M. Golden, Duncans, S. C., in which he states, that, accompanied by Roberson Smith, Manly F. Smith, W. R. Bailey and W. W. Moore, he visited the supposed spot where the Hampton family were buried and on opening the same, they found at the west end of the grave a part of a skull bone containing teeth, and further eastward they found two thigh bones of a man, and two more thigh bones of a lesser size, lying across the larger two. They also found a razor, a buckle or two—which proved to be suspender buckles--pieces of broken dishes, bottles, home-made nails and a quantity of charcoal and ashes.

Mr. Golden further states that from all appearances, the grave was not dug in any regular order, but was only a rough hole not more than two feet deep, the bodies having been hurriedly thrown in and covered up. After careful examination everything was nicely replaced in the grave, except the razor, which is now in the possession of Mr. Golden. The ground was cleared off, head and foot stones were placed and the mound was covered with white sand. Mr. Golden further states that Mr. Roberson Smith settled the place on which the grave was located, in 1827, and is now residing there, at the advanced age of 90 years. While clearing the land near the grave, soon after he settled the place, an old lady by the name of Bridget Bright came along hunting her cows, and admonished him not to clear the spot on the top of the hill, as it was the place where the Hampton family was massacred, their house burned and their bodies buried in the yard. The place had been pointed out to Bridget Bright by her father, who lived one mile below on Middle Tyger, and who assisted in the burial of the Hampton family. A public road now runs by this sacred spot, which is surrounded by huge oaks, and there is a flourishing academy near by.

CHAPTER VII.

INTRODUCTORY TO THE BREAKING OUT OF THE REVOLUTION.

IT is unnecessary to enter into the minute details of the causes which brought about the revolutionary struggle. It is well understood that principal among the causes—after the repeal of the memorable Stamp Act—was an act passed by the British Parliament imposing a duty on glass, paper, tea, paints and other articles. This duty, however, was removed on every article except tea. But the people, *on principle*, resolved that they would not submit to this unjust taxation imposed by the Parliament. They became jealous of the designs of the Mother Country. Cargoes of tea sent to Charlestown, Boston and other places, were stored and the consignees were restrained from exposing it for sale. The fact is well known in history that at Boston, a few men disguised as Indians, entered a ship and threw into the water all that had been exported to that place by the East India Company. This trespass on private property provoked to wrath the British Parliament and caused that body, first to pass an act to virtually blockade the Boston port, and later to pass another "act for the better regulating the government of Massachusetts," which meant to altar the charter of that province, remove the executive power from the hands of the people and thus leave the appointment of all officers to the King. As soon as the facts were made known to the people of Massachusetts and the other colonies, meetings were everywhere held to deliberate on the alarming state of affairs. At one of these meetings, held May 13, 1774, it was resolved and recommended that Massachusetts and the other colonies put a stop to all exportation and importation to Great Britain till the blockading act was repealed. A copy of the resolutions were sent to South Carolina and other provinces. Upon its arrival in Charlestown, it was presented to a number of gentlemen, who were of the opinion that the principles of policy and self-preservation made it necessary to support the people of Boston. It was thought best to call a meeting of the inhabitants. Letters were sent to every parish and district in the province. This meeting was held on the 6th of July, 1774, at Charlestown, and was composed of persons from every part of South Carolina.

The situation in Boston, where General Gage was collecting a large army to force the people into submission, and the affairs of Massachusetts, generally, were fully discussed. Strong resolutions were passed and delegates were appointed to attend the Continental Congress, which met in Philadelphia in October, 1774. This body having finished its business, the South Carolina members returned home and gave to the people an account of their proceedings.

To give strength to the action of the deputies from South Carolina, it was determined to convene a Provincial Congress, or what would now be called a *State Convention*. Delegates from every parish and district in South Carolina were elected to attend this Congress. This body had its first meeting January 11th, 1775. The proceedings of the Continental Congress were submitted to their judgment. Resolutions of approval were passed, a Council of Safety and a General Committee were appointed. The same delegates were appointed to the next Continental Congress. The inhabitants were recommended to be diligent and attentive to learn the use of fire-arms, and the 17th day of February, 1775, was set apart and recommended to them for observance as a day of fasting, humiliation and prayer before Almighty God, and on that day the people were to devoutly petition Him "to spare the King with Wisdom, etc."

How long this Congress remained in session, we are not informed. We notice another meeting of the same body in June of the same year. At this time the news of the battles of Lexington and Bunker Hill, and the general uprising of the people of Massachusetts and other colonies, had been received. They resolved that an association was necessary. Up to this time opposition to British authority had been conducted entirely on commercial principles, but Great Britain turning a deaf ear to the petitions and remonstrances of the colonists, determined to force their obedience to whatever laws she saw proper to enact. There was left no alternative but a mean submission or a manly resistance. The question before the people now was, "Shall we live slaves or die free men?" The instrument to be signed by the association was first signed by the President (Henry Laurens,) and members of the Provincial Congress, and was after wards presented to the inhabitants throughout the entire province for their signatures. Those who signed it pledged themselves to resist force by force and to unite under every tie of religion and honor. They further pledged themselves to "be ready to sacrifice life and fortune to secure the freedom and safety of South Carolina, holding all persons inimical to the liberty of the colonies who shall refuse to subscribe to this association." The Provincial Congress further resolved, since opposition to British authority was greater than was at first intended when they were elected, that the people should have fresh opportunity to express their opinion on the state of public affairs. They therefore determined that their existence as a public body should expire on the 6th day of August, and that a new election should be held on the two succeeding days for a new Provincial Congress. On the 22d dav of June, 1775, they adjourned, having delegated a greater part of their authority to the Council of Safety and the General Committee, composed of about fortv members. The former was to be in the nature of an executive and the latter a legislative body. It was during the sitting of the Provincial Congress that Lord William Campbell, Governor of the province of South

Carolina, arrived. The executive authority had been, for a time, vested in Lieutenant Governor Bull, a native of the province. Governor Campbell was received with demonstrations customary on such occasions. He was waited upon with an address from the Provincial Congress, who assured him, among other things, that the people of South Carolina only desired to secure their invaluable rights upon constitutional principles, and that they wished nothing more than a speedy reconciliation with the Mother Country. The Governor replied that he knew of no representatives of the people except those constitutionally convened in the General Assembly, and further, that he was incompetent to judge of the merits of the disputes between the Government of Great Britain and the American colonies. Under the constitution, the governor was Commander-in-chief of the militia; he also had the power to convene or dissolve the General Assembly at will. It was soon discovered, however, that he was plotting against the patriot cause. To his supposed friends he secretly gave out word "that His Majesty was determined to speedily send out troops from one end of the continent to the other." Through John Stuart, Superintendent of the Cherokee Nation, and Alexander Cameron, Deputy Superintendent of the same, he conspired against his province, the sequel of which will be presently explained.

Soon becoming distrustful of his personal safety in Charlestown, Governor Campbell retired to a sloop-of-war—*Tamar*—first issuing a proclamation to dissolve the General Assembly, and carrying off with him the great seal of the province. A fortnight afterwards he was waited upon by a committee, who invited him to come ashore, promising him that his person and character should be respected. He deemed it prudent, however, to remain on the vessel.

Stuart, very early in the contest, retired to Florida. He was an officer of the Crown and wholly devoted to the Royal interest. For several years the management of the Indian tribes had been committed to him. He pretended that he conceived it his duty to attach the Indians to the Royal cause. He prejudiced their minds by the non-importation agreement, which had been adopted by the colonies. This wholly deprived him of the opportunity of supplying their wants, and also precluded the possibility of giving Royal presents, as had been previously done. This interruption gave him an opportunity to exasperate the Indians against the friends of the patriot cause. A secret plot was on foot among Campbell and all the Royal Governors, to land an army in Florida, and in conjunction with the Tories and Indians, to fall upon the frontier settlements of South Carolina and other Southern provinces. A fleet and army were, at the same time, to invade from the coast. Moses Kirkland, a Tory from the back settlements of South Carolina, was sent to communicate this plan to General Gage, at Boston. Fortunately, the vessel that was sent to convey him was captured, with Kirkland on board. The letters found on his person unfolded the whole plan, which, by order of Congress, was published to the people. This convinced the minds of the Americans that the British authorities had employed the Indian savages to indiscriminately murder men, women and children on the western frontiers, of which the early settlers in the present counties of Spartanburg and Union were a part. A lot of powder which had been started from Florida by Stuart to the Cherokee country, was captured The news of this fortunate capture and the exposing of the nefarious plot soon spread over the country, and for a time, put a quietus to the Tories and Indians and prevented what might otherwise have been, during the year 1775, a terrible disaster to the border settlements.

The second or new Provincial Congress of South Carolina, met on the 1st day of November, 1775, composed of delegates from all over South Carolina.

It would be impossible here to give a general summary of all of the proceedings of this important gathering of patriots. The defenses around the city of Charlestown were ordered to be put in repair. At this time they were threatened by two British sloops of war—*Cherokee* and *Tamar*—lying inside of the harbor.

This Provincial Congress elected a new Council of Safety and enlarged their powers. That part, however, of their proceedings which directly concerned the people of the up-country was the dividing of the country between the Broad and Saluda rivers into three congressional or election districts. We prefer to quote the record as we find it. (See Drayton's Memoirs, vol. ii, page 154).

No. VII.—In Congress.

Resolved, that the district heretofore described between the Broad and Saluda rivers be now divided into three, as well for the convenience of electors in Congress, as on account of the happy influence which it may have upon the peace and union of the inhabitants.

That the *Lower District*, commonly called Dutch Fork, shall have the following boundaries. viz: From fork where Broad and Saluda Rivers meet, up Broad River to where Tyger River falls into Broad River, thence up Tyger River to the ford crossed by the old Saluda road, thence along said road to where it crosses Saluda at the place usually called Saluda Old Town, thence down the confluence of Saluda and Broad Rivers: that the election of members of Congress for said district be held at the meeting house nearest to the home of Adam Summers.

That the *Little River District* be bounded as follows: By Saluda River to Saluda Old Town to where the said river crosses the Indian boundary line; by the said Indian line to where it crosses the Enoree River, thence down the Enoree to road above described, which bounds the lower district, the election to be held at Hammond's old store.

That the *Upper* or *Spartan District* be bounded by Tyger River from its confluence with Broad River up to where said Tyger River is crossed by the Saluda old road, thence by the old road to where it crosses Enoree, thence by the said Enoree River to the Indian line [the present line between the counties of Greenville and Spartanburg] to the Colony line; thence by the Colony (the state line between North and South Carolina) to where it intersects with Broad River; thence by Broad River to its confluence with the Tyger; the place of election to be at the meeting house, near the house of Joseph Kelsey, and that the district as now divided be allowed and do respectively elect four members of Congress and ther representatives."

NORTH CAROLINA.

GREENVILLE Co.

UPPER or SPARTAN DIST.

York Co.

Chester Co

Lancaster Co.

Fairfield Co.

Kershaw Co.

MIDDLE or LITTLE RIVER DIST.

Lower Dutch Fork Dist.

Abbeville Co.

96 Court House

Saluda River.

Richland Co.

Sumter Co.

EDGEFIELD Co.

LEXINGTON Co.

AIKEN Co.

Orangeburg

GEORGIA

Savannah River.

State Line.

Actual Co. Line.

District Line

96

It will be seen that the present counties of Union and Spartanburg composed the Upper or Spartan District, with only one voting precinct for the entire district. The presumtion of the writer is that this was somewhere in Union County.

The most important work, however, of the Provincial Congress of South Carolina, was the adoption of a new and independent constitution. After much debate, this was adopted early in 1776. While this debate was in progress, an express arrived from Savannah, bringing a copy of the Act of Parliament, passed December 21st, 1775, confiscating American property and throwing all of the colonies out of His Majesty's protection. This quickly put an end to all further debate; the body became at once revolutionized and solidified. They voted themselves at once to be the *General Assembly of South Carolina*, elected thirteen of their ablest members to be a Legislative Council, and also elected a president and vice-president; six privy counselors to advise the president; a chief justice and three assistant judges; an attorney-general, secretary, ordinary, judge of the admiralty and register of mesne conveyance.

The first president under the new constitution was John Rutledge. The first vice-president was Henry Laurens and the first chief-justice was William Henry Drayton.

We have thus briefly noticed the changes as they rapidly took place, and in which the people of the up-country, doubtless through their representatives, took part. It was the extinction of Royal authority in South Carolina.

CHAPTER VIII.

INTRIGUE OF GOVERNOR CAMPBELL WITH THE PEOPLE OF THE BACK COUNTRY.—COMMISSIONERS SENT BY COUNCIL OF SAFETY TO THE UP-COUNTRY.

DURING the session and after the adjournment of the Provincial Congress already referred to, Lord William Campbell, claiming his authority as Governor of South Carolina, was unremitting in his efforts to persuade the uninformed of the back settlers that the power of Great Britain could never be effectually resisted by the American colonies; that the whole dispute was about a trifling tax on tea, which they were not in the habit of using, and the matter was of little or no interest to them. Through his emissaries, he insisted that *the gentlemen* on the sea coast, in order to obtain their tea free, were willing to involve the people of the back country in a quarrel that would deprive them of salt and other imported necessaries, and that the expenses of an insignificant tax on tea was nothing as compared to the expenses of a war with the mother country.

These well-paid emissaries had no trouble in distracting the minds of very many of the back country people, who had not been settled more than fifteen or twenty years. They were persuaded that the instrument which had been prepared by the association (referred to in the preceding chapter) for their signatures, was intended only to dragoon them into submission. This aroused in the bosoms of many, a spirit of resistance and independence, and instead of signing the document by which the people of the lower country had pledged their lives and fortunes to each other in open opposition to Royal authority, they signed other papers, as we will see further, at their general musters and other public gatherings, declaring their unwillingness to concur in the measures recommended by the Provincial Congress. These papers charged the patriots with motives and designs that were dishonorable. The country soon divided in sentiment. While there were many that were sincerely devoted to the cause of Liberty, there were others who were stubborn in their opposition to the new provincial authority, which then existed. Camps were soon formed of the opposing parties and both were quickly in arms. The Tory element in the lower part of the District of Ninety-Six* were headed and led by two brothers, Patrick and Robert Cunningham, while the same element was led, in a large measure in the Upper or Spartan District by Colonel Thomas Fletchall, who resided on Fair Forest. This influence which he possessed over the people of his section was due to the fact that he was Colonel of the militia. His regimental district, before the Revolution, included all the country between the Broad and Saluda rivers in South Carolina, and embraced the three districts (Lower or Dutch Fork, Middle or Little River and Upper or Spartan) referred to in a former chapter, which were created by the Provincial Congress in 1776. The regimental parade ground of Fletchall's regiment was at Ford's, on the Enoree.

The Provincial militia of South Carolina in the early part of 1775, consisted of twelve regiments. One of these in the upper part of the province was commanded, as we have already said, by Fletchall. It was through the Colonel's command of the different regiments, that the instrument of the association was transmitted to the people for their signatures. Fletchall's conduct gave great uneasiness to the Council of Safety. An effort was made to induce him to join the common cause or to make

*The old district of Ninety-Six, before and during the Revolution, was composed of the present counties of Spartanburg, Laurens, Union, Newberry, Abbeville and Edgefield. The county site was at Cambridge or Ninety Six, in Abbeville county, not far from the present Ninety-Six depot. The three last named counties were laid out in 1783, the former remained as the county of Ninety-Six, with a change of the county site to Pinckneyville, on the Broad River, in Union county, until 1785. The old official records of Cambridge are now at Abbeville court house, while those of Pinckneyville are at Union court house.

known his sentiments on the situation of affairs. He was written to by the Council of Safety on the 14th day of July, 1775. In his reply on the 24th of the same month, he claimed that many reports had been maliciously circulated against him by the General Committee, which he could prove to be false; that upon the desire of John Caldwell, Lieutenant-Colonel of his regiment, he had called the same together on the 13th inst., when he proceeded to every company and caused Major Terry of his regiment to read the instrument of the Provincial Association to them, but not one of them signed it and he could not compel them; that the people then agreed to sign an association of their own and Major Robinson, then on the ground, was applied to, who drew up articles of an association suitable to their wishes, and which had been generally signed from Broad to Savannah rivers. Fletchall warned the Council of Safety of some of their *highland gentlemen*, as he called some in the interior, who were aspiring and fond of commissions, and who, to gain favor with *the gentlemen* in town, would say anything but the truth. Fletchall expressed a concern that he was looked upon as an enemy to his country, and thought the government had greater cause to complain of some who were less suspected than himself. Upon the main subject upon which he had been approached by the Council of Safety, Fletchall declared that he would not take up arms against his King, until it became his duty to do so, and he was convinced of the propriety of the measure.

We have mentioned some particulars of this correspondence to show the unwholesome influences that were at first brought to bear upon the minds of the people of the up-country of South Carolina, by leaders in official authority. Let it be remembered, as we have said, that the boundaries of Fletchall's regiment embraced a large scope of country, between the rivers—Saluda and Broad—to the North Carolina line. So large was it, as we have shown in a preceding chapter, that the Provincial Congress passed a resolution March 23d, 1776, to divide this regimental district into three, the boundaries of one of these to embrace the *Upper* or *Spartan* District. (See Drayton's Memoirs, vol. xxi, page 155).

The Council of Safety feeling the necessity of a full explanation to the people of the nature of the dispute between the colonies and the mother country, sent to the country between the Broad and Saluda rivers, where the disaffection seemed greatest, the Hon. William Henry Drayton and Rev. William Tennant. The mission of these gentlemen was to pacify the inhabitants and bring them into co-operation with the Council of Safety and General Committee. They set out on their journey in August, 1775. The first section visited by them was the Dutch Fork, near the junction of the two rivers mentioned. Their first meeting was at a German muster. These people were so warmed by the eloquence and reasoning of Drayton, that many of them shed tears and nearly all signed the instrument of the association. Some few, however, refused at first, and an amusing scheme was adopted by Drayton to bring them to terms. In the presence of some of their leaders, he wrote to the Council of Safety, requesting them to keep a constant guard at the town gate at Charlestown and to inquire of all wagoners from the Congress (the fork of the Saluda and Broad Rivers) for certificates showing that they had joined the association. Upon their non-production of the same, he suggested that they be required to return.

Mr. Drayton separating himself for a time from Mr. Tennant, who traveled through other sections of the country, continued his journey up the Saluda River, accompanied by Mr. Kershaw, of Camden. At King's Creek, he addressed a large gathering. All seemed pleased with his reasoning and eloquence, but when about to sign the association, a messenger arrived and said that Cunningham was on hand and would like to address the meeting. This brought everything to a pause, the people now indulging the idea of having both sides discussed. The report was circulated that Cunningham had in his pocket a proclamation from the King, showing the fallacy of the American proceedings. Upon Cunningham's arrival, he and his company were invited to dine with Mr. Drayton, where dinner had been ordered. After this was over, Mr. Drayton took Cunningham aside and spoke to him seriously and politely, respecting the questions before the people. Cunningham would not, however, be drawn from his purpose. In the afternoon, when the people had reassembled to receive Cuunningham's communication, one of his companions, Thomas Brown, a Scotchman, who had been tarred and feathered at Augusta, Georgia, for making fun of the American cause in a toast at a dinner party, read "Dalrymple's Address from the People of England to the People of America," which had been transmitted, through the Governor, Lord William Campbell. Brown performed the part of an orator on this occasion and read the address aloud from beginning to end. Mr. Drayton, having determined to follow him in all his windings from beginning to end, applied ridicule when he thought it would have effect, which made the people laugh heartily, and to which Cunningham and Brown made no reply. Demolished and beaten from the field, Cunningham and his friend of tar and feather memory, quietly stole away. Mr. Drayton and Mr. Kershaw, after visiting the settlements along the Saluda, crossed the Enoree and came into the settlements which now belong to the territory of Union and Spartanburg counties. They arrived at the house of Colonel Fletchall* on the 17th of August, where they found Thomas Brown, Cunningham and Robinson who had arrived the evening before, as had also Mr. Tennant and Colonel Richardson. The respective heads of parties as they there stood, had

*The writer is informed by Hon. John L. Young, of Union, S. C., that Fletchall's place was afterwards known as the Murphy Mill place, on Fair Forest, about five miles south-west of Union. Later it was a part of the McBette estate, and is now owned by Murphy & Nicholson. Colonel Fletchall left the country and went to the West Indies after the revolution. His estate was confiscated and taken posession of by Colonel Brandon, who was a sort of "Willie the Conqueror" of that section.

now met together for the first time since the Commissioners (Mr. Drayton and Mr. Tennant) had commenced their mission. Mr. Tennant, in a letter to the Council of Safety (August 20, 1775), writes, "We have at length visited the mighty Nabob Fletchall. We found him surrounded by his court, viz: Cunningham, Brown and Robinson, who watch all his motions and have him under great command. We soon found the unchangeable malignity of their minds, and the inexpressible pains they were at to blind the people and fill them with bitterness against *the gentlemen*, as they are called. General Gage's pamphlet is raging through the district and greedily read. The leaders * * * * keep the people ignorant and in general they firmly believe that no man, that comes from below, and that no paper printed there, can speak the truth. This is necessary to prevent anything we can say from taking place. We soon found that reasoning was vain with those who were fixed with Royal emoluments, but perceiving that Fletchall expected (?) to play between, we let him know that we had discovered things which he thought were a profound secret and surprised him much. He confessed receiving a letter from the Governor within five days last and offered to swear there was no harm in it and that he would not take arms against the country. But we surprised him into a promise to assemble his regiment next Wednesday at Ford's, which highly affronted Cunningham and the rest of the upper house, some of whom treated us with insolence upon it. We expect to meet the regiment accordingly, and many of our friends whom I have advertised of it.

In the meantime Mr. Drayton has gone up to his iron works (*) "and to the people about Lawson's Fork, where we will do something."

On the 21st of August, Mr. Drayton wrote a letter from Lawson's Fork to the Council of Safety giving the particulars of what had passed while the commissioners were at

---

*Buffington or Wofford's Iron Works, near Glendale, referred to,

Colonel Fletchall's. In his letter he says: "I reached Colonel Fletchall's last Thursday morning before breakfast, and Mr. Tennant and myself, after breakfast, engaged him in a private conversation, during near three hours. We endeavored to explain everything to him and endeavored to show him that we had confidence in him. We humored him, we laughed with him, then we recurred to argument, remonstrances and intreaties, to join his country and all America. All that we could get from him was this: '*He would never take up arms against his King or his countrymen, and that the proceedings of the Congress at Philadelphia were impolitic, disrespectful and irritating to the King.*' We charged him with having written to the Governor (Lord William Campbell) and with having received an answer; he confessed both. * * * We named the method by which he received it, concealed in a cane; he appeared confounded but after a pause, he attempted to laugh off this last particular." Drayton says further of Robinson, "This man's looks are utterly against him; much venom appears in Cunningham's countenance and conversation. Neither of these say much, but Brown (the same who was tarred and feathered at Augusta) is the spokesman; and his bitterness and violence are intolerable. He has, in various ways, insulted us during our twenty-four hours stay at Fletchall's, as if he wanted to provoke me to violence. * * * * Before this happened we engaged the Colonel in the private conversation to call out his regiment on the 23d instant; upon our return to the house where this Cunningham, Brown and Robinson were, he mentioned what he had promised. All three of them were opened mouthed against the measure and Mr. Tennant had much to do to keep the Colonel to his promise. This meeting of the regiment will be at Ford's (on Enoree River) and I am not without some apprehension that some violence will there be used against us. * * * And besides this it is my firm belief, that Brown, Cunningham and Robinson will do everything in their power to bring things to extremities; for they are clearly of the opinion that they can beat the colony. These men manage Fletchall as they please, when they have him to themselves."

The reader would naturally infer from what has already been said, that the infant settlements of the Upper or Spartan district were influenced almost entirely by Fletchall and his associates, to take sides with the Royal authority in opposition to the common cause of America. While this was true, with reference to the settlements in the middle and lower portion of the district of Ninety-Six, it was not true of the early settlers of Spartanburg County, which was then the upper portion of the said district and next to the Cherokee Indian Nation. In the same letter of Mr. Drayton, already referred to, written on Lawson's Fork, August 21, 1775, the writer says: "I had this day a meeting with the people in this frontier. Many present were of the other party; but I have the pleasure to acquaint you that those became voluntary converts. Every person received satisfaction and departed with pleasure. I finished the day with a barbacued beef. I have also ordered matters here, that this whole frontier will be formed into volunteer companies; but as they are at present under Fletchall's command, they insist upon being formed into a regiment independent of him; and I flatter myself you will think this method of weakening Fletchall, to be considered sound policy. *These people are active and spirited; they are staunch in our favor;* are capable of forming a good barrier against the Indians, and of being a severe check upon Fletchall's people, on whom they border, if they should think of quitting their habitations under the banners of Fletchall or his companions. For these reasons and to enable them to act with vigor, I shall take the liberty of supplying them with a small quantity of ammunition; for they have not one ounce, when they shall be formed into regular companies. Several companies will be formed by this day week. (See Drayton's Memoirs, vol. i, page 374).

We have quoted from Mr. Drayton's letter to prove the spirit of patriotism that belonged to the people of the old

Spartan District, few in numbers, as they were, at the dawning of the Revolution. Let their descendants of the present day read with pride the indelible testimony preserved and handed down to us.

Not long after the departure of Messrs. Drayton and Tennant a regiment was organized within the present limits of Spartanburg County and made up of inhabitants from both sections of Union and Spartanburg, under the command of Col. John Thomas, Sr. This was called the *Spartan Regiment.* Of what number of men composed it we are unable to determine, but the supposition is that it was small, perhaps not more than two or three hundred, judging from the following letter, which we find recorded in Gibbs' Documentary History of the American Revolution, 1764 to 1776, page 170.

"Mr. Thomas, of the Spartan Regiment, to Mr. Drayton. (Original Ms.*)

SPARTAN REGIMENT, Sept. 11, 1775.

TO THE HONORABLE WM. H. DRAYTON, ESQ.:

May it please Your Honor;—I this moment received Your Honor's favor of the 10 inst., and very fortunately, the command for this district was just assembled at my house in order to address the Council of Safety almost on the very purport of Your Honor's letter, as we had all the reason in the world (and still have) to believe from good information, that the malignants are forming the most hellish schemes to frustrate the measures of the Continental Congress, and to use all those who are willing to stand by those measures in the most cruel manner. Your Honor will be fully convinced of the truth of this by perusing the papers transmitted herewith, to which I refer Your Honor.

I shall comply with Your Honor's orders as far as is in my power; Your Honor must suppose it impossible to raise the whole regiment, as several have families and no man be left about the house, if they should be called away. I shall take as large a draft as possible from every company, and in short, do everything to the utmost of my power, and when encamped shall transmit to Your Honor, as quick as possible, an account of my proceedings. JOHN THOMAS."

*The original manuscript of this letter has been recently reported as among the South Carolina colonial records in London. The legislature of South Carolina, at its session of 1891-2, made an appropriation to bring the records from the London office to Columbia, to be placed among our State records.

We will show in a succeeding chapter that Colonel Thomas' Spartan Regiment soon entered active service, and participated in scenes mentioned further on.

The commissioners (Mr. Dravton and Mr. Tennant) in the course of their journeyings met again, agreeably to appointment, on the 23d of August, at Ford's, which was the parade ground of Fletchall's regiment. Mr. Drayton says that this place is on the Enoree River in the fork of Cedar Creek and Enoree. The Cedar Creek referred to is doubtless the same as the present Cedar Shoal Creek running west of Cross Anchor. This was the day that Fletchall had promised to assemble his regiment.*

The commissioners when they arrived found Colonel Fletchall, Kirkland, Brown and the Cunninghams already on the ground industriously working among the people. By the contrivances of these men, the people had, as much as possible, been kept away. Not more than two hundred and fifty had assembled where one thousand or fifteen hundred men usually met at a regimental muster. Cunningham told the commissioners that he had told his men "that if they were satisfied with their present opinions, there was no occasion for them to come to hear the addresses." Some of the captains of companies had told their men that "the colonel left it to them, to come or not as they pleased, and if they stayed away he would not be angry with them."

It was some time in the day before the people assembled. Good order generally prevailed. Kirkland and Brown demanded a part of the time of the commissioners, which, of course, for the sake of peace, had to be granted. Brown read the address (Dalrvmple) from the people of England to the people of America. It had lost its credit and few listened to it. Kirkland, in his talk, abused the Provincial Congress, Council of Safety and General Committee, and was so insolent to Mr. Drayton that a per-

*Mr. B. G. Lambright informs the writer that Ford's old muster ground place is between Enoree and Cedar Shoal Creek, at or near the old Davis Newman place. It is not far from Musgrove's battle ground.

sonal altercation came very near taking place, but the people pressed around Mr. Drayton and gave him to understand that he was in no danger of assault. Mr. Drayton in his progress always had about his person a dirk and a pair of pocket pistols to protect himself from insult or for the defense of his life. He wrote next day (24th) to the Council of Safety referring to the speeches of Brown and Kirkland. He says: "Imagine every indecency of language, every misrepresentation, ungenerous and unjust charge against the American politics that could alarm the people and give them an evil impression of our designs against their liberties and the rights of Great Britain. Imagine all vou can on these points, and you will not exceed what we heard as well from Kirkland as from Brown. Our indignation was painful, but we were obliged to conceal it and our situation was as disagreeable as you can well conceive. Brown loudly declared that when the King's troops arrived he would join them against us; and he hoped every other person in these parts would do the same."

Kirkland and the Cunninghams on this occasion appeared with arms, sword and pistol. The small audi ences, however, for the speeches of Brown and Kirkland, showed that the commissioners had won the day. Several of Fletchall's captains came over to Dravton's side and signed the instrument of the association. At this meeting there were strong friends to the American cause who had come from distant homes.

The commissioners now turned their backs upon Colonel Fletchall and his party, to visit other sections in the up-country.

CHAPTER IX.

THE ASSEMBLING OF THE KING'S MEN.—MR. DRAYTON ISSUES A PROCLAMATION.—RESORTS TO OTHER MEANS THAN DISCOURSES.—THE MILITIA AND RANGERS RALLY TO HIS AID.

MR. DRAYTON and Mr. Tennant continued the progress of their mission but a few days after the meeting at Ford's muster ground. On the 29th of August they received information that Kirkland had taken up arms, and was collecting men for the purpose of attacking Forts Charlotte and Augusta. Fort Charlotte was situated on the Savannah River, about twenty or thirty miles above Augusta, and about twenty miles south-west of Ninety-Six Court House. The malcontents, or King's men, as they were called, were to meet at a designated place about twenty miles above the residence of a Mr. Hammond, called Snow Hill. In their progress, Mr. Tennant and Mr. Drayton had separated, as we have already said, the former visiting the Long Cane settlements on the Saluda. Mr. Drayton sent a messenger to him directing him to trace his steps at once down the Savannah.

The King's men met according to appointment, but dispersed again during the night, having arranged to meet again in three or four days with guns and ammunition, for the purpose of attacking Fort Charlotte. Mr. Tennant, as he passed down the river by that place, ordered Captain Caldwell, the commandant of the fort, to erect platforms for fighting with the cannon as expeditiously as possible, and to mount two of the best four pounders for field use, and to advance sentinels and patrols. The Indian corn growing in front of the fort was ordered to be cut away, and what was left was to be bladed and topped so as to give the approaching enemy no advantages of shelter. He was cautioned as to letting persons into the fort, and was ordered to send the troops of horses some distance away for pasturage. In case of the enemy's approach, Captain Caldwell was ordered to fire a signal gun for the volunteers to assemble and commence their march. Captain Caldwell was further ordered to let those companies have powder and lead, which were organized for the protection of that part of the district.

To counteract the schemes of the King's men, Mr. Drayton commenced his march for Ninety-Six Court House on the 6th of September, with one hundred and twenty men and four swivels (small cannon turning on pivots). His intention was, with his militia and rangers, to march against Fletchall's quarters and demand the surrender of the principal offenders. A special detail was sent to Capt. Robert Cunningham, but it was found that he had quitted his residence the day before. His papers, however, were taken possession of, among which were two letters from Fletchall.

Mr. Drayton and Mr. Tennant, before leaving Charlestown, had been empowered with authority by the Council of Safety, to call upon every officer of the militia and rangers for assistance, support and protection. Mr. Drayton received advices of the continued uprising of the King's men. His own force of volunteers, which at first amounted to but little more than one hundred men, now began to increase, one hundred men having arrived from Augusta. Major Williamson, of the Ninety-Six regiment, soon arrived with three hundred men. He was ordered to Harlin's Ford, on the Savannah River, about thirty miles above Augusta. Colonel Thomson had also arrived with his rangers and three hundred men, and was ordered to take post at a place called "The Ridge." Colonel Richardson, with three hundred men, was ordered to take post near the mouth of the Enoree, to be a check on Fletchall's people in case they showed any intention of assisting Kirkland.

Mr. Drayton having now determined to resort to other means than discourses to the people, issued a proclamation in which he warned all persons to forthwith desist from following the counsels of Moses Kirkland or others in hostility to the lawful authority, and all such persons found in arms or in company with, or by the instigation of the said Kirkland, would be deemed public enemies, to be suppressed by the sword. This proclamation, which we are not able to publish in full, disconcerted and paralyzed Kirkland's exertions. The intended meeting of the King's men with arms and provisions did not take place. Kirkland sent his brother to Mr. Drayton with offers to surrender on promise of pardon. Mr. Drayton, knowing his character and reputation, demanded his surrender without promise to comply with his request. Kirkland's heart failed him, and he sought safety in flight. In planning the means of doing so, he looked about for several days, after which, with the assistance of two trusty friends, he fled in disguise to Charlestown. From thence he was sent, privately, to the sloop-of-war, *Tamar*, where he met Governor Campbell. Not long after this, he started on a vessel to General Gage, at Boston, which was captured and thus was exposed a nefarious plot to fall on the frontier settlements—the circumstances of which are recorded in the former chapter

After Kirkland's flight, Mr. Drayton received information that the King's men were collecting at O'Neal's Mill. He at once sent one hundred men to disperse them, who on their way, heard that Colonel Fletchall had arrived at that place with a large party of men. After consultation with Major Williamson and Major Mayson, the principal officers, Mr. Drayton decided (of the different propositions that had been made) to surprise the march of the King's men at night, during which they would be in a confused order, and a general rout would, in all probability, ensue.

To establish a strong reserve, and at the same time to secure a good position to fall back upon, four swivels were planted in the four windows of the gaol at Ninety-Six, so as to command every approach. A sufficient number of men were here placed with a supply of provisions and water. This post could not be forced except by firing the shingles on top of the building. One hundred men were then advanced to Island Ford, six miles above Ninety-Six Court House, on the Saluda River, where the King's men must be sure to pass. These were under the command of Major Mayson, who placed them in ambush so as to give a diagonal fire on Fletchall's men, if they should attempt to cross the river. One hundred men were also stationed about half way between Island Ford and Ninety-Six Court House. About ten o'clock at night, Mr. Drayton and Major Williamson went to see if the disposition of troops had been made as ordered. They waited at Island Ford until about two o'clock in the morning, when Mr. Drayton received certain accounts that the alarm was false in a measure, as only Cunningham was at O'Neal's Mill with about one hundred men. However, to be on the safe side, Major Mayson remained in position until daylight, while Mr. Drayton and Major Williamson returned to Ninety-Six Court House about 4 o'clock in the morning with the rest of the troops.

The one hundred men which Cunningham had ordered to O'Neal's Mill, were but the first of a large party, which had been summoned to rendezvous there. By the 17th of September, Mr. Drayton's forces were increased by the addition of Colonel Thomson's cammand, which consisted of a few militia and rangers. In two days afterwards, he was joined by a number of Major Williamson's militia. Colonel Fletchall had, in the meantime, arrived at O'Neal's Mill and his forces were increasing fast in number.

Mr. Drayton marched within about three-quarters of a mile of Ninety-Six Court House and formed a camp. Fletchall moved his camp to within four miles of the Saluda River, which now divided the opposing forces, now only about ten miles apart. Fletchall's forces amounted to upwards of twelve hundred, while Mr. Drayton's hardly reached a thousand. They were in good spirits, however, well disciplined and well officered, while on the contrary, Fletchall's men were under poor command, with no regular supplies. They could not have been kept together very long. Mr. Drayton's men were anxious to be led against the King's men. Had this been done, doubtless many lives would have been lost. With the approbation of the officers of the different commands, Mr. Drayton decided to remain in camp and watch Fletchall's movements. He put everything in practice to give Fletchall to understand that he would persevere in his bold determination to meet and confront him. As a cunning device, he sent a letter directed to Col. Richard Richardson, written for deception, in order that it might be intercepted. This weakened the impulses of the King's men and caused delay. In the meantime, Mr. Drayton's forces were fast approaching twelve hundred, while Fletchall's were diminishing. Mr. Dravton felt that it was an opportune time to attempt to heal the dissensions. He put forth another declaration on the 13th of September, 1775, which was sent to Fletchall's camp and publicly read.

This declaration is too lengthy for publication in full here. Mr. Drayton called attention to the fact, that the liberties of America were being treacherously and cruelly violated bv an abandoned administration in Great Britain, surrounding the throne, and deceiving majesty for their own corrupt purposes; that thirteen American colonies were successfullv confederated to hazard their lives and fortunes to wrest from the hands of traitors those invaluables which they had ravished from them and which the Americans had endeavored to recover by every peaceable means.

In this declaration he called the attention of the people to the fact that men of low degree, though of eminence in the new country, men totally illiterate, were trying to rise in the world by misleading their honest neighbors, and whom His Excellency the Governor, had amply promised to reward. He showed that these wicked men, by misrepresentation, were trying to sell their country in opposition to the voice of America. He stated further, that Mr. Tennant and himself had made progress through the disturbed parts of the country "to explain to the people at large, the nature of the unhappy disputes between the American colonies and Great Britain;" that thousands had heard and believed them. He stated emphatically the terms upon which the peace and safety of the country might be enjoyed. He declared that it should be his duty to march against and attack, as public enemies, all and every person in arms in that part of the country in opposition to the measures of Congress. This plain, outspoken official declaration, backed as it was by a large body of troops, some of whom were Provincials, made an impression upon the malcontents in Fletchall's camp and caused them to pause. Hence, after consultation, they sent a deputation to Mr. Drayton's camp, near Ninety-Six Court House, to confer with him. Soon after, Colonel Fletchall and other malcontent leaders also arrived in his camp with full powers to treat and conclude terms of pacification. Before Mr. Drayton could, however, treat of this matter, it became necessary that he should understand precisely how far he was actually authorized, by the Council of Safety, to act on so important an occasion. Satisfying himself on this point, he proceeded to carry his plan into execution with Colonel Fletchall and the other leaders. Articles of treaty were drawn up and signed on the 16th day of September, 1775. (See original articles, Drayton's Memoirs, vol. i, page 399). After this treaty, by which the peace and harmony of the up-country appeared to be restored upon a just and honorable basis, Colonel Fletchall and the rest of his deputies returned to their camp beyond the Saluda River, where the treaty, which had just been concluded, was made known. Some of the principal leaders who had remained in camp, became wrathy and declared that they would not abide by what had been done. As Mr. Drayton had before predicted, they were divided among themselves. The whole camp, therefore, broke up, except

Robert Cunningham and about sixty of his followers, who declared that they were not included and would not be bound by the terms of the treaty. When Mr. Drayton heard of this he wrote to Cunningham, which brought a reply from him, dated at Page's Creek, October 6th, in which he stated he would not abide by the instrument of peace. He accused Mr. Drayton of making the bargain to suit himself, and of taking advantage of men half scared out of their senses, at the sight of liberty caps and sound of cannon, "as seeing and hearing had generally more influence with some men than reason."

Cunningham and his men did not remain in their camp very long. They soon dispersed, as they were obliged to submit to the necessity of the case.

The affairs of the up-country being adjusted by Mr. Drayton, he had no further use for military support. He discharged the troops under his command, then about eleven hundred strong, with thanks. Major Williamson was ordered to transmit suitable returns to the Council of Safety, of money and rations disbursed, etc. In making his return, October 16th, Major Williamson closed with the following complimentary words: "And it is but justice to those patriotic troops who had come forth at their country's call, to say, that during the whole time this army lay encamped near Ninety-Six Court House, they were patient under all the difficulties and deprivations they experienced. During most of the time, their huts and dwellings were penetrated by heavy rains, but discontent was not seen among them, for, satisfied with the cause in which they were engaged and with the leaders who commanded them, they submitted to such military regulations as the occasion required. In the camp good order was preserved and without it the advanced posts were duly and regularly stationed and relieved."

The mission of Mr. Drayton and Mr. Tennant to the people between the Broad and Saluda rivers now closed and happily, in a different manner from what many at first supposed. By a preconcerted plan, Mr. Drayton had arranged through Mr. Richard Paris to assemble the warriors from the Cherokee Nation at Congaree Store. This store was just below old Granby, on the west side of the Congaree River, and not far from the city of Columbia. Mr. Drayton met the warriors on the 25th of September and explained to them in a talk, suitable to the occasion, the nature of the dispute between Great Britain and America. He exhorted them to hold fast to the chain of peace and friendship with the people of the colony, assuring them that they should receive such supplies of ammunition and other articles, both for pleasure and comfort, as could be spared by the Provincial Congress and Council of Safety. He made them presents suitable to the occasion after which they took leave and returned home apparently satisfied.

In the distribution of presents, Mr. Drayton endeavored to impress upon the Indians the importance of patience and economy under existing circumstances. He pulled his coat off and presented it to them and said, "for my part in this unhappy time, I will be content to wear an Osnaburg split shirt." These split shirts were worn much in the up-country at this time. They were split or opened in front and ornamented, and like a summer coat, were worn, says a writer, over their dress. Mr. Drayton thought proper to adapt his dress to the customs of the people he was among, and when he returned to Charlestown, which he did in a short time, he occasionally wore the split shirt merely to introduce it to the people where merchandise was scarce and economy was important.

CHAPTER X.

CAPTAIN ROBERT CUNNINGHAM ARRESTED AND CARRIED TO CHARLESTOWN AND INCARCERATED.—CAPTURE OF ONE THOUSAND POUNDS OF POWDER BY PATRICK CUNNINGHAM WHILE ON ITS WAY TO THE CHEROKEE NATION.—KING'S MEN MARCHING AGAINST MAJORS WILLIAMSON AND MASON WHO ARE BESEIGED IN STOCKADE FORTS AT NINETY-SIX.—TERMS OF CAPITULATION AGREED UPON.

THE fact was stated in the former chapter that Captain Robert Cunningham and his followers refused to abide by or consider themselves included in the treaty as made between Mr. Drayton on one side, and Fletchall, Ford, Greer and other leaders of the King's men, on the other.

Robert Cunningham still expressing himself as being in open opposition to the Provincial authority, was arrested in pursuance of the orders of Major Andrew Williamson, who remained in command of the Ninety-Six District after the departure of Mr. Drayton and Mr. Tennant. This arrest was grounded on an affidavit made by Cap tain John Caldwell, of the rangers, before Richard Rapley Esq., of Ninety-Six, on the 23d of October, 1775, charg ing the said Cunningham with the use of seditious words. Had Cunningham kept still, the troubles which we relate in this chapter would have been averted at least for a time. He was sent to Charlestown where he appeared before the Provincial Congress. The affidavit being read to him, he was thereupon questioned by the president of the body. Cunningham said, that he could not deny that he had made expressions somewhat like those mentioned in Captain Caldwell's affidavit, which had just been read to him; that he believed that Captain Caldwell had not perjured himself; and though he did not consider himself bound by the late treaty at Ninety-Six, yet, had constantly behaved himself as peaceably as any man; and although he had opinions, he had expressed them only when asked. After this explanation of himself, Cunningham was committed to jail in Charlestown in pursuance of an order from the Congress, by a warrant under the hand and seal of the president of that body. Thomas Grimball was at that time sheriff at Charlestown. He was directed "to afford to the said Robert Cunningham every reasonable and neccessary accommodation at the public charge; but that he should not suffer the said Cunningham to converse or correspond with any person whatsoever; nor was he to have the use of pen, ink or paper, unless by express leave of Congress, or authority derived from them.

The arrest and imprisonment of Robert Cunningham appears to have been a mistake, as it caused another insurrection in Ninety-Six District. The people of the up-country were greatly incensed, or at least some, who were in sympathy with the Royal authority, but were willing to submit to the powers that be.

When Mr. Drayton gave a talk to the Cherokee chiefs at the Congaree store, already alluded to, he promised to send them powder and lead as the situation of the colony's funds would permit. On the 4th of October, 1775, a vote passed the Council of Safety to supply the Cherokee Nation with one thousand pounds of powder and two two thousand pounds of lead. Accordingly, a wagon was dispatched with it as a present to the Cherokees, under the escort of a subaltern officer of the rangers and twenty privates.

The arrest of Robert Cunningham aroused his brother, Patrick Cunningham, who, gathering a body of friends composed of about sixty, pursued his brother Robert, with the expectation of recapturing him. Failing to overtake him, they turned their attention to the powder which was on its way to the Indians. They succeeded in taking it

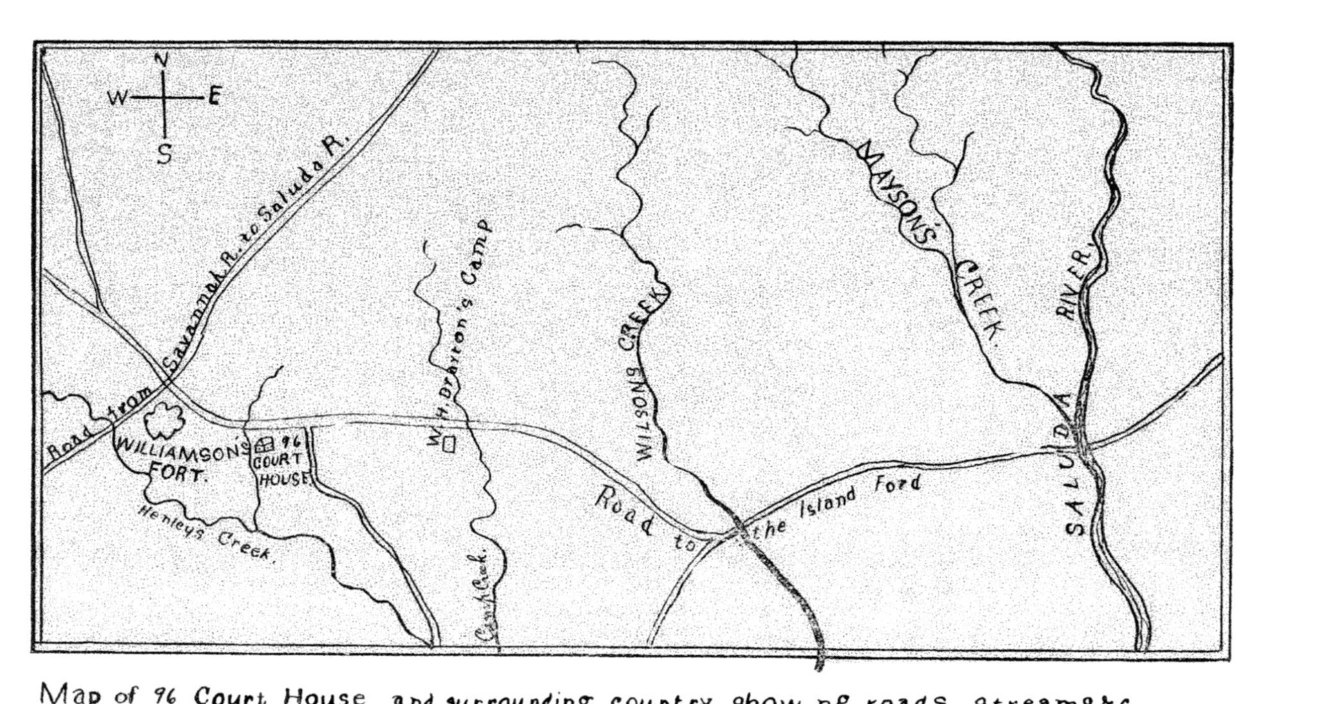

Map of 96 Court House and surrounding country show ng roads, streams &c., together w th Williamson's Fort.
"Th s map s copied from one found n Drayton's Memo rs.

at Mine Creek, between the Ridge and Ninetv-Six Court House, on the 3d day of November, 1775, causing the guard to surrender, and the ammunition to be immediately seized and carried off. A report was thereupon industriously circulated that the powder was sent to inflame the Indians to rise upon and massacre all those who refused to sign the document of the association. Captain Richard Paris, who had forsaken the patriot cause and joined the insurgents or King's men because he had not been noticed in the late appointments and promotions in the military arrangements of the Provincial Congress, not only circulated this report, but averred in an affidavit, that the ammunition taken by Patrick Cunningham was for that purpose. He abused outrageouslv Mr. Drayton, at whose hands he expected promotion, and to lessen his consequence among the people, he urged that the recent meeting with the Cherokee warriors at the Congaree store, which he was instrumental in bringing about, was for the purpose of cutting off all who were considered as disaffected persons or King's men.

Such reports as these, of course, exasperated the ignorant multitude and roused them to commit acts, which placed them in open arms against the country.

Major Williamson went in pursuit of the Loyalists who had captured the powder, but was compelled to retreat before superior numbers. The Insurgent or Loyalist element was speedily swelled in numbers, while Williamson's militia came in very slowly. Although the insurgent forces were rapidly increasing, Williamson could not be made to believe that they would dare to attack him. He continued in camp, laboring under this impression until about the 18th of November, when he received information that the insurgents were in full march upon him and had already crossed the Saluda River at Island Ford, in order to attack him. At this time, Major Williamson was joined by Major Mayson who had been in the neighborhood of Island Ford with thirty-seven rangers. Major Williamson wanted to march at once and attack the insurgents, but yielded to the judgment of Major Mayson, who advised him to retreat to the cleared ground of Colonel Savages' plantation. This was separated from Ninety-Six Court House and gaol by a ravine and spring supplying the inhabitants with water, affording a place where they might erect breastworks and from whence they might use their swivels to advantage. They also thought they would be more likely to receive reinforcements at this place. Colonel Thomson was already on the way to them with his rangers. According to this agreement Major Williamson took up his line of march and arrived at the proposed ground about daybreak on Sundav, the 19th of November, with troops, live stock, provisions and baggage.

A square of about one hundred and eighty-five yards was taken in and fortified as well as time and means would allow. The men worked unceasingly for about three hours and a temporary stockade fort was made of fence rails, straw and beeves' hides, with such other materials as they could put their hands on. The defenses extended from a barn and store to some outhouses, and at a distance of about two hundred and fifty yards from the jail.

Williamson and his men had hardly enclosed themselves in this rustic fortification when the insurgents appeared with drums beating and colors flying and taking possession of the court house and jail, they advanced troops and completely invested the stockade fort of Major Williamson's forces. Immediately upon their arrival, Major Williamson dispatched an officer with a flag to know what their intention was. Major Robinson and Captain Patrick Cunningham, who appeared to be the leaders, refused to have a conference with any one but the commanding officers. Major Mavson and Captain Bowie were then sent to them. They met the insurgent leaders—Robinson, Cunningham and Evan McLauren—on half-way ground between the two bodies of troops. The parties had about fifteen minutes conversation. Major

Mayson and Captain Bowie returned and reported to Major Williamson that the insurgents demanded his immediate surrender and disbanding, hinting, at the same time, that it would be necessary for the men to keep inside of the fort for safety. Just at this time, two of Williamson's men near the fort were seized by the insurgents, upon which Major Williamson gave orders to rescue them. A general firing took place from the fort with swivels and small arms, which was answered by the insurgents with rifles and muskets from behind trees, houses, logs, stumps and fences. For two hours and a half the firing was incessant on both sides and continued at intervals until night. The garrison, including fifty-five officers, consisted of five hundred and sixty-two. (See Drayton's Memoirs, vol. ii, page 150.)

During the night the fort kept up a firing, lest the insurgents in the darkness should endeavor to creep near and fire the fort. On the next day (Monday) the firing was commenced and continued as had been kept up the evening before. The beseigers constructed something which they called *mantelets* for the purpose of approaching the fort to set it on fire, but not being able to advance them in their front so as to hide their approach, they were destroyed. The firing only slackened with the day, Monday; it was revived and continued on Tuesday and lasted all day until about sun down, when the insurgents displayed a white flag from the jail building and called a parley. To this, an answer was given that if they wished to send an officer or messenger he would be received with perfect safety. Some time during the night a messenger was seen approaching the fort carrying a lighted candle as a protection, charged with a letter from Major Robinson, directed to Colonel Mayson, who was Lieutenant-Colonel of the Ninety-Six regiment of militia of which Williamson was then acting as Major. But the Council of Safety had placed Major Williamson in command on this occasion, as he was more influential in that part of the country.

This letter reiterated the former demands to surrender, allowing only one hour for an answer. To this Majors Williamson and Mayson replied that they were determined never to resign their arms. This was transmitted by Captain Bowie. In two hours he returned with the original demand, accompanied by Captain Patrick Cunningham. Williamson met them about fifty yards in front of the fort and after some conference, Cunningham went with them into the fort. Here they entered into a discussion as to the claims and rights of each party, after which, it was decided that a conference should take place the next morning. Accordingly, at the appointed hour, Majors Williamson and Mayson and Captains Williamson and Bowie met Major Robinson and Captains Cunningham, McLauren and Pearis. It was agreed that hostilities should immediately cease; that the garrison should be marched out of the fort and their swivels given up. By a secret understanding, those swivels were to be restored privately in a day or two; that the fort should be destroyed flat without damaging the house therein; that the differences should be submitted to Lord William Campbell, the Governor, on the part of the insurgents and to the Council of Safety on the part of Major Williamson and those under his command; that each party should send its messengers to their superiors and be allowed twenty days to return; that Major Robinson should withdraw his men over the Saluda River and there disperse them as he pleaseth or keep them embodied until His Excellency's orders be known; that no person should, in the meantime, be molested in returning home; that should reinforcements arrive they should be bound by the treaty; that all prisoners be immediately set at liberty; that the fortifications be leveled, and the well, which had been dug in the fort, be filled up.

Such was the end of an affair which might have produced the most alarming consequences. It is said, however, with such an army as Major Robinson commanded, he could not have made much more out of it, as it was composed of undisciplined and discordant elements. It was made up of inferior leaders among the old insurgents, of a class of people who from ignorance, believed Paris' affidavit with respect to the purpose for which the powder was sent to the Indians. Many of the insurgents joined from timidity, seeing that party so rapidly increase in a short space of time. None of those who had signed the treaty at Ninety-Six took part in this insurrection, except McLauren, although history records the fact that Colonel Fletchall gave private encouragement to this bold attempt of the insurgents (or *Tories* as they should be more properly called) to upturn the existing Provincial authority.

The casualties were very slight in this beseigement. Of Major Williamson's party, only one man was killed and twelve wounded. On the other side, several were killed and about twenty wounded. The insurgents could not have been very courageous in the affair since they failed to attack this stockade fort, the construction of which only consumed three hours. The account which we find says, that during the whole time of the firing, they continued almost out of gun shot range, except those who were stationed in the brick jail at Ninety-Six. These alone annoved the troops of Major Williamson, while the others, as we have said, kept themselves posted behind logs, fences, and other securities, and this accounts for the small execution which was affected upon them during a firing of small arms and swivels for three days.

Says a writer of this affair: "Major Williamson's men had suffered great hardships during the time they had been cooped up in this temporary fortress, being obliged to lay by their arms during the nights, to be ready against surprise, and their tour of duty being frequent and heavy; and particularly experiencing the total want of water from Sunday morning to Tuesday afternoon. However, during this severe trial, not only of courage but constitutional energy, they did not murmur; but while some fought the beseigers, fatigue parties were digging a well; and at length, after penetrating through a very tenacious clay soil forty feet deep, water was obtained, which relieved the necessities of the garrison. In addition to these difficulties; they had nearly exhausted all their powder; for of 200 pounds weight which they had at the commencement of the firing, only thirty pounds weight remained, except what each man had in his powder horn."

The small quantity of powder which remained was only known to Major Williamson and one other person. This was the principal cause why the fort surrendered, for Major Williamson expressly states in his official report (see Dravton's Memoirs, vol. ii, page 2), on the the 25th of November, that he had in the fort thirty eight barrels of flour, four live beeves, and very good water from the well which he had dug, and but for powder he could have maintained his post for a considerable time.

CHAPTER XI.

THE FAMOUS SNOW CAMPAIGN.

THE recent success of the insurgents in the seige of Williamson's fort at Ninety-Six had emboldened them to continue their opposition to the Provincial authority. The time had arrived, however, when either the Provincial or Royal authority must predominate in South Carolina. The Council of Safety, under the authority of the Provincial Congress, had determined from the first to take no backward steps. The people must be made to understand and recognize the existing authority. Up to this time the steps taken by the Council of Safety to resist oppression, redress wrongs and enlist the people on the side of liberty, had been prudent and cautious. Mr. Drayton and Mr. Tennant had visited Ninety-Six District and by eloquent and persuasive arguments had pointed out to the people the nature of the controversy between America and Great Britain. We have seen the results in former chapters. There was no longer any necessity for this sort of work. The time had now come when the people must be taught the lesson of the fable of the man who found a boy upon one of his trees stealing apples. The Tories or Insurgents in this fable represent the character of the young "sauce box," who did not respect the rights of the old man (South Carolina). The Council of Safety determined to "fetch him" down. Up to this time this body had only been throwing "tufts of grass." This had only intended to increase the obstinacy of the insurgent elements and make them laugh, as it were. Now it became necessary "to see what virtue there is in stones." In other words, the discordant elements of the up-country had to be taught the moral of this fable "if good words and gentle means will not reclaim the wicked, they must be dealt with in a more severe manner."

While Major Williamson was beseiged by the insurgents at Ninety-Six, Colonel Richardson had commenced his march against them in pursuance of orders he had received from the Provincial Congress, and in doing so, he was directing his course towards the middle or upper part of Colonel Fletchall's regimental district, which embraced, before divided into three, the country between the Broad and Saluda Rivers.* But as soon as he heard of Major Williamson at Ninety-Six, he changed his route. He appears to have started from Charlestown, and by forced marches reached the Congaree River about the 27th of November, 1775. At this time his command consisted of about one thousand men. Col. John Thomas, Sr., was however, with his newly organized Spartan Regiment, pressing forward, the account says from the northwestern portion of the colony (now Spartanburg County) to meet him.

At his camp on the Congaree, Colonel Richardson wrote to the Council of Safety, giving them an account of the situation in the up-country. He states in his letter that the insurgents were much elated by their success at Ninety-Six; that his men desired to be led against them and would not be satisfied unless they were allowed "to finally subdue and to effectually put down the opposition." In this letter he warned Congress that it was a matter of necessity to silence the discontents of the back country and that although in doing so, the expense would be great, still the crisis at hand demanded prompt and decisive action.

Colonel Thomson, who belonged to Colonel Richardson's command, also wrote to the Council of Safety as follows: "Several of the officers and men declare that they will never take up arms again unless they have liberty to subdue America, as they observe that those who are not for America are undoubtedly against it."

Colonel Richardson remained in his camp on the Congaree until about the 30th of November, for the purpose of

---

* See map.

conveying his wagons and baggage across that river and also for the purpose of collecting the various bodies of militia that were marching to him. When he was ready to maich his army consisted of about fifteen hundred. Before leaving his camp his officers held a council of war and decided that they were not bound by the recent treaty of cessation of arms at Ninety-Six. The army marched to the Saluda River, and crossed the same into Dutch Fork (between Broad and Saluda Rivers). On the 2d of December, it encamped at McLauren's store, fifteen miles from Saluda River. At this camp several of Fletchall's disaffected captains were brought in as prisoners, among whom were John Mayfield, William Hunt and others. Colonel Richardson's command was here joined by Colonel Thomas' Spartan regiment, with two hundred men; Colonel Neel two hundred (Colonel Neel came from the "new acquisition" territory of South Carolina); Colonel Lyles one hundred and fifty men—which, together with Colonel Thomas' regiment of rangers, increased Colonel Richardson's command to about two thousand and five hundred. This did not include the command of Colonel Polk from North Carolina, which consisted of six hundred men, and which were in full march to join Colonel Richardson's forces. At this time, it is said, the insurgents were hovering about with little confidence in their leaders, not more perhaps than four hunded of them were assembled in arm, and of these, constant desertions were taking place, leaving their number so small that they retrograded towards the sources of the Saluda River and the Cherokee Nation.

On the 4th of December the Council of Safety wrote a letter to Colonel Richardson desiring him to publish a declaration inviting the insurgents "to lay down their arms" and to promise "the strictest neutrality," and upon doing this to grant terms of mercy and protection." Before this request was received from the Council of Safety, however, Colonel Richardson, anticipating their wishes, issued the following declaration:

"SOUTH CAROLINA:

Whereas, on the 3d dav of November last past, Patrick Cunningham, Henry O'Neal, Hugh Brown, David Reise, Nathaniel Howard, Henry Green, and sundrv other persons did, in Ninety-Six District, raise a dangerous insurrection and commotion, and did, near Mine Creek in said district, feloniously take and carry away a quantity of ammunition, the property of the public, and in contempt of public authority; and did also with further and by force of arms on the 19th, 20th and 21st days of said month of November, at Ninety-Six, in the district aforesaid, attack, beseige, kill and wound a number of good people of this colony, and in manifest violation of peace aud good order, and breach of a solemn treaty, entered into on the 16th day of September, made and concluded between the Hon. William Henry Drayton on the one part and Col. Thomas Fletchall and others on the other part, thereby becoming guilty of the attrocious crimes of robbery, murder and breach of peace.

To satisfy public justice, in the first punishment of all which crimes and offenses as far as the nature of the same will admit, I am now come to these parts in the name and behalf of the colony, to demand of the inhabitants the delivering up of the bodies of all principal offenders herein, together with the said ammunition, and full restitution for the ravages committed, and also the arms and ammunition of all the aidors and abettors of these robbers, murderers and disturbers of the peace and good order as aforesaid. And in case of neglect or refusal for the space of five days, I shall be under the necessity of taking such steps as will be found disagreeable; but which I shall certainly put in execution for the public good.

Given under my hand this the 8th day of December, 1775.

RICHARD RICHARDSON."

In consequence of this declaration numbers came in and delivered up their arms and received the promised protection. This, however, did not include capital offenders. No leaders were surrendered by the insurgents. Colonel Richardson conducted himself with prudence and humanity towards those who came in to surrender themselves, dismissing them with soft words and kind admonitions. "The army," says a writer, "still advancing and increasing in numbers, struck terror into the insurgents and the disaffected, and they constantly retreated, keeping about twenty miles in advance of Colonel Richardson's army. They now perceived that they had been deceived by their leaders as to the strength and means of the Provincial Congress and the Council of Safety; while at the same time, they found no promises or assistance to be relied upon as coming from Lord William Campbell." "Weak as a rope of sand," says Ramsay, "they could neither face the invading army nor fall upon any measures for maintaining themselves in the land of their fathers. At one time they would take heart and threaten to stand and give battle; but so soon as the army commenced its march upon them, cowardly councils and guilty consciences obliged them to turn and retreat. In this manner the operations were principally carried on; a steady pursuit, detachments taken prisoners and sometimes recovering portions of ammunition which Patrick Cunningham had taken; being mostly the services in which they were engaged." (See letter from Colonel Richardson to Colonel John Laurens, Gibbs' Documentary History, 1764-1776, page 241).

By December 12th Colonel Richardson's army numbered three thousand men, and account says they penetrated the interior as far as the great survey (the Cherokee boundary line) on Duncan's Creek (in Laurens County). They had now several prisoners which, as Colonel Richardson to the Council of Safety said, were "of the first magnitude." Among these were Colonel Thomas Fletchall, Captains Richard Paris, Jacob Frey, George Shuburg and John McWilliams. The last named was the person who constructed the mantlets which they endeavored to use against the stockade fort at Ninety-Six. These were sent to Charlestown under a suitable guard commanded by Captain Richard Richardson, Jr.*

*Captain Richardson was the husband of Mrs. Dorcas Richardson, one of the heroines of Mrs. Ellet's "Women of the Revolution." Her residence was in Clarendon. She was the daughter of a prominent Irish gentleman whose name was Captain John Nelson, who married a Miss Browning, of South Carolina. A ferry over the Santee River, established and kept by them, is still known as Nelson's Ferry. Their

Colonel Fletchall, when he was captured was hid in a cave on Fair-Forest Creek, above its junction with Tyger River, from which he was unkenneled by Colonel Thomson's rangers, who had been sent to scour that part of the disaffected district, and to beat up Fletchall's quarters where he resided. (See Colonel Richardson to Henry Laurens Gibbs' Documentary History, (1764-1776), page 239)

John Drayton, LL.D., author of "Memoirs of American Revolution" says, (vol. ii, page 129), that in 1829 he received a letter from Spartanburg District, stating that there was a large sycamore tree with a hollow seven or eight feet wide on the north side of Fair Forest Creek, two and a half miles below Brandon's mills, in which Colonel Fletchall occasionally secreted himself. The letter stated that it was from this tree Fletchall was taken. The

---

descendants are numerous in that section. It is said that Cornwallis in his march through the interior of South Carolina, after the fall of Charlestown, established his headquarters at the house of the widow Nelson, near the ferry. She received and entertained him on condition that her property should be protected. When a quantity of her valuable plate had been discovered and claimed by its captors, she reminded Cornwallis of his promise. His Lordship refused to have the plate restored to her, replying that his promise had reference only to things above the ground.

Dorcas married at the age of twenty in 1761, and removed to her husband's plantation about twenty miles up the river, near the junction of the Congaree and Wateree. Here she lived in affluence with her husband until the storm of the Revolution began. When the Loyalists in the upper districts in South Carolina were incited by the royal governor, Lord William Campbell, three regiments were organized to march against them. These were commanded by General Richardson, father of Captain Richardson. After the famous "Snow Campaign" General and Captain Richardson were both retained in office on account of their great popularity with the troops. Edward, a younger brother, was appointed captain of rangers under Colonel Thomson.

A regiment of riflemen was raised in March of the following year. This was commanded by Col. Thomas Sumter and one of the companies in the same by Captain Richardson. From this time and during the remaining six years he was at home but very little with his family. After the fall of Charlestown, he, his father and brother were

tree was at that time standing, while the cave referred to was filled up.

Some valuable papers were captured with Colonel Fletchall. He, it is said, was the depositary of Lord William Campbell's correspondence and secrets. These papers were transmitted by Colonel Richardson to the Council of Safety. While Colonel Thomson's rangers were at Fletch all's place, Captains Plummer and Smith, with thirty of their men, surrendered themselves with their arms, &c.

Still following the trail of the insurgents, Colonel Richardson pressed forward through all the inclemencies of the weather. His men were thinly clothed and poorly provided for; but they determined to stay not their steps until the object of their expedition was completed. Arriving at Liberty Hall, on the line between Newberry and

---

taken prisoners. In violation of the terms of capitulation, Richard was taken to John's Island, a military station, where he very quickly fell a victim to small pox. As soon as he had sufficiently recovered, he made his escape and returned to the neighbood of his home, where he concealed himself in the Santee Swamp. At this time the British troops had overrun the State, and Colonel Tarleton had made the house of Captain Richardson, with some others, a station for his regiment of cavalry. They lived sumptuously on his richly stocked and well cultivated plantation, while Mrs. Richardson was restricted to a single apartment, with a scanty allowance of her own stores. From this she sent food to her husband in the swamp by a negro servant in whom she had implicit trust. Mrs. Richardson occasionally ventured to visit her husband, taking with her her little daughter. Captain Richardson's chosen place of retreat was on a little knoll or elevation in the swamp, which he called "John's Island."

When the British got wind of Captain Richardson's escape, they made a diligent search for him and offered rewards for his capture. One day while a British officer was caressing the little child, she was asked when she had seen her papa. The mother grew pale, as it had only been a short time since she had seen him. The thoughtless pratler replied that she had seen him only a few days before on "John's Island." The officer concluded the child had been dreaming and knowing of but one "John's Island," near the sea coast, replied, "Pshaw, that was a long time ago." The little telltale was not trusted with another visit to her father.

Mrs. Richardson's feelings were often terrified by the threats of the British, as to what they would do with Captain Richardson in case of

Laurens counties, and four or five miles from the Enoree River, south of Duncan's Creek, the army encamped for a few davs. It was from this place, the prisoners referred to were sent to Charlestown, they being considered by the officers and people of that part of the country as offenders, whose active conduct against the patriot cause and the association of congress did not justify their being longer at large.

Colonel Richardson's army up to this time, numbered about five thousand, and consisted of his own regiment, Colonel Thomson's light horse, Colonel Thomas' Spartan regiment, Colonel Neel's, Colonel Polk's and Lieutenant-Colonel Martin's, Colonel Rutherford and Colonel Graham's troops from North Carolina. In a letter to the Council of Safety, Colonel Richardson says, of the

---

his capture. On one occasion the officers displayed in her sight their swords reeking with blood—probably that of her cattle—and told her it was the blood of Captain Richardson, whom they had killed. She remained in a state of cruel suspense for several days. One day while the troops were absent Captain Richardson ventured to visit his home. Before he was ready to return to the swamp, however, a patroling party appeared unexpectedly at his gate. He was saved by Mrs. Richardson's presence of mind and calm courage. Seeing the British soldiers about to come in, she appeared busy at something about the front door, thus retarding their progress while her husband made his escape by the back door.

Captain Richardson subsequently united with Marion's command. One day he returned to his home accompanied by an escort. In a short time the British and Tories were seen advancing. All of Richardson's men mounted and made their escape, except a young man named Roberts, with whom Mrs. Richardson was well acquainted. In vain did she beg with streaming tears to the British officers to spare his life. He was hanged to a walnut tree only a few paces from her door. Mrs. Richardson was told that she "would soon see her husband kick like that fellow."

After the return of peace Mrs. Richardson continued to reside at the same place with her family. She survived her husband many years and died in 1834, at the advanced age of ninety-three. Through all the trials and vicissitudes in life her reliance and consolation was in her religion. It was her hope and triumph in the hour of death.

commands of Colonels Rutherford and Graham numbering five hundred men, that "to their honor they stepped forth unsolicited to aid this colony in the cause of liberty." We would also mention that about the 20th of December, Colonel Richardson's army was joined by Major Andrew Williamson, Captain Hammond and a small party of Colonel Stephen Bull's regiment.

The presence of such a large army had a good effect on the feelings of the disaffected people in that part of the colony. They were much terrified and came in with fear and trembling, giving up their arms with deep contrition for their late conduct. The spirit of discord was much abated. Most of the captains came in with a good portion of their companies. The District of Ninety-Six was now clear of any organized body of insurgents, but a camp of the principal aggressors still existed four miles beyond the Cherokee boundary line, at a place called the *Great Cane Brake*, on the Reedy River, about twenty-five miles from Hollingsworth's Mill. Colonel Richardson determined to break up this nest of sedition and turbulent spirits and for this purpose he detached from this army at Hollingsworth's Mill, about thirteen hundred cavalry and infantry under the command of Colonel William Thomson. All of these were volunteers, and among them were Colonels Martin and Rutherford, Neel, Polk and Lyles and Major Williamson and other officers of distinction. This command set out in the night on the 21st of December and after a tedious march of near twenty-three miles, Colonel Thomson with his command got within sight of the camp fires of the insurgents at a distance of about two miles. A halt was taken for a short time, after which, towards daylight on the 22d of December, they moved forward to attack the camp. They had nearly surrounded it when they were discovered. A flight immediately took place from the side which had not yet been surrounded. Patrick Cunningham escaped on a horse barebacked, telling every one as he galloped away "to shift for himself."

The troops were much enraged against the insurgents or King's men, as they preferred to call themselves, and had it not been for the humanity of Colonel Thomson, great slaughter would have taken place. The pursuit was continued for some distance and five or six of the insurgents were killed. Their camp consisted of about two hundred men, about one hundred and thirty of whom were taken prisoners. All their baggage, arms and ammunition remained in possession of the victors. None of the colonial troops were killed and only one was was wounded. This was a son of Colonel Polk, a youth of promise, who was shot through the shoulder.

On the 23d of December, Colonel Thomson with his detachment returned to Richardson's camp. Soon after this it commenced snowing and continued without intermission for thirtv hours. The account says, (see Drayton's Memoirs, vol. ii, page 122), that the ground was generally covered for two feet. The army was without tents. Their shoes and clothing being much worn, they were badly prepared to encounter such dreadful weather. For this reason, Colonel Richardson kept his troops longer in the field, but the insurrection having now been crushed, he proceeded to dismiss his commands. On Christmas day he returned his thanks to the officers and men. He first dismissed the North Carolina troops under Colonels Rutherford, Martin, Graham and Polk's commands, afterwards the commands of Colonels Neel and Thomas and Major Williamson, giving to each and all instructions during their homeward march to pursue such measures as would confirm the principles of those favorable to the American cause and to awe and work upon the fears of the disaffected elements. He delivered to Colonel Williamson six kegs of gunpowder, which he had taken from the insurgents and which he directed to be sent to Mr. Wilkerson, one of the Indian agents at the Cherokee Nation, as a part of the present the Council of Safety had sent them, but which had been seized by Patrick Cunningham and his party. Colonel Richardson during his march had succeeded in recapturing most of this powder. In a letter to the Council of Safety he reports, January 2d, 1776, the amount taken at different times to be two barrels and seven kegs.

The camp at Hollingsworth's Mill was now broken up. Colonel Williamson with the remaining portion of his command took up his march towards the Congaree. During his march his troops suffered extremely. They were poorly clad, their clothes being nearly worn out. They had no tents, and by reason of the snow, they did not set foot on the earth for seven days. When they halted they had to clear away the snow as well as they could before thev could make fires to cook their victuals, warm themselves and make places to sleep after a toilsome march. Many of us, who at a later day in the history of our country, endured like hardships and fatigue around the camp fires, can fully appreciate the sufferings of our forefathers, the veterans of the great American Revolution.

On the eighth day of Colonel Richardson's march a heavy cold rain fell, accompanied with sleet. Through all these difficulties the soldiers continued their march. They were glad to reach their old camping ground on the Congaree once more on the 1st day of January, 1776. Here Colonel Richardson after having taken steps for arranging the accounts and expenditures of the expedition, dismissed his soldiers to return to their homes. The stands of arms amounting to several hundred were sent to different places; some to Fort Charlotte on the Savannah, some were deposited at the Congaree and some sent to Camden. The prisoners were sent by water to Nelson's Ferry and escorted thence to Charlestown. The guard was commanded by Captain (afterwards General) Thomas Sumter. The prisoners consisted of ten captains and one hundred and twenty-six men. Of these thirteen were old offenders, having been with Cunningham when he seized the ammunition on its way to the Cherokee Indians, and also with Robinson when he beseiged Williamson at

Ninety-Six. Fifty-five had been at the seige of Ninety-Six and at the Cane Brake, and seventy-two were only at the seige of Ninety-Six. All the leaders of the insurgents had been captured except Major Robinson, Captains Patrick Cunningham and McLauren, and two or three others who fled the country. The Council of Safety, after considering the cases of the prisoners, released nearly all of them, except a few who had been most active in bringing about these disturbances. Colonel Richardson, in a letter to the Council of Safety, makes honorable mention of Colonel Thomson for his excellent conduct and support, during this expedition, which history has designated as the *Snow Campaign*, in commemoration of the hardships and sufferings which were borne by the soldiers with a devotion worthy of themselves and the cause in which they were engaged.

On this expedition Captain Thomas Sumter acted as Adjutant-General to Colonel Richardson; and Major Joseph Kershaw, whom we have before mentioned as accompanying Mr. Drayton on his mission, acted as treasurer and commissary general. These two officers filled these positions in a manner highly commendable to themselves.

Colonel Richardson deserved the thanks and applause of the country for the mild manner in which he conducted the expedition. Notwithstanding this, however, he deemed it prudent to adopt some measures by which the insurgents would in the future be held in check. He caused many of them to sign an instrument of writing, by which they imposed upon themselves the penalties of forfeiting their estates, real and personal, should they ever take up arms again or disturb the peace and tranquility of the colony.

The snow campaign against the insurgents between the Broad and Saluda rivers was now ended. In a concluding letter to the Council of Safety, dated January 2d, 1776, Colonel Richardson says: "The people are now more convinced than ever of their being wrong. The lenient measures have had a good effect, the spirit and power is gone from them. And I am sure (if not interrupted by designing men) that the country which I had it in my power to lay waste (and which the people expected) will be happy, and peace and tranquility take the place of ruin and discord. On the rivers, had I burnt, plundered and destroyed, ten thousand women and children must have been left to perish, a thought shocking to humanity."

The Provincial Congress met in February, 1776, soon after the expedition of Colonel Richardson. After the accounts of the campaign were audited and arranged, this body resolved that their thanks be presented through their president, by letter, "to Colonel Richard Richardson for the very important and signal services he has rendered to his country and to the common cause, by putting a stop to the late dangerous and alarming insurrection which the enemies of America had excited in the interior parts of the colony; desiring the Colonel to signify the thanks of this congress also to the officers and men who were under his command upon that expedition."

For sometime after Richardson's expedition, a system of disarming such of the insurgents as were discoved in Ninety-Six District prevailed. But in February, 1776, the Provincial Congress took this matter under consideration and ordered that the same be suspended. It was at this session of congress that this body also resolved, "as well for the convenience of electors of members of congress as on account of the happy influence which it may have upon the peace and union of the inhabitants" to divide the district heretofore spoken of as under Colonel Fletchall's command into three election districts or regimental divisions. The Lower or Dutch Fork comprehending one, the country below Little River another, and the Upper or Spartan District the third.

CHAPTER XII.

PATRIOTISM OF EARLY SETTLERS OF SPARTANBURG AND UNION COUNTIES.—INDIAN OUTRAGES, 1776. LETTER FROM PROF. MORRISON.

IN the preceding chapters we have shown that while the people in the interior of Ninety-Six district were divided in sentiment on the American cause for liberty, the people along the borders in the upper or Spartan District were, according to Mr. Drayton's account, "active and spirited." To quote again Mr. Drayton's words, he said of these people in a letter to the Council of Safety, written on Lawson's Fork: "They are staunch in our favor; are capable of forming a good barrier against the Indians and of being a severe check upon Fletchall's people on whom they border, etc." (See Drayton's Memoirs, vol. i, page 374).

Notwithstanding, that the first settlers of upper South Carolina sympathized, for the most part, with the patriot cause, yet it is doubtful, after the recent unhappy difficulties with the Cherokees, whether they were willing to engage in warfare with any people. Living as they did, on the borders of civilization in South Carolina, they fully realized the dangers to which they would be exposed in the event of war between the colonies and the mother country. The Indians, under tempting bribes, would, in all probability, side with Great Britain. They knew, too, the power of Great Britian, her armies and fleets, and that her flag waved in triumph over her vast empire throughout the four quarters of the globe. On the first appearance of a rupture between Great Britain and the American colonies, both parties were engaged to secure the friendship of the Indians, and but for the interference and intrigues of John Stuart, superintendent, and Alexder Cameron, deputv superintendent, among the Cherokees, these people might have remained in a quiet and neutral condition. Mr. Drayton says that "the Insurgents (in 1775) had, in vain, endeavored to induce the Cherokee Indians to come down and join them, but the Indians said they were satisfied." (See Drayton's Memoirs, vol. ii, page 131).

Perhaps the troubles which we are now to relate, were due, more than to anything else, to the intrigues of Alexander Cameron who, it appears, lived among the Cherokees.

This man Cameron, who was under the influence of John Stuart, was a bad and dangerous man. Besides his secret designs in the abominably wicked plot which has already been related in Chapter vii, he held a meeting with the Cherokee warriors, about four hundred in number, in the early part of 1776, in which he exhorted them that the people of America had used the King verv ill and had killed a considerable number of his army; that the King was to send out more soldiers to suppress them; that they (the Indians) ought not to turn against their father, the King, but that they should join his army against the people of America. To this the Indians replied that they could not fight, as they had no gunpowder. Cameron assured them that this apparent obstacle should not be in the way, for he would supply all their wants in this respect. He did all he could to induce the Indians to join the King's forces against the people of South Carolina. At the conclusion of his remarks, the Indians turned their backs upon him and discharged their guns. The whole assembly set up the war whoop, which was a signal that they approved of his discourse. (See Drayton's Memoirs, vol. i, page 414).

As we have already said, the frontier settlements, believing that the Indians might take the side of Great Britain, and in this event they would be exposed to impending danger, an effort was made to enlist them on the side of the patriots or else make such terms with them as would cause them to remain neutral during the approaching hostilities.

Among those who were delegated on a mission of this kind to the Cherokee Nation, was Captain Edward Hampton and his brother Preston. They were sent by the people of the frontier settlements who resided within the present limits of Spartanburg county. They were sent to see if by a suitable "talk" with the Indians, they could not be made to comprehend the cause of differences growing between the colonies and the Mother Country.

We have shown in a former chapter that the Council of Safety, appreciating the importance of maintaining a true friendship with these people, very unwisely, as the sequel proved, sent to them a thousand pounds of powder, intending the same as a present only, believing that the Cherokees would prize this above everything else.

Edward and Preston Hampton, upon their arrival in the Indian country, found Cameron and other British emissaries at work among them. Cameron made prisoners of them, and gave their horses, guns, and a case of pistols and holsters to the Indians. By some means they managed to escape with their lives. Returning home, they reported to the people of the settlements the result of their mission. The people grew alarmed for their safety. They sought safety in the old forts that were already con structed and perhaps in others that were hurriedly con structed. Through the machinations of the British emis saries, the Indians commenced their marauding expeditions in 1776 in western North Carolina and along the frontier settlements of South Carolina.

It is our purpose only to bring to the eye of the reader such of the outrages as accurred in our vicinity, some of which are recorded in history, while others are only traditional.

The first which we propose to mention as happening during the year 1776 was the murder of the Hampton family. This, as we understood it, was not far from the site of Wood's Fort, between Middle and South Tyger rivers, and near what is known as the Asa Cunningham place, on the line between the counties of Greenville and

Spartanburg, which was then the east line of the Cherokee Nation. Anthony Hampton (says Dr. Howe in his history of the Presbyterian Church of South Carolina) with his wife and daughter, Preston, Henry and Edward, his sons, and James Harrison, his son-in-law, moved to what was afterwards Spartanburg District, about the year 1774. It is said that the Indians were seeking a different settlement which they had located. As they approached Mr. Hampton's house, some of their men recognized the face of Preston Hampton, whom, as we have already stated, had just returned from the Indian towns and had given warning of their intended rising. Some of the children of Mr. Hampton were sent to give warning to the neighbors. Mr. and Mrs. Harrison were, at the time, absent for a short distance. Old Mr. Hampton, it is said, met the Indians cordially. He gave the chief a friendly grasp of the hand, but had not more than done this when he saw his son, Preston, fall from the fire of a gun. The same hand which he had grasped a moment before sent a tomahawk through his skull. In the same way his wife was killed. An infant son of Mr. and Mrs. Harrison was dashed against the wall of the house, which was spattered with its blood and brains. The Indians then set fire to the house of Mr. Hampton. Mrs. Hampton, on coming up, seeing her father's house in flames, came very near rushing into the midst of the savages. Her husband, anticipating what the trouble was, held her back until the savages were gone. Edward Hampton was, at the time, at the house of his father-in-law, Baylis Earle, on the North Pacolet.

The writer is indebted to Prof. Wm. S. Morrison, whose residence near Welford, S. C., is not far from the scene of this massacre, and who had taken great pains to investigate the circumstances according to the traditions of the neighborhood. We take pleasure in inserting his letter, which letter explains itself·

WELFORD, S. C., JULY 27, 1891.

Dr. J. B. O. Landrum, Landrum, S. C.

Dear Sir:—I have looked carefully into the matter of the place of the murder and burial of the Hampton family as you requested. I am satisfied I have found the burial place. Am not so sure as to the place of the massacre, though I believe it was near the graves.

Mr. Roddy Smith, now eighty-four (84) years old, lives in the the western part of Spartanburg county on the Saluda Gap road, between Duncan's Station on the Air Line, and Arlington or Cedar Hill Factory, about two miles from each place. Mr. Smith moved to the place where he now lives in 1830. Soon after he moved there while he was one day at work cleaning up an old field, Mr. Isham Evans came to him and asked if he knew where the 'Hampton graves' were. Upon Mr. Smith answering that he did not, Mr. Evans led him to the graves but a few yards distant and pointed out the spot where the Hamptons were buried—all in one large grave—by the side of which a child, whose name Mr. Evans did not call, was buried. Mr. Evans told Mr. Smith the spot had been shown him by a woman named Bridget Bright, daughter of James Bright, an old Revolutionary soldier who had helped bury the Hamptons. Mr. Smith says the signs of the two graves were then plainly to be seen. The spot had never been cleared, though the land around it had been in cultivation. Mr. Smith has never allowed the place to be cleared or worked over in any way.

A week ago, under Mr. Smith's guidance, I visited the spot. It has the appearance of an old grave yard. Trees mark the graves. These are on the highest point of a hill. This bill top is about three-eights of a mile back of Mr. Smith's house, some 300 yards from South Tyger River, one and one-half miles from Greenville and Spartanburg county line, seven-eights of a mile North of the Air Line Road at its nearest point, and about one and one-half miles from the railroad bridge over South Tyger River.

A short distance from "the graves" there used to be signs of a house. At the foot of the hill is a spring with large rocks around it. Near the spring, on another hill, stood a house, the chimney place of which may yet be seen. Mr. Smith has not allowed any changes to be made about the spring, which he says looks now just like it did 61 years ago. Along the hill, in 1830, was a dense swamp or thicket, which extended up the spring branch and between the two houses named.

I have talked with several old people whose lives have been spent in the immediate vicinity. There seems to be no difference of opinion--seems there has never been any—as to the precise location of the rude grave of Anthony Hampton and his family. As to his dwelling place, there is some difference of opinion. Mr. James R. Dickson (Mr. Dickson has since died) over 80 years old, says that he moved to the place where Mr. Jack Green now lives, in 1835. Within a few yards of the house rises a little stream known as the "Hampton branch," which is about three miles long. About midway of its course, this branch crosses the county line. A few hundred yards below the line, it crosses the Saluda Gap Road very near the residence of the late Asa Cunningham, whose spring is called the Hampton spring. On the same side of the road as the Cunningham house, where some locust trees are growing stood a house where some think the Hamptons lived and were murdered. Mr. Dickson has often seen the chimney place. He learned from two old men, Alex. and Joseph Thomson, and from a woman named Kizzey Mobley, that two children of Wade and Betty Hampton, were there murdered by the Indians and buried on an opposite hill, between the branch and Beaver Dam Creek. Kizzey Mobley told Mr. Dickson she had often seen the rail pen around the little grave. The father was absent. The mother fled through Beaver Dam Swamp. Several days afterward, she was found wandering through the woods near where Holly Spring Church now stands—then a wilderness—her clothing torn to rags, and taken to Wood's Fort, near Milford Presbyterian Church, on Beaver Dam Creek. Mr. Dickson knew nothing of the murder of the elder Hamptons. He says he was always told that the 'old people were buried two or three miles further down the river.' This agrees with Mr. Smith's statement as to the graves.

Some older people say this 'Hampton Branch Story' is a new thing, of which they heard nothing until after Wade Hampton's election as Governor, in 1876.

I am satisfied Mr. Smith has shown me the burial place. I believe that the murder was committed near the graves. No coffins were used. It is not likely bodies would be carried several miles. I have written *curente calumus*. The information is reliable. Work it up to suit yourself. * * * I am so glad you are writing a history of the county. You are the very man for the work. I want a copy.

Kind regards to Mrs. L. Yours truly,

WM. S. MORRISON.

Until the writer met Mr. Jas. K. Dickson in Greenville city, a few days prior to the reception of Mr. Morrison's letter, he had never heard of Wood's Fort*. It doubtless, like the others we have mentioned, had a history. There are many *little things*, as they were, which was once considered, were related by the early settlers of our country which have been lost in tradition, owing to the unpardonable indifference of the generations that followed to preserve and transmit them in the pages of history.

---

* In Johnson's Traditions (page 439) there are two forts mentioned as belonging to Spartanburg county, of which the writer can gather

But to return to the Indian depredation of 1776, we would further state that about the time of the Hampton massacre just related, James Reed, of North Carolina, had just come into the Tyger settlement on business connected with their safety. "He was attacked," says Rev. R. H. Reid in the Spartanburg Express, 1854, "at the old ford on North Tyger River, a short distance below Snoddy's Bridge. He was shot through the breast and thigh. He snatched the tomahawk out of the Indian's hand that had come up to scalp him. The Indian being disarmed, now fled." Reed escaped to Prince's Fort, which was again occupied by the terrified white people, where he remained until his wounds were healed.

The writer is also indebted to the writings of Mr. Reid for the account of the killing of Mr. John Miller.

Mr. Miller, it appears, had just returned with his family, from Poole's Iron Works, and while crossing Middle Tyger at Buffalo Bridge, at or near what is now known as Barry's Bridge, he was shot down and very soon expired. He had been, it is said, to the house of a neighbor and was returning with two other persons, whose names were Orr and Leach. As soon as Miller fell, these men attempting to escape by running up the south side of the river. The Indians, who were under the bridge, commenced to fire upon them. They ran to a marsh, which further hindered their progress. Orr being the stronger

---

little or no information concerning their history. One of these is Wood's Fort or Thomson's Station, and the other is Jamison's Fort on South Pacolet. Wood's Station stood near Beaver Dam Creek, between Middle and South Tyger rivers, and not far from what is known as "Granny" McMakin's Bridge. It being near the Cherokee Indian boundary line, it was doubtless built by the early settlers against the encroachments of the Indians. Fort Jamison, according to our best information, stood near the Blackstock Road, in the John Rudisil plantation (now Crawford Earle's place) on the south side of South Pacolet. It is stated in Johnson's Traditions that this fort was once commanded by a Captain McJunkin, of Colonel Thomas' regiment, who afterwards served, for a time, at Woods' Fort or Thomas' Station.

of the two, jumped over, while Leach fell in and lying quiet, the Indians thought him dead. They continued to pursue Orr, whom they killed and scalped, and after they had passed, Leach made good his escape. Orr was buried by the neighbors, in the bottoms where he was shot. Miller was buried about a quarter of a mile from him in the fork of North and Middle Tyger rivers, on a plantation now owned by Mr. David Anderson. "He was," says Mr. Reid, "buried without coffin or shroud, in the dress he had on. A brick wall encircling his grave marks his last resting place." We would here remark that the John Miller referred to by Mr. Reid was the father of *Sheriff* Sam Miller, whose name and character is well known to many of the older citizens of Spartanburg county. His widow subsequently became the wife of Hon. James Jordan, grandfather of the late Judge T. O. P. Vernon and Dr. J. J. Vernon, well known and popular citizens of Spartanburg county.

The following was gathered up several years ago by the writer as a neighborhood tradition, the same having happened in the neighborhood where he was born and raised.

Near Shiloh Church, on what is known as the Adam Greenling place, lived a Mr. Bishop, whose house during these troublesome times, was visited by the Indians. Mrs. Bishop had gone to visit some friends in Fort Prince and on this account her life was saved. She had left her husband at home with her three children—Isaac, Rachel, and another daughter, and a little colored boy, Simon. The Indians, as soon as they came to Mr. Bishop's house, murdered him and plundered his house, cutting open his bed ticks and scattering the feathers over the house. They then carried the three children off with them. The little colored boy Simon hid between the treadles of the loom and escaped their notice. The children remained in the hands of the Indians for six months, and after they had been subdued to submission, Mr. Davy Lewis, learning that they were still alive and their whereabouts, collected a party of friends and went to the Indian Nation, where he found them. The two elder ones recognized him and went and met him, while the third ran off with some frightened Indian children. The children being surrendered by the Indians to Mr. Lewis, were brought back to the bosom of the agonized mother.

Mrs. Phatome Alverson, who recently passed away at a bright old age, first related this circumstance to the writer. She said that the stolen boy, Isaac Bishop, married a Miss Frankee Ballenger, an aunt of hers. Mrs. Alverson further stated that Mr. Bishop had often related to her how the Indians treated him and his little sisters while they were held as captives. He was required in their long tramps to carry a *pappoose* (an Indian babe.) Sometimes his burden would become so heavy that he would, in his stubbornness, fall down in the mud. For this he was cruelly whipped by the Indians. He also said that he and his little sisters would almost die from hunger, and that when the Indians would fall asleep around the venison which they were hanging in the sun to dry, he would steal for himself and his little sisters. *

The late Mr. Isaac Pollard, who passed away only a few years ago, at the advanced age of about ninety years, has recalled to the writer the same facts and circumstances as given by Mrs. Alverson. He stated that the negro boy Simon lived in his neighborhood to a bright old age, and on account of this circumstance which occurred in his boyhood, and of which he maintained a vivid recollection in his old age, he was generally the center of attraction at log rollings and other gatherings where many delighted to interrogate him.

There were many of these Indian outrages which are lost in tradition. Some, however, were so glaring and cold-blooded that they have been handed down to us. One of these was the Hannon massacre on North Pacolet an account of which we will relate in the next chapter.

---

* Mr. Davy Lewis, who recovered the stolen children, was a brother-in-law of Mr. Bishop. He was also the father-in-law of Mr. Albery Wingo (father of Mr. John W. Wingo) who yet lives at an extreme old age.

CHAPTER XIII.

INDIAN INVASIONS AND MASSACRES OF 1776 CONTINUED.—HANNON MASSACRE.—MURDER OF MR. ANDERSON AND OTHERS.—MAJOR HOWARD'S VICTORY OVER "BIG WARRIOR" AT ROUND MOUNTAIN.—MAJOR WILLIAMSON'S CAMPAIGN AGAINST THE CHEROKEES IN 1776.

DURING "the days of 1776" or "days that tried men's souls," the frontier settlements along the borders of upper South Carolina, by reason of their close proximity to the Indian country, as already stated, were in constant dread of attack in any locality. The hostilities which had already sprung up between the two races, only increased the alarm of those infant and isolated settlements for their safety. The present line separating the counties of Greenville and Spartanburg was the same which divided the colony of South Carolina from the Cherokee Nation, and it is said that along this line there was for a distance a beaten pathway, over which the people would go in search of Indian trails, which could be seen by reason of the high grass and wild pea vines which grew in that day. Mr. O. P. Earle informs the writer that at one time his grandfather, Mr. Baylis Earle, was traveling this pathway for the reason stated. At one time he had occasion to leave his horse for a short distance, which ran away from him. He followed for some distance in expectation of overtaking him, but being unable to accomplish this, he shot to "crease"* him, but the ball ranging too low killed him. As wild or branded horses were plentiful he did not grieve, but con-

*To graze the crest or foretop.

soled himself that he had saved a new saddle, which at that time was worth almost the price of the horse.

Notwithstanding the vigilance of the people, the border settlements were occasionally visited by the Indians without a moment's warning. This was the case as to the settlements on the North Pacolet, to which Mr. Earle belonged, where occurred the massacre of the Hannon family, in 1776. As we have only a traditional account of this raid, it is impossible now to know the extent of the barbarities that were at that time committed. The Indians were no doubt encouraged and emboldened in their bloody work, as subsequent events proved by the, Tories, in and beyond the mountains, who were plotting against the Whig families on North Pacolet and other places.

The Hannon family lived on the banks of the North Pacolet River, on the plantation now owned by Henry Morgan, in Polk County, North Carolina. It is said that at the time this family was subjected to the merciless fury of the Indians, Mr. Hannon and the larger members of the family were but a short distance from the house, planting corn. The Indians, as soon as they came, killed Mr. Hannon and the older members of the family. Edwin his son, a boy about ten years of age, ran with his little brother John to the river. He was so hotly pursued that he had to drop his charge and escape across the stream. He had not more than cleared the bank when he heard the lick that ended the life of his poor little brother. While the murdering was going on in the field near by, Winnie, a girl of seven or eight years, seized her infant brother William, and ran off and concealed herself in a dense cane brake not far away, where she remained until the savages went away. The terrified people of the neighborhood gathered at the house of Mr. Baylis Earle for the purpose of making the best possible defense. Captain Thomas Jackson (father of the older Jacksons on North Pacolet, Thomas, John, James, Andrew, Samuel and Robert), a militia captain, summoned his company to resist the approach of the Indians, who advanced no further than the bank of Wolf Creek and North Pacolet, which is said to have been a camping ground of theirs years before.

Of the surviving members of the Hannon family, Edwin, Winnie and William, became the adopted children of Colonel John Earle*. Winnie was a cripple and never married. Edwin and William when they grew up became sons-in-law of Colonel Earle. Edwin was the proprietor of a valuable estate on North Pacolet, now owned by John B. Cleveland, Esq. He was the father of the late Mrs. Betsy Mills (wife of William Mills, deceased), and father-in-law of James Miller, one of the first citizens of the city of Spartanburg, who resided near the present residence of Dr. Jesse F. Cleveland.

William Hannon was also a man of fair circumstances, of intelligence and influence, and a minister of the Gospel. He was the first (and for a long number of years) pastor of Wolf Creek Baptist Church, near Landrum, S. C., organized in 1803.

A strange and merciful Providence seems to have spared him to do a good work in the Master's cause. His memory still lives in the affections of the older citizens of the community in which he lived.†

It was during the trouble with the Indians in 1776 that old Mr. Anderson was killed. He was a staunch patriot and a friend to the Whig cause. The Indians scalped and split his head with a tomahawk. After firing the house of his son David, near by, they murdered an old man and his son in the same settlement. It is stated that his

---

*Grandfather of Major John Earle Bomar.

---

†To N. H. Hill, Esq., of Columbus, N. C., (son-in-law of William Hannon), to Miss Sallie Henderson, an aged and pious lady who died a few years ago, and to Mrs. Candses Daniel, 85 years old, now deceased, the writer is indebted for the particulars of the "Hannon massacre."

brother, David Anderson, was at Fort Prince with his family when his house was burnt, which was in the night time.

Major William Hoy, in a recent communication to the Spartan, speaks of a murder by the Indians of an old man by the name of Shatteen, who was a Baptist preacher. It may be that this occurred during the Indian invasions and massacres of 1776 already referred to.

On account of the Indian depredations occurring at different points along the outer settlements on the frontier, it became necessary that the constituted authorities take steps to protect the people. Among those who were the first to throw themselves into the breach to resist the Indian invasions and depredations was a Captain Howard (father-in-law of the late Elias Dill, who died at the advanced age of 80 years), one of the early adventurers and pioneers of North Greenville (dark corner) County. Captain Howard, with a small command, marched from the old Block House Fort, already referred to, and against the Indians and Tories, who had banded themselves together and were in a gap in the mountains, since known as *Big Warrior*, named in honor of the Indian chief who commanded these forces at the time. In his march Captain Howard was guided bv a friendly Indian whose name was Schuyuka (pronounced Skywicca) who led him through another gap in the mountain, since known *Howard's Gap*, which enabled him to gain the rear of the Indians and their Tory allies. This gap was east of Warrior's Gap, the trail across the mountain leading through the latter at the time.

Captain Howard attacked his enemy fiercely, who were expecting him in their front, killing and wounding a number of them. The surviving Indians buried their dead on the battle field. The rock-covered mounds are still to be seen there near the present residence of Mr. Wash Fisher.

There is a tradition that not long after the engagement referred to, the Tories and Indians captured and hung Schuyuka, the friendly Indian, at the foot of Tryon

Mountain, on the banks of the beautiful running stream which now bears his name, and which enters into the North Pacolet River only a short distance below Bell's (or McAboy's) Hotel.

Let the immortal name of *Schuyuka* be preserved in the annals of our country's history. It was the first name suggested for the present county site of Polk, North Carolina. Afterwards it was proposed as a suitable name for the present village of Tryon, in the same county and only three or four miles, and in full view of the battle ground referred to, which is known in tradition as "*The battle of Round Mountain.*" For some reason the name, in both instances, for the towns referred to was abandoned.

The battle and victory of Captain Howard was not sufficient to subdue the Indians. It was necessary for the Carolinians to take more decisive steps to conquer them. Perhaps the people were encouraged in this undertaking by the news of Colonel Moultrie's victory on Sullivan's Island, and also by the news of the Declaration of Independence, which at this time had been received throughout the country. To accomplish the desired end and to finally put down the insurrections, two expeditions were organized and sent against the Indians. One of these was from South Carolina, under the command of Colonel Andrew Williamson, and the other was from North Carolina, under the command of Colonel Griffith Rutherford. Colonel Williamson's command consisted of about twelve hundred men. With a detachment of three hundred horses, he advanced upon the Indian forces at Oconorie Creek. His approach was known to the Indians, who were waiting for him in ambush. He suddenly found himself engaged in a desperate conflict, for which he was only partially prepared. His horse was shot from under him, an officer slain by his side, and under a dreadful fire, his army was thrown into disorder. It was rallied by Colonel Hammond. The thicket was charged and the day retrieved. Colonel Williamson then proceeded across the Smoky Mountains and down the valley of Little Tennessee River and began to penetrate the country of the Indians where their people were most numerous.

The command of Colonel Rutherford crossed the Blue Ridge mountains at Swannanoa Gap, and passed down the French Broad River and crossed at a ford which is to this day known as "War Ford." He then passed up the valley of Hominy Creek and crossing Pigeon River, proceeding in the direction of the valley of Little Tennessee. He burnt to ashes the Indian towns of Watonga, Estoetoa and Elijay. At the last named point his command united with that of Colonel Williamson who assumed command of the whole. Entering a narrow defile enclosed by mountains on each side, a second ambuscade awaited him. Twelve hundred warriors were secreted in the surrounding heights and poured a constant fire on Williamson's men, from which they were only saved by a charge with bayonets. The Indians fled. Williamson's command continued the work of devastation, destroying the Indian towns and their growing crops in the beautiful valleys. All of the country lying east of the Appalachian mountians being laid waste, the conquered Indians sued for peace. A treaty was made by which they ceded all of their lands south east of the mountains of Unacaya. By this treaty the present counties of Greenville, Anderson and Pickens (the two last once forming old Pendleton district) were gained to the territory of South Carolina. That portion which the Indians reserved to themselves embraces, for the most part, the present county of Oconee.*

This placed the country of the Indians so far away from the settlements that they gave no more trouble until just at the close of the Revolution (1781), of which we shall speak further on.

After the close of the Revolution, only a few years, the Indians sold the remainder of their reservation in this treaty to the State of South Carolina, the Legislature

*See map, frontispiece, Ramsay's History of South Carolina.

making a special appropriation for the purchase of the same.

In the last affair with the Indians, Colonel Williamson captured thirteen white men, disfigured, disguised and painted so as to resemble the Indians, thus proving what has already been said, that the trouble with the Indians during the year 1776 was, in a great measure, instigated by the Tory emissaries of the British.

Colonel Williamson's command was made up for the most part in the district of Ninety-Six but contained in part brave men from all the settlements in upper Carolina, among whom we would mention the name of Capt. John Collins, from the settlement on Middle Tyger, to whom reference will again be made.

Among those who belonged to Colonel Rutherford's command were Colonel Martin, who commanded a regiment from Guilford; Lieutenant (afterwards General) Lenoir and Col. Joseph Graham.

It is recorded that when this command set out it was almost destitute of clothing and tents. Their uniforms were principally of rude cloth made from hemp, tow and wild nettle bark, and, as a sample of the uniforms worn by the officers, Colonel Rutherford's consisted of a tow hunting shirt dyed black and trimmed with white fringe.

CHAPTER XIV.

INTERVAL OF QUIET.—PROPOSITIONS FOR PEACE WHICH ARE REJECTED.—BRITISH RENEW THEIR EFFORTS TO CONQUER THE PROVINCE.—GENERAL LINCOLN IS APPOINTED BY THE CONTINENTAL CONGRESS TO TAKE COMMAND OF AMERICAN FORCES IN SOUTH CAROLINA HIS CAMPAIGN AND SURRENDER AT CHARLESTOWN, SOUTH CAROLINA.—EXPEDITION OF MAJOR FERGUSON TO NINETY-SIX DISTRICT.—MANY INHABITANTS SEEK BRITISH PROTECTION, &c.—RENEWING HOPES AND PREPARATIONS FOR DEFENSE.

A PERIOD of four years transpired between the ending of the Indian troubles of 1776, which we have just narrated, and the visit of Maj. Patrick Ferguson to the district of Ninety-Six.* During this interval the pages of history are silent as to the events which transpired in the upper portion of South Carolina. It was during this time that an effort was made to win over South Carolina to the British cause. Commissioners were sent over to negotiate a reunion of the colonies with the mother country. A flag was sent with an address separately to the Governor, the Assemblymen, the Clergy, the Military, and in fact, to the whole people of South Carolina, making overtures of peace, which meant nothing short of absolute submission to British rule. President (Governor) Lowndes convened his council and the leading men of the different orders to whom the address was made. It is useless to say that the propositions were rejected, the flag ships were dismissed, and the Commissioners were reprimanded for having violated the Con-

* Comprising the present counties of Spartanburg, Union, Laurens, Newberry, Abbeville and Edgefield. See map.

stitution in their endeavor to treat with the colony in its separate capacity.

The Government of Great Britain being convinced of the worthlessness of their negotiations, set to work in earnest to subjugate the province of South Carolina. The reduction of Savannah by Colonel Campbell, in 1778, and the successful conquest of Georgia, made South Carolina, as it were, an exposed frontier. The close proximity of the enemy admonished the people to redouble their energies for defense.

By request of the South Carolina delegation in Congress, Major General Lincoln was ordered to take charge of the defenses of South Carolina. He was second in command when General Burgoyne surrendered his army to General Gates at Saratoga. Bringing with him a great reputation, he assumed command of the Southern department and preserved, for some fifteen months, the reputation of the State. In his department he had officers of reputation, such as Generals Moultrie, Williamson, Rutledge and Count Pulaski. At the close of the campaign in 1779, after several encounters, of which time and space will prevent any particular mention, * no decisive advan-

---

* One of the engagements deserving of special notice as occurring about this time is mentioned in an article to the Carolina Spartan, May 23 1894, called "The Battle of the Canebrakes," from the pen of Col. Thomas J. Moore, Moore, S. C., in which Mr. David Anderson (father of the late Tyger Jim Anderson) figured prominently. Says Colonel Moore in his article: "It seems after the fall of Savannah, to encourage the Loyalists and to awe the Republicans in that quarter, Colonel Campbell was ordered by General Prevost, to advance upon Augusta with two thousand regulars and Loyalists. He sent emissaries among the South Carolina Tories, saying, that if they would cross the Savannah and join him at Augusta, the republicans might be crushed and the whole South freed from their pestilential influence. This encouraged about eight hundred Tories of North and South Carolina, who collected on the west side of Broad River, under Colonel Boyd, and marched along the frontier of South Carolina towards the Savannah. They must have marched through or near this section. At this time the regions below and above Augusta were completely at the mercy of

tage had been gained on either side. The French fleet under the command of Count D'Estang had co-operated with Lincoln in the seige against Savannah and but for the delay of one day, in which the British garrison was allowed to consider a demand to surrender, subsequent affairs might have been different. As it was, the seige was a failure. Count D'Estang had announced his intention of remaining only fifteen days on shore. The seige was raised after an unsuccessful assault against the batteries of the enemy. D'Estang re-embarked his troops, artillery and baggage, and left the continent. The militia of General Lincoln dispersed and went to their homes, while he, with the rest of his army, marched to Charlestown. By a series of engagements and disasters during the year 1780, at Monk's Corner and other places, he found himself at last within the confines of the City of Charlestown, confronted by a superior and overpowering army and fleet under the command of General Clinton. For three long months he was beseiged. Failing to extricate himself or to receive reinforcements in due time, he was at last compelled to capitulate, May 12th, 1780.

---

the enemy. The Whigs who could leave their families crossed over to the Carolina side. Colonel Dooly, Colonel Pickens and others were active on the Georgia side in organizing forces to repel the British. Colonel Pickens, who was beseiging a fort on the Georgia side, abandoned the effort upon learning of the approach of Colonel Boyd and his eight hundred Loyalists from South Carolina. He crossed with his force the Savannah into Carolina, in Abbeville county, near Fort Charlotte, when Colonel Boyd hastened toward the Cherokee Ford on the Savannah. At the ford was a garrison of eight men with two swivels, who successfully disputed the passage of Colonel Boyd. He marched five miles up the river and crossed on rafts. He was pursued by a detachment of Americans under Captain Anderson, who attacked him in a cane brake. A severe fight ensued. Colonel Boyd lost one hundred men—killed, wounded and missing. The American party lost sixteen men, killed, and the same number of prisoners. This occurred in February, 1779. Colonel Boyd hastened forward after this defeat by Captain Anderson, but was closely pursued by Colonel Pickens, who had crossed the Savannah lower down, be-

His army of Continental troops numbered less than two thousand. The number surrendered amounted to about five thousand, which, besides the Continental troops, included about five hundred sick in hospitals and about five hundred who were citizens of the town and sailors, who had been taken from the shipping and placed in the batteries.

These events have been, in outline, briefly mentioned to show that this was a gloomy hour for South Carolina. The British believed that the colony was thoroughly conquered. Subsequent events proved that they had only conquered the territory and not the people. Soon after the surrender of Lincoln, Sir Henry Clinton departed from Charlestown, leaving Lord Cornwallis in charge of the Southern department. Cornwallis determined to follow up the success already attained and to press the conquest into the neighboring province of North Carolina. To accomplish this end, three expeditions were formed. The first was toward the river, Savannah, in Georgia. The second was placed under the command of Colonel Tarleton, who was ordered to scour the country between the Cooper and Santee rivers. In this expedition, Tarleton

---

tween him and Augusta, to the Georgia side with about three hundred militia, marching in battle order. Colonel Dooly commanded the right wing, Lieutenant Colonel Clarke the left, and Colonel Pickens the center. Colonel Boyd, ignorant of the proximity of his opposers, halted on the banks of Kettle Creek and commenced to slaughter cattle for his army, and turned his horses out to graze in a neighboring swamp. In this condition he was attacked. His pickets fired and fled to the camp. The utmost confusion prevailed and Colonel Boyd commenced to retreat, skirmishing with his assailants. The contest lasted about two hours. About seventy of the Tories were killed aud seventy-five made prisoners. The Americans lost nine killed and twenty-three wounded. Colonel Boyd was severely wounded and expired that night. His whole force was scattered to the winds. The seventy-five prisoners were carried to South Corolina, tried for high treason and condemned to death. Five of the most active men were hanged, the balance were pardoned. This was one of the severest blows Toryism had yet received in South Carolina.

encountered a body of Whigs, who had been marching to the succor of General Lincoln, but who were now retreating by forced marches. He fell upon them and the carnage was dreadful. He butchered many who offered to surrender. This horrible massacre gave a bloody turn to the war. The Americans remembered this engagement with horror, and from that time it became a proverbial mode of expressing the cruelties of a barbarous enemy to call them *Tarleton's Quarter*. The third expedition was that of Colonel Ferguson to the District of Ninety-Six, already referred to. All of these expeditions were, for a time, successful, and many of the inhabitants flocked from all parts to meet the Royal troops, expressing a desire to return to their ancient allegiance and offering to enlist to defend the Royal standard. A proclamation had been issued soon after the surrender of Lincoln at Charlestown, by General Clinton, offering a full and absolute pardon to those who would immediately return to their duty, promising that no offenses or transgressions heretofore committed in consequence of political troubles, should be investigated. Many of those who had heretofore been faithful and active leaders in the patriot cause, now took Royal protection and availed themselves of the proclamation, among whom we would mention the names of Gen. Andrew Williamson, Gen. Isaac Huger, Colonels Andrew Pickens, John Thomas and Isaac Hayne. Others, however, preferred to brave the popular tide and remain in open partisan warfare, among whom were Francis Marion, Thomas Sumter, the Hamptons, Williams and others.

Ferguson was dispatched to the up-country on the 18th day of May, 1780. His command consisted of from one hundred and fifty to two hundred men of the provincial corps. His route to the up-country was via Nelson's Ferry, Beaver Creek, Congaree Store, crossing Saluda above the mouth of Broad River, thence to Little River and Ninety-Six Court House, where he arrived on the 26th of June. His orders were to apprehend all prominent

Whigs on the way, and to have a watchcare over the entire district.

Ferguson's march to Ninety-Six alarmed the patriots of the up-country for their general safety, being now too weak to offer a general resistance, but we have accounts of small gatherings here and there. In the sketch of Mrs. Jane Thomas in Mrs. Ellet's "Women of the Revolution," Vol. i., we are informed that by a preconcerted arrangement between Colonels John Thomas, Giles and Brandon (the two latter from the Union County section) the scattered patriots of the country were to be brought together for resistance. Each of these officers were to have designated points for recruiting. That of Colonel Thomas was at Cedar Spring, as we will see later. The Tories, however, flocking to Colonel Ferguson's camp, kept him posted as to the whereabouts of the Whig encampments. Ferguson sent a detachment to Brandon's camp. The latter was not prepared for resistance, and the attack being unexpected, he and his command were put to flight.

Ferguson, after remaining a fortnight at Ninety-Six, resumed his march. Advancing only about sixteen miles, he selected a good location on Little River, where he erected field works, and then with the most of his provincials, advanced to the plantation of Col. James Williams, in the Fair Forest region. Here the British and Tories maintained a post for sometime. This was most of the time under the command of General Cunningham.

This was indeed a dark hour for South Carolina, whose condition was generally regarded as hopeless. The territory was now completely under the control of Royal authority, with the British troops scattered all over the State. The people felt that there was no other alternative but absolute submission. Both Georgia and South Carolina were considered as conquered provinces, and so predominant was the idea, that Mr. Madison introduced resolutions in the Continental Congress to treat with

Great Britain by surrendering these two States as conquered provinces. *

An address was prepared by several hundred citizens of Charlestown and presented to Lord Cornwallis, congratulating him on the conquest of the State. It was during this period that many of the Whigs, together with many of the prominent leaders to whom we have referred, took British protection by reason of the duties and responsibilities that confronted them. The Tories who espoused the Royal cause, were men of no moral or political principle, their greatest ambition being plunder and robbery. The unfortunate condition of affairs encouraged them to commit the most atrocious acts all over the country. Many who had hitherto feigned a devotion to the cause of Liberty now pressed from every quarter to ingratiate themselves in favor of the victors and to offer their services to the Royal government. Not content with going themselves, they dragged in their train, in some instances, the friends of Liberty, whom they had lately obeyed with such parade and zeal and whom they now denominated as their oppressors. Ferguson, upon his arrival to the up-country, issued a proclamation, in which he said: "We came not to make war upon women and children, but to relieve their distress." The Tories flocked by the hundreds to his camp, inspired by such leaders as the Cunninghams, Fletchall, Paris, David Fanning and others. Many of these were thoroughly disciplined. Indeed it is said that Ferguson possessed a talent and qualification in this direction. Being a man of magnetism and large experience, he had unlimited influence over his men.

But while, as we have hinted, Ferguson exercised a commanding influence over certain sections in South Carolina, and especially in the lower and central portions of the district of Ninety-Six, we have unmistakable evidence on

---

* See sketch of Benj. Roebuck by Gevernor Perry—"Eminent Men and Statesmen."

record, that the settlements in the extreme up-country did not take to him. We have already shown the spirit of patriotism that prevailed in the upper or Spartan Congressional district when Mr. Drayton and Mr. Tennant visited that section in 1775. The people of this section were still disposed to maintain a stubborn resistance to Royal authority. Says Ramsay (page 216): "Opposition to British Government was not wholly confined to the parties commanded by Marion and Sumter. It was at no time altogether extinct in the extremities of the State."

Further, it is stated that Colonel Ferguson had undertaken to personally visit those disaffected to the Royal authority, thus showing that there was still existing in the up-country an element true to the cause of Liberty, to whom his mission was especially directed.

Among those who were associated with Major Ferguson in the up-country was Major Hanger. He was ordered to repair "to the interior settlements," says Draper, "and jointly or separately to organize, muster and regulate, all volunteer corps and inspect the quantity of grain and number of cattle, etc., belonging to the inhabitants, and report to Cornwallis." He was alsc ordered to administer oaths of fealty, and to thoroughly drill the young men fitted for recruits for Cornwallis' diminished forces.

Nor were these the only powers vested in Ferguson and Hanger. Believing the province of South Carolina subjugated, beyond any question of doubt, and all Royal authority having for several years been superseded by the newly created government of the province, these officers had superadded to their *military* authority, *civil* powers, and among other things, the right to perform the marriage ceremony.

Major Hanger did not remain with Ferguson very long. While he found many that were loyal to his standard, he met with many rebuffs and uncivil receptions on the part of many of the ladies of the up-country. To gratify a spiteful revenge, he published what he intended as a slur upon their sex. "In the back parts of Carolina," says the Major, "you may search for an angel with as much chance of finding one as a parson. There is no such a thing—I mean when I was there." But it is said that "the darkest hour is sometime just before daylight." While it was admitted that the territory, as we have said of South Carolina, was completely subjugated to British authority, and the people were at first disposed to submit to the powers that be, their minds were quickly changed by unlooked-for circumstances. This was especially the case in the extreme upper portion of the State, where we have hinted that the Whig settlements were more numerous. The principal cause for this revulsion of sentiment was a proclamation which was issued, by which British commanders absolved prisoners from their parole and restored them to the condition of British subjects in order to compel them to join the British army. This raised the mettle in the bosom of the Carolinians. General discontent prevailed everywhere. Most of the people, since they had lost what they believed to be the cause of Liberty, desired to remain at least in tranquility at their homes, thus conforming themselves to the circumstances and submitting to a necessity. If this repose had been granted them, they would, in all probability, have remained quiet, and perhaps little by little would have accustomed themselves to the new order of things, and to some extent, would have forgotten the past. But this proclamation rekindled their rage and they cried with one voice, "If we must resume arms, let us rather fight for America and our friends than for England and strangers." They meant what they said and carried the same into execution. Being released from their parole, they considered themselves at liberty to go where they pleased. They determined to venture all to serve their cause and many by unfrequented and circuitous routes made their way into North Carolina to join the American standard. Of course the greater part

Map showing location of BATTLE FIELDS in upper SOUTH CAROLINA and other points of historical interest.
BATTLE FIELDS. ⚑ OTHER PLACES by a +
-.—.—. State Line.
.... County Line.

of the people remained at home determining to protect their property until ordered bv the British authority to take the field. Perhaps this resolution appeared as an expediency. They were in dread of persecution by the English and a false report was then being industriously circulated that Congress had come to the determination to no longer dispute with the English about the Southern provinces.

During all the while that Ferguson was recruiting and preparing to retain complete and absolute control of the affairs of upper Carolina, both civil and military, the gallant spirits of Marion, Sumter, Roebuck and others who defied Royal authority, had been all the while at work to arouse the Whigs to continued action and resistance. Their commands, which had been reduced to mere handsful of patriots, began to swell and soon they had respectable and well organized commands. The hopes of the people began to revive, and in small bodies they began to rendezvous and arm themselves for resistance. In the up-country among recruiting camps established were Earle's Ford and Cedar Spring. The brave and devoted partisans were soon in a better shape for resisting the British and Tory invasion. Before the closing of the same year, 1780, the following battles were fought and victories won, viz: Cedar Spring, Thickety Fort, Wofford's Iron Works, Earle's Ford, Musgrove's Mill, Blackstocks' Ford and King's Mountain, and in January of the following year, Cowpens.

All of these, except King's Mountain, which is less than fifty miles from Musgrove's, was fought within the borders of the old *Spartan* district. The writer, in this narrative, proposes to treat of each of these separately, and to give to them their importance and the place they justlv deserve to occupy in history, and to prove that these battles and victories, insignificant as they may appear at the present day as compared with some of the modern battles, went very far during the stormy period of the Revolution, towards deciding the destiny of the great American Republic.

CHAPTER XV.

FIRST BATTLE OF CEDAR SPRINGS.—GENERAL UPRISING OF THE WHIGS.—CONTINUED MARAUDING, PILLAGING, &c., BY FERGUSON AND HIS MEN.

THE general uprising of the people in upper South Carolina during the summer and fall of 1780 set Ferguson and his compeers, the Cunninghams, Fletchall, Robinson and Paris, to work to counteract the prominent patroit leaders. Among the latter class was Col. John Thomas, Sr., of the Fair Forest settlement, whom we have already introduced to our readers as among the first in the up-country at the breaking out of the Revolution to arouse the liberty-loving people to a sense of their duty. It will be remembered that John Thomas, Sr., was the organizer and first colonel of the old Spartan Regiment, which participated in the famous "snow campaign" five vears before this period, and also in "Williamson's campaign against the Cherokees in 1776." After the fall of Charlestown, Colonel Thomas took British protection, but by reason of the proclamation already referred to as emenating from the British authorities, he was again iu open hostility to the further progress of that authority. Although now quite an old man, he was arrested and hurried off with other prisoners to Ninety-Six. He was soon followed to this place bv his devoted wife, who went to administer such comforts as was in her power to bestow, and for this purpose she rode nearly sixty miles. While at Ninetv-Six she overheard a conversation between some Tory women to the effect that "the Loyalists intend tomorrow night to surprise the rebel camp at Cedar Spring." Her son, Col. John Thomas, Jr., who had succeeded his father to the command of the Spartan (called by Draper the Fair Forest) regiment, was encamped at that place with about sixty men. Other friends and neighbors of Mrs. Thomas were there also. This brave heroine, knowing that there was no time to be lost, started early on horseback the next morning, and after a fatiguing ride, reached Cedar Spring in time to give to Colonel Thomas and his men warning of the impending danger. This was on the 13th day of July.

Colonel Thomas, on receiving this information from his mother of the intended British attack, lost no time in making preparations to meet the same. After a brief consultation it was decided to retire a short distance to the rear of his camp fires and await the arrival of the British force. Among those who belonged to Major Thomas' command at this place was Major McJunkin, of whom mention will be made later. During the night, as anticipated, the British and Tories, about one hundred and fifty strong, came. They expected to find the rebels, as they called them, asleep—but to their utter astonishment they found them wide awake. They experienced a warm reception with a volley of balls from Colonel Thomas' men. The engagement was short, quick and decisive. The enemy soon retreated, leaving several of their dead on the battle field. Among the latter was a Tory, named John White, well known to Major McJunkin. This man White, it is said, in the early struggles with the Indians, refused to fight for his country, claiming as he did to be a non-combatant. The importance of this little engagement, which is known in history as the first battle of Cedar Spring, cannot be over estimated, as it was the first show of resistance to the overpowering influence and strength of Ferguson in the up-country. The precise spot where it took place is not known, but is supposed to be on the rising ground a short distance north of Cedar Spring. It was here that Prof. N. F. Walker unearthed an old gun barrel, supposed to have been used in Revolutionary times.

It was fortunate that this was a night affair, as it gave the enemy no opportunity of judging of the strength of Thomas' forces. It gave new life and courage to the whigs, who continued to rally to the American standards. Some came from other States, among whom was Col. Elijah Clarke, of Georgia, recorded in history by Ramsay as the first settler of the present territory of Spartanburg County. When Georgia was overrun by the British it became unsafe for him and other Whigs to remain there. He and his little band determined to cross the border line where they knew they would find other Whigs who would operate with them in making a stand against a common enemy. Others from that State had already gone and connected themselves with the command of Col. Joseph McDowell in North Carolina.

Ferguson, in the meanwhile, was moving along with renewed energies to counteract the general uprising of the Whigs all around him. He was sending detachments in every direction and himself marched into Union District, with a force of about fifteen hundred men, and encamped on the south side of Tyger River, about a half mile below Blackstock's Ford. Here he was observed by a cripple spy, whose name was Joseph Kerr, who immediately reported to Colonel McDowell the extent of his observations. This man Kerr was a noted spy during the Revolution. His Ms. personal statements appear in Hunter's Sketches of Western North Carolina.* From Blackstock's Ford, Ferguson passed into a settlement called "Quaker Meadows," or "Meadow Woods," and from thence to Sugar Creek, a southern tributary of Fair Forest, where the Whigs were numerous. After camping awhile at this place and at Fair Forest Shoal and other places, he finally located for three weeks at the Dr. John Winsmith place, two miles south of Glenn Springs, now the home of Mr. Elias Smith. During all this time the Tories were scouring the country, plundering and robbing the people of cattle, hogs, horses, beds, wearing apparel,

*See Draper's "King's Mountain," page 224.

bee gums, grain, vegetables, and everything imaginable, even to finger rings which they took from the ladies. This only tended to strengthen the American cause. The American officers were either paying for the supplies in the currency of the country, or else they were giving proper vouchers, while Ferguson supported his army by pillage. He turned his horses loose in fields of grain that happened to be most convenient. He continued the work of apprehending the Whigs, not even excepting those that had taken British protection. These he hurried to a dirty and loathsome prison at Ninety-Six, where they remained for some time, incarcerated and well-nigh dying for want of sustenance. Nor could anything else be expected of Ferguson with his surroundings. Says Irving, "Ferguson had a loyal hatred to the Whigs, and to his standard flocked many rancorous Tories besides outlaws and desperadoes, so that with all his conciliating intentions his progress through the country was attended with many exasperating excesses." Says the Hon. Lyman C. Draper in his "King's Mountain and its Heroes" of Ferguson and his men, "The desperate, the idle, the vindictive who sought plunder or revenge, as well as the youthful Loyalists whose zeal or ambition prompted them to take up arms, all found a warm reception in the British camp; and their progress through the country was marked with blood and lighted with conflagration." Says the same writer further, "The Tories were soon as heartily despised by the British officers as by their own countrymen—the Whigs. But Ferguson was not the man to be diverted from his purpose by any acts of treachery or inhumanity. He knew that the "defender of the faith" generally gave much more cash and more honors for a single year of devoted service in military enterprises than for a lifetime spent in such pursuits as exalt and ennoble human nature."

CHAPTER XVI.

THE BRITISH OUTPOSTS IN SUMMER, 1780.—CONCENTRATION OF WHIG FORCES AT EARLE'S FORD AND CEDAR SPRING.—RETREAT OF COLONEL JONES FROM GEORGIA.—NIGHT ATTACK ON SMALL BODY OF TORIES AT GOWEN'S FORT.

DURING the summer of 1780 two of the most important British outposts in our up-country were Prince's and Thickety Forts. The construction and location of the former (Prince's Fort) has been described in a former chapter of this work. It was at this time garrisoned by Tories and Loyalists, under the command of Colonel Innes, who was in command of a regiment called by some writers the "Queen's Rangers," by others the "Queen's American Regiment." Prominent among the officers of this regiment was Major Dunlap, whose character and whose career as a soldier will claim further attention. Also among the officers of the garrison was Col. Ambrose Mills, who commanded the Loyalists at this place. Thickety Fort was in command of Col. Patrick Moore. Between the forts and other points that were garrisoned, the British were constantly plying, committing their acts of pillage and marauding.

In striking distance of these forts (Prince and Thickety) were two places, Cedar Spring and Cherokee Ford, the former already mentioned, where the Whigs were concentrating for defence The command of the troops at Cherokee Ford was under Col. Charles McDowell, "who," says Draper, "was then embodying a force on the south-western borders of the North Province."

The retreat of Col. Elijah Clarke, already referred to, from Georgia to South Carolina was preceded by a small command under Col. John Jones, of Burke County.

Clarke and his associates had decided before starting for South Carolina, to scatter for a few days to visit their families, and then re-unite and take up the line of march. On the 11th of July one hundred and forty well-mounted and well-armed men met at the appointed place of rendezvous, and after a quiet crossing at a private ford on the Savannah at night, they learned that the British and Loyalists were in force in front of them. They considered it hazardous to continue their retreat further on account of the smallness of their numbers. As they were only an independent body of volunteers they could not be forced against their inclinations. Colonel Clarke was induced to return to Georgia and allow his men to disperse for awhile. This retrograde movement, however, was opposed by Colonel Jones, who proposed that if the men would follow him he would carry them through the woods to North Carolina, where the patriots were rallying for defence. Thirty-five men volunteered to go with him. He was chosen as leader, while John Freeman was chosen second in command. Among this party was a South Carolinian by the name of Benjamin Lawrence, who was a superior woodsman and well acquainted with the country. He rendered a valuable service as guide on this retreat.

The only account we find of Colonel Jones' retreat from Georgia is in Draper's "King Mountain and its Heroes," and in Schenck's "North Carolina." In order to point out what appears to be some inaccuracies, the writer will quote from the pen of that eminent historian, Draper. Referring to the route by which Colonel Jones and his party traveled, he said · "Passing through a disaffected region they adroitly palmed themselves off as a Loyalist party, engaged in the King's service. and under this guise, they were in several instances furnished with pilots and directed on their route.

"When they had passed the head waters of the Saluda, in the northeastern part of the present County of Greenville, one of the guides informed them that a party of rebels had, the preceding night, attacked some Loyalists a short distance in front and defeated them, doubless the British repulse at Cedar Spring, as already related and which occurred some twenty-five miles away. Jones expressed a wish to be conducted to the camp of these unfortunate Lovalist friends that he might aid them in taking revenge on those who had shed the blood of the King's faithful subjects. About 11 o'clock on that night, July 13th, Jones and his little party were conducted to the loyalist camp, where some forty men were collected to pursue the Americans who had retreated to the North. Choosing twentv-two of his followers and leaving the baggage and horses in charge of the others, Colonel Jones resolved to surprise the Tory camp. Approaching the enemv with guns, swords and belt pistols, they found them in a state of self-security and generally asleep. Closing quickly around them they fired upon the camp, killing one and wounding three, when twenty-two, including the wounded, called for quarter and surrendered. Destroying the useless guns and selecting the best horses, the Loyalists were paroled as prisoners of war, when the pilot, who did not discover the real character of the men he was conducting until too late to have even attempted to prevent the consequences, was now required to guide the Americans to Earle's Ford, on North Pacolet River, where a junction was formed the next day with Colonel McDowell's forces."

Draper says that Colonel Jones in this retreat crossed the head waters of the Saluda. This is a mistake. To have crossed the head streams of this river would have brought him across the Saluda Mountain, in the vicinity of the present town of Saluda, N. C., on the Asheville and Spartanburg railroad. Besides, the different prongs of the Saluda are in the northwestern and not in the *north-eastern* portion of Greenville County. Draper, doubtless, when he referred to the Saluda, meant the Tyger River. The present road from Tygerville to Gowensville, in Greenville County, passes the head waters of Tyger. There is a church on the way called "Head of Tyger." It is doubtful whether Colonel Jones passed through any white settlements until he reached the District of Ninety-Six, now Spartanburg County. The country between this and the Savannah River had been obtained by treaty from the Cherokees only four years before. The Indians were still occupying a large portion of it, and it is not likely that it was settled so early.

Draper fails to locate the place where Colonel Jones made this night attack on the Loyalists' camp, but the writer has good reason to believe that it was at Gowen's Old Fort, on the old Blackstock Road, near South Pacolet River. We have shown that other forts built in early times as a defence against the Indians were at this time occupied by the British and Tory forces, and it is reasonable to suppose that the same may have been the case as to this fort. It was on the line of way between the Savannah and Earle's Ford. Draper says that when Jones attacked the camp of Loyalists he found them "in a state of self-security and generally asleep," thus implying that they might have been protected by some fortress or enclosure. He further says that Cedar Spring was some twenty or thirty miles from this place. This would make it the more probable that it might have been at Gowen's Fort, as the distance from the latter place to Cedar Spring is about twenty-five miles.

CHAPTER XVII.

BATTLE OF EARLE'S FORD, ON NORTH PACOLET.

FROM researches into our local history we find but a meager account of the little engagement at Earle's Ford, which, like the affair at Cedar Spring, occurred in the night time. It seems to have been overlooked by all the writers of Revolutionary events in our State, and but for the careful researches of that eminent historian, Lyman C. Draper, who has, to a great extent, reproduced our history during the last years of the Revolution, much that is now known and understood of this battle would have faded away forever, ever in tradition.

During the year 1867, the writer had for the first time, the pleasure of meeting the Venerable William Prince on North Pacolet, who died in 1878, at the advanced age of ninety-five years. Mr. Prince was a son-in-law of Col. John Earle, a soldier of the Revolution, of whom we shall speak later. He was well posted in all the local and traditionary events of his neighborhood. In answer to some interrogations by the writer, he said: "There was a fight down close to your house," and stated further, that some of the Hamptons were killed and buried in a burial ground on a wooded hill near by, where there are still occasional burials. This is all that the writer can recollect of the conversation with Mr. Prince about this engagement. A few years later when his attention was called to an article in the press giving an account of the murder and burial of the Hamptons, near the Greenville County line (the particulars of which are already given) he had come to the conclusion, until he had the pleasure of reading Draper's "Kings Mountain and Its Heroes," that Mr. Prince was mistaken.

We merely mention this to show that outside of Mr. Draper's work, a tradition has been handed to us by an aged citizen which leaves no doubt as to the certainty and place of this battle. The writer has recently made an effort to gather up the traditionary information concerning the battle of Earle's Ford, the most reliable of which is embraced in the following letter from Mr. O. P. Earle* grandson of Baylis Earle, whose residence was near the ford and battle ground ·

EARLESVILLE, S. C., July 4th, 1891.

DOCTOR LANDRUM:

I do not know just where the battle of Earle's Ford was fought, but have understood that the Tories came from the direction of Prince's Fort, and crossed Pacolet north of grandfather's house, which stood very near my old stable, and after crossing the river turned to the right and attacked the Whigs on the ridge east of where the Gibbs family now live. Those who were killed in this skirmish were buried near by. I suppose all the Whigs were buried there.

The neighbors came to grandfather's house on some occasion for protection, though Earle's Fort was at Colonel John Earle's, where W. L. Prince now lives. After the fight was over, the Tories came back to graddfather's house, the Whigs in pursuit, and went in the direction of Prince's Fort again. Yours, &c., O. P. EARLE.

It will be presently shown that this traditionary account of Mr. Earle of the fight corresponds very much, as far as it goes, with Draper's account, and also with the statement of Mr. Prince as to the place where the fight occurred, and as to the killed, who were buried near by.

In a former chapter we have described the location and previous history of Prince's Fort, referred to in Mr. Earle's letter. The old site is near the Blackstock Road, about three-fourths of a mile below Mount Zion Church, and near Gray's Creek, one of the prongs of North Tyger River. Its location is about twenty miles from Earle's Ford. It was, as previously stated, in 1780 occupied by a British and Tory force under the command of Colonel Jones.

McDowell's camp was on rising ground on the eastern side of North Pacolet River, which runs here in a southeastern direction. In order that the reader may better

---

*Now deceased.

understand the precise location of this camp, we will state that it was on the former plantation, and near the residence of the late Rev. John G. Landrum, who resided on North Pacolet for several years after the late war. It is now the property of his daughter, Mrs. E. E. Bomar. The homstead residence was burned down several years ago, and another built on the same spot, which is now occupied by the Gibbs family, referred to in Mr. Earle's letter. For two years the writer tramped over the grounds, the scenes of other days, entirely unconscious of the sacred and hallowed associations that clustered around it. This was what Mr. Prince meant when he said that "there was a fight down close to your house."

Innes, unapprised of McDowell's approach on North Pacolet, and hearing of the audacious operations of Colonel Jones, detached Major Dunlap with seventy dragoons, and Col. Ambrose Mills with a party of Loyalists to go in pursuit and attack him. Dunlap with his command set out on their journey. Reaching the vicinity of Earle's Ford, on the west side of the stream, during the night, Dunlap supposed that he was confronted only by Jones' small command on the opposite side of the stream. He decided at once to attack it. When he had commenced to cross thestream, which was not very wide, the American sentinel fled and gave the alarm in camp of the enemy's approach. The account in McCall's History of Georgia savs that he fired his gun. This is denied, however, by James Thomson, one of McDowell's men, and is corroborated by the complaint of Colonel Hampton, that if the camp had been properly guarded it would not have been surprised.

Dunlap as soon as he had crossed the river, dashed instantly with his dragoons and Tories with drawn swords into McDowell's men, while but few of them had been aroused out of their sleep. The Georgians were nearest to the ford and were the first attacked. They lost, two killed and six wounded; among the latter was Colonel Jones, who received eight cuts on the head from the enemy's sabres. Freeman, with the remainder of the

Georgians, fled back about one hundred yards, where he was joined by Major Singleton who was forming his men behind a fence, while Colonels McDowell and Hampton were forming the main body of their men to the right of Singleton. Being thus rallied and formed the Americans were ordered to advance. Dunlap, discovering his mistake as to numbers, made a hasty retreat across the river, which, Draper savs, "was fordable in many places." This is unquestionably a mistake. The bottom lands here from one side to the other have a stretch of a mile at least. These must have been covered at this time with a dense growth of cane and trees. The banks of the stream are precipitous and there are today but few fordings on the stream, and these, with the slightest flush from rains become dangerous and uncertain. It is very evident, therefore, that Dunlap with his command recrossed the same ford over which he had just crossed to attack McDowell. This corresponds with Mr. Earle's statement, who says the Tories came back to his grandfather's, house which stood near his present residence on the west side of the stream, and on the road leading from the ford. It may have been that on account of the condition of the country along the river in front, below and above, that Colonel McDowell selected this place to make a stand to resist the threatened invasion of North Carolina by Ferguson, which took place a few months later. It will be remembered that he went as far as Gilberttown, near Rutherfordton. Besides the casualties sustained by the Georgians, six of McDowell's men were killed, and eighteen were wounded. Among the former was Noah Hampton, a son of Col. Edward Hampton, and also a comrade of his whose name was Andrew Dunn. Young Hampton when aroused from his sleep was asked his name. He replied "Hampton" The very name enraged the Tories, who cursed him for a rebel and ran a bayonet through him. Young Dunn met with the same cruel treatment. The particulars of the killing of these young men have been furnished by Ms. communications of Adam, Jonathan and James J. Hampton, grandsons of Col. Edward Hampton. It is said that Colonel Hampton felt hard towards Colonel McDowell for not placing videttes on the opposite side of the river to warn the camp of the enemy's approach. Colonel McDowell would doubtless have taken this precaution, had it not been that he had sent his brother, Maj. Joseph McDowell, with a few men to scout the country in his front and ascertain where the Tories lay. Not returning to camp at nightfall, he naturally concluded that everything was all right, that no part of the enemy's forces was near him. His men being tired and footsore he allowed them to take their repose. It appears, however, that Major McDowell in returning lost his direction, and while wandering in the night the enemy passed him unnoticed, to surprise and attack McDowell's camp.

There is some discrepancy in history as to when this battle was fought. Draper and most of the writers of Revolutionary history, however, put it down on the night of the 15th of July, 1780. Allaire, a British officer in his diary, however, appears to refer to it as having taken place on the night of the 14th.

The reader can scarcely conceive the salutary effect of this temporary repulse of the British and Tory forces at Earle's Ford. This, together with the capture of Fort Thickety, which occurred only a short time afterwards, the affair at Wofford's iron works, and the success of Colonel Jones which we have already mentioned, had a tendency to revive the desponding hopes of the Whig people in the upper portion of South Carolina. These little successes, doubtless, counteracted in a large degree the depressing effects of Gates disastrous defeat near Camden, and other reverses which the American arms were sustaining.

Draper says that McDowell's camp near Earle's Ford, was "on the eastern side of North Pacolet, in the present County of Polk, North Carolina, near the South Carolina line." Judge David Schenck in his "North Carolina," a recent work which he has published, being a history of the invasion of the Carolinians by the British army under Lord Cornwallis, 1780-1, notices this engagement between McDowell's and Mills' forces and says the junction formed between Jones' and McDowell's forces was "at Earle's Ford, on the Pacolet, in what is now Polk County."

It will be seen that both of these eminent gentleman place this revolutionary spot in North Carolina. This is unquestionably a mistake, according to the location of the present State line, though, it may have at one time been on the North Carolina side. Draper, in his "King's Mountain," (page 16), presents a map of localities in revolutionary times in the western portion of North and South Carolina. On this map the residence of Baylis Earle (homestead residence of O. P. Earle, deceased), is placed in North Carolina, which is half a mile south of the present State line, which at that point runs due east and west. According to Draper's map the line between the States at this point is northeast and southwest. The same was corrected in 1815, (see Sim's history of South Carolina, page 328, appendix) on the part of commissioners from North and South Carolina. This change placed the scene of the engagement at Earle's Ford, a few hundred yards south of the State line and within the limits of the present County of Spartanburg.

CHAPTER XVIII.

RETREAT OF DUNLAP AND HIS FORCES.--SKIRMISH AT FORT PRINCE.

IT will be seen by reference to Mr. Earle's letter in the former chapter, that the Tories after the battle of Earle's Ford, returned to his grandfather's house and went in the direction of Fort Prince. The old road from the old Baylis Earle homestead (now O. P. Earle's or Earlesville) to Prince's Fort ran in Revolutionory times for several miles on the dividing ridge between the rivers —North and South Pacolet. It ran near the blue pond, which is near and in the rear of the residence of Mr. Hampton Alverson, who lives at the Smith old field place. It continued to diverge to the right between the Alverson place and the Doctor Compton old place. The old road bed can be distinctly traced to the present day. Continuing in its course, it crossed South Pacolet near Compton's bridge and then ran perhaps with or near the present ridge road by the town of Inman, intersecting the old Blackstock Road at the Frank Bush place, near Shiloh Church. We have said before that the Blackstock Road ran by Prince's Fort. It was doubtless over this road that Dunlap and Mills advanced to, and retreated from, Earle's Ford. It is very probable too, from circumstances which we will presently show, that Dunlap and his forces remained in the vicinity of Baylis Earle's place until the morning after the battle. Draper's account corroborates the traditionary account of Mr. Earle. He says, "before sunrise the ensuing morning, fifty-two of the most astive men, including Freeman and fourteen of his party, mounted on the best horses in camp, were ordered to pursue the retreating enemy." This command was placed underCol. Edward Hampton. Had the forces of the enemy retreated immediately after the fight, it would have been impossible for Colonel Hampton's command to have overtaken them. They must have stopped somewhere to rest. The account of Draper says that Colonel Hampton "after a rapid pursuit of two hours overtook the enemy fifteen miles away; and making a sudden and unexpected attack, completely routed the enemy, killing eight of them at the first fire."

Some ten years ago the writer, who was engaged in preparing a series of articles for the county press, took it upon himself to visit the home of Mr. Isaac Pollard some three miles south of the present village of Inman. Mr. Pollard passed away about three years ago (1889) at the advanced age of ninety years. He was was generally regarded by his neighbors as the best-posted man on the local traditions of the county. He was fond of conversing on these matters and repeating what had been told to him by the older people who had passed away. The purpose of the visit referred to was to interview him in reference to the traditions of this little running fight and the retreat of Dunlap's men to Fort Prince. Mr. Pollard had never seen nor heard of any published account of the affair, but what he said corresponded precisely with Draper's account, only that he had an impression that the enemy's forces were commanded by "Bloody Bill" Cunningham. He said that the enemy was first overtaken and attacked near Shiloh Church. This is five miles above the site of old Fort Prince, about fifteen miles from Earle's Ford. Mr. Pollard said the fight with the enemy continued along the road until Fort Prince was reached. He said further that several men fell dead at different places on the road—one near the John Bush place, one on the roadside which ran through his plantation, and another at the Lawrence place, near Mount Zion Church. He said that the man who was killed near the John Bush place lay for several days by a large oak tree, which was standing only a few years ago, without being buried. The neighbors concluded at last they would dig a hole and roll him in it. Mrs. Bishop, whose husband was killed by the Indians several years before and whose children had been stolen from her (the circumstances of which we have already given) happened to be passing by. Moved to sympathy by the unnatural and inhuman mode of burying, she took off her apron and spread it over the face of this unfortunate victim.

Draper savs that Dunlap, unable to rally his terrified men when attacked by Hampton's men, made a hasty and precipitate retreat to Fort Prince, during which several of his soldiers were killed, thus corroborating Mr. Pollard's statement. The pursuit of Colonel Hampton's forces was continued within three hundred yards of the fort, in which three hundred men were posted. Hampton did not pursue them any further. By two o'clock in the afternoon, he had returned to McDowell's camp, with thirtyfive good horses, dragoon equipage and a considerable portion of the enemy's baggage, as trophies of the victory, and all this too, without the loss of a single man. Draper says this was a "bold and successful adventure, worthy of the heroic leader and his intreped followers."

Mr. Pollard said to the writer in his conversation about this matter that it was a surprise to the neighborhood that the Tories in the fort, who were four or five times stronger than the attacking party, did not march out to meet the advancing Whigs. They were evidently struck with the same terror that Dunlap's forces were, who had been stampeded for five miles. By reference to Allaire's diary too, it is plain to be seen that thev were deceived as to the number of Hampton's command. Under the date of July 15, (the date of the battle of Earle's Ford) this officer, after referring to a dinner party at Colonel Fletchall's and a visit to his mill, says, "Returning to camp were informed that Captain Dunlap had been obliged to retreat from Prince's Fort. Captain Dunlap made an attack upon the rebels,* drove them from their

*Referring to his attack on McDowell at Earle's Ford.

ground, took one prisoner, who informed him that the rebels were four hundred strong. Upon this information Dunlap thought proper to retreat, as his number was only fourteen American volunteers and sixty militia. We lost two, killed, a sergeant and a private wounded, and one prisoner. The loss of the rebels is uncertain—reports are twenty to thirty killed. Upon this news arriving Captain DePeyster ordered the American volunteers and militia to get in motion to support Dunlap. Capt. Frederick DePeyster with one hundred militiamen, marched twelve miles to McElrain's Creek where they met Dunlap."

From the information here contained in the entry of Allaire, there is a wide discrepancy in the British and American account of Dunlap's strength at Fort Prince, and also as to the casualties sustained by McDowell's men.

It is very evident that Allaire made the entry in his diary merely upon rumors which had reached him. It is likely, however, from the report of the prisoner which Allaire says Dunlap captured, who stated "that the rebels were four hundred strong," that Dunlap thought McDowell's whole command was upon him instead of the small detachment under Colonel Hampton. It is not surprising, therefore, that he beat a hasty retreat from Fort Prince, leaving according to the traditionary account of Mr. Pollard, his dead along the road unburied. The following is the entry of Allaire for Sunday, the 16th of August: "Dunlap with the men under his command marched down to Stephen White's plantation, where the American volunteers and militia lay."

It will thus be seen that this daring expedition of Col. Edward Hampton drove back for a time the British and Tory forces, to the happy relief of the people of the surrounding country. In another place, we will give a sketch of the brave and patriotic officer, who, like others we will mention, has never received the place he rightly deserved to occupy by the writers of the Revolutionary history of our country.

CHAPTER XIX.

SHELBY AND SEVIER UNITED WITH McDOWELL AT CHEROKEE FORD.—COLONEL CLARKE RETREATS FROM GEORGIA AND JOINS SUMTER'S COMMAND.—CAPTURE OF THICKETY FORT.

COLONEL McDOWELL remained encamped at Earle's Ford a few days and then changed to Cherokee Ford, on Broad River. Seeing that Ferguson's movement to the northwestern portion South Carolina threatened North Carolina, he dispatched a messenger with the alarming intelligence to Cols. John Sevier and Isaac Sevier, on Watonga and Holston; then in the western portion of North Carolina but now East Tennessee. He urged these noted leaders to come at once and bring to his aid all the riflemen that they could gather. In the meanwhile he continued to recruit his command with volunteers from the thinly populated settlements on the headwaters of the Catawba, the Broad and Pacolet Rivers.

When the messenger reached Colonel Sevier he felt unable to leave the frontier exposed to the inroads of the Cherokees. He responded to the appeal, however, by sending Maj. Charles Robertson with a part of his command. Colonel Shelby it appears was more remote than Colonel Sevier, but hastened to McDowell's relief as early as possible. He was a few days later than Sevier, but by the 25th of July arrived at McDowell's camp, near Cherokee Ford, with two hundred mounted riflemen.

It will be remembered that the fact was stated in a former chapter that Colonel Jones left Colonel Clarke in Georgia. The latter did not remain very long after Jones left. While remaining in Georgia he and his comrades had to secrete themselves in the woods and be fed by friends. When his command reassembled, however, its numbers had increased. It was the desire of all that Colonel Clarke should lead them to North Carolina. The command set out at once, passing along the eastern slope of the Blue Ridge Mountains. On the way Colonel Clarke was joined by the command of Capt. Joseph McCall, consisting of about twenty men, and later he was joined by Jones' command near Cherokee Ford, but for want of confidence in the activity of McDowell, he pushed on and joined Colonel Sumter on or near the Catawba.

These different commands having come together under brave partisan leaders, it was impossible for military operations to remain still. The next event of importance after this union of their forces was the capture of Fort Thicketv or Anderson, under the command of Capt. Patrick Moore, a noted Loyalist, who was born within a few miles of the present town of Lincolnton, North Carolina. He was a son of another noted Loyalist of that region, and a brother of Lieutenant-Colonel John Moore of Colonel Hampton's North Carolina regiment of Lovalists, whose behavior at the battle of Ramsour's Mill on the 20th of June, 1780, was such, that when, after the battle, he returned to Cornwallis' camp near Camden, he was threatened with court martial for disobedience of orders and was treated with disrespect by the British officers, which placed him in a disagreeable suspense.*

It is said that Capt. Patrick Moore escaped from the slaughter of the battle of Ramsour's Mill, when his brother with a few men retired to Cornwallis' camp. Among the Whigs there was a great anxiety to capture Moore, whose influence and mischief was damaging the American cause. Maj. Joseph Dickson, Capt. William Johnson and the veteran William Martin, who had served in the French and Indian wars, were sent with a party to capture him. On Lawson's fork, near Wofford's old iron works (now Glendale), the parties met and a skirmish ensued, in which Capts. Johnson and Moore had a per-

*See Wheeler's History of North Carolina, (Lincoln County), Page 231.

sonal encounter. Moore was finally overpowered and captured. It was, however, a desperate contest, in which Johnson received several sword wounds in the head, and one on the thumb of his right hand. While conducting his prisoner towards the Whig lines, a short distance away, he saw several British troops approaching him. He attempted to fire his loaded musket at them, but the blood from his bleeding thumb wet his priming. This misfortune on his part enabled his prisoner to escape, and perceiving his own danger, he fled to a thicket near by, thus eluding the grasp of his pursuers. Shortly afterwards he joined his command. It was soon after this time that Moore had command of Thickety Fort. This fort is situated near Goucher Creek, and about two and a half miles above the mouth of this water course which enters into Thickety Creek, being a western prong of said creek, and uniting with it a few miles above its junction, with Broad River.*

It is reported to have been a strong fortress, built a few years before as a defense against the Cherokees, and was surrounded by strong breast timbers well fitted for a vigorous and successful resistance. Draper states that among the spoils taken at King's Mountain was a fragment of a letter without date or signature, probably a dispatch from Ferguson to Cornwallis, in which this account is given of the construction of Thickety Fort. "It had an upper line of loop holes and was surrounded by a strong abatis, with only a small wicket to enter by. It had been put in thorough repair at the request of the garrison, which consisted of the neighboring militia that had come to the fort, and was defended by eighty men, against two or three hundred banditti without cannon, and each man was of the opinion that it was impossible for the rebels to take it."

*In a recent conversation with Mr. Edward (Pompey Ned) Lipscomb, he informed the writer that the old site of Thickety Fort was within a few steps of the residence of his son-in-law, Mr. Ben Bonner.

It was from Thickety Fort that Moore and his Tory associates would sally forth to plunder Whig families in the surrounding country. Women and children were often left without clothing, shoes, bread, meat and salt. We find in Mrs. Ellett's "Women of the Revolution" some particulars recorded of their depredations. Says an author, "In the absence of Capt. Nathaniel Jeffries of that region, one of the plundering parties visited his house, appropriated such articles as they chose, built a fire on the floor, abused Mrs. Jeffries as the meanest of all rebels, and drove off the horses and cattle. On another occasion, the house of Samuel McJunkin, in Union district, a warm patriot, but too old for active military service, was visited by a party under Patrick Moore. They staid all night, and when about to depart, stripped the family of bed clothes and wearing apparel. A noted Tory, Bill Haynsworth, seized a bed quilt and placed it upon his horse, when McJunkin's sturdy daughter Jane snatched it and a struggle ensued for the possession. The soldiers amused themselves by exclaiming, "Well done woman!" "Well done Bill!" For once, Moore's gallantry predominated over his love of plunder and he swore roundly if Jane could take the quilt from Haynsworth she should have it. Presently, in the fierce contest, Bill's feet came in contact with some dirty slime in the yard and slipped from under him, and he lay prostrate and panting on the ground. Jane, quick as thought, placed one foot on his breast and wresting the quilt from his grasp, retired in triumph, while poor Bill sneaked off defeated and crestfallen. This brave woman was a sister of Major McJunkin."

The same author states that the Tories visited the Irish settlement on Fair Forest and that Miss Nancy Jackson kicked a Tory down the steps as he was descending loaded with plunder.

In Draper's "King's Mountain," the following story is related: Sam Brown, known as Plundering Sam, and another whose name was Butler, went to the house of

Josiah Culbertson, son-in-law of Col. John Thomas, in the Fair Forest region, where he mistreated Mrs. Culbertson. Her husband coming home at night, was informed of Brown's insolence and unbecoming conduct. His temper was so aroused that he determined to capture or kill him and thus rid the country of a bad man. Selecting a man by the name of Charles Holloway, he started at once in pursuit. Early next morning they were joined by William Neel, William McIlhaney and one, Steadman.

It is stated that these determined men pursued Brown some ten miles, and as they were passing the house of Dr. Andrew Thomson on Tyger River, they discovered in the stables the horses of Brown and Butler. Retracing their steps they concealed themselves near the stables. Very soon Brown and Butler appeared at the door, when Culbertson leveled his rifle on him and sent a ball into his body which killed him. Holloway, who was near him, fired at Butler but missed his aim and Butler made good his escape.*

*Col. T. J. Moore, of Moore, S. C., in a communication to the *Carolina Spartan*, April 7th, 1894, stated that he has investigated and found the scene of the murder of Sam Brown. Colonel Moore states that the house where Dr. Thomson lived is the present Pinson or "tin roofed" house, now occupied by Mr. Newton Bearden, a mile or two from Oats' Shoal going east, and on the road from Walnut Grove to Marches' Shoal bridge, in the direction of Woodruff.

This old historic house is built of hewn logs, has two large rooms below, flight of stairs and two rooms above. Long years ago it was weatherboarded which preserved the logs. The same floor is in it now as was then. The planks are wide and notched down at every sleeper to make it level and true. There is a cellar in the middle of one room. The nails used were wrought ones. The hewn logs for the most part are in a good state of preservation. The old fire place is ten feet wide and ten feet thick between the rooms. It is further stated in Colonel Moore's article, that the blood of Brown is still on the door and floor near it, and that for a long time the hole of the bullet that was shot at Butler and which struck the house was seen, and that until the past few years the tree under which Culbertson and his friends were concealed was standing.

Sam Brown's grave is about a mile from the place where he was killed, across a branch and near a shoal on the branch, and directly between the houses of Mrs. Trail and Belton Steadman. Colonel Moore visited the grave, which was pointed out to him by Mr. George P. Moore and Mr. Steadman, both of whom were familiar with the tradition of the killing of Sam Brown.

Returning to Moore we will say that the inroads of this noted character and his Tory associates, reaching the ears of Sumter, this officer directed Colonel Clarke and his Georgians to gather together such persons in his camp as resided in that region and desired to aid in its protection against the outrages of the Tories. Among those who availed themselves of this privilege was Capt. William Smith* and his company. Arriving at Cherokee Ford, they met Colonel McDowell just as he was, with Colonels Shelby, Clarke, Andrew Hampton and Major Robinson, of Sevier's regiment, organizing a force of six hundred men to surprise and capture Thickety Fort not many miles away. They took up their line of march about sunset on the evening of the 25th of July, 1780, and surrounded the fort the next morning at daybreak. Colonel Shelby sent in Col. William Cocke (afterwards United States Senator from Tennessee), to make a peremptory demand for the surrender of the garrison. Moore replied that he would defend the place to the last extremity. Shelby then drew his lines within musket shot of the enemy all around and to avoid what appeared to be an unnecessary effusion of blood on both sides, made a second demand of Moore to surrender. Shelby's gallant "six hundred" presented such a formidable array that Moore relented. He doubtless had in his mind the recent onslaught against the Tories at Ramsour's Mill. He agreed to surrender the fort on condition that the garrison be paroled, not to serve again during the war unless exchanged; which was agreed to very willingly on the part of the Americans, as they did not care to be encumbered with prisoners.

Moore surrendered ninety-three Loyalists and one British Sergeant-Major, who had been sent to this place to drill and discipline them. Not a gun was fired. Among the trophies of the victory were two hundred standof

---

*William Smith was afterwards one of the early judges for Spartanburg County, of whom further notice will be made.

arms, all loaded with ball and buckshot and so arranged at the port holes that they could have resisted double their number had the besieged party been headed by a brave commander such as Ferguson or DePeyster.

Moore was greatly censured by the British authorities in South Carolina for not defending Thickety Fort. In the same fragment of letter already referred to in this chapter were these words: "The officer next in command and all the others gave their opinion for defending it, and agree in their account that Patrick Moore after proposing a surrender, acquiesced in their opinion and offered to go and signify as much to the rebels, but returned with some rebel officers whom he put in possession of the gate and place, who were instantly followed by their men, to the surprise of the garrison. He plead cowardice I understand."

Shelby and his men, loaded with the spoils of victory, returned at once to McDowell's camp near Cherokee Ford.

Wheeler, in his history of North Carolina, makes a slight mention of the capture of Thickety Fort, but does not give the date of its capture. The date we have given however, (26th day of July, 1780), is doubtless correct. According to Allaire's diary it took place on the thirtieth of November, 1780, which is a mistake.

CHAPTER XX.

SECOND BATTLE OF CEDAR SPRING OR WOFFORD'S IRON WORKS.

AFTER the capture of Thickety Fort, McDowell continued to hold his position near Cherokee Ford, which was considered the most formidable that could be selected as a base for future operations. His forces numbered about one thousand, including Colonel Clarke's command, which it appears, had now shifted from Sumter's to his camınand. The command of Ferguson numbered about eighteen hundred. On account of this difference in strength it was the policy of the Americans to maintain a strong position and guard against surprise.

Very soon after the Thickety expedition, Colonel McDowell detached Colonels Shelby, Clarke and William Graham, with their forces combined, amounting in all to about six hundred mounted men, to watch the movements of Ferguson's men, and whenever possible, to cut off and capture his foraging parties. The general plan, it seems, was a change of position by moving down Broad River some twenty-five miles to Brown's Creek, in Union county, believing this to be a good position whence to watch the movements of the British and Tories. But before all the troops could be collected at this point, a superior force of the enemy forced them to retire some thirty or forty miles to the Fair Forest settlement, within the present limits of Spartanburg county. They were solid and eager for the onset, which they knew was not far off and were now watching their opportunity to gain some decided advantage over their enemy, which they knew were in large numbers in that quarter. It was their policy to establish no permanent camp, but to keep moving about here and there. Ferguson, finding that he was confronted by these bold Rebels, made several ineffectual efforts to surprise them. But, says Draper, "Our frontier heroes were too watchful to be caught napping." Having no fixed camp, Clarke and Shelby were all the time on the alert. It was with difficulty that they could be located. It was not long before the hostile forces met, and their first meeting brings us to the consideration of the second engagement near Cedar Spring, known also in history as the battle near Wofford's Iron Works. We pause here to state that history is so conflicting as to the time and place of this little battle, and the several traditionary accounts which have been published are so inconsistent with the main facts recorded, that it is almost impossible, at the present time, to present a truthful account of it. After careful examination, however, into the conflicting authorities and traditions, we give to the reader what we believe to be the most trustworthy facts on record.

The old site of Wofford's Iron Works spoken of in Ramsay's history as *Buffington's*, and in Johnson's traditions as *Burwick's Iron Works*, was just above (at the upper shoal) of the present manufacturing village of Glendale, known in former times as Bivingsville. As this place is some three miles to the east of Cedar Spring, the question is naturally asked, where did the engagement referred to take place? We think we can answer so as to satisfy the reader's mind.

On the Spartanburg, Union and Columbia Railroad, four miles below the City of Spartanburg, are the ruins of an old station building, on the right passing down the road, known in former times as "Cedar Spring Station." In after years a larger structure was built some three or four hundred yards below this, on the left. This, at present, is known by either the names Glendale or Cedar Spring station, being the most convenient point to reach either of these places from the railroad. Just north of this station building, about one hundred yards or more, is a clump of large and stately oaks, standing on a spot of ground which gives every appearance of an ancient dwelling place and which is known as the old Thomson place. Just here, in Revolutionary times, two roads came together. One was the road from Pinckneyville, on Broad River, and the other was from North Carolina via Cherokee Ford and Wofford's Iron Works. From this point the road ran in the direction of Georgia. Leaving Cedar Spring about one mile to the left, it ran by the old Anthony Foster place, * the late residence of E. H. Bobo, Esq., by the home of the late Isham Hurt, by Bethlehem Church, Dr. Miller's old place, Capt. David Anderson's, Maj. Frank L. Anderson's, and on in the direction of Georgia, via Simpsonville, in the lower portion of Greenville county. Like the old Blackstock, this is one of the oldest roads in Spartanburg county. It has been known in the neighborhood, through which it passes as the "Old Georgia" or "Pinckneyville" road. It was at the crossing of this old road over Fair Forest, near Mr. Will Wood's, where the plantations of the late Capt. A. Copeland and Capt. John Blassingame came together, that Clarke and Shelby, on the 7th of August, stopped for refreshment and to encamp for the night if not disturbed. This was about two miles west of Cedar Spring. Scouts were sent out to make a reconnoisance, who returned before day and reported that the enemy were only about a half a mile distant. About this time the report of a gun was heard in the direction in which the British were reported coming. It was afterwards ascertained that this gun was fired by one of Dunlap's men, "who," says Draper, "felt some compunctions of conscience at the idea of surprising and massacring his countrymen.

Shelby and Clarke, on receiving this intelligence, decided to retreat at once. Their route was over the old road referred to, in the direction of Wofford's Iron Works. Reaching the old Thomson place, the location of which has already been described, they formed a line of battle

* This is the old Anthony Foster brick mansion. This and the Price building, on the Tyger (the former residence of Capt. George B Dean) are said to be the two oldest brick buildings in Spartanburg County.

on what they believed to be the most favorable ground to meet the approaching enemy, who had followed in pursuit. Scarcely had these preliminaries been completed when spies came running in and reported that the enemy's horses were almost in sight. Very soon they came and the action commenced. The enemy's forces were strong and consisted partly of colonial dragoons and partly of mounted militia. They were headed by the same Major Dunlap, whom we have introduced to the reader in former chapters of this work. Both sides—the Whigs and British—were anxious for the fray. The latter being over-confident, rushed forward as if victory was already assured. Dunlap's mounted riflemen, it is said, were in front and at the very first fire of their opponents. they recoiled and gave back. It was with difficulty that their commander could rally them. Having succeeded, however, he placed himself at the head of his dragoons with broad swords and led them forward to renew the contest. He was followed by the mounted riflemen, who were too timid to come in close contact with their opponents. Shelby's and Clarke's men stood their ground with firmness and were kept busy picking them off as they advanced. Dunlap was, at length, beaten back with considerable loss. In "Mills' Statistics" we are informed that he was pursued about one mile, but could not be overtaken. About two miles from the battle ground, Dunlap met Ferguson with his whole force advancing against Shelby and Clarke. This compelled the latter to make a hasty retreat in the direction of Wofford's Iron Works, leaving one or two of their wounded behind them who were humanely treated by Ferguson when he came up. Not having the time or convenience to care for them, he left them where he found them. By adroit management, Shelby and Clarke had captured about fifty prisoners, mostly British, including two officers. Ferguson was restless to recapture these, but he soon found a stubborn resistance to his further progress. The account says that "the American leaders retired slowly, forming frequently on the most advantageons ground to give battle and so retarding pursuit that the prisoners were finally placed beyond recapture."

With the exception of a bold stand for a half hour or more at the Thomson old place, where Dunlap's forces wére repulsed, this engagement was a running fight from the point where it commenced to Wofford's Iron Works and farther on. For this reason it has been called by some writers, the "battle of Cedar Spring,"—it being only one mile from this to the place where the action commenced—and, by other writers, "the battle (or skirmish) at Wofford's Iron Works. Ferguson's forces continued the pursuit to the fording on Pacolet River, three miles northeast of Wofford's Iron Works, "just beyond which," says Draper, "skirting its northeast border, rises a steep and rocky hill fifty or sixty feet high, so steep where the road passed up at that dav, that the men, in some instances, had to help their horses up its difficult ascent. Along the crest of this hill Shelby and Clark displayed their little forces, and when Ferguson and his men came in view, evincing a disinclination to pursue any further, the patriots from their vantage ground bantered and ridiculed them to their hearts' content. Ferguson having maintained the chase for four or five miles, now abandoned it with nothing to boast of save his superior numbers." This was the end of this spirited engagement. We have already intimated that we have other accounts of the same engagement, differing from those which we have presented. Rev. James H. Saye, it is said, spent his life of over seventy years gathering up the traditions of the country from surviving soldiers of the Revolution. These he published about fifty years ago. The battle of Cedar Spring is described as "the battle of the *peach orchard*," which he says was "upon a parcel of land extending down a hollow which was cleared and planted in fruit trees prior to the Revolutionary war." This was near and northeast of the Thomson place and along the old road leading to Wofford's Iron Works. "In this orchard," says Mr. Saye, "the patrol parties met from the adverse armies. The party from Dunlap's camp were in the orchard gathering peaches; the liberty men fired on them and drove them from the place. In turn the victors entered the orchard, but the report of their guns brought out a strong detachment from the Cedar Spring, as well as a reinforcement from Shelby. The commander of the patrol, when he saw the enemy approaching, drew up his men under the cover of a fence along the ridge just where the old field and woodland now meet, and where the traces of an old residence are now visible. Here he awaited their approach." Mr. Saye further narrates other particulars of the engagement which, differing from those we have already given, we will not reproduce here.

Mr. Draper thinks that this tradition, as presented by Mr. Saye, may very properly be a supplement to the narrative just given and that the meeting of the hostile forces in the peach orchard was probably but one of the episodes of the exploits of that day. Mr. Draper also very properly observes, that this account of Mr. Saye is only a local tradition, and that local tradition is extremely liable to error and confusion, as the actors are sometimes from other States and strangers to the neighborhood.

There are several interesting incidents connected with this battle worthy of notice. In an article published by Governor Swain, of North Carolina, in the University Magazine, in 1861, recently reproduced in Schenck's "North Carolina," we find the following in reference to Colonel Clarke's conduct at the battle of Cedar Spring: "It was in the severest part of the action that Colonel Shelby's attention was arrested by the heroic conduct of Colonel Clarke. He often mentioned the circumstance of pausing in the midst of the battle to look with astonishment and admiration at Clarke's fighting." Draper says that in the fierce hand to hand contest, which Clarke was maintaining in the unequal struggle, he received two sabre wounds—one in the back of his neck, and the other on his head, his stock buckle saving his life; that he was even for a few minutes a prisoner in the hands of two stout Britons, but having confidence in his own strength, he knocked one of them down while the other fled. Mc Call, in his "History of Georgia," says that both Colonel Clarke and his son were wounded in this action.

Among the heroes of this battle was Capt. William Smith, whose biography will claim further notice. Another was Josiah Culbertson, also a native of Spartanburg county.

Before Clarke and Shelby left their temporary camp on Fair Forest, Josiah Culbertson, who has been described as one of the bravest of young men, obtained permission to visit his home only two or three miles away. His object was to make such observations and gain such information as he could in regard to the location, position and strength of the enemy. About daylight the next morning he rode fearlessly and unconcernedly into the camp he had left the evening before, supposing it to be still occupied by his friends, not knowing that Clarke and Shelby had decamped and that Dunlap had taken possession of it. Discovering his mistake, he leisurely rode out of camp until out of sight and then spurred forward rapidly to give Clarke and Shelby notice of the nearness of the enemy.* As he passed through the camp he noticed that the dragoons were getting their horses in readiness. He knew from this and other preparations which were being made by the enemy that they were making ready to renew their line of march. He could only guess as to the route Shelby and Clarke had taken, and when he overtook them, he found them already in line of battle on chosen ground ready for the onslaught.

During the progress of the fight, Culbertson had a personal adventure worthy of special notice. "Meeting a dragoon," says Draper, "some distance from support, who imperiously demanded his surrender, the intrepid American replied by whipping his rifle to his shoulder and felling the haughty Briton from his horse. When the

* See Johnson's Traditions, page 422.

dead were buried the next day, this dragoon was thrown into a hole, where he lay, and covered with earth. He happened to have some peaches in his pocket at the time, from which a peach tree grew and for many years afterwards bore successive crops." It is said, upon the authority of Prof. N. F. Walker, at Cedar Spring, that this grave can yet be pointed out, though the peach tree has long since disappeared. This fact was stated to Professor Walker by an aged gentleman in the neighborhood, who died a few years ago at the advanced age of nearly one hundred vears and who had, in early life, eaten fruit from that tree.

The second battle of Cedar Spring or of Wofford's Iron Works as erroneously called by some writers, was fought on the 8th day of August, 1780. There are different statements as to the time of day when the engagement commenced. Mills places it before day, when it was so dark that it was hard to distinguish friend from foe. This is a mistake, as we will prove. He doubtless has reference to Dunlap's attack on Colonel Thomas' command at Cedar Spring one month before, the particulars of which we have given in a former chapter and which occurred in the night time. McCall states that it occurred in the afternoon. Governor Perry in his articles states, upon the authority of Capt. William Smith, that it was the morning or forepart of the day. This is correct. The account which we have given states that Clarke and Shelby stopped for refreshment on Fair Forest, where the old road referred to crosses that stream, and to encamp for the night if not disturbed. In Governor Perry's article to *The Magnolia* 1842,* the fact is stated that Colonels Clarke and Shelby were alarmed by the firing of a gun of one of Dunlap's soldiers already referred to. They immediately decamped in the night time and took up their line of march to the Thomson place, where morning found them. Dunlap, with a detachment from Fer-

* See Johnson's Traditions, page 422.

guson's command, marched into his encampment and remained there until morning, when Culbertson found him. It is probable that the fight commenced about eight or nine o'clock in the morning and it may have been in the afternoon before the skirmishing which occured between the Thomson place and the crossing on Pacolet ended. The historical accounts which we have before us differ as to the numbers on each side in this engagement, and also as to the casualties of both. Mills states that Clarke's force numbered one hundred and ninety-eight, but does not indicate the number of Shelby's and Graham's forces. He places Dunlap's advance force as consisting of sixty dragoons and one hundred and fifty mounted volunteer riflemen, and that his force combined with Ferguson's numbered between four and six hundred. He states further that the Americans had four killed and twenty-three wounded, all by the broad sword, while Dunlap lost twenty-eight of his dragoons and six or seven of his Tory volunteers killed, besides several wounded. Shelby in "Haywood's Tennessee," states that Ferguson's full force amounted to about two thousand, of which Dunlap's advance force consisted of about seven hundred. He places the strength of the American forces at six hundred, and states that ten or twelve of the latter were killed and wounded. He does not give the enemy's loss, but Colonel Graham states that it was heavy. Governor Perry in his writings states that as late as 1842 there were seen as many as twenty or more graves of the dead who fell in this battle. Dr. Geo. Walker, of Glendale, informs the writer that inside of a rough rock wall near the site of Wofford's Iron Works are several graves, which tradition says, contained the bodies of some of the dead who were killed in the skirmish near that place. It is stated upon the authority of Maj. A. J. Wells, of Alabama, a former resident of Spartanburg county, near Cedar Spring, that after the war the widow of a Tory came to the place where the dead were buried and had the bodies disinterred, from which she selected the remains of her husband, who was six and one-half feet high. She carried off the remains for a more decent interment. * In a former chapter, in giving an account of the first engagement near Cedar Spring on the 12th of July, we stated that Mrs. Thomas rode nearly sixty miles from Ninety-Six, where her husband was incarcerated to inform her son, Col. John Thomas, Jr., that the Loyalists intended to attack him the same night. This, in Mills' statistics, has been accorded to Mrs. Mary Dillard. In Col. Samuel Hammond's note on the battle of Cedar Spring, he states that this lady, about a half hour before day, came in full gallop to one of the videttes, who conducted her to Colonel Clarke. † She told him to be in readiness to fight or fly, as the enemy would be upon him, and they were strong. It may have been that the intelligence conveyed by this lady aroused Clarke and Shelby in their camp on Fair Forest instead of the firing of the gun by the Tory, as stated, or else it may have been that after they had retreated from Fair Forest on the night of the 7th of August, and had taken their position at the Thomson place on the morning of the 8th, that Mrs. Dillard came to convey the intelligence of the near approach of the enemy. The account as recorded in history, states that soon after Clarke and Shelby formed their line of battle at the Thomson place, spies (not scouts) came running in and reported that the enemy's horses were almost in sight. Hammond states that as soon as Mrs. Dillard de-

---

* In January, 1893, the writer was on a visit to Union, S. C., and called on his venerable friend, Gen. B. B. Foster, then seventy-five years of age. General Foster is a native of Spartanburg county and was born at the old Anthony Foster place near Cedar Spring. In referring to the battle at the old Thomson place the General stated that he heard Mr. John Bagwell say that after the battle referred to, the Tories were put in one hole, but so shallow that the wolves scratched them out and that he (Bagwell) with his mother and sister, cut brush and piled on the graves to prevent any further molestation by the wolves.

† See Johnson's Traditions, page 507. Colonel Clarke was not in the first engagement at Cedar Spring.

livered her message to Colonel Clark, "every man was, in an instant, up and prepared and the enemy entered our camp in full charge." We believe the statement as to Mrs. Thomas to be unquestionably correct. As to the honor accorded to Mrs. Dillard, we leave the reader to form his own conclusion. The point that we make, is, that since it has been proven that there were, at different times, two engagements near Cedar Spring, it is not impossible that both Mrs. Thomas and Mrs. Dillard performed the heroic deeds which historv has accorded to them.

Draper thinks that it was a mistake that Mrs. Dillard carried the intelligence to Cedar Spring of the enemy's approach, as she lived south of the Enoree, in Laurens county, fully thirty miles south-east of Cedar Spring, but says that she lived on the route Tarleton pursued when on his way to attack Sumter at Blackstocks, on Tyger. Tarleton relates that "a woman on horseback had viewed the line of march from a wood, and by a nearer road had given intelligence" to Sumter. This, he says, was Mrs. Dillard.

The writer has been asked if he knew where the *Battle of Buffington* was fought. This doubtless has reference to the same engagement which we have just narrated. Prof. N. F. Walker, of Cedar Spring, informs the writer that he has in his possession the old Buffington land papers or grants which cover a large section around him. It is probable that the first owner of Wofford's Iron Works was a Buffington. Ramsay, in his history of the upper country of South Carolina, (see appendix, page 307) says that "the first iron works in South Carolina were erected by a Mr. Buffington, in 1773." These, he says, were destroyed by the Tories in the Revolutionary war.*

---

* Mr. Allen Thomason informed the writer a short time ago, that they were destroyed by "Bloody Bill" Cunningham during his raid in November, 1781. Mr. Thomason has since died at the advanced age of about ninety years. He was well posted on the Revolutionary traditions in Spartanburg county.

The history of the battle of Cedar Spring, or Wofford's Iron Works, has been neglected by the writers of Revolu tionary history in South Carolina. Ramsay, Lee's Me moirs and Johnson and Greene do not notice it, while other writers barely touch upon it.

The people of Spartanburg county, and all of South Carolina, owe a debt of gratitude to that eminent historian, Lyman C. Draper, for the pains and interest which he has devoted to minute details, and to him the writer is indebted in the main for the facts which are here presented.

CHAPTER XXI.

EXPEDITION AND BATTLE OF MUSGROVE'S MILL.—SKETCH OF ISAAC SHELBY AND OTHERS.

IN a few days after the Fair Forest expedition Colonel McDowell removed his camp from Cherokee Ford to Smith's Ford, which is some seven or eight miles lower down on Broad River. This was better perhaps for obtaining forage for his horses and supplies for his command, and better at the same time for resting his men after an active campaign of several weeks. Shelby and Clarke, however, were not the men to remain idle. The term of enlistment of Shelby's men was about to expire, and it was necessary to strike another blow at the enemy before they were disbanded to depart for their homes.

Colonel McDowell was very vigilant to learn the exact whereabouts and position of the enemy. Bv his faithful scouts he learned that Ferguson's camp was at Fair Forest Shoal, in the Brandon settlement, some twenty-six miles from his encampment, and that at Musgrove's Mill, on the Enoree River, about forty miles from Smith's Ford and some fourteen miles southwest of Ferguson's camp, there were about two hundred Loyalists encamped. These were stationed on the south side of the stream to guard the rocky ford at that place, which was regarded as a vulnerable point. To march against and attack these, and at the same time escape the notice of Ferguson, was an important feat to be accomplished, and the fact that it was accomplished, and the brilliancy of the expedition and the victory which was won in the battle, will always reflect glory upon the hills of Musgrove, and upon the names of the heroes who participated in that little struggle for American Independence.

There were several reasons why it was preferred to attack this force of Loyalists at Musgrove's Mill to Ferguson's forces, which lay between Musgrove's Mill and Smith's Ford. In the first place the Loyalists were less trained and disciplined than the regular British forces, and it would be easier to overcome these than Ferguson's forces, which were composed of some good fighting material. In the second place, if this fording on the Enoree could be successfully carried the way would be open to Ninety-Six, where a British garrison was stationed and which might be stormed and captured. It was rumored also in McDowell's camp that a military chest was being conveyed from Ninety-Six via Musgrove's Mill to Ferguson's camp, and to intercept and capture this was a matter of great importance to the American troops.

It appears that the troops which were organized for this expedition were volunteers from the camp of Colonel McDowell, whose forces, according to different statements, amounted to from one to two thousand.* Colonels Shelby and Clarke had charge of the expedition. There were several officers of distinction who volunteered their services on this occasion, and among whom was Colonel Williams, whose home was in the region of Ninety-Six. Also Capt. James McCall, of Georgia, and Capt. Samuel Hammond, from near Ninety-Six. Besides these were Colonels Thomas Brandon and Steen and Majs. McJunkin and Joseph McDowell, brother of Colonel McDowell; also Capts. David Vance† and Valentine Sevier, the latter with a number of riflemen from the valleys of the Watauga and Nolachucky. There are different estimates as to the number which composed this expedition. Draper says that Shelby's command consisted of two hundred adventurous followers. The account in O'Neal's "Annals of Newberry" places the number at seven hundred. Judge

---

*See Draper's "King's Mountain," page 89; also O'Neal's "Annals of Newberry," page 320.

†Grandfather of United States Senator Z. B. Vance and Hon. Robert B. Vance.

Schenck in his recent work "North Carolina" refers to Governor Swain's article published in the University Magazine in 1861, which states that the most correct account of the expeditions of 1780 is found in the "National Portrait Gallery." From this Judge Schenck copies in full "Col. Isaac Shelby and Col. Charles McDowell's campaign in 1780." This account states that "General McDowell, having received information that five or six hundred Tories were encamped at Musgrove's Mill, on the south side of Enoree, about forty miles distant, again detached Colonels Shelby, Clarke and Williams, of South Carolina, with about seven hundred horsemen to disperse them." Col. Samuel Hammond, an active participant in the battle of Musgrove's Mill, gives an interesting account of this affair in "Johnson's Traditions." (See page 519). Colonel Hammond does not indicate the number in the expedition, but alludes to it as "our little band." It is very reasonable to suppose from the number of the enemy met in battle, and from the fact that this expedition had to place itself between Ferguson's command and the enemy at Musgrove's Mill, that McDowell would not have sent out a weak force to contend with either or both, as circumstances might necessitate.

There is a discrepancy in history as to the precise day on which the battle of Musgrove's Mill was fought. Colonel Hammond intimated that it was fought on the 19th of August. He says: "We marched twenty or twenty-five miles on the 16th, halted, fed and refreshed for an hour, and after dark set out on our march again. In the course of the night Colonel Bratton turned off the line of march, intending to pass through his own neighborhood and to fall in with us before day. This was injudicious in every point of view, for it afforded more than a double chance to the enemy of gaining intelligence of our approach and a probability of our not falling in with them or of their aiding us in the affair; and this proved to be the case, for they did not rejoin us until the affair was over. General McDowell advanced a few miles, but declined joining the enterprise. Our march was silently and skillfully conducted and we arrived near the post about day."

Judge Schenck fixes the day of the battle of Musgrove's Mill on the 19th of August. The account which he presents in his recent work states that "the American commanders took up their line of march from Smith's Ford, on the Broad River, just before sun down, on the evening of the 18th of August, 1780, continued through the woods until dark and then pursued a road, leaving Ferguson's camp about three miles to the left. They rode hard all night, frequently in a gallop, and just at the dawn of day about a half mile from the enemy's camp, met a strong patrol party. A skirmish ensued and several were killed." Wheeler's "History of North Carolina" fixes the time of this battle on the nineteenth of August, while Draper places it on the eighteenth. Savs this emi nent author: "Secrecy and dispatch were necessary to success. A night march was therefore chosen, as less likely to be observed and cooler for the horses to travel. Shelby and his two hundred adventurous followers left camp an hour before sun down on the seventeenth of August." The writer is disposed to adhere to the opinion of Draper, as he states that Colonel Williams with a few followers joined McDowell on the sixteenth.

The expedition when it set out was piloted by William Brandon, and the men were well acquainted with the countrv and knew the best route to take to effect their designs upon the enemy. Says Draper: "They traveled all night through the woods until dark, much of the way in a canter, and without making a single stop, crossing Gilky's and Thickety creeks, Pacolet, Fair Forest and Tyger, with other lesser streams, and passing within three or four miles of Ferguson's camp on the left." The American forces reached a point within one mile of Musgrove's Mill near the dawn of dav. Halting in an old Indian field, a party of five or six scouts were sent forward to reconnoitre the situation. They crossed the mouth of Cedar Shoal Creek, near the Spartanburg and

Union County line, just below the mill, and proceeded by a by-road up the river as far as Head's Ford, which is about a mile above Musgrove's Mill. Here they crossed the river and proceeded cautiously until they came in sight of the Tory camp. Making such observations as they thought necessary, they recrossed the river by the same route. When they had reached the top of the ridge west of Cedar Shoal Creek, they encountered a small Tory patrol which had crossed over Musgrove's Ford, above, during their absence, and had thus gained their rear. A sharp fight took place in which one of the enemy was killed and two wounded. The other two fled precipitately to the Tory camp. It is stated in Sckenck's work and also in Wheeler's history that while this skirmish was going on a countryman living near by informed the American commanders that the enemy had been reinforced the evening before with six hundred regular troops, under the command of Col. Alexander Innes, (called Enines in O'Neal's Annals). This was called the Queen's American Regiment from New York. * Draper says that the countryman living near by gave intelligence of a reinforcement of the enemy the evening before of only three hundred, (two hundred men of the provincial regiments and one hundred Tories). A British writer represents Colonel Innes as having command of a detachment instead of a regiment, and consisted of a light infantry company of the New Jersey volunteers, under Capt. Peter Campbell; a company of DeLancey's provincial battalion, under Capt. James Kerr, together with about one hun dred mounted men of his own regiment, the South Caro lina Royalists. The garrison which was already sta tioned there consisted for the most part of Tories of that region under the command of Col. Daniel Clary, though it appears that the garrison was commanded by a Major

*See Wheeler's "History of North Carolina," page 100. Also Schenck's "North Carolina," page 79, also O'Neal's "Annals of Newberry," page 321.

Fraser, whilst it is also stated that Capt. Abraham De-Peyster, * of the King's American Regiment, and Capt. David Fanning, a noted Loyalist, were there.

With this strong force confronting Shelby and his associates, they instantly concluded that there was no alternative but to fight. "Death was before them and destruction was behind them," says Wheeler. Should Ferguson have gotten wind by accident or otherwise of this night raid so near his encampment, he doubtless would have pounced upon the rear of Shelby and Clarke, and their whole command would have been in danger of being cut off or captured. They could not, therefore, afford to remain inactive many hours. It was necessary to bring on an engagement at once, and in order to do this they resorted to stratagem. Capt. Shadrack Inman, a brave officer from Georgia, who had figured prominently in battling with the British and Tories of that State, was selected to perform a responsible duty. He had under his command twenty-five picked mounted men. His orders were to fire upon and provoke the enemy to cross and skirmish with them at his discretion and to retire, drawing them if possible into a general engagement with Clarke and Shelby's whole command.

In the meanwhile, Shelby and Clarke had taken position on a timbered ridge, a short distance east of Cedar Shoal Creek, and only about a half mile from Musgrove's Mill and Ford. The horses, says Colonel Hammond, were picketed about three hundred yards in the rear beyond the hill and placed in charge of sixteen men. The men then set to work to improvise a breastwork of logs and brush and make the best possible defense. This was accomplished in about thirty minutes. It was semi-circular in shape and stretched across the main road leading to the ford. The troops being placed in position, Shelby took command of the right wing, Clarke the left, while Colonel Williams was stationed in the road, in the center, without

*Second in command to Ferguson at the battle of King's Mountain.

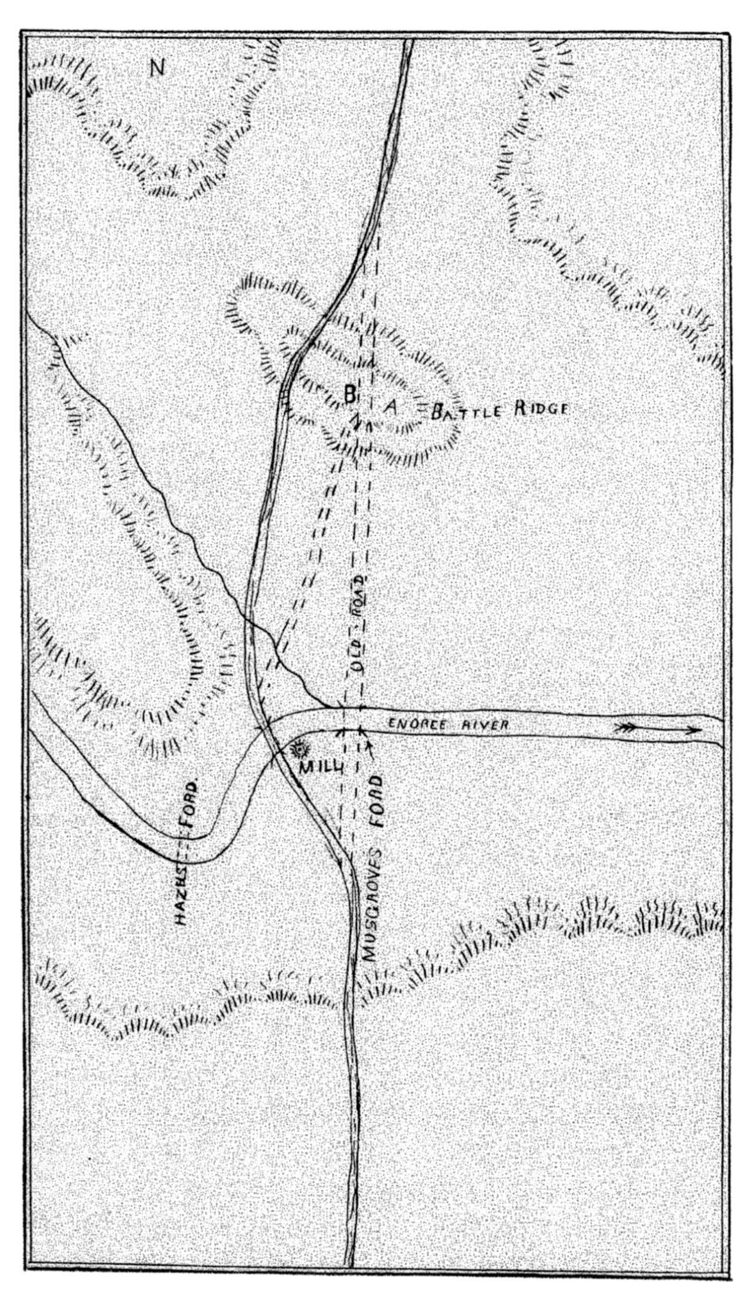

PLAT OF REGION NEAR MUSGROVE'S MILL. A GRAVES.
B WHERE CAPT. INMAN WAS KILLED, AT THE JUNCTION OF THE OLD AND NEW ROADS.

a separate command. A party of about twenty horsemen were placed on each flank. Josiah Culbertson had command of that on Shelby's right. Colonel Clarke had a reserve of about forty men within calling distance. Colonel Hammond, who was present, refers to this, giving the number on each flank as sixteen instead of twenty, and says these were ordered to fire upon the flanks of the enemy who might follow Captain Inman as he was retreating.

The stratagem which Inman had himself suggested worked well. The British infantry seemed elated with their success in driving him before them at the point of the bayonet. Captain Inman only intended to keep up a show of fighting and retreating merely to bring the enemy into the net which Shelby and Clarke had so adroitly prepared for them. Perhaps not more than an hour elapsed from the time Captain Inman was sent out with his command to skirmish with the enemy's forces on the banks of the Enoree before they crossed over to the north side of the stream. "The sound of their drum and bugle horns soon announced their movements," says Governor Swain. The pursuit of Inman's command was rapid and in great confusion, the enemy doubtless believing that the whole American force was routed. They came shouting, "Huzza for King George." * Says Draper, "While the enemy were yet two hundred yards distant from the American breast works, they hastily formed into a line of battle; and as they advanced fifty yards nearer they opened a heavy fire, pretty generally overshooting their antagonists. When trees were convenient the frontiersmen made use of them, while others were sheltered behind their rudely constructed barrier, and to some extent availed themselves also of a fence extending along the road. The Americans had been cautioned to reserve their fire "till they could see the whites of the Tories' eyes," or as another has it, "till they could distinguish the buttons

---

*See O'Neal's Annals of Newberry, page 322.

on their coats" nor even then to discharge their rifles until orders were given, when each man was "to take his object sure." These orders were strictly obeyed. Colonel Hammond says * that Shelby's and Clarke's men "were placed in one line in scattered or open order and were ordered not to fire until the enemy were within fifty yards, and also to be governed by a single shot from Colonel Shelby; to be steady and take good aim. They came flushed with the hope of an easy victory, in full trot." Colonel Hammond further states that the enemy advanced in three columns. The regulars, commanded by Major Fraser, the militia on the right and left "advancing." Says Colonel Hammond, "They deployed and gave us a fire which was not returned but from our flanking parties. They then advanced with trailed arms, their columns displayed, and were allowed to come within forty yards, when the signal was given and their ranks thinned." At the first fire they recoiled, but the superiority of their numbers enabled them to continue the attack, notwithstanding the Americans had the advantage of the temporary breastwork. A strong force of Provincials, led by Colonel Innes and Major Fraser, concentrated on the enemy's left wing and drove the right wing, under Shelby, from their breastwork. A desperate struggle ensued. Shelby's men contending against great odds, were forced to give back. The left and center, however, stood their ground. The left wing under Clarke was opposed by Tories. This officer, seeing the right wing under Shelby forced back, ordered his small reserve to march at once to his aid, which proved to be a most timely relief. Says Draper, "at this critical moment, as Innes was forcing Shelby's right flank, the British leader was badly disabled and fell from his charger and was carried back, shot it was reported by one of the Watauga Volunteers, William Smith, who exultingly exclaimed: "I have killed their commander." Shelby rallied his

*See Johnson's Traditions, page 520.

men who raised a regular frontier Indian yell and rushed furiously upon their enemy, who were gradually forced back before the exasperated riflemen. Culbertson's flanking party acted a conspicuous part on this occasion." The Tories on the enemy's right wing failed to make any impression on Clarke's line. Many of their men and several officers were killed. They began to show signs of wavering when Captain Hawsey, a noted leader among them, who was trying to re-animate them and retreive the fortunes of the day, was shot down. In the midst of this confusion Clarke's men, seeing Shelby's men pressing on the right, followed their example. There was a general forward march on the part of the Americans. The British and Tories were now in full retreat, closely pursued by the intrepid mountaineers. In the pursuit the brave Captain Inman was killed while pressing the enemy in a hand-to-hand fight. Manv of the British and Tories threw down their arms and surrendered. In the melee, two Whigs seized the bridle bits of Colonel Clary, a noted Tory. He extricated himself from his perilous situation by his ingenuity and presence of mind, exclaiming: "D—n you, don't you know your own officers." He was instantlv released and fled at full speed with the rest of his comrades, who had ceased to offer further resistance. Says a writer: "The yells and screeches of the retreating British and Tories as they ran through the woods and over the the hills to the river, loudly intermingled with the shouts of their pursuers, together with the groans of the dying and wounded, were terrific and heartrending in the extreme. The smoke as well as the din and confusion rose high above the exciting scene. The Tories ceased to make any show of defense when half way from the breast works to the ford. The retreat then became a perfect rout, and now with reckless speed they hastened to the river, through which they rushed with the wildest fury, hotly pursued by the victorious Americans with sword and rifle, killing, wounding and capturing all who came in their way."

The British and Tories before their final rout fought bravely. Their dragoons lately raised and poorly disciplined behaved with becoming gallantry, fighting on the left under Colonel Innes. They all exhibited more or less the training they had received from Ferguson, who has already been represented as a superior training master.

The British loss in this engagement in proportion to their number engaged was heavy. Sixty-three were killed, about ninety were wounded and about seventy were made prisoners. Many of both the British and Tories were shot down as they were retreating pell mell across the Enoree at the Rocky Ford. According to the best accounts their whole attacking force could not have amounted to more than five hundred, of which number it will be seen their total loss was not far from two hundred and twenty-three. Besides, the notorious Tory Captain Hawsey, was killed on their right wing. Several of their officers were killed and wounded on their left in the desperate encounter with Shelby's forces. The most prominent among their officers wounded besides Colonel Innes, who was shot down by Smith, was Major Fraser,* who was wounded by Robert Beene, another Watauga rifleman. He was seen to reel from his horse. Captain Campbell and Lieuts. Camp and William Chew were also numbered among their wounded officers.

The American loss was only four killed, including the brave Captain Inman, and eight or nine wounded. Captain Inman was killed near the junction of the old and new roads between the battle ridge and Musgrove's Ford, while pressing them in a hand-to-hand fight. He received several shots from the Tories, one shot piercing his forehead.

The firing was continued for sometime after the enemy had recrossed the river. While this was going on, Capt.

---

*In Colonel Hammond's account in Johnson's Traditions he states that Major Fraser with eighty-five others were killed. Draper says he was only wounded.

Sam Moore, a bold and fearless scout, led a small party consisting of only ten or twelve, up the river and crossed over at Head's Ford. From this place he rushed down with such audacity and impetuosity as to impress the British and Tories with the idea that the whole American forces were swooping down upon their flank. They made a precipitate flight in front of Moore, while this gallant officer with his little band retraced their steps across the river to join their victorious comrades.

There are some interesting incidents connected with the battle of Musgrove's Mill, which we must not fail to notice. It is related that while the battle was in progress, as many as possible of the British and Tories remaining in camp, climbed on top of Musgrove's house to witness the result. They never doubted for a moment that the troops of King George would sweep everything before them like an avalanche. When they saw Captain Inman deliver his successive fires near the river and retreat, being hotly pursued by their troops, they threw up their hats and set up a wild huzza that made the hills around them resound with echo and re-echo in commemoration of an imaginary victory. They supposed that this little force under Inman constituted the entire forces of the Americans. Great, however, was their consternation and disappointment when they saw their forces driven back and routed by the Whig forces, who had been concealed behind their breastworks. It is said that about fifty of these were paroled prisoners doing duty, contrary to the laws of war. Dreading the consequences of a possible capture by the Americans, they raised a cry of despair. With pale and trembling faces they exclaimed, "We are beaten—our men are retreating," and long before the British and Tory forces had recrossed the river they had repacked their knapsacks and were in post haste for Ninety-Six.

It is said that after the British and Tories were fairly over the river one of their number, to exhibit his bravado, turned his body in an insulting position in derision at the Americans. "Can't you turn that insolent braggart over?" said a Whig officer to Golden Tinsley. "I will try," said Tinsley, and with cool and deliberate aim he soon brought him down. He was picked up by his comrades and carried away. Another instance of the accuracy of the sharpshooting is mentioned. Thomas Gillespie, a Watauga rifleman, shot and killed a Tory across the river, whose body was partially exposed from behind a tree. Many of the enemy took refuge in the mill, from which place a few shots were fired.

"The battle of Musgrove's Mill," savs a writer, "was one of the hardest ever fought in the country with small arms alone; the smoke was so thick as to hide a man at the distance of twenty rods." It was, no doubt, fortunate for the Americans that only small arms were used. Had Ferguson, who was only about fifteen miles in their rear, caught wind of the pealing of cannon, he doubtless would have marched with his whole command against the troops of Shelby and Clark, who being thus placed between two bodies of their enemy, would have found it difficult to extricate themselves. Another fortunate circumstance intervened which was in favor of the Americans, Says a writer, a large patroling party which had been down the river near Jones' Ford, heard the firing and came dashing back at full speed, and while descending the steep hill east of the old Musgrove domicile, their bright uniforms and flashing blades and scabbards, reflected the rays of the morning sun, just rising in its splendor. They reined up their panting steeds before Musgrove's—the commanding officer eagerly inquiring what was the matter. A hurried account of the battle, which had terminated so disasterously some thirtv minutes before, was given, when rising in his stirrups and uttering deep and loud imprecations, the cavalry commander ordered his men to cross the river. They dashed at full speed over the rocky ford, splashing the water which, with the resplendent sun-rays, produced miniature rainbows about the horses. They were too late, for the victorious Americans had retired with their prisoners, leaving to the British troopers the melancholy duty of conveying their wounded fellows to the hospital at Musgrove's."

Let us now note the movements of the two respective armies immediately after the action at Musgrove's Mill. As to the movements of the British and Tory forces the accounts are conflicting. The Tory leader, David Fanning * says that after the battle the British retreated a mile and a quarter, where they halted for the day and at night continued their retreat to Ninety-Six, under the command of Captain DePeyster. It is also stated upon the authority of a British writer, McKensie, that the retreat of the defeated British and Tory forces was con ducted to the south side of the river by Captain Kerr. Of this officer, says McCall, the Georgia historian: "Find ing that resistance would be in vain and without hope of success, he ordered a retreat, which was effected for four miles." This statement is hardly probable, as Draper observes that "the larger portion must have remained, if for nothing else, at least to take care of the their wounded." It is probable that most of the enemy remained after the fact had been discovered by the foraging party already referred to that the American forces had already departed. The command which left under Colonel DePeyster probably referred to only a part of the enemy. It has also been stated that the enemy's forces were reinforced at Musgrove's Mill soon after the battle at that place by Cruger's forces at Ninety-Six, but of this we have no positive information.

Governor Swain's article in the University Magazine, republished by Judge Schenck, states that the Americans, after pursuing their enemy across the river, returned to their horses and mounted with a determination to proceed to Ninety-Six, at that time a weak post, and distant only about twenty-five or thirty miles. They could easily reach that place before night and were anxious to im-

---

*See Draper's "King's Mountain," page 113.

prove the advantage they had already gained. After the horses were mounted and Shelby and Clarke were consulting together, an express, whose name was Francis Jones, arrived in great haste from Colonel McDowell's headquarters, with a letter written to him by Governor Caswell, * informing him of Gates' disastrous defeat near Camden, S. C., on the sixteenth. It appears that Caswell had shared in this defeat. The letter advised Colonel McDowell and all officers commanding detachments to get out of the way at once, as they were in danger of being cut off. McDowell sent word that he would move at once in the direction of Gilberttown. Governor Caswell's handwriting was fortunately familiar to Colonel Shelby, and he at once realized that this was no Tory trick. The further advance to Ninety-Six was therefore abandoned. Shelby and his associates saw at once the danger they were in. They could not retire to McDowell's camp at Smith's Ford, for his force was no longer there. Gates' army, except that portion which was either killed or captured, was scattered. Ferguson was on the flank and Cruger in the rear at Ninety-Six, with whatever troops of Innes and Fraser that remained. There was but one alternative and this to take a northwesterly direction and thus elude Ferguson. The prisoners were hurriedly brought together and distributed one to every three of the Americans, who carried them alternately on horseback, the prisoners being required to carry a gun deprived of the flint. In a short time, the whole cavalcade was ready to beat a hasty retreat, as it was well understood that Ferguson, as soon as he was apprised of their success, would make a vigorous effort to overtake and defeat and recapture the prisoners.

The writer has been at a loss to understand the route by which Shelby and Clarke retreated from Musgrove's Mill. Colonel Hammond says: "Our retreat

---

* At that time Governor of North Carolina. Draper refers to him as General instead of Governor Caswell.

was hasty and continued without halting day or night to feed or rest for two days and nights." We entered North Carolina and passed down towards Charlotte with our prisoners. Colonel Shelby left us near Greenville (?) and we encamped near Charlotte with a few Continental troops, who had escaped Gates' defeat." Draper says that this pretended narrative of Hammond in Johnson's traditions was not relied on by him in his account of the affair at Musgroves' Mill. This writer says: "The Whig troopers, encumbered with their prisoners, were hurried rapidly away in a northwesterly direction, towards their old encampment. They passed over a rough, broken country, crossing the forks of Tyger, leaving Ferguson on the right and heading towards their own friendly mountains." It is probable that the retreat of the Americans was in the direction of Hobbyville and from thence in the direction of Moore's, Capt. C. A. Barry's and to Capt. David Anderson's Mill. Here this little command doubtless fell into the old Georgia road (already described) to Wofford's Iron Works, where, Draper says, Ferguson attempted to capture the prisoners. This route sets out in a northwesterly direction and crosses the three branches (South, Middle and North) of Tyger River. In Mr. John P. Kennedy's narrative of "Horse Shoe Robinson," he states that the course of Clarke and Williams, after the engagement at Musgrove's Mill, "lay towards the head waters of Fair Forest in the present region of Spartanburg." It may have been that the army of Clarke and Shelby, after crossing North Tyger at Anderson's Mill, fell into the old Blackstock road, which ran by Prince's Fort, Gowen's Fort, the Blockhouse to the mountains. It will be remembered that the present Blackstock road runs by Fair Forest Station, which, at this place, is the original road of Revolutionary times. This is within one mile of Fair Forest Creek, which heads on what is known to the older citizens as the Herbert Hawkins plantation near the present residence of Mr. James Lowe.

Wearied as the men and horses were from the previous night march, with scarcely a particle of food for either, Shelby would not permit them to stop while danger lurked on the way. Only once or twice were they allowed to stop and feed and rest their jaded horses. During the active march the men subsisted on peaches and green corn, which they pulled from the stalks and ate in its raw state. It was no doubt well for Shelby and Clarke that they adopted this rapid retreat. for as they expected, they were hotly pursued by a strong detachment of Ferguson's command. Savs Draper: "Late in the evening of the eighteenth, Ferguson's party reached the spot where the Whigs had, less than thirty miuutes before, fed their weary horses; but not knowing how long they had been gone, and their own detachment being exhausted, they relinquished further pursuit. Not aware of this, the Americans kept on their tedious retreat all night, and the following day, passing the North Tyger * and into the confines of North Carolina. Sixty miles from the battle field and one hundred from Smith's Ford (via Musgrove's Mill), from which they had started, these brave heroes had marched without making a stop save long enough to defeat the enemy at Musgrove's. It was a remarkable instance of unflaging endurance, in the heat of a Southern summer, encumbered as they were with seventy prisoners. No wonder that after forty-eight hours of such excessive fatigue, nearly all the officers and soldiers became so exhausted that their faces and eyes were swollen and bloated to that degree that thev were scarcely able to see."

---

*North Tyger River is made up of two main streams, viz: Jammie's Creek and Jordan's Creek. These come together at Benson's (now Turner's) Mill. The former heads just above Hannon's Mill, in the vicinity of Holly Springs, the latter one or two miles above Howell's Mill. Both of these streams head south of "New Cut" road, running from Shiloh to Gowensville. North and Middle Tyger Rivers come together in Captain Anderson's bottoms. So we have an idea as to the route of Shelbv's men.

This heroic band, exhausted and worn out, reached the mountains in safety, where they met Colonel McDowell's party, considerably reduced in numbers. It was now proposed by Colonel Shelby, which seems to have met with the approbation of all, that an army be at once raised on both sides of the mountains in numbers sufficient to cope with Ferguson. The officers and privates were both consulted, and all agreed on the propriety and feasibility of the undertaking. It was agreed that the over-mountain men should at once return to their homes to recruit and strengthen their numbers, as the term of their present service had expired. Colonel McDowell in the meanwhile, was to remain in front of Ferguson and to watch and obtain information of his movements and to keep the over-mountain men apprised of them. He sent an express to Colonels Cleveland and Herndon, of Wilkes, and to Major Winston, of Surry, inviting them to join in the expedition soon to be organized against Ferguson.

Knowing that subsistence for the proposed expedition would be an absolute necessity, he set to work to devise the best means to preserve the beef stock of the Whigs of the Upper Catawba valleys and coves, which would be an object of Ferguson's greed.

Shelby and Clarke, after their reunion with McDowell's command near Gilberttown, now parted company. Colonel Shelby and Major Robinson, with their Holstein and Watauga volunteers, took the trail which led to their homes over the Alleghanies. The Musgrove prisoners were turned over to Colonel Clarke, who after continuing some distance on his route in the direction of Charlotte, now concluded to return to Georgia by the mountain trails. The prisoners were turned over to Colonel Williams, who, with Captain Hammond, conducted them safely to Hillsboro, N. C.

Let us now return to the condition of affairs on the battle field of Musgrove's. It is said that the scene there on the day of and after the battle was one that beggared description. "For many miles around," says a writer, "every woman and child of the surrounding country who were able to leave their homes visited the battle ground, some for plunder, some from curiosity and others for a different purpose. It was chiefly a Tory region, the few Whigs having retired from motives of personal safety, joining Sumter and other popular leaders. The most of these visitors were Loyalist families; and it was interesting to witness them as well as the few Whig leaders present turning over the bodies of the slain, earnestly examining their faces to see if they could recognize a father, husband, son or brother. Not a few went away with saddened hearts and eyes bedewed with tears."

The British and Tories gathered their wounded and carried them to Musgrove's house and Mill which were, for a time, turned into hospitals. It is said that the few wounded Americans left behind were humanely cared for by the British, and especially by the Musgrove family. Among them was a soldier whose name was Miller, shot through the body and whose injuries were believed to be mortal. A silk handkerchief was drawn through the wound to cleanse it. Notwithstanding the British surgeons gave him every needed attention, his parents, who resided somewhere in the present County of Laurens employed Dr. Ross, an old physician, who gave him his time and attention. He fully recovered.

Captain Inman, who, as before stated, was killed, was buried near by. He fell at the base of a Spanish oak that stood where the modern road leaves the old Mill road and where his grave, only a few years since, was still pointed out. It is said that sixteen Tories were buried in one grave near the mouth of Cedar Shoal Creek, the particular spot long since obliterated and forgotten. Several were buried between the battle ground and ford, but a short distance from where George Gordon lived some forty years ago, which was on the west side of the old road, while others were buried in the vard of the late Capt. Philmon Waters, midway between the ford and battle field, opposite the dogwood spring, while others yet were buried in a graveyard just below Musgrove's house.

After the lapse of more than a hundred years, it may be interesting to the reader to enquire something more into the location and situation of Musgrove's Mill and mansion near by, and also into the character and history of the propriotor of these premises. Mr. Kennedy, in his tale of "Horse Shoe Robinson," has given a beautiful and romantic description of Musgrove's house and mill. Says this writer: "On the banks of the Enoree, in a little nook of meadow formed by the bend of the stream which, fringed with willows, swept around it almost in a semicircle—the inland border of the meadow being defined by a gently rising wall of hills, covered with wood—was seated within a few paces of the water a neat little cottage, with a group of outbuildings presenting all the conveniences of a comfortable farm. The dwelling house itself was shaded by a cluster of trees, which had been spared from the native forest and within view were several fields of cultivated ground, neatly enclosed with fences. A little lower down the stream, and within a short distance of the house, partially concealed by the bank, stood a small, low browed mill built of wood."

Mr. Draper says that the man who perpetuated the name of the battle, fought near his residence, was Edward Musgrove, a native of England. He was one of the earliest settlers of upper South Carolina, his home being on the south side of Enoree river in Laurens county. He bore the title of Major Musgrove, and was said to be a man above medium height, of slender form, prematurely gray, and a man of firmness and decision of character. It is further stated of him that he was possessed of a fine education and was bred to the law. He also possessed fine abilities as a lawyer, and was noted for his hospitality and benevolence. He was a useful and indispensable man in the community in which he lived, giving as he did to his neighbors good legal advice, and executing business papers to all who needed them for many miles around him. He had passed the period of active life when the Revolutionary War commenced, and was then living with his third wife. He was, says Mr. Draper, the father of Mary Musgrove, "the renowned heroine of Kennedy's popular story of 'Horse Shoe Robinson.'" By reference to Mr. Kennedy's work, however, we find the name of the proprietor of Musgroves given as Allen instead of Edward Musgrove. The name may have been fictitiously assumed by Mr. Kennedy, but we can see no reason for this. He is represented by the writer as bearing traces of age, though still robust and muscular His head was partially bald, and his whitened locks played in the breeze. He is also represented by the same writer as being a Presbyterian and an humble Christian one who during the trying scenes around him would assemble night after night, his family around the hearth stone and adjusting his eye glasses read from the Book of Truth. Then on bended knees he would offer up his petition to the Lord of Hosts, *to stay the hand of the destroyer and let the angel of peace again spread his wing over our racked and wearied land, to take from the wicked heart his sword and shield and make the righteous man safe beside his family hearth; to shelter the head of the wanderer, and guide in safety the hunted fugitive, who flies before the man of wrath; to comfort the captive in captivity, and make all hearts in this rent and sundered province to know and bless Thy mercies forevermore.*

Especially did this venerable saint pray, *to give the victory to him that hath right to establish the foundations in justice and truth, giving liberty of conscience and liberty of law to those who know how to use it.*

The history of the battle of Musgrove's Mill would be incomplete without an inquiry into history of the principal actors on both sides, in this brief but bloody encounter for American liberty. We present only such as come within our possession.

ISAAC SHELBY.

Isaac Shelby, was a son of the distinguished Gen. Evan Shelby,* a native of Wales, whose life and distinguished services are recorded in the pages of history.

Isaac Shelby was born in Maryland on the 11th of December, 1750, and was not quite thirty years of age at the battle of Musgrove's Mill. Born amid the excitements of Indian wars, he received only an ordinary education. In 1771, he was engaged in herding and feeding cattle in the extensive ranges west of the Alleghanies. The same year the Shelby connection moved to the Holston country. In 1774, when the Indians became troublesome, he was commissioned as a lieutenant and served with distinction under his father, being second in command of his father's company in the celebrated battle at the mouth of the Kenhawa, October 10, 1774, on the Ohio River—the most severe and sanguinary conflict ever maintained with the northwestern Indians, called the Shawnees. The action was from sun rise to sun set, with varied success, but finally ending in the abandoning of the ground by the celebrated chief Corn Stalk, who commanded the Indians. Point Pleasant was then made a garrison, where he re-

---

*During the month of June of the present year (1891), the writer while on his way to the commencement exercises at Glade Spring, Va., where his children were in school, had the pleasure of meeting on the train between Morristown and Bristol, Judge R. R. Butler, ex-Congressman from East Tennessee District, who stated in the conversation that General Shelby was buried in the country where the City of Bristol was afterwards located. His grave, covered with a rough iron slab, being in the middle of one of the main thoroughfares, it was decided after many years to remove the remains to the cemetery near by. When the grave was opened nothing was found except a few teeth, coffin nails, and a few metal buttons. The writer having a few hours in Bristol, visited the cemetery and found this old iron slab almost covered up, wedged between other graves. Up to this time he was under the impression he was visiting the grave of Isaac instead of Evan Shelby, whose grave it really was. The following was the inscription in raised letters: "General Evan Shelby, born 1720, died 1794."

mained in service until July, 1775, when Governor Dunmore ordered its disbandonment lest the troops might become obedient to the Whig authorities.

He was, after this, employed as surveyor, under Judge Henderson's company and resided in the wilderness of Kentucky, which was at this time, a dark and bloody ground. Being exposed to dangers, privations and difficulties for nearly a year without bread or salt, his health gave way and he returned home During his absence in July 1776, he had been appointed Captain of a minute company, by the committee of safety in Virginia.

In 1777, Patrick Henry, then Governor of Virginia, appointed him commissary of supplies for an extensive body of troops to guard the frontiers, and also the commissioners who had been appointed to form a treaty at Long Island of the Holston River, with Cherokees. In 1778, he was a member of the Virginia Legislature from Washington county, and was appointed by Thomas Jefferson, then Governor of Virginia, a major in the escort of guards to the commissioners for extending the line between Virginia and North Carolina. By this line of division, he was found to be in North Carolina (now Tennessee) and was appointed by Richard Caswell, then Governor of North Carolina, Colonel in Sullivan county.

We have already stated, in a former chapter, that he was, in the summer of 1780, engaged in Kentucky, surveying, locating and securing the lands which he had previously marked, when news of the disastrous surrender of Charlestown reached him. This intelligence roused his daring spirit. He immediately returned home, determined to enter the service of his bleeding country, and never to leave it until her liberty and independence was secured. On his return home to Sullivan county, he found, as we have already stated, a requisition from Col. Charles McDowell to furnish all the aid in his power to check the enemy who had conquered South Carolina and Georgia, and who now, flushed with success, had entered North Carolina. He immediately called up all the militia in

Sullivan and in a few davs crossed the Alleghany at the head of three hundred mounted riflemen. He reported to Colonel McDowell at his camp at Cherokee Ford (three miles east of Gaffney City) on the 25th of July, 1780. He led in the expeditions against Thickety fort, Cedar Spring or Wofford's Iron Works and Musgrove's Mill, and the conspicuous part which he performed in these engagements have already been minutely detailed.

The culminating point of his success and glory as a warrior, however, was at the battle of King's Mountain, which was one of the most brilliant achievements of the Revolution. Here he is numbered as among the most prominent of the heroes of that engagement, a fact so well known that we will not comment on him here. Soon after this, the Legislature of North Carolina voted a splendid sword and their thanks to Colonel Shelby.

In 1781 Colonel Shelby served under General Marion. He with Colonel Mayhew were ordered to take a British post at Fair Lawn, near Monks Corner, under the command of General Stuart. On attacking this post it surrendered with one hundred and fifty prisoners. Immediately after this the whole British force retreated to Charlestown. Colonel Shelby soon after this obtained leave of absence from Marion to attend the session of the North Carolina Legislature, of which he was a member from Sullivan county. In 1782 he was again a member and was appointed a commissioner to settle the pre-emption claims upon the Cumberland, and lay off land to the officers and soldiers south of where Nashville now stands. He performed this duty well, and, the war being now over, he returned to Boonesboro, where he married a Miss Susanna Hart. After the war he devoted himself to his farm, on the first pre-emption and settlement granted in Kentucky.

He was a member of the convention in Kentucky to obtain a separation of that State from Virginia; was a member of the convention that framed the Constitution of that state; was elected the first Governor of Kentucky and served four years, proving to be a model chief magistrate of that State. He was three times chosen Presidential elector and supported Thomas Jefferson for President.

When the second war with England in 1812, burst upon the country, Shelby was again chosen Governor of Kentucky. Though now sixty-three years of age, his spirit was not calmed by the frosts of age. By request of the Legislature, he was placed at the head of four thousand men and marched under General Harrison in 1813 to Canada, closing with the victory of the Thames. For this patriotic service, Congress in 1817 voted him a gold medal.

The revival of the war spirit in 1812 reminded North Carolina of her ancient pledge of a sword to Shelby. This was presented to him in 1813.

In 1817, President Monroe called him to the Department of War, but on account of his advanced age he declined this honor.

In 1818 he was appointed by the President with General Jackson to form a treaty with the Chickasaw Indians by which they ceded their lands west of the Tennessee River. This was his last public service. He was stricken with paralysis in 1820, but his mind remained unimpaired until July 18, 1826, when he was again stricken with paralysis sitting in his chair, with only his venerable companion present. Thus this hero of many wars passed away, at the advanced age of seventy-six years.

Such is the record of Isaac Shelby, the hero of Musgrove's Mill, fought on the soil of Spartanburg County. Let his name and character be preserved in the region that witnessed his patriotism and valor.

JAMES WILLIAMS.

"James Williams, son of Daniel and Unsala Williams, natives of Wales, was born near Old Fork Church, Hanover County, Virginia, in November, 1740." His education was limited, his parents dying early. In early life he migrated to Granville county, North Carolina, where his brother, Col. John Williams, a distinguished jurist, was residing." He married a Miss Clarke in 1762, and ten years later settled on Little River in Laurens county, where up to the beginning of the Revolution, he was engaged in the vocations of farmer. miller, and merchant.

Taking sides with the colonies in the dispute with the mother country, he was, in 1775, chosen a representative to the Provincial Congress from the section of country between Broad and Saluda Rivers. Soon afterwards he was appointed one of the local committee of safety, and in the famous Snow Campaign, served as captain. In 1776, he was made lieutenant Colonel and served this year in Williamson's campaign against the Cherokees, and was engaged for awhile in guarding prisoners at Ninety-Six. In 1780 he served under Sumter as commissary in his expeditions against Rocky Mount and Hanging Rock. Afterwards he rejoined, as we have already stated, the expedition against Musgrove's and commanded the center which stood firm in this battle. Soon after this he was commissioned a Brigadier General by Governor Rutledge, but because this commission did not eminate from Congress, his authority was not recognized by Sumter and others. This did not deter him from his duty, however. His eventful and useful life was closed at the battle of King's Mountain, receiving there a mortal wound, of which he died the next day.

Thus perished this gallant patriot and hero. While possessing some miner faults, he was, says Bancroft, "A man of exalted character, of a career brief but glorious."

The biography of COL. ELIJAH CLARKE, another of the heroes of Musgrove's, is reserved for another place in this work.

We regret that we are unable to gather any information as to the early life of CAPT. SHADRACK INMAN. He was a Georgian, probably a member of Colonel Clarke's command and had figured prominently in battling with the British and Tories of that State at Savannah and other points.

SKETCHES OF BRITISH OFFICERS.

COLONEL INNES was a Scotchman, *a protege* of Alexander Cameron, the British agent among the Cherokees. Cameron, of whom we have spoken in former chapters, was also a Scotchman. Innes was an assistant in the commissary department at the Long Island of the Holston, at one time, but returned to Cameron in the Cherokee Nation in the fall of 1777. He received his commission as Colonel of the South Carolina Royalists, January 20, 1780. In 1782 he was made Inspector General of the Loyalists forces. After the Revolution he was retired on half pay.

COLONEL CLARY, who was in command of the Tories at Musgrove's before he was reinforced by Colonel Innes' command, was a prominent citizen of Ninety-Six District; and surviving the war remained in the same section. It is said of him, that notwithstanding he sided with the Tories, he was greatly respected. He was, with the exception of the error referred to, a good citizen, and left behind him a line of worthy descendants, living mostly in Edgefield county.

CHAPTER XXII.

SOUTH CAROLINA OVERRUN.—BLOODTHIRSTY ORDERS OF CORNWALLIS TO CRUGER AT NINETY-SIX.—SHELBY, CLARKE AND WILLIAMS RETIRE TO NORTH CAROLINA.—PROPOSITION TO RAISE AN ARMY ON BOTH SIDES OF THE MOUNTAINS.—A STORM BEGINS TO GATHER.—FERGUSON THE UNDISPUTED MASTER OF THE UP-COUNTRY.—HIS PLUNDERINGS.—STORY OF DUNLAP.

IT WAS a dark and doleful period for South Carolina, after the disastrous defeat of General Gates near Camden and Sumter's disaster at Fishing Creek, August 18, 1781. The latter engagement was an offset to the American victory at Musgrove's, which occurred on the same day. McDowell, Shelby, Clarke and Williams, had now retired to the back parts of North Carolina. The term of enlistment of nearly all of McDowell's men had expired. This officer retired to the mountain regions of Burke and Rutherford counties, with his force dwindled down to about two hundred. The province of South Carolina was apparently subjugated. The British flag floated in triumph over Charlestown and Savannah. The troops of Cornwallis, with all pomp and circumstance, advanced from Camden to Charlotte. "Like a mastiff fed on meat and blood," Cornwallis, on account of his success at Camden, was all the more fierce for further strife and carnage. Two days after Gates' defeat he wrote to Cruger at Ninety-six as follows: "I have given orders that all the inhabitants of this province, who had not submitted and who had taken part in this revolt, should be punished with the greatest rigor; that they should be imprisoned and their whole property taken from them and destroyed. I have likewise directed that compensation should be made out of their effects to the persons who have been plundered and oppressed by them. I have ordered in the most positive manner, that every militia man who had borne arms with us and had afterwards joined the enemy; *should be immediately hanged.* I have now, sir, only to desire that you will take the most vigorous measures to extinguish the rebellion in the district in which you command, and that you will obey in the strictest manner, the directions I have given in this letter, relative to the treatment of the country."

It is unnecessary to state that these sanguinary orders were most faithfully carried out by Tarleton, Rawdon, Balfour and Brown, which only demonstrated their fitness to enact scenes too black, bloody and heart rending to claim space in this work.

In a former chapter it is stated that Shelby, after his retreat from Musgrove's and just before leaving McDowell's camp to visit his home for a short time, proposed that an army be raised on both sides of the mountains* in numbers sufficient to cope with Ferguson. It was true that the sky was gloomy, but the darkest hour is sometimes just before dawn. From the scattered whig settlements in the old Spartan District, from the fastnesses of the mountains, from the valleys of the Holston, Watauga and Catawba, a storm was gathering which was soon to descend in all its fury upon the heads of the enemies of our country. It was no small matter in that day to oppose and confront the authority of Great Britain, the mightiest monarchy on the face of the globe, one on whose dominions the sun never sets, and from whom men and means could still be collected to prosecute the war in America.

Notwithstanding these facts glaring them in the face, the brave spirits of our country did not despair. Like Warsaw's "last champion" stood the stalwart soldiers of that day.

---

* See Draper's "King's Mountain," page 118.

"Oh Heaven!" they said, "Our bleeding Country save!
Is there no hand on high to shield the brave?
What though destruction sweep these lovely plains?
Rise fellowmen! Our country yet remains;
By that dread name—we waive the sword on high,
And swear for her to live—for her to die."*

Let us now briefly notice the movements of the enemy, immediately after the retirement of McDowell, Shelby, Clarke and Williams to North Carolina. It has already been stated that the term of enlistment of the different commands under these officers had, for the most part, expired. McDowell, Shelby, Clarke and Williams, having now retired, as we have said, most of their men had returned to their homes, many of whom lived in Washington and Sullivan counties in North Carolina, now East Tennessee.

Thus was Ferguson left for a short time the undisputed master of the country. He improved every moment of his time. "He marched," savs Judge Schenck, "into Union District on the Tyger river, and thence northward through Spartanburg district to the 'Quaker's Meadows,' in Burke county North Corolina, the home of Col. Charles McDowell. The Tories as they went, plundered the citizens of cattle, horses, beds, wearing apparel; even wresting rings from the fingers of ladies, until they were heartily despised by the British officers as well as their own countrymen who were contending for liberty." Says Draper: "The desperate, the idle, the vindictive, who sought plunder or revenge * * * all found a warm reception in the British camp and their progress through the country was marked with blood and lighted with conflagration."

Ferguson following in the direction of McDowell, Clarke, Shelby and Williams, encamped for awhile at Gilberttown, three miles north of the present village of Rutherfordton. Here he issued a proclamation calling upon the citizens to flock to his standard. His bold display of Royal au-

*Cambell's Pleasures of Hope.

thority intimidated many, as all hope seemed to be gone. The only remaining continental army (under Gates) had been routed and put to flight, and there seemed to be no alternative but for the Whig families to seek British protection in order that they might save their cattle and other property. In the midst of these trying times honor is due to Col. Charles McDowell because he was the first, with a mere handful of men, to confront the authority of Ferguson who was ravaging the country with impunity. Ferguson with a detachment marched against him. To his surprise he found him ambuscaded at Bedford Hill, three miles southwest of Brindletown, North Carolina, near Cowen's ford, a crossing on Cane Creek. While the British were crossing this ford, the Whigs fired upon them, severely wounding Major Dunlap, whom we have before mentioned and who was a favorite of Furguson and one of the most energetic officers belonging to his corps. Several were killed in this engagement and Ferguson, it is said, was forced to retire to Gilberttown to save his own life.

"McDowell being unable," says Judge Schenck "to resist the large British force now in North Carolina retreated across the Blue Ridge to the 'Watauga settlement,' then the homes of Sevier and Shelby." He informed the latter of the desolation that followed the track of Ferguson and urged them to join the mountain men on the other side, to resist further invasion. Ferguson continued his headquarters at Gilberttown.

Major Dunlap, who was wounded at the engagement referred to, was on crutches at the house of William Gilbert, a Loyalist. He is described as being the most hardened of all the Tory leaders, and Johnson in his "Life of Greene," says "he rendered himself infamous by his barbarities." Draper relates numerous instances of his oppression and cruelty while at Gilberttown and thus describes an attempt on Dunlap's life: "When Ferguson suddenly left Gilberttown on the approach of the overmountain men, Dunlap was left behind. The avenger of blood was nigh. Two or three men from Spartanburg rode to the door of the Gilbert house, when the leader, Captain Gillespie, asked Mrs. Gilbert if Major Dunlap was not up stairs. She frankly replied that he was, supposing the party were Loyalists and had some important communication for him. They soon apprised her of their character and mission, for they declared that he had been instrumental in putting some of their friends to death and, moreover, had abducted the beautiful Mary McRea, the affianced of Captain Gillespie, and because she would not encourage his amorous advances, had kept her in confinement, trusting that she would in time yield to his wishes; but death came to her relief; she died of a broken heart. They had now come for revenge, Gillespie particularly uttering his imprecations on the head of the cruel destroyer of all his earthly hopes. So saying thev mounted the stairs. Gillespie abruptly appoached Dunlap as he lay in bed, with the inquiry, "Where is Mary McRea?" "In heaven," was the reply. Whereupon the injured Captain shot Dunlap through the body, and quickly mounting their horses, Gillespie and his associates, bounded away to their Spartanburg homes." *

The impression has lived in tradition that Dunlap was killed outright by Gillespie, and was buried three hundred yards south of the Gilbert house, where a grave is still seen with a granite rock at the head and foot, and which is pointed out as his grave.

This information was obtained from Maj. James Hol-

---

*The old Gilberttown house, afterwards the property of the Hampton family, stood for nearly a hundred years after the Revolution. The stain of Dunlap's blood was discernible on the floor as long as it stood and was always pointed out to visitors. It is said that the early courts of the county were held in this ancient building, and when about to fall from age, it was taken down by its present owner, J. A. Forney, Esq. During the summer of 1892, the writer was on a pleasure excursion with a party to Rutherfordton. While there he had occasion to drive over to the old historic place—Gilberttown. On returning to the city he received a polite letter from Mrs. Forney (Mr. Forney being away) accompanied by a piece of the blood stained plank

land, a Congressman from North Carolina from 1795 to 1797, who lived at Gilberttown for many years. The same information was conveyed to Draper by Ms. letters of Adam, James J. and Jonathan Hampton, sons of the patriot Jonathan Hampton, Sr., and also from the late M. O. Dickerson, Esq., W. L. and Dr. T. B. Twitty and others.

It appears, however, that Dunlap was not killed by Gillespie, and when shot, he was either left unconscious or feigned death, and for his safety was reported dead and buried near by, this report being circulated by his friends. As soon as he was able to travel he was conveyed to Ninety-Six, and in March 1781, he had sufficientlv recovered for active service. He was sent on a foraging expedition, when he renewed his former habits of plunder ing and marauding. General Pickens hearing of this, detached Colonel Clarke and Major McCall to attack him. These officers came up with him on the 24th of March, encamped on Little River, some twenty.two miles from Ninety-Six. Dispatching a party to secure a bridge over which Dunlap would have to pass, the main body advanced and took him by surprise. He sought shelter with his men at Beattie's Mill near by, in some outhouses, but these were too open for protection against riflemen. Dun-

---

referred to. Mrs. Forney has since "crossed over the river," but her letter and relic will be sacredly preserved as mementoes of her kindness.

The writer, however, has grave doubts as to the name of the affianced of Gillespie being Jane McCrea. The "Story of Jane McCrea," is a familiar one to every reader of Revolutionary history. While Gates and Burgoyne were confronting each other near Saratoga, Jane McCrea a young, beautiful and amiable lady, a daughter of a Royalist, but living inside of the American lines, became engaged to a British officer, who offered to two Indians a ransom to bring her through the opposing lines, his purpose being to marry her. The Indians succeeded in coaxing her from her home, but on the way fell out as to who should be the first to deliver her. The quarrel resulted in splitting her head with a tomahawk. This circumstance led to angry correspondence between Generals Gates rnd Burgoyne.

lap resisted for several hours, until thirty-four of his men were killed and wounded, himself among the latter. A flag of truce was finally hung out, else all, in all probability would have been either killed or wounded. This was the end of Dunlap. He died of his wounds the ensuing night. The prisoners were sent to the Watauga settlement in East Tennessee for safe keeping.*

But let us return to Gilberttown. It is said that while Ferguson was encamped here, he found a case of small-pox developing itself. This must have been a mild attack however, as he was not encamped at this place more than thirty or forty days, which was between the time of the battles of Musgrove's Mill and King's Mountain, fought respectively August 18th and October 7th, 1780. Says Draper, "It was one of his officers who was left in a deserted house taking his favorite charger with him. And there the poor fellow died in this lonely situation; and it is said his neglected horse lingered around till he, at length, died also. It was a long time before any of the country people would venture to visit this solitary pest house.

> "And there lay the rider distorted and pale,
> With dew on his brow and the rust on his mail."

---

* See Draper, 163.

CHAPTER XXIII.

FERGUSON TARRIES AT GILBERTTOWN TO CUT OFF THE RETREAT OF COLONEL CLARKE FROM GEORGIA TO NORTH CAROLINA.--CRUELTY TO PRISONERS BELONGING TO CLARKE'S COMMAND.—SAMUEL PHILIPS PAROLED BY EERGUSON WITH A MESSAGE BY THE LATTER TO THE OVER-MOUNTAIN PEOPLE.—SHELBY AND SEVIER MEET AND CONFER.—LETTERS AND MESSENGERS SENT TO COLONELS CAMPBELL, CLEVELAND AND OTHERS.—AN EXPEDITION AGREED UPON.

THE question may be asked by the reader why was it that Ferguson remained encamped so long at Gilberttown when confronted by little or no force in any direction. Being thoroughly posted on the situation of affairs south of him, by Cruger at Ninety-Six and Cornwallis at Charlotte, he little dreamed of the storm that was gathering north and west across the mountains, and of his impending danger. He had furloughed a large number of his Tory followers to visit their homes on promise to return to him at the shortest notice. His tarrying so long at Gilberttown had its meaning. He had hopes of intercepting Colonel Clarke, who had laid seige to Augusta, Georgia, from the 14th to the 16th of September, and would have succeeded completely in his undertaking had not Colonel Cruger arrived with a relief force from Ninety-Six, thus compelling Clarke to make his way northward along the eastern base of the mountains. The route over which Ferguson expected to meet and encounter Clarke was doubtless along or near the public dirt road running from Greenville to Rutherfordton via Gowensville, Landrum, O. P. Earle's (the old Baylis Earle place) and Sandy Plains in Polk County, North Carolina. The remnant of Clarke's command was small. In the pursuit that followed his retreat, quite a number of his men were killed and taken prisoners, the latter being cruelly treated by the British, Tories and Indians. Some were hanged under the eves of Colonel Brown, the British commandant at Augusta. Thirteen were delivered to the Cherokees, and were killed either by tomahawk, torture or in flames. Thirty, altogether, were put to death by the cruel and vindictive Brown, which was but the carrying into effect the inhuman orders of Lord Cornwallis to Balfour and Brown, already noticed in the preceding chapter.

It has been suggested by Draper that Ferguson's idea in furloughing so many of his men while at Gilberttown to visit their homes, was to obtain, if possible, an early notice of the approach of Clarke's men. This watching and delaying to accomplish this object, as the sequel shows, proved his destruction.

Soon after Ferguson took post at Gilberttown, smarting under the annoyance the British had suffered at Fort Thickety, Wofford's Iron Works and Musgrove's, he paroled Samuel Philips, a distant relative of Col. Isaac Shelby, whom he had taken as a wounded prisoner, either at Wofford's or Musgrove's. By Philips he sent a verbal message to the officers on the western waters of Watauga, Nolachuckev and Holston that "if they did not desist from their oppression to the British arms, he would march his army over the mountains, hang their leaders and lay their country to waste with fire and sword." This threat on the part of Ferguson accomplished more than he bargained for. Philips resided very near Colonel Shelby, and on reaching home he went directly to the latter with Ferguson's message, giving him at the same time, such intelligence as he could impart concerning the position, strength and locality of Ferguson's command. Philips further conveyed the information that a Loyalist belonging to Ferguson's command, had a few months before received a coat of tar and feathers by the light horsemen of Capt. Robert Sevier on Nolachuckey, and had proposed, in resentment, to pilot Ferguson across the mountains to the Watauga settlements, since he was familliar with all the passes through the mountains.

A few days after this message was received, Shelby rode some forty miles to a horse race, to a spot near the present site of Jonesboro, Tennessee, to confer with Colonel Sevier, whom he informed of Ferguson's threatening message, and to consult as to the best methods for resisting this threatened invasion. The result was that these brave men agreed that they would at once call out their own forces and endeavor, if possible, to procure the assistance of Col. William Campbell of Virginia. Their plan was to raise all the men they could and with proper assistance to surprise and attack Ferguson in his camp, before he could have time to cross the mountains into their country. There was, however, no time to lose. The place of rendezvous was at Sicamore Flats, on the Watauga River, where the troops were ordered to assemble on the 25th of September. Colonel Shelby prepared a letter which he at once sent by his brother, Capt. Moses Shelby, addressed to Col. William Campbell, residing forty miles away, informing him of the situation of affairs, and urging him to come to the rescue of the people of his section. The Burke men also were there as exiles, ready at any moment to join the expedition against Ferguson.

It appears that it was a part of Cornwallis' plan, in his march from Salisbury, to form a junction with Ferguson preliminary to the invasion of North Carolina and Virginia. This officer had also ingeniously incited, through his emissaries, the southern Indians to invade not only the Holston and Watauga settlements, but also to proceed, if possible, as far up into southwest Virginia as Criswill's Lead Mines and destroy all the works and stores there, where large quantities of lead were produced for the supply of the American army. When Shelby's letter reached Campbell, the latter had just been engaged for several weeks in putting down a Tory insurrection in his country. It appears that he fully understood Cornwallis' plan, At first, the proposed expedition of Colonels

Shelby and Sevier did not strike him very favorably and he declined to take part in it. Touched, however, by the appeal to his generosity, he decided, after consultation with his field officers to divide his militia, one-half remaining to repell the anticipated Indian invasion and the other half to join Shelby and Sevier. At the time of this arrangement, Colonel Campbell sent an express to Col. Benjamin Cleveland, of Wilkes county, North Carolina, apprising him of the situation and requesting him to meet them on the eastern side of the mountain, with the militia of his county. The place indicated for this meeting was at "Quaker Meadows," in Burke county, North Carolina, two miles north of Morganton, which was the home of the McDowells.

To raise funds sufficient to defray the expenses of the proposed expedition against Ferguson was a serious question. The people had but little money. Colonel Shelby applied to the entry taker of Sullivan county—now East Tennessee—for the sale of North Carolina lands, for the loan of funds. The name of this agent was John Adair. His reply to Shelby, who wanted the money to meet a public exigency, is worthy of a patriot. Said he, "I have no authority by law to make that disposition of this money; it belongs to the impoverished treasury of North Carolina, and I dare not appropriate a cent of it to any purpose; but if our country is over-run by the British, our liberties are gone. Let the money go too. Take it. If the enemy, by its use, is driven from the country, I can trust that country to justify and vindicate my conduct. So take it.*"

By this loan about twelve thousand dollars was raised. This patriotic act of Agent Adair was afterwards legalized by the State Legislature.

The appointments which had been made to assemble at Sicamore Flats were faithfully kept. Here on the 25th of September Colonel Campbell appeared with two hundred

*See "Knoxville in Ye Olden Times," Harper's Magazine, April, 1885.

men, while Colonels Shelby and Sevier also appeared each with two hundred men. At this place the party of Colonels McDowell and Hampton had been encamped for some time. The whole force now amounted to about eight hundred and fifty. They were mostly mounted men, and armed with the deadly Deckard rifle, without bayonets. The men had neither baggage, wagons, quartermaster stores nor commissary stores. The wallet, which contained a supply of parched meal, and a tin cup and blanket completed the outfit. The men wore hunting shirts manufactured by their wives and daughters, and fur skin caps, which were common in that day. At their side in a belt were the tomahawk and knife.

Early on the morning of the 26th of September, when the army was about to move, Colonel Campbell appeared in camp at the head of about two hundred men. The whole force now numbered about one thousand and fifty, and made, says a writer, "The welkin ring with their glad acclaim." Being now ready for the line of march, it was necessary at this critical hour to invoke the blessing of God, and to supplicate His divine protection. The Rev. L. Samuel Doak, a missionary in the Watauga settlements, was present, who offered up a fervent prayer for the protection of the people from the dangers to which they were exposed from marauding hosts of the British in their front and barbarous savages in their rear. "He remembered," says a writer, "that because of the Midianites the children of Israel had holes in the mountains, and the greatness of God's deliverance; and pausing for a moment, he exclaimed, 'The sword of the Lord and of Gideon.' Tears stole down the furrowed cheeks of the rough skinned men of the forest, but their faith was strengthened. The preparation was over. The march began." It was through a solitary wilderness along the mountain trails. A distance of about twenty miles was made the first day, when camp was struck. The native grass which was then growing luxuriantly afforded abundant food for the horses. The next day, the 27th, there was delay in order to slaughter some beeves for the journey. This was near the base of Round and Yellow mountains.

The march was resumed on the 28th. The mountains were ascended and when the top was reached, they found a bold spring, surrounded by hundreds of acres of beauti ful level land. Here camp was struck the second night. The men fired off their guns, cleared out and reloaded, and here also, a circumstance occurred that came well nigh foiling the whole plan of the expedition. Two men deserted and made their way to Ferguson's camp. Their names were James Crawford and Samuel Chambers. This treachery made it necessary to take a different route from the one first chosen, so as to baffle any spy Ferguson might send to watch their movements. The march was down Roaring Creek via the mouth of Grassy Creek and up this creek to its head and over Gillespie's Gap on the Blue Ridge. Here the command divided. Campbell following a trail six miles south of Wofford's Fort, the other to Hunnycut Creek. As soon as Colonels McDowell, Shelby and Sevier had decided to march against and attack Ferguson, Colonel McDowell hastened across the mountains in advance of the over-mountain men, to encourage and arouse the people, and to obtain as much information as possible of Ferguson's movements and whereabouts, and to hasten the march of Cleveland and Winston, to the appointed place of rendezvous, "Quaker Meadows." Having performed this duty he rejoined one wing of the over-mountain men at Hunnycut Creek. On the 25th of September, the over-mountain men reached "Quaker Meadows," the hospitable homes of the brothers, Col. Charles and Maj. Joseph McDowell. Here it is recorded that the "fatted calf" was killed and the smoke-houses were thrown open. It was not long until the glad tidings were announced of the approach of Colonel Cleveland and Major Winston with three hundred and fifty men from the counties of Wilkes and Surry, North Carolina. A shout of welcome rent the air. Soon the troops were mingling joyfully together, with bright and bouyant hopes of success. The whole army now amounted to about thirteen hundred and eighty. Sunday morning, October 1st, was bright and fair; the men were rested, cheerful and full of spirit, the horses fresh and active. The march was resumed. They felt that Ferguson was almost in their grasp. They were eager to overtake him. At noon-day they passed Brindletown, near a gap in South mountain, where McDowell had only a few weeks before engaged and repulsed Ferguson. That evening it rained for the first time since they started.

Monday, October 2d, it rained all day and the troops remained in camp. They were now within sixteen miles of Gilberttown. Up to this time no commander for the army had been chosen or agreed upon. A conference of the different commanders was held. It was agreed that Col. Charles McDowell should visit at once the headquarters of General Gates at Hillsboro, with the request that he send them a general officer. It was hoped that Colonel McDowell would return very soon with General Morgan, who had recently won laurels at Saratoga, and whom the troops preferred above all others. Colonel Campbell, although the youngest of all the commanders, was requested to assume the chief command until Colonel McDowell should return. There was no time to lose. At this critical juncture celerity and despatch of movement were all important. It was supposed that the decisive battle between the Whig and Tory forces would be fought at Gilberttown. The former, as we have already said, felt an abiding confidence in their success. Before the men took up their line of march on October 3d, Colonel Cleveland, who had the happy faculty of inspiring his troops, made a short address to them. He said, among other things, "The evening is at hand; we must be up and at them. I will be with you when the pinch comes. If any of you shrink from the battle glory, you now have an opportunity to back out and leave, and you may have a few minutes for consideration. You, who wish to back out will, when the word is given, march three steps to the rear and stand." There was a pause of three minutes, the word was given, but not one man moved. They were dismissed with orders to prepare rations and to be readv for marching in three hours, at the end of which time, the line of march was taken up. They reached a point near the mouth of Cane Creek and near Gilberttown on the 4th of October. Here they met Jonathan Hampton, who gave them the first information of the flight of Ferguson. Their hopes and expectations were temporarily thwarted, but we shall see further that they proved themselves equal to the emergency which confronted them.

CHAPTER XXIV.

GATHERING OF OTHER CLANS FOR THE EXPEDITION AGAINST FERGUSON.—COLONEL WILLIAMS COMMISSIONED A BRIGADIER-GENERAL BY GOVERNOR RUTLEDGE.—MOVEMENTS OF HILL, LACY AND WILLIAMS.—ROUTE OF FERGUSON FROM GILBERTTOWN TO KING'S MOUNTAIN.

IN order to bring the reader's attention to all the ingathering clans engaged in the expedition against Ferguson, it will be necessary to leave the over-mountain men at Cane Creek to notice other bodies destined to become allies in the famous campaign.

It has been stated in a former chapter that the prisoners captured at Musgrove's were escorted to Hillsboro, North Carolina, by a detachment under the command of Col. James Williams. While at this place Colonel Williams met Governor Rutledge, of South Carolina, a refugee, and gave him the first news of the American victory at Musgrove's Mill.

While the credit of this victory is given in the main by Draper and others to Colonels Clarke and Shelby, yet, to the mind of the impartial observer, much credit is due to Colonel Williams in this spirited engagement, who commanded the center and who made a firm stand, while Shelby was being pressed back on the right. This in a large measure saved the battle to the American arms. Governor Rutledge, who was clothed with dictatorial powers, doubtless thought Colonel Williams deserved promotion and commissioned him a Brigadier-General.

General Williams, before entering the field again, sought and obtained permisssion from Governor Nash, of North Carolina, to recruit one hundred men from that province for his skeleton command. Though now a citizen of South Carolina, he had some claims on North Carolina, having been born and reared in Granville County in that State. This call for one hundred men was made on the 23d of September, and the place of their rendezvous was at Higgin's plantation, in Rowan County. Prominent among his officers were Colonel Brandon and Major Hammond. At this time a detachment of Sumter's army, under the immediate command of Colonels Hill and Lacy, were encamped between the main Catawba and the "South Fork" of that stream.

It was not long before General Williams had obtained his allotted number of men, and with his command he repaired at once to the camp of Colonels Lacy and Hill, where he exhibited his commission as Brigadier-General, and ordered that they at once place themselves under his command, which they absolutely refused to do. Hot words ensued, which resulted in Williams separating himself from them. It was the intention of Lacy and Hill to attach themselves to General Davidson's command, and to accomplish this end they dispatched a messenger to him who soon returned with the information, received through Col. Charles McDowell, that a large party of mountain men were marching against Ferguson for the purpose of attacking him. On this same day they were reinforced by fifty or sixty more men, under the command of Col. William Graham and Lieutenant-Colonel Hambright, of Tyron County. The plan of joining General Davidson's command was at once abandoned and it was decided to join the over-mountain men in their expedition against Ferguson without delay. In these trying times, however, co-operation with bands of patriots was necessary. Having refused to place themselves under the command of General Williams it was necessary, lest they might encounter some superior force of the enemy, to make some honorable proposition to that officer. It was proposed that the troops marching to the assistance of the over-mountain men should be arranged in three divisions: The South Carolinian's proper; Graham and Hambright's party; and Williams' followers, who at this time were reinforced by Capt. Benjamin Roebuck's command from the region of the present County of Spartanburg, South Carolina. This command consisted of about thirty. The proposition was at first refused by General Williams, he by virtue of his commission claiming the right to command the whole, but his patriotism in this trying hour caused him to yield and accept the terms offered. It was arranged that a commanding officer should be chosen for the whole, but the orders and movements of the corps were to be delivered by all the officers. This party of South Carolinians marched through Lincoln County, near Ramsour's Mill, on the south fork of the Catawba, thence in a southwesterly direction, crossing Buffalo and First Broad Rivers to Cherry Mountain (near Cherryville, N. C.) Here they struck camp for a few days to await further developments of the plans and movements of the men of the mountains. While at this camp they were visited by Col. Charles McDowell on his way to Hillsboro to General Gates' headquarters. He was not prepared, however, to communicate the plans which were afterwards agreed upon to push for Ferguson, and very soon set out in continuation of his mission.

Let us now before we return to the movements of the over-mountain men, whom we left at Cane Creek, examine briefly the movements of Ferguson.

We have already stated that this officer tarried for sometime at Gilberttown in the hope of intercepting Colonel Clarke, whom he had been informed had been repulsed at Augusta, Georgia, and was retreating towards North Carolina. To place himself where he felt sure of cutting off retreat, he left Gilberttown on the 27th of September, and marched to Green River, in what is now Polk County, and struck camp at James Step's. Here on the 30th of the same month the two deserters referred to, Crawford and Chambers, reached him, apprising him that the over-mountain men were on his track. Ferguson became alarmed. His ranks were thin, many of his Tory allies being on furlough. Messengers were sent in every direction to hurry them in, and a dispatch was sent to Lord Cornwallis at Charlotte informing him of his danger.

Ferguson now gave out that he was in full retreat for Ninety-Six merely to delude the Whigs. On the first day of October, the day that the over-mountain men left "Quaker Meadows," he was at the house of Baylis Earle on North Pacolet, near the scene of the battle of Earle's Ford, which had occurred only a short time before. The old Baylis Earle place is now the home of his grandson, O. P. Earle, on the present Greenville and Rutherfordton road—the road over which Ferguson was expecting to meet Colonel Clarke and his retreating forces.

In a Ms. letter of Baylis Earle, dated September 11, 1814,* to Maj. John Lewis and Jonathan Hampton, he stated the fact that Ferguson while at his house killed a steer, destroyed four or five hundred dozen sheaves of oats, and plundered at his pleasure.† From this place he marched in a northern direction to Dennard's Ford, on Broad River, which was about a half a mile below the present Twitty's Ford, in Rutherford County. Here, realizing his impending danger, he issued an address to the inhabitants of the country, in which he warned them of the approach of the men under Shelby, Hampton, McDowell and Cleveland, and telling them to grasp their arms "in a moment and run to camp" if they did not wish to be pinioned, robbed and murdered, and see their wives and daughters in four days abused by the dregs of mankind."

Ferguson was now only about fifteen or twenty miles from the forces of McDowell, Shelby and Sevier. Anticipating an attack from them he moved with his command on Monday, October 2d, about four miles and lay on his arms all night. On the 3d of October, he marched through the present County of Rutherford, crossing Second Broad River at Camp's Ford, and Sandy Run Creek

---

*Baylis Earle lived until 1828.

†See Draper's "King's Mountain," page 203.

six miles further, at Armstrong's. Here, after resting awhile he moved seven miles further, to Tate's place, on Buffalo Creek, which is said to be in the southeastern portion of the present County of Cleveland. At Tate's place Ferguson tarried the 4th and 5th of October, doubtless, to gain intelligence of the movements of the Whigs and to communicate with Cornwallis at Charlotte, only about thirty-five miles distant. The following is a copy of the original dispatch to Cornwallis:

"My Lord. I am on my march to you by a road leading from Cherokee Ford north of King's Mountain. Three or four hundred good soldiers would finish this business. *Something must be done soon.* This is their last push in this quarter." "PATRICK FERGUSON."

It would appear from the movements of Ferguson up to this time that he was trying to reach Cornwallis and outstrip the pursuit of the over-mountain men. This idea, however, appeared distasteful to him. Whatever may be said of the character of Ferguson, he was no coward. It is said that his pride outweighed his judgment, and he determined to risk a battle rather than enter Cornwallis' camp, a fugitive from the very men he affected to dispise. He knew, however, that his destiny was sealed one way or the other. He knew the character and spirit of the men who were marching against him and he resolved to fight. But where should he select his ground? The King's Mountain stood out invitingly before him as a favorable position. To this place, which was sixteen miles southwest of Tate's place, he marched on the 6th of October. He passed near Whittaker's, on the present Air Line Railroad, moving in the direction of Yorkville. On this road after crossing a creek he came to "King's Mountain" in the afternoon. Here he pitched his camp and said he "had selected his ground and that he defied God Almighty and all the rebels out of hell to overcome him."

CHAPTER XXV.

FURTHER MOVEMENTS OF OVER-MOUNTAIN MEN.—INFORMATION OBTAINED BY A SPY OF FERGUSON'S MOVEMENTS.—LACY VISITS THE CAMP OF THE OVER-MOUNTAIN MEN.—A SPECIAL NOUNTED FORCE SELECTED TO OVERTAKE FERGUSON.—JUNCTION OF OVER-MOUNTAIN MEN AT COWPENS WITH HILL, LACY, WILLIAMS AND GRAHAM.—THE MARCH RESUMED AT NIGHT TO OVERTAKE FERGUSON.

HAVING followed the movements of Ferguson in the last chapter, let us now return to the over-mountain men, whom we left at Cane Creek, not far from Gilberttown. Sore indeed was their disappointment when they learned that the "game had fled." Ferguson had given out word that he was in full retreat for Ninety-Six. The Whigs having nothing but rifles, knew that they would not be able to make much impression on Ferguson if he were allowed to reach this stronghold. A council of officers was held. It was determined to follow Ferguson even to Ninety-Six, and strike him as best they could. Taking up their line of march on the 4th day of October, they did not tarry at Gilberttown, but followed Ferguson's track to Dennard's Ford on Broad River. Here they lost his trail for a time. It is stated on good authority that Ferguson marched his men down in the stream to elude their pursuit, coming out below the ford and then bore down the stream, thus proving clearly that Ninety-Six was not his objective point.

The Whigs continued their march across Dennard's Ford until they reached Alexander's Ford on Green River. It is said that being baffled in their efforts to overtake Ferguson, many of them became discouraged and uneasy. Many of the men were foot sore from travel, and some of the horses were jaded and broken down. It would never do, however, to give up in despair. A council was called and it was determined to select their best men, best horses, and best rifles, and press the pursuit, leaving the weaker to follow. It was necessary, however, before this march should commence to find out more of Ferguson's movements and whereabouts. This information was very soon obtained mysteriously in the following way: While Ferguson was encamped at Tate's place on Buffalo, "an old gentleman called on him, who disguised the object of his visit." Impressing upon the mind of Ferguson that he was a faithful Loyalist to the British cause, he obtained from that officer the information that he had sent to Cornwallis for reinforcements, and that he "had selected his ground (King's Mountain) and that he defied God Almighty, and all the rebels out of hell to overcome him." On the next day, October 5th, this faithful old patriot rode twenty miles in a northeast direction to the camp of Hill, Lacy and Williams, on Cherry Mountain, where we last left them, to communicate this information. That night Colonel Lacy made his way with a guide to the camp of the over-mountain men where he communicated to Colonel Campbell and others the important information which he had received from the old gentleman. For awhile Lacy thought him to be a spy, but finally he was enabled to impress upon Campbell the genuineness of his person and the truthfulness of his statements. It was agreed between them to form a junction without delay at Cowpens and march on Ferguson at once.

"On the 5th of October," says a writer, "and nearly all the night following, at Green River, the Whig officers and Campbell's command were busy choosing the select men, rifles and horses for the pursuit. Seven hundred were chosen, leaving six hundred and ninety or more in camp, others of the command having fallen by the way from weakness or sickness. These numbers are approximately correct.

Just before the beginning of this march the Whigs were

joined by Major William Chandler and Captain Johnson, with about thirty Georgians from Colonel Clarke's forces retreating from Georgia. They had received news of the expedition against Ferguson and felt a desire to participate in it. Colonel Clarke had advanced further west, making his way across the mountains to the Watauga settlement, and carrying his own and other Whig families with him.

The expedition was soon ready for a new start to overtake Ferguson. Major Henderson, of Cleveland's regiment, was left in command of the foot men, with Capt. Neal in special charge of the Virginians who were to fol low. Their orders were to set out at once, hurry their march as much as possible and to follow in the footsteps of the mounted men in order to be able to support them in case they should meet with disaster. The seven hundred mounted men set out from Alexander's Ford on the morning of the 6th of October (1780) and marched down the old Cowpens ridge road from the present site of Columbus and of Mill Springs to Cowpens battle ground. They went by way of Sandy Plains, Arrowwood Church (Thorne's) reaching Cowpens on the afternoon, after having traveled about twenty miles. Here they found in waiting Williams, Hill, Lacy and Graham, with their respective commands, they having marched on the same day direct from Cherry Mountain to Cowpens, a distance of some twenty miles or more. Their combined forces amounted to about four hundred, a large number of whom were South Carolinians.

Says Draper, "For an hour or two on the evening of the 6th, there was a stirring bivouac at the Cowpens. A wealthy English Tory, named Saunders, resided there, who reared large numbers of cattle, having many pens in which he had his stock, hence the derivation of Cowpens. Saunders was at the time in bed, feigning sickness, from which he was unceremoniously pulled out and treated pretty roughly. He was ordered to tell what time Ferguson had passed that place, to which he declared that he had not passed at all; that if his word could not be taken there was plenty of torch pine in the house, which they could examine for themselves and further, if they could find any track or sign of an army they might hang him or do whatever they pleased with him. The old Tory had spoken the truth fully. Search was made but no signs of an army passing there could be found. Several of his cattle were at once shot down and slaughtered for the supplv of the hungry soldiers, and in a few hours the army was well supplied with cooked beef, which was to support and strengthen them in the performance of a glorious work in store for them on the following day. About fifty acres of corn, which been planted near by, was harvested in about ten minutes, and soon fed to the weary horses.

It appears that the Whigs on their way to Cowpens passed near where several large bodies of Tories were assembled; one numbering about six hundred, at Major Gibbs'* about four miles to the right. Says Draper, "The only account we have of this enterprise is preserved in Ensign Campbell's dairy: 'On passing near the Cowpens, we heard of a large body of Tories about eight miles distant, and although the main enterprise was not to be delayed a single moment, a party of eighty volunteers, under Ensign Robert Campbell, was dispatched in pursuit of them during the night. They had, however, removed before the mountaineers came to the place, and who, after riding all night, came up with the main body the next day.'" Ensign Campbell further adds, "That a similar expedition was conducted by Captain Colvill, with no better success, but without causing delay."

Having arrived within full view of King's Mountain,

*The writer has tried in vain to learn the whereabouts of the ancient homestead of Maj. Zachariah Gibbs. He has examined the records at the office of the Clerk of Court at Spartanburg, but the name does not appear, nor does it appear in census of 1790. From the description of the locality Major Gibbs must have resided in the vicinity of Martinsville or Cash's store.

the most important duty devolving on Colonel Campbell, the commander of the expedition, was to find out the exact location and position of Ferguson. This he obtained from Joseph Keer, a cripple spy, at that time a member of Colonel Williams' command, at Colonel Williams camp at Flint Hill, on Cherry Mountain. Kerr had been sent to gain intelligence of Ferguson and found him temporarily encamped at Peter Quinns,' on the 6th of October, six or seven miles from King's Mountain. This being a region of Tories, Kerr was not suspected and found no difficulty in gaining access to Ferguson's camp. He was not suspected of being a spy, having been a cripple from infancy. He made anxious inquiries relative to taking protection and appeared gratified on learning the good news of the King's prospects in the future. Learning that Ferguson intended to march to King's Mountain the same afternoon, and managing by his good sense and natural shrewdness to make all the necessary observations, he quietly slipped off, making his way by a circuitous route to rejoin his command, which he overtook at Cowpens. He at once communicated the information he had obtained to the Whig chiefs. It was necessary, however, to keep posted with regard to the continued movements of Ferguson, and to gain further intelligence of his present position. Enoch Gilmer, of South Fork, was proposed for this undertaking by Major Chronicle for, said he, " Gilmer can assume any character that occasion may require; he could cry and laugh in the same breath, and all who saw it would believe he was in earnest; that he could act the part of a lunatic so well that no one could discover him; above all, he was a stranger to fear." Gilmer set out at once. He called at a house of a prominent Tory only a few miles in advance, and represented that he belonged to Ferguson's command and was waiting to join this officer on his supposed march from Dennard's Ford to Ninety-Six. The Tory, not suspecting his true character, frankly told him all he knew and understood concerning Ferguson's movements and intentions; that after he had crossed Broad River at Dennard's Ford, he received a dispatch from Lord Cornwallis, ordering him to rejoin the main army at once; that the plan was to defeat the army of General Gates the second time and overrun and subdue North Carolina. Gilmer returned to the Cowpens the same evening with this intelligence, but this did not give to the Whig leaders the intelligence they were most anxious to find out concerning Ferguson's present plans and whereabouts. A council of war had in the meanwhile been held, all the newly joined officers participating except Williams. It was agreed that Colonel Campbell should remain in chief command. By nine o'clock, the men and horses refreshed, the command set out to find Ferguson. It was a very dark night and soon after they left a drizzly rain set in. The roads were pretty good, however, and they had guides acquainted with the country. But owing to the extreme darkness the pilots of Campbell's men lost their way and that corps became much confused and dispersed through the woods, so that when the morning light dawned the rear portion was not more than five miles from Cowpens. When the absence of the Virginians was discovered next morning, runners were sent in different directions till they were at length found, having taken a wrong road. They were quickly piloted to the main column. Once reunited the command pressed forward uncommonly hard. It was the intention to cross Broad River at Tate's, since known as Deer's Ferry, but for fear that British troops might be stationed on the east side of the river to retard their progress, the troops bore down the stream to Cherokee Ford two and a half miles, where they crossed. Before crossing, however, Gilmer was sent forward about daylight to reconnoitre this ford and discover, if possible, whether the enemy might not be waylaying, with the view of attacking the troops while they were crossing. In the meanwhile the men were ordered to keep their guns dry, for it was yet raining. It was not long before Gilmer's familiar voice was heard singing "Barney Linn," a favorite song of that day, in the hollow near by. This was sufficient notice that the way was clear. It was about sunrise when the troops crossed the river. They had now marched about eighteen miles from Cowpens and were only about fifteen miles from King's Mountain. As soon as Broad River was crossed, Gilmer was again sent forward to make discoveries and dashed off at a full gallop, while the troops with the officers at the head, moved on in a slower gait. After traveling some three miles they came to Ferguson's former encampment, above Cherokee Ford. Here they halted for a short time to partake of a snack, such as their wallets and saddle bags afforded. Some who were without food would pull corn along the roadside and cut the raw corn from the cob for sustenance. During the forenoon of the march the rain continued to fall so heavy that Colonels Campbell, Sevier and Cleveland concluded that it would be best to halt and refresh themselves, as the men were weary and the horses jaded. To this proposition Colonel Shelby, when apprised of the views of the other officers, would not consent, replying with an oath, "I will not stop until night if I have to follow Ferguson into Cornwallis' lines."

The march was continued. The men could only keep their guns dry by wrapping their bags, blankets and hunting shirts around the locks. By noon, however, the rain had almost ceased to fall. After traveling about a mile from the proposed halt, the troops reached Solomon Beason's, who was said to be half Whig and half Loyalist, as occasion required. From him they learned that Ferguson was only eight miles in advance. At this place they also had the good fortune to capture two Tories, who, at the peril of their lives, were ordered to pilot them to Ferguson's camp on King's Mountain.

When the Whigs had advanced five miles further, they reached the house of a Loyalist where some of Sevier's men called. The only information they could get was that Ferguson was not far away. As the soldiers left the house, however, the daughter of this Loyalist, who was in sympathy with the Whig cause, inquired: "How many are there of you?" "Enough to whip Ferguson if we can find him," was the reply. "He is on that mountain," she said, pointing her hand to the eminence.

After traveling several miles further the officers saw the horse of Gilmer, the scout, fastened to a gate in front of a house about three-fourths of a mile ahead. Colonel Campbell concluded to test the scout's ability to sustain his assumed character as a Tory. Providing himself with a rope he and others put whip to their horses and rode at full speed up to the house, where they found Gilmer seated at the table partaking of a good meal and hurrahing for King George. Campbell caused him to be dragged from the house, and fixing a running noose, he threw it over Gilmer's neck, swearing he would hang him on the bow of the gate. Gilmer was marched up the road to be hung while the old woman and the girls were weeping and begging for his life. Gilmer, after getting out of sight, began to laugh heartily and said: "Colonel, I found them such Loyal friends I couldn't help from giving them all a sympathizing smack."

The information which Gilmer had gathered with reference to Ferguson's numbers and axact position, was the most valuable that had been obtained up to this time. One of the girls just mentioned told him that she had been to Ferguson's camp that morning with some chickens; that he was only three miles away and was posted on a ridge between two branches, where some deer hunters had had a camp the fall before. Major Chronicle and Captain Mattocks said they knew the place precisely; that the camp referred to where Ferguson had taken post was theirs, and that it was a spur of King's Mountain.

The officers now came together for consultation again, and agreed upon a plan of attack, which was to surround Ferguson's camp on the hill and destroy him there. The plan was freely communicated to the men for their encouragement, assuring them that by this course of action, they would all the while be shooting up hill and there would be no danger of hurting their comrades on the other side, and that the British would likely overshoot, in shooting at them down the mountain. When within a short distance of the battlefield Col. William Graham was overtaken by a messenger, who informed him that his wife was at the point of death. With Campbell's advice he left at once. The next ranking officer was Colonel Hambright, but as Hambright was an old man, his command was given to Major Chronicle. The patriotic old Dutchman took no offense, as Major Chronicle was better acquainted with the ground over which the battle was to be fought

When within about two miles of the battle field, the Whigs captured a lad named James Ponder, a youth of some fourteen years of age. Colonel Hambright, knowing that this lad had relatives in Ferguson's camp, caused him to be searched. On his person was found a dispatch from Ferguson to Cornwallis, informing him of his situation and imploring his assistance at once. Ponder, on being questioned in regard to Ferguson's dress, said that he was the best uniformed man in camp, but that he wore a checked shirt over it. Colonel Hambright, who was a German, laughed and said: "Poys, hear dot, shoot for the man mit the pig shirt."

When within one mile of Ferguson's camp the troops met George Watkins, a Whig prisoner, whom Ferguson had just released. He was able to give the very latest information, with the positive assurance that Ferguson still occupied his position on the mountain. A brief halt was here made. Up to this time the men had not been riding in order, but now they were drawn up in two lines two men deep. The officers again agreed to surround the mountain and to do this successfully the men, after they had formed two lines were divided, Colonel Campbell leading the right line and Colonel Cleveland the left. Major Winston was detached with a portion of the Wilkes and Surry troops to make a detour south of the quarry road in order to gain Ferguson's right and cut off his retreat if necessary. While these movements were taking place no talking was allowed. The marches of the different lines were made as noiselessly as possible.

It was about three o'clock in the afternoon when the Whigs neared Ferguson's camp. The rain had ceased and a stiff breeze was blowing. Says Draper: "In the rear of trees and bushes on the east side of King's Creek, a little above where the quarry road passes that stream, the mountaineers arrived." They were ordered to, first, "dismount and tie horses," next, to "take off and tie up great coats and blankets, &c., &c., to your saddles." A few men were selected to take charge of the horses. Then came the final order, "Fresh prime your guns, and every man go into battle firmlv resolved *to fight till he dies.*"

CHAPTER XXVI.

BATTLE AND VICTORY AT KING'S MOUNTAIN, OCTOBER 7, 1780.—DEATH OF FERGUSON.—DETAILS OF THE SURRENDER.—INTERESTING INCIDENTS.—THE WHIGS RETRACE THEIR MARCH WITH PRISONERS FROM KING'S MOUNTAIN TO NORTH CAROLINA, RESTING FOR A TIME AT GILBERTTOWN.—EXECUTION OF COLONEL MILLS AND OTHERS AT BICKERSTAFF'S.—MARCH CONTINUED.

AS the battle of King's Mountain was the end of the bold and daring Ferguson, and also the end of his plundering and marauding expeditions, this narrative would not be complete without a brief history of this brilliant engagement and victory for American Liberty.

It is impossible, as already intimated, to present any thing more than an outline, following as we are doing, in the line of other writers, but for a fuller and more comprehensive account of this battle and of the many little interesting incidents connected therewith, the reader is referred to that splendid work, "King's Mouutain and Its Heroes," by the Hon. Lyman C. Draper, who spent more than twenty years with tireless energy and industry in getting up a work perfect in all its parts, evincing a research hitherto unsurpassed by any American writer of Revolutionary historv.

"Ferguson," says a writer, "was on King's Mountain in his lair like a wild beast that had been brought to bay." He showed no signs of fear. His little army was drawn up along the crest of one of the lateral spurs of King's Mountain, which extends in length about sixteen miles in a northeast and southwest course. While the main range is in North Carolina, the battle ground now famous and sacred in the annals of our history, was in York County, South Carolina, about one and a half miles south of the North Carolina line, and about six miles from the pinnacle of King's Mountain. This hill or stony ridge was about sixty feet above the level of the surrounding country. It was about six hundred yards long and about two hundred and fifty yards wide from one base across to the other; or from sixty to one hundred and twenty yards wide on the top. The Mountain tapered rather to the southeast. Ferguson's forces consisted of about eleven hundred and twenty-five and were made up of Provincials and Loyal militia, usually called Tories. The Provincials or Rangers, as they are called by Tarleton in his Memoirs, numbered only about one hundred, and were made up from other Provincial bodies, the King's American Regiment, raised in and around New York, the Queen's Rangers and the New Jersey Volunteers. These troops wore scarlet coats. They were well trained and disciplined and well armed with muskets and bayonets, the use of which they fully understood.

The Loyal militia had been recruited from both North and South Carolina. Many of them were from the same insurgent element that resided in the region of Ninety-Six, and whose conduct at the breaking out of the Revolution has been described in former chapters. They were drilled and disciplined as far as their personal character would permit. Many of them had guns without bayonets. Ferguson, to meet this deficiency, provided each with a long knife made by the blacksmiths of the country, the butt end of the handle of which was filed the proper size to insert snugly in the muzzle of the rifle, with a shoulder or button two inches or more from the end, so that it would answer in place of the bayonet.

The two armies were about equal in numbers, the ad vantage being in favor of Ferguson, who had chosen his ground of defense; his men being well rested and fed. Neither had artillery or cavalry. It was a contest of the bayonet and musket on one hand and the Deckard rifle on the other.

It is useless to contrast the two armies and the motives

which had prompted each to take part in this engagement. While the regular British soldiers, few as they numbered on this occasion, fought for the honor of their King, but a small number of the Tories were conscientious in taking part with them, against the cause of the Patriots. It was either disappointment, ambition, fear of punishment, or opportunity to plunder, that caused them to enlist under Ferguson's banner. "No noble sentiment was found in their hearts," says a writer, "and they felt the disgrace of taking up arms in behalf of oppression and wrong.'

The Whigs, on the other hand, fought for freedom, and to prevent the invasion of their peaceful homes, which had been threatened. They had firmly implanted in their bosoms principles of religious liberty and independence. They were prompted by no mercenary motive; unlike the great armies of Napoleon in Egypt, they had no Pyramids to look down on them to incite them to glory; no Forty Centuries of battle to provoke them to emulation. Being out in an open and lonely wilderness, they had no maiden hands to crown them as victors; no applauding thousands waiting to honor them as survivors of a victorious battle for Liberty; no titles of nobility or badges of knighthood to animate them. They were simply fighting for their country's cause; for their homes and firesides and for the dear ones they had left behind them. The great Spectator of the occasion was the God of battles, who had already heard and recorded in Heaven, the prayer of the Pioneer Missionary in the Watauga Settlements. The answer, we shall see, came through fire and smoke on King's Mountain.

The battle was well planned on the part of the Whig commanders. Their forces were drawn up at the southwestern end of the Mountain, where the slope was gentle, and the army was divided into two corps, which moved off in different directions to surround Ferguson and his army. Says Draper: "Campbell was to lead his Virginians across the southern end of the ridge and southeast side, which Shelby designated as the column of the right-center; then Sevier's regiment, McDowell's and Winston's battalions, were to form a column on the right wing, northeast of Campbell and in the order named, under the command of Lieutenant-Colonel Sevier. Of these, Winston, it will be remembered, made a detour some distance to the south of Ferguson in order the more promptly to gain the position assigned him and peradventure lend a helping hand in retarding the enemy, should they conclude that a hasty retreat was the better part of valor.

Shelby's regiment was to take position on the left of the mountain, directly opposite to Campbell, and form the left center, Campbell's left and Shelby's right coming together; and beyond Shelby were respectively Williams' command, including Brandon, Hammond and Candler; then the South Carolinians under Lacy, Hathorne and Steen, with the remainder of the Wilkes and Surry men under Cleveland, together with the Lincoln troops under Chronicle and Hambright, all under the direction of Colonel Cleveland. By this disposition the patriot force was arranged in four columns, two on either side of the mountain, led respectively by Colonels Campbell and Sevier on the right, and Cleveland and Shelby on the left. It is reasonable to presume that as Winston had been detached when a mile away to gain his assigned position on the right, that Hambright and Chronicle were also early ordered to gain the extreme left portion of the mountain so that the two parties should meet each other and thus encompass the enemy on that end of the ridge."

While these movements were taking place and the Whig forces were gathering around Ferguson, this officer viewed them with firmness and courage, but not with confidence and indifference. His last dispatch to Cornwallis, committed to the care of John Ponder, who was captured, indicated his apprehension of defeat.

Shelby and Campbell, being on the opposite sides of the mountain, began the attack. As soon as the approach of the Americans was discovered by Ferguson, he caused the drum to beat to arms in his camp. His shrill whistle was heard all around. His men were soon in line of battle. Says Draper: " Orders had been given to the right and left wings, that when the center columns were ready for the attack thev were to give the signal by raising a regular frontier warhoop after the Indian style, and rush forward, doing the enemy all the injury possible, and the others, hearing the battle shout and the reports of the rifles, were to follow suit."

The first firing of the enemy was on Shelby's column on the north side of the mountain. Shelby's men were not yet in position and it was with difficulty that this officer could restrain his men from returning it until the proper time. " Press on to your places," he cried, " and your fire will not be lost." Before Shelby's men got into position, however, Campbell had wheeled his men into line. He exclaimed at the top of his voice, " Here they are mv boys; Shout like h—l and fight like devils." The Indian war whoop reverberated all around and the battle was begun.

Campbell's line in pressing forward was delayed in its march about ten minutes by a swampy marsh in front. Shelby's men received the first bayonet charge from the enemv. They were driven down the hill for a short distance, but quickly reloading, they poured a galling fire into the British ranks, which drove them up the hill again.

The trees which retarded the charge of the British Rangers down the hill, afforded protection to the riflemen in their advance up hill. From behind these, they took steady aim, each ball doing its deathly work, as the crest of the mountain was bare and the British, when in column, were unprotected. Harry Lee said of King's Mountain, " It was more assailable by the rifle than defensible with the bayonet."

The battle now raged with fury from every side of the mountain. " As the coil drew nearer, Ferguson dashing from one side to another to rally his men or lead a charge, was typical of Satan when he cried, " Which way I flv is hell."

The rattle of musketry, the keen cracks of the rifles, the daring charges made by the assailants with their yells and whoops, the groans of the dying, doubtless made a discordant noise around this little mountain, which can be better imagined than described. Many heroic and daring deeds are recorded by Draper, which time and space will not allow us to reproduce. Hand to hand conflicts and splendid shots occurred on every side. The Whigs as they advanced up the mountain leaped from rock to rock for shelter. The trees were peeled with bullets intended for the men behind them; the wounded were scrambling away for safety, whilst the dead were lying all around. But in the midst of all this the coil drew nearer still. "As the British bayonets drove the men down one side, the Whigs from the other shouted, 'They retreat,' and rushing to the British rear they poured in the bullets like hail on their backs."

Every charge and countercharge upon the British Rangers and Tories caused their ranks to grow thinner and thinner. Colonel Sevier's command was the first to reach the top of the mountain and hold its position. Sheltered as they were by the rocks around, they continued to pour a destructive fire into the British ranks.

The coil continued to get smaller and tighter around the crest of the mountain. At times both Whig and Tory would be making for the same rock. The countersign of the Whigs was "Buford" in remembrance of "Tarleton's quarter" to this officer and his command at the Waxhaws.

When this Shibboleth was not given on demand up went the rifle to the shoulder, and he who was quickest was the survivor. The Whigs wore a white paper in their hats, while the Toties wore a pine top. The cloud of smoke was, however, too dense at times for these to be discerned.

As the British and Tories were driven closer together, the columns of Shelby and Campbell united on the summit of the mountain. Cleveland, Winston and McDowell led their men up the steep acclivity and were in the rear of

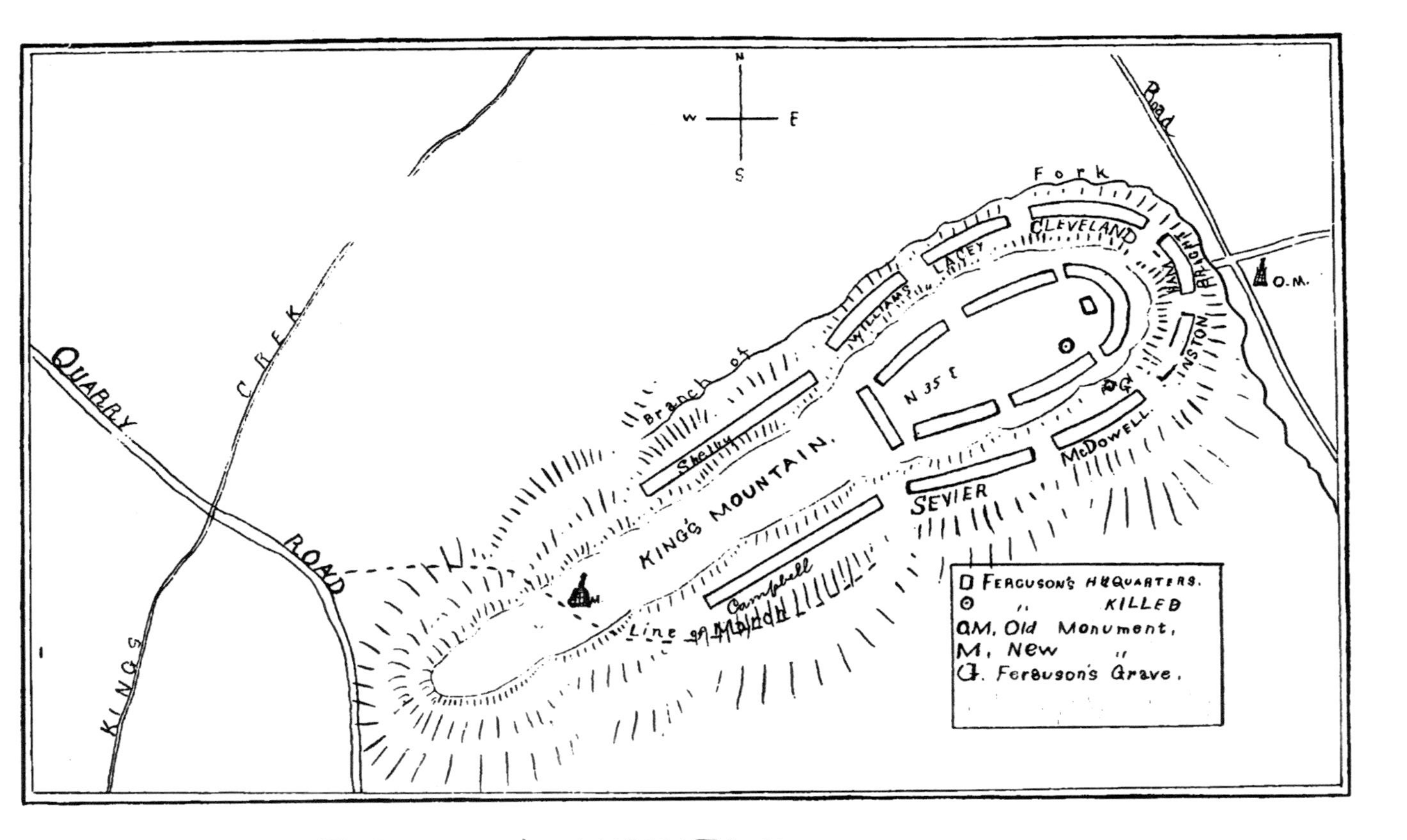

DIAGRAM o the BATTLE of KING'S MOUNTA N.

Ferguson's line which was facing the united columns of Campbell and Shelby.

At last the British were so closely enveloped and the fire so hot from every quarter, that they were unable to renew the charge. Two white flags were raised in token of surrender. which Ferguson cut down with his sword. He was remonstrated with by one of his officers, but he swore he "would never surrender to such banditti." At length, being satisfied that all was lost, "Ferguson," says Draper, "with a few chosen friends made a desperate effort to break through the Whig lines on the southeastern side of the mountain and escape.

It had been announced to the Whigs beforehand that Ferguson wielded his sword in his left hand and that he wore a light or checked duster or hunting shirt over his uniform, called by Hambright, "the pig shirt." They were on the *qui vive* for him. "The intrepid British leader made a bold dash for life and freedom with his sword in his left hand, cutting and slashing till he had broken it." To pass through the Whig lines was an impossibility. He was first recognized by Gilliland, one of Sevier's men, who leveled aim on him, but his gun missed fire. Next Robert Young of the same corps fired and Ferguson tumbled from the saddle. The small party which had resolved to follow consisted of about twenty—a cavalry detachment under Lieutenant Taylor. These, however, were picked off by the Whig marksmen as fast as they mounted. Driven to desperation, Ferguson attempted to make his escape with only two officers, Colonel Vazey Husband and Major Daniel Plummer,* both of whom were killed

Ferguson was unconscious when he fell and lived only a few minutes. A number claimed the honor of having

*Maj. Daniel Plummer, a Loyalist, lived between Fair Forest and Tyger, in Spartanburg County. He is represented as having been "honest and open," kind and considerate to all. His estate was confiscated. His faithful devotion to his commander (Ferguson) at King's Mountain, was worthy of a better cause.

shot this fallen chief. His body was pierced with seven or eight wounds, and one through the head.

White handkerchiefs were now seen displayed from the British ranks everywhere, but those who raised them simply became targets for the infuriated Whigs. "Buford!" "Buford!" "Tarleton's Quarters!" "Tarleton's Quarters!" rang with fearful tones in the ears of the wretched survivors of the Rangers and Tories. "All order and organization were lost and the wretched beings stood like a herd of deer in a corral and were slaughtered in their tracks." In vain were the white handkerchiefs raised. The scene was too sad to contemplate; the curtain must fall. Major Evan Shelby shouted to the victims, "Throw down your arms!" This was instantly done. Shelby rushed forward and implored his men to shoot no more. Captain De Peyster, second in command, now displayed a white flag to Colonel Campbell, who came riding to the front. The firing had almost ceased, but as stragglers, or those who were too weak to be in front, gained the crest of the hill, they emptied their rifles into the British ranks.

Colonel Campbell cried out to his men, "For God's sake quit!" "It is murder to shoot any more." Captain DePeyster, who was sitting on a gray horse, rode up to Colonel Campbell and expostulated with him. Referring to the firing on his flag, he said: "Its d——d unfair." Colonel Campbell did not bandy words with him, but simply ordered him to dismount, and called out, "Officers, rank by yourselves—prisoners, take off your hats and sit down!" The flags formed a continuous circle around the prisoners until finally, as the latter were brought closer together, they were four deep. The space occupied by the enemy at this time was about sixty yards in length and about forty in width. Colonel Campbell then proposed three cheers for *Liberty*. The hills resounded with huzzas and shouts of victory, which was a welcome and glad acclaim by the victorious Americans.

Just here an unfortunate occurrence took place, which

is unpleasant to relate. Says Draper: "A small party of Loyal militia, returning from foraging, unacquainted with the surrender, happening to fire on the Rebels, the prisoners were immediately threatened with death if the firing should be repeated." It was about this time that Colonel Williams was mortally wounded. It is not positively known whether he was struck by the foraging party, which scampered off in the same direction from which it came, or whether he was shot by a ball from some of the prisoners, who, in a huddle, became exasperated that proper respect had not been paid to their flag.

Colonel Williams was riding at the time toward the British encampment; wheeling around he said to William Moore: "I'm a gone man." Colonel Campbell was near at hand when the unfortunate event transpired. It is supposed that he reasoned that if this shot came from an outside party it was a precursor of the approach of Tarleton's men. If it came from the Tories, there was danger that they would spring a trap by shooting down the Whig leaders and make a desperate effort to escape, their arms being still in their hands. Campbell, acting upon the spur of the moment, resolved to quell what appeared to be a mutiny. He instantly ordered the men near him, the men of Williams' and Brandon's command, to fire upon the enemy. The order was obeyed.

It is not known how many were killed by this volley. Joseph Hughes,* of Brandon's commands, said: "We killed about one hundred of them." It was an unfortunate and hasty affair, to say the least of it, and Colonel Campbell, it is said, deeply regretted the order he had given to fire upon an unresisting foe.

The game being bagged, the arms were removed from the prisoners and strongly guarded in order that they might not be able in a moment of confusion to grasp them.

---

* Joseph Hughes went from the section of Union County which was then a part of the Upper or Spartan District.

Accounts differ as to whom De Peyster delivered his sword. One account states to Colonel Campbell, while another says it was to Maj. Evan Shelby.

Most of the officers surrendered their swords to Campbell, who was stalking around among the enemy in his shirt sleeves, with his collar open. From his unmilitary plight, it was hard at first to make the British officers believe that he was the commander of the Whig forces at that place.

Ferguson was buried near where he fell. He was enclosed in a beef's hide and buried in a hole made in a ravine. He was despised by the Whigs whom he had wronged and their cravings for revenge was insatiable. His personal effects were distributed among the officers. His sword was given either to Cleveland or Sevier—probably to the latter. His horse, by common consent, was given to Cleveland, who had lost his in battle. His official correspondence and papers were taken charge of by Colonel Campbell. His silver whistle dropped from his pocket in his last desperate effort to escape. It was picked up by a Tory named Powell, who lived in Caldwell County, N. C. It was preserved by the family until 1832, when it fell into other hands.

So great was the curiosity of the Whig soldiers to see the dead body of Ferguson, that many of the wounded soldiers had their friends to convey them to the spot that they might gaze upon it.

Ferguson had two witnesses with him; one a red-haired woman whose name was "Virginia Sal," who was killed; and another whose name was "Virginia Paul," who appeared indifferent as to his fate.

The battle lasted only about fifty minutes, certainly not more than an hour. Not one of the enemy on the hill escaped after the battle opened up. A foraging party went out the same morning, consisting of about two hundred, which did not return.

The loss of the enemy, in killed and wounded, were heavy. According to the most trustworthy information, the casualties in Ferguson's corps, the Rangers, were thirty killed, twenty-eight wounded and fifty-seven prisoners. The loss of the Tories was one hundred and twenty-seven killed, one hundred and twenty-five wounded and seven hundred and six prisoners—total, one thousand and sixteen (1016). The American loss was twenty-eight killed and sixty-two wounded.

Among the prominent that were killed, were Col. James Williams, of South Carolina; Major Chronicle and Captain Mattocks, of Lincoln County, North Carolina; Captain Edmondson, of Virginia. Among those that were wounded were Lieutenant-Colonel Hambright, Captain Sevier, Captain Moses Shelby, Captain Epsey and others.

Amidst the natural rocky defenses along the crest of the mountain, where many of the Tories had sought shelter, some twenty or more of their bodies were found jammed together. Most of these were shot through the head as if their death had been the deliberate work of massacre.

Dr. Johnson, of Ferguson's corps, it is said, acted the part of the good Samaritan after the battle was over by rendering every possible attention to the wounded both of the Whigs and Provincials, while the wounded of the Tories were left pretty much to their fate.

It has been observed that rarely, if ever, did a body of eighteen hundred men come into conflict with so little provisions to supply their wants. The Americans in their hasty pursuit had provided themselves with almost nothing, while Ferguson had been improvident in supplying his army. It was for this reason, no doubt, that the foraging party of two hundred already referred to, had been sent out by Ferguson.

We who witnessed and survived the scenes of other conflicts at a later day in the history of our country, can fully realize how awful must have been the scenes at King's Mountain after the carnage of the dreadful day—the piteous groans of the wounded and the constant cry throughout the night succeeding the battle for Water! Water!

It is recorded that in the hurry, confusion and exhaus tion of the Whigs, these cries that were emanating from the Tories were but little heeded. While many hearts were touched, others were hardened. In the eyes of the Whigs, the Tories had brought upon themselves their wretched condition. They believed it a righteous retribution from Heaven, for opposing their countrymen in their efforts to throw off the chains of political bondage which had been forged by the oppression of the British Government.

During the long night, the weary Whigs guarded by turns the prisoners and cared for their own wounded. They were keeping at the same time a close watch lest Tarleton should unexpectedlv dash upon them. "It was a night," says Draper, "of care, anxiety and suffering vividly remembered and feelingly rehearsed as long as any of the actors were permitted to survive." The reader is referred to "King's Mountain and Its Heroes" for an account of many little particulars and battle incidents connected with this contest for freedom and independence.

After a night of confusion and only a partial repose for the Whigs, they were ready by ten o'clock to commence a tedious march, encumbered by their wounded and about six hundred prisoners. Much of the morning had been consumed in preparing litters to convey the wounded. Rumors were prevalent that Tarleton's cavalry were pressing on, and while it was only a rumor brought in by the people of the surrounding country, the Whigs deemed it wise to waste no time.

"When the army marched at ten o'clock in the forenoon, Colonel Campbell remained behind with a party of men to bury their unfortunate countrymen." Two large pits were dug upon a small elevation some eighty or a hundred yards southeast of Ferguson's headquarters, where the slain were placed side by side with blankets spread over them. The British dead were placed in one pit and the Tories in the other. They had but a very shallow covering, however, for soon the wolves and vultures of the surrounding country were attracted to the places of interment by the smell of flesh and blood. Some were overlooked and were unburied. The rest were scratched out of their resting places by these scavengers of the wilderness.

After the army had marched some twelve miles from the battle ground it encamped that night near the eastern bank of Broad River and a little north of Buffalo Creek. The Whigs had reached a good camping ground at a deserted plantation of a Tory whose name was Walden or Fondren. Happily thev found a sweet potato patch which supplied the whole army. The patriots were joined during the evening by Colonel Campbell and party and also by the footmen whom they had left at the ford of Green River, and who had made fine progress in following the footsteps of the mounted advance. These had, fortunately, secured a few beef cattle on the way, which went far towards supplying with food the almost famished Whigs.

The army continued its march, reaching on Wednesday, 11th, Colonel John Walker's place, who resided some five miles west of Gilberttown, on the east side of Cane Creek. While on the way to this place, the army marched through Gilberttown and rested awhile. Says Draper: "The prisoners were placed in a pen in which Ferguson, when stationed there, had confined captured Whigs, when the British had full sway in that quarter. A Tory woman there was asked what the leaders were going to do with their rebel prisoners in the bull pen. "We are going," she tartly replied, "to hang all the d——d old rebels and take their noses and scrape their tongues and let them go."

The same woman now visited the same pen and saw her husband among the prisoners captured at King's Mountain. "What are you soldiers going to do with these poor fellows?" said she to James Gray with eyes filled with tears. "We are going to hang all the d——d old Tories," said he. "take their wives, scrape their tongues and let them go." This retort in her own coarse language, caused her to go quietly away.

The country around Walker's was so thinly settled, it having been plundered for two months, provisions could not be obtained for love or money. Not the prisoners only, but the whole army came, in the language of Thomas Young in his narrative, "near starving to death." The army, therefore, moved to Bickerstaff's or Biggerstaff's Old Fields, since known as Burnt Chimneys, (now Forest City) which is some nine miles northeast of the present town of Ruthfordton, N. C.

While encamped here, Colonel Campbell issued a general order deploring the many desertions from the army and appealing to the officers to exert themselves in suppressing the degrading habit of plundering indiscriminately, both Whig and Tory families by soldiers "who issue out of camp, etc." He further ordered that none of the troops be discharged until the prisoners were transferred to a proper guard: the sequel proved that some of the prisoners were to be disposed of in a manner not anticipated when this order, just issued, was made known to the army.

We come now to the closing of what appears to be the most sickening of the many scenes that overshadowed the British-Tory defeat at King's Mountain. It appears that while the army was encamped at Bickerstaff's the officers of the two Carolinas united in presenting a complaint, "that there were, among the prisoners, a number who were robbers, house burners, parole breakers and assassins." Colonel Campbell, on the strength of these reports, was induced to order a court of inquiry. "The Carolina officers urged," says Draper, "that if these men should escape, exasperated as they now were by the consequence of their humiliating defeat, they would commit other enormities worse than their former ones." We have shown in a former chapter that the British leaders at Augusta and Ninety-Six, in a high-handed and summary manner, hung not a few of the captured patriots; the same was done at Camden. The time had now arrived to adopt a severe retaliatory measure that would have a healthful influence on the Loyalists and put an end to their atrocities.

A copy of the law of North Carolina was obtained, which authorized "two magistrates to summon a jury, and forthwith to try, and if found guilty, to execute persons who had violated its precepts." This law, which provided for capital punishment, had reference to those guilty of murder, arson, house-breaking, riots, etc.

As most of the North Carolina officers were magistrates at home the court martial was *technically* a *civil* one, composed as it was, of field officers and captains. The jury was also composed of twelve officers. The court was conducted in an orderly manner; the witnesses were called in each case and examined; the consequence was that "thirty-six men were tried and found guilty of house-breaking, killing the men, turning the women and children out of doors and burning the house."

The trial was brought to a close about nightfall. A suitable oak was selected, and upon a projecting limb the executions were to take place. Only nine were executed. Their names were Col. Ambrose Mills, Capt. James Chitwood, Captain Wilson, Capt. Walter Gilkey, Captain Grimes, Lieutenant Lafferty, John McFall, John Biddy, and Augustine Hobbs. All the rest were pardoned, except one Isaac Baldwin, who made his escape in the darkness of the night. The pardoning power seems to have been exercised by Colonel Shelby, who was a magistrate at home. Says Draper: "While all eyes were directed to Baldwin and his companions, pinioned and awaiting the call of the executioner, a brother of Baldwin's, a mere lad, approached, apparently in sincere affection, to take his parting leave. He threw his arms around his brother and set up a most piteous screaming and lamentation, as if he were going into convulsions, or his heart would break with sorrow. While all were witnessing this touching scene, the youth managed to cut the cords which bound his brother, he darted away, breaking through a line of soldiers and easily escaping under the cover of darkness into the surrounding forest."

The unfortunate condemned were to swing off three at a time. It is stated upon the authority of Allaire, a British officer, that Mills, Wilson and Chitwood, died like Romans. Among those who were condemned and not executed was James Crawford, who with Samuel Chambers, an inexperienced youth, deserted the over-mountain men, while at Bald or Yellow mountain on their outward march, and gave Ferguson the first information of the storm that was gathering to overwhelm him.

Captain Grimes, one of the executed, had been a leader of a party of Tory horse thieves and highwaymen in East Tennessee, where some of his band were taken and hung. He had fled to escape the same punishment that overtook him in the end.

During the same night of the execution, one of the reprieved Tories, with a heart full of gratitude to Colonel Shelby, went to this officer and made this revelation: "You have saved my life," said he, "and I will tell yon a secret. Tarleton will be here in the morning—a woman has brought the news." Thc Whig leaders, upon receiving this information, deemed it prudent not to risk another engagement, but to retire with the prisoners to a place of safety. The camp was instantly aroused and every preparation was made for an early start next morning, which took place at five o'clock.

The poor Loyalists were left still swinging to the sturdy oak, which was known for years afterwards as the Gallows Oak. As soon as the Whigs were gone, Mrs. Martha Bickerstaff, wife of Capt. Aaron Bickerstaff, who had served under Ferguson and was mortally wounded at King's Mountain, with the assistance of an old farmer near by, cut the bodies down; eight of them were buried in a shallow trench some two feet deep, while the remains of Captain Chitwood were conveyed by his friends on a blanket to a graveyard about a half mile away.

In the year 1855, a party of road workers concluded to exhume the remains of Colonel Mills and his companions, as the place of burial was well known; only four of the graves were examined. The bones crumbled on exposure. Several articles were found in a good state of preservation: a butcher knife, a small brass chain about five inches in length, a large musket flint, thumb lancet and other articles.

Most of these were, a few years ago, in the hands of the late M. O. Dickinson, Esq., of Rutherfordton, N. C.

We cannot further pursue the army of Colonel Campbell in detail, having already devoted so much space to the battle of King's Mountain.

The army continued its march to the Catawba River, at Island Ford, where the stream was forded breast deep. They bivouacked on the western bank of the river at Quaker Meadows, already mentioned as the home of Major McDowell. Here the half-starved men obtained provisions, and were fed and rested. By the 16th of October the army had reached the head of the Yadkin. By the 18th it had reached Wilkes Court House. Some of the wounded Americans were left in Burke County, eight or twelve miles above Morganton, and committed to the care of Dr. Dodson, who had some eighteen under his care at one time.

About the 20th of October the command of Colonels Sevier and Lacy branched off. By the 24th the official reports of the battle of King's Mountain was made out and signed by Colonels Campbell, Shelby and Cleveland. * By the 26th, while the army was encamped at Bethabara, near Salem, N. C., Colonels Campbell and Cleveland repaired to the headquarters of General Gates, at Hillsboro, to consult as to what disposition should be made of the prisoners, while Colonel Cleveland was left in com-

---

* See Wheeler's History of North Carolina, Part II, Page 104.

mand of the troops and prisoners. Most of the British officers were paroled. It was intended to send the prisoners to secure regions in Virginia, but a great many escaped, including the officer, Allaire. Says Draper in reference to the prisoners: "Prior to the 7th of November, one hundred and eighty-eight who were inhabitants of the western country of North Carolina, were taken out of Colonel Armstrong's charge by the civil authorities and bound over inferentially for their appearance in court or for good behavior; some were dismissed; some paroled; but most of them enlisted; some in the three months militia service, others in the North Carolina continentals and others still in the ten-months' men, under Sumter." Colonel Armstrong, under whose care the prisoners had been placed, was made to answer for his conduct by General Gates and for the injury done to the American cause. The remaining prisoners, amounting to about one hun dred, were then marched under a strong guard to Hills boro.

A large portion of the mountaineers who had volun teered for the expedition, returned home, while many joined the American army, south, under General Gates, who was in a short time afterwards superseded by General Greene.

Thus ended the great and glorious expedition and battle of King's Mountain, a victory of which the historian, Banroff, said, "Was like the rising of Concord, and in its effects like the success at Bennington," and changed the aspects of war. The Loyalists no longer dared to rise.

It fired the patriots of the two Carolinas with fresh zeal. The fragments of the defeated and scattered American army now came together and organized.

"That memorable victory," Jefferson declared, "was the joyful annunciation of that turn of the tide of success which terminated the Revolutionary War with the seal of independence."

CHAPTER XXVII.

SKETCHES OF THE PROMINENT HEROES IN THE SCENES AT KING'S MOUNTAIN.

GENERAL WILLIAM CAMPBELL

WAS born in western Virginia, Augusta County, in 1754. He was a son of Charles Campbell, of Irish birth, a prominent man in his day and time, who died in 1767, leaving the care of his wife and four daughters to his son William. Soon after this William, when only about twenty-two years of age, migrated with the family to a fine tract of land called Aspenvale, near Abingdon, Virginia.

In 1773 he was appointed one of the earliest judges of Fincastle County, and in 1774 a militia captain. Soon after this he participated in the Indian war against the Shawnees, being a part of Colonel Christian's regiment. which was a part of the forces of Lord Dunmore.

He early espoused the American cause. In 1775, he, with his hunting-shirt riflemen, formed a part of the first Virginia regiment, under the command of Col. Patrick Henry.

It was not long after this that he married Miss Elizabeth Henry, a sister of the famous Patrick Henry.

Troubles on the borders in 1776 caused him to resign and return to his home. In January, 1777, Washington County was organized. Colonel Campbell was continued a member of the justice's court and was at the same time made Lieutenant-Colonel of the militia in a regiment commanded by Evan Shelby.

In 1777 he was appointed a commissioner to run the boundarv line between the Cherokees and Virginia. In 1779 he was engaged in suppressing a partial uprising of the Tories in Montgomery County. In April, 1780, he was promoted to the full rank of colonel in place of Col.

Evan Shelby, whose residence was now determined to be in North Carolina. The same year he served a term in the Virginia House of Delegates. Soon after he returned home he engaged large bodies of Tories, who, at the instigation of British officers, were endeavoring to seize the lead mines near Wytheville; returning from this expedition he led four hundred brave riflemen from Washington County to meet Ferguson and his command of united rangers and Tories who were advancing in the direction of his section of the country. This expedition and the final overthrow of Ferguson has been briefly related. Too much praise cannot be accorded to the memory of the "Hero of King's Mountain" for his gallant bearing in the campaign generally, and especially for his conduct in battle.

Hurrying home after the battle of King's Mountain, he found the Cherokees at work on the border. Raising additional troops he marched to the assistance of Col. Arthur Campbell, Colonel Shelby and Major Martin, who had preceded him to quell this insurrection. The Cherokees were pursued, many of their warriors killed and their settlements desolated.

On the thirteenth of January, 1781, General Greene wrote to Col. William Campbell reminding him of the glory he had already acquired, and urging him to "bring without delay one thousand good volunteers from over the mountains." Notwithstanding the fact that the troubles in his own country with the Indians and Tories were not yet settled, Colonel Campbell raised over a hundred of his picked riflemen and moved forward on the twenty-fifth to the assistance of General Greene. Others joined him on the way and when he reached the army of General Greene, which was about the second of March, he had a command of about four hundred. He fought gallantly in the battle of Guilford and his services in the campaign are conspicuously recorded. Returning home after the battle of Guilford, he was again chosen to represent Washington County in the Virginia House of Delegates. He served on important committees with Patrick Henry and others. By this body he was created a Brigadier-General of the militia, to serve under Marquis De LaFayette, then commanding in Virginia. He at once repaired to LaFayette's camp for service. He became a favorite of this gallant nobleman, who appointed him to command a brigade of light infantry and cavalry. His career, however, in this campaign was destined to be short. He was taken with a complaint in his breast and after a few days illness expired, August 22d, 1781, in his thirty-sixth year. General LaFayette issued a general order announcing the sad event and characterizing Colonel Campbell as "an officer whose services must have endeared him to every citizen, and in particular to every American soldier. The glory which General Campbell acquired in the battles of King's Mountain and Guilford Court House will do his memory an everlasting honor, and insure him a high rank among the defenders of liberty in the American cause." The remains of General Campbell were at first interred at Rocky Mills, in Hanover County, Virginia. Here they reposed until 1823, when his relatives had them removed to his old Aspenvale homestead on the Holston, in southwest Virginia, to rest beside his mother, little son and other relatives. His widow, a son and a daughter survived him. The widow subsequently united in marriage to Gen. William Russell; the son died young; the daughter Sarah, became the wife of Gen. Francis Preston and mother of Hon. William C. Preston, Gen. John S. Preston and Col. Thomas L. Preston. General Campbell's widow lived until 1825, to the age of about eighty years, and the daughter, Mrs. Preston, lived until 1846, to the age of about seventy years. The name of William Campbell should never be forgotten by the rising generations of our country. Says a writer, "Whenever the story of King's Mountain and Guilford is read and the services of their heroes fully appreciated, it will be found that William Campbell has 'purpled o'er his name with deathless glory.'"

COLONEL BENJAMIN CLEVELAND.

The Clevelands, it is said, were an ancient family deriving their name from a tract of country in the north Riding of Yorkshire, England, still called Cleveland. In history there are two Alexander Clevelands mentioned. The junior of this name was father of John Cleveland, who was the father of Benjamin, the subject of this sketch.

John Cleveland early migrated to Virginia and married a Miss Martha Coffee. He settled on the famous Bull Run, in Prince William County. It was here that Benjamin Cleveland was born on the 26th of May, 1738. His early educational advantages appear to have been limited. Much of his early life was spent in hunting. It is said by a writer, that he, "like Daniel Boone, had an unconquerable aversion to the tame drudgery of farm life." His favorite resort in early youth was in the wilderness where he secured pelts and furs, which found a ready market. He was also fond of hunting deer by torch light, commonly called fire hunting. In early manhood he married Miss Mary Graves, of Orange County. It is said that he participated in the French and Indians wars, but this is not proven in history, and that his marriage did not tame him. He was fond of horse racing, gaming and other wild sports common on the frontiers. During harvest times the neighbors would be invited. A fiddler and plenty of liquor were provided, and the day's work usually ended in a debauch.

To brake away from these habits and associations, Benjamin Cleveland moved with his family to Roaring Creek, in Wilkes County, North Carolina. Here he opened up a farm and devoted much of his attention to stock raising and hunting. In 1772, in company with a party of friends, he set out to Kentucky in quest of Daniel Boone. On the way he and his friends were captured and deprived of their horses, guns, ammunition and shoes. In this pitiful and almost starving condition they returned home. Several months after this Cleveland raised a select party and visited the Cherokee country and recovered the stolen horses. In this he was aided by a friendly chief, Big Bear, who furnished him an escort to visit the several towns and assist in recovering the stolen property.

He early espoused the patriotic cause and on the first of September, 1775, was appointed an ensign in the second North Carolina regiment, under the command of Col. Robert Howe. This honor, however, he declined, preferring rather to serve with the militia from his own locality.

During 1775 Cleveland's neighbors had occasion to go to Cross Creek to purchase their supplies of iron, sugar and salt, and other necessaries. They were compelled before they could buy or sell to take the oath of allegiance to the King. Cleveland, hearing of these acts of tyranny, swore that he would dislodge those Scotch scoun drels at Cross Creek. He raised a select party of riflemen and marching down upon them soon scattered them. He scoured the country, captured several of the outlaws, one of whom he executed. The name of this party was Jackson, who had set fire to the home and store house with merchandise of one Ransom Sunderland.

In the campaign of Colonels Williamson and Rutherford against the Cherokee Indians, in 1776, Cleveland, as captain of a company in the Surry Regiment served gallantly, sharing all the hardships and privations which the soldiers had to undergo.

In 1777, Captain Cleveland again led his company to the Watauga settlements against the yet troublesome Cherokees, where he served at Carter's Fort until a treaty of peace was concluded in July of that year.

In 1778, the new County of Wilkes, North Carolina, was organized. Cleveland was placed at the head of the commission of justices and was made colonel of the militia. In the fall of this year he was chosen to represent his county in the Legislature of North Carolina. *

In 1778, when the Britsh forces invaded Georgia, Colonel Cleveland served in this campaign, his regiment being

* See Wheeler's History of North Carolina, Wilkes County, page 468.

a part of General Rutherford's command. Returning home from this service he was elected to represent his county in the State Senate.

In the summer of 1780 he was actively engaged in suppressing the Tories at different places; first in marching against the Tories assembled at Ramsour's Mill, arriving there shortly after their defeat; second, in chasing Colonel Bryan's forces from the State, and finally in scouring the region of New River, checking the Tory rising in that region. In some instances some of their notorious leaders and outlaws were hanged.

The distinguished services of Colonel Cleveland in the famous King's Mountain campaign have already been noticed. Just before the opening up of the battle of King's Mountain he delivered an address to the troops in plain, unvarnished language, which did much to inspire their courage and patriotism on this occasion, and doubtless added greatly to the triumphant success of the Amercan cause.

Draper, in his biography of Cleveland, gives an extended account of a narrow escape by him not long after the King's Mountain expedition. It appears that on one occasion he captured two Tory outlaws, Jones and Carl, and hung them. Soon afterwards and whilst all alone, he was captured bv a gang of Tories. His life hung on a thread. His name and influence was worth everything to the Tories, who decided before they executed him to require him to write passes for them, certifying that each was a good Whig, to be used when in close quarters. Cleveland was a very poor scribe and wrote passes very slowly, believing they would kill him as soon as he fin ished this work. While he was thus engaged a party of Whigs came up, under the command of his brother, Capt. Robert Cleveland. and he was fortunately recaptured. Riddle, who commanded the Tory company which cap tured Cleveland, was afterwards captured with his son and another follower and carried before Cleveland, and by his orders all three of them were hung near the present town of Wilkesboro, North Carolina.

It is said of Cleveland that while in many instances he résorted to the severest measures of punishment against the outrages and maraudings of the Tories, he yet exercised a commanding influence over them and caused some of them to abandon their Tory associations and unite under his standard. Says a writer, "Cleveland was literally all things to all people." By his severities "he awed and intimidated not a few, restraining them from lapsing into Tory abominations; by his kindness, forbearance and even tenderness, winning over many to the glorious cause he loved so well."

Cleveland's last military service was in the autumn of 1781. He performed a three months tour of dutv on the Little Pee Dee, in South Carolina. His command of mountaineers routed the Tory detachments. After this was accomplished he returned home.

At the close of the war Cleveland lost his handsome plantation, called "Round About," by reason of a defective title. His attention had been attracted to a beautiful country in the Cherokee Nation, while participating in the expedition of Colonels Williamson and Rutherford against the Cherokees in 1776. Though the the Indian title was not yet extinguished he resolved to become among the first squatters of that country. He visited the Tugaloo Valley in 1784, and selected for his future home a magnificent body of land lying between the Tugaloo River and Chauga Creek, in the present County of Oconee, S. C. To this place Cleveland removed about the year 1785 or 1786.

To the history of Col. Ben Cleveland's life after his removal to the Tugaloo, much is due to his biography by Governor Perrv in his "Sketches of Eminent Statesmen." It was not long after his removal to his new home until his services were called into requisition. When the new "County Court Act," of which Judge Pendleton was the author, went into force Col. Benjamin Cleveland,

Gen. Andrew Pickens and Gen. Robert Anderson were appointed judges of the court for Pendleton County. Colonel Cleveland was no lawyer, though a good judge of right from wrong. He had a contempt for the technicalities of law and its delays. He was fair in the administration of justice, and after hearing the evidence his mind was quickly made up. He did not consult books, but decided according to his sense of justice and right.

It is stated bv Governor Perry that Colonel Cleveland grew very corpulent during the latter days of his life, weighing some four or five hundred pounds. It is further stated by this eminent writer, that his (Perry's) father, visited him one bitter cold morning and found him sitting in his piazza with nothing on but a thin calico gown, and that his legs were of a purple color. Mr. Perry said to him, "This is a very cold morning, Colonel Cleveland." "No," replied the colonel. "It's a very fine morning, and I have come out to enjoy the fresh morning air." It is further related by him that by reason of his fleshiness, he would while sitting on the bench take a snooze, while the lawyers were rendering their arguments, and would sometimes snore so loud as to interrupt the proceedings of the court.

Governor Perry gives an interesting account of the descendants of Col. Benjamin Cleveland. Two brothers, John and Robert, and one sister are named. John Cleveland was a Baptist preacher of good standing, influence and ability. He was pastor of a church on Chauga River, in Oconee County. In referring to the "General History of the Baptist Denomination of America," published in Boston, in 1813, a copy of which is in possession of the writer, his name appears as pastor of Chauga Church, Sarepter Association. Membership, 265, founded 1783. The sister referred to, married a Mr. Franklin, brother of Governor Franklin, of North Carolina.

Robert Cleveland, brother of Col. Benjamin Cleveland, was a soldier of the Revolution and was a captain in his brother's regiment at King's Mountain. He was the father of Capt. Jeremiah Cleveland, of Greenville, South Carolina, and of Jesse Cleveland, one of Spartanburg's early and most successful merchants, who was the father of the late John and Dr. Robert E. Cleveland, the latter the father of the present Dr. Jesse and John B. Cleveland, Esq.

The remains of Colonel Cleveland were buried on his farm which belonged, in 1887, to Dr. William Earle. Governor Perry states that he visited, when a boy, the grave of this immortal hero. It was much neglected, brambles, briers and bushes having grown up around it. Some years afterwards some one built a square pen around it of pine saplings, which soon rotted down. A few year ago, under the leadership of one of his descendants, Vanoy Cleveland, Esq., a handsome monument was placed over the last resting place of Colonel Cleveland by his relatives.

It has been truly said of Colonel Cleveland, that he "was one of nature's great men—great in every respect, great in person, great in heart and great in mind. He was honest, truthful and honorable, and discharged his duties frankly and fearlessly. He was a man of extraordinary judgment, good sense and practical wisdom." Let his name and glory stand among the memories of other heroes that are being perpetuated.

COLONEL JOHN SEVIER.

Son of Valentine and Joanna Sevier, was born in the village of New Market, Rockingham county, in the Valley of Virginia, on the twenty-third day of September, 1745. After the Indian war of 1755, the family removed for safety to where John was placed at school. He was afterwards sent to school at Staunton, and while there was accidentally saved from drowning in a mill-race by the heroic efforts of two young ladies, one of whom became the wife of George Matthews, a colonel of the Revolution and Governor of Georgia. In early life, John Sevier was engaged with his father in trade and at the age of seventeen he married a Miss Sarah Hawkins. He opened up a farm, engaged in merchandising and occasionally participated in excursions against the Indians. On one occasion he and his companions narrowly escaped an ambuscade which had been set for them.

Late in 1773, John Sevier removed his family to the Holston country (now East Tennessee) within a few miles of the Shelbys. Before his removal from Virginia, he was commissioned a captain, by Lord Dunmore.

The wife of John Sevier being delicate, she never moved from Virginia, and died there soon after the birth of her sixth child.

John Sevier was at Watauga Fort when attacked by the Indians in July, 1776. A large number of people had gathered there and at davbreak, when the women were outside milking the cows, a large body of Cherokees fired on the milkers, but fortunately they all escaped to the fort, the gates having been thrown open for their reception. Among the girls who were engaged in milking was a Miss Catherine Sherrill. It seems that the gates were accidentally shut against her before she reached the fort. She was equal to the emergency, however. She threw her bonnet over the pickets and climbed over herself and fell into the arms of John Sevier, who subsequently became her husband. The attack on the fort was successfully resisted.

We have shown that John Sevier was among the first in the defense of the settlements on the Watauga and Nolachuckey. He was elected clerk of the first self-constituted court in 1775, and in 1776 was chosen one of the representatives of the united settlements to the North Carolina Convention, at Halifax. During this session he secured the establishment of the district of Washington. After his return he served in Christian's expedition against the Cherokees, at the head of a spirited company of riflemen. He remained in the service until the treaty of Holston, at Long Island, July, 1777. In the fall of this year he was appointed Lieutenant-Colonel of Washington County. His principal duty from 1777 to 1779 was to guard with vigilance the Tories, Indians and horse thieves that infested the country.

During the year 1780 he participated in the expedition against Ferguson. His gallant services at King's Mountain have already been noticed and cannot be too highly extolled. In December of the same year he defeated the Cherokees at Boyd's Creek, killing thirteen and taking all their baggage. After this he joined Col. Arthur Campbell in an expedition against the hostile towns.

In February, 1781, he was made a full colonel. In March of this year he led a successful expedition against the middle Cherokee settlements, killing about thirty of their warriors, capturing some prisoners, burning six towns and bringing away about two hundred horses. In the autumn of this year he served under Generals Greene and Marion in South Carolina. In November, 1784, he was appointed Bregadier-General, which honor he declined, because of his leadership in the proposed republic of Franklin, or, as Wheeler has it, *Frankland.* During the period of its existence he was made its Governor and principal defender. He was apprehended by the North Carolina authorities, headed by Governor Tipton, and carried to the court at Morgantown under the charge of rebellion. He was rescued by a party of his friends. He bore the sobriquet of "Nolachuckey Jack" at home. Returning home from Morgantown he led a campaign against the Indians. The people of East Tennessee being divided in sentiment, the State of Frankland ceased to exist, after a stormy career of about four years.

In 1789 General Sevier was chosen a representative to the Legislature of North Carolina, when an act of obliv ion was passed. He was thereupon reinstated Brigadier General.

In 1790–1 he was elected to represent the East Tennes see district of North Carolina in Congress, and when Ten nessee was organized into a territory he was appointed by President Washington a Brigadier-General of the militia. He continued to protect the frontier settlements, carrying on the Hightower campaign against the Cherokees in 1793. In 1798 he was made a general in the provisional army of the United States. On the organization of the State Government of Tennessee, in 1796, Gen. John Sevier was chosen its first governor and continued in this office until 1801. In 1802 he served as commissioner to run the boundary line between Tennessee and Virginia. He was again chosen governor from 1803 to 1809 and then served a term in the State Senate. In 1811 he was again chosen to a seat in Congress, and served on the committee on military affairs until 1815, when he was appointed by President Madison one of the commissioners to ascertain the boundary of the Creek territory, and died while on this service, near Fort Decatur, Alabama, September 24th, 1815, at the advanced age of seventy years.

"General Sevier," said the distinguished Hugh L. White, who had served under him, "was considered in his day among the most gallant, patriotic and useful men in the country in which he lived." For a long number of years his remains rested in a neglected and almost forgotten grave, with no stone to point to the sacred spot. Not many years ago, however, they were removed to the court house grounds in Knoxville, Tennessee, where a handsome monument with appropriate inscriptions, marks their final resting place. *

In another part of this work will be found a sketch of Col. Isaac Shelby and also Col. James Williams, of South Carolina.* Soon after the fall of the latter on the battle field of King's Mountain, he was carried into the British

---

*Under a government appointment to Oklahoma Territory, the writer had the pleasure of visiting this monument while passing through Knoxville, Tennessee.

* See Musgrove's expedition and battle.

lines and placed under the care of the British surgeon, Dr. Johnson, of whom it is said that he did all the service he could to Whigs and Provincials alike. When the army took up its line of march the following day, the wounded were placed on horse litters and the tenderest care was taken of the heroic Colonel Williams. Says Draper: "In the early part of the afternoon, when about three miles south-west of the battle ground, on the route towards Deer's Ferry on Broad River, the little guard having him in charge, discovering that life was fast ebbing away, stopped on the road-side at Jacob Randall's place, since the homestead of Abraham Hardin, where he quietly breathed his last. His death was a matter of sincere grief to the whole army. His friends resolved at first to carry his remains to his old home, near Little River in Laurens County, but soon after changed this determination. Marching some twelve miles from the battlefield, they encamped that night near the eastern bank of Broad River and a little north of Buffalo Creek on the road leading to North Carolina, and within two miles of Camp's Creek. Here, at the deserted plantation of Waldron or Foundron, they found a good camping ground." As no suitable conveyance could be found, the next morning the friends of Colonel Williams concluded to bury his remains near by. They were accordingly interred with the honors of war between the Whig camp and the river, a little above the the mouth of Buffalo Creek, on a plantation that afterwards belonged to Capt. J. B. Mintz. Repeated efforts were made by different ones, and by the descendants of Colonel Williams years after, to locate this sacred spot, but without success. Many years afterwards Captain Mintz employed some men to shrub off the ground where the long forgotten grave was supposed to be, and sure enough a grave was discovered with a head and foot stone of a different kind of rock from any to be found near by. This is unquestionably the last resting place of Colonel Williams. It is an irreparable shame to our American Republic that the last resting places of many of her heroes have been neglected and forgotten. Be this as it may, their memories and glorious deeds will be preserved and perpetuated through long succeeding ages.

Time would fail us to present sketches in detail of Col. Charles McDowell, Lieut.-Cols. Frederick Hambright, Benjamin Herndon, Edward Lacy and Majs. Joseph Winston, William Chronicle, Even Shelby, Jr., Joseph McDowell, and many of the list of devoted patriots of King's Mountain, whose names have been preserved and whose valorous services, together with those whose names are not given to us, will be forever preserved and perpetuated in the annals of our country's history.

BRITISH AND LOYALISTS LEADERS.

COLONEL PATRICK FERGUSON, commander of the British and Loyalists forces at King's Mountain, was no ordinary man. He was a finished soldier and his bearing throughout his military career proved him as brave as a lion. He was a Scotchman by birth and son of James Ferguson, an eminent Judge, Lord of Sessions and Justiciary. He was a nephew of a great nobleman whose name was Patrick Murrv (Lord Elibank), a man of eminent literary talents who was deemed by other writers and contemporary sages equal to the best authors of the Scottish Augustan age. Patrick Ferguson early acquired an education, possessing as he did, a vigorous mind and brilliant parts. At the age of eighteen he entered the army in the German war and was distinguished by his cool and determined courage. It is said that he early displayed inventive genius, sound judgment and intrepid heroism, and all the essential qualifications which constitute the successful soldier. He was the inventor of a new species of rifle that could load at the breach and fire seven times a minute with accuracy and precision. He participated in the battle of Brandywine in 1777, and used with his corps his invention with fatal effect.

In 1779 he distinguished himself on the North River, and was sent soon after to aid General Clinton in the

South. He rendered signal service in the reduction of Charleston, May, 1780, and received complimentary notice in the dispatches of his Commander-in-Chief. He was pleasant and conciliatory in manner, and was well calculated to gain friends. It was for this reason, after the fall of Charleston, that he was dispatched to the district of Ninety-Six, to win the inhabitants to the British cause. The record is that he displayed much tact and judgment. He published an address to the inhabitants in which he said, "We come not to make war upon women and children, but to give them money and relieve their distresses." In another place we have stated the circumstances of his fall at King's Mountain. It seems that Providence assigned to him a sad fate. His talents, patriotism and devotion to his King and superiors were worthy of a better cause.

CAPTAIN ABRAHAM DE PEYSTER was second in command at King's Mountain, and surrendered the army after the fall of Ferguson. He was born in New York in 1753. He descended, it is said, from an ancient and influential family. He entered the Royal service as Captain in the New York Volunteers; served in the seige of Charleston, at Musgrove's Mill and in Ferguson's operations during the summer and autumn of 1780—distinguishing himself at King's Mountain, where his life was saved by a doubloon* in his vest pocket, which stopped a rifle ball, though the coin was bent by its force. He retired on half pay to New Brunswick, where he was treasurer and colonel in the militia, dying about 1798. He is represented as a brave, vigilant and enterprising officer.

COLONEL AMBROSE MILLS, who was captured at King's Mountain and executed at Bickerstaffs, was born in England about 1722, and while yet young, was taken to Maryland. He married Miss Mourning Stone, and first

---

*A Spanish or Portugese coin, of the value of from $15 to $60.
—*Webster*.

settled on James River. Afterwards he removed to the frontiers of South Carolina, where his wife was murdered by the Indians during the Indian War of 1755 to 1761, leaving an only son William. He subsequently married Miss Annie Brown, a native of the present region of Chester, South Carolina, a sister to the wife of Col. Thomas Fletchall, whose character as a Loyalist and whose residence on Fair Forest region has been already mentioned. Colonel Mills by his second marriage had three sons and three daughters. In 1765, he settled on Green River, in the present county of Polk, North Carolina. In 1776, he served against the Cherokee Indians. He appears to have been all right until 1778, when he united with the notorious David Fanning in raising a corps of five hundred men, the object of which was to join the Royal standard at St. Augustine. One of the party betrayed their plans. Mills and sixteen others were apprehended and taken to Salisbury, where they were placed in jail. Fanning with a small party endeavored to rescue him on the way, but their efforts were unavailing. Mills, after a time, was released. He joined Ferguson when he visited his region in 1780. He fought at Earle's Ford and at King's Mountain. "Viewed a century afterwards," says Draper, "he was too severely dealt with at Bickerstaffs." His execution was doubtless, to a great extent, intended as a retaliatory measure. He was, when well advanced in years, at the head of a lawless, plundering and marauding band of Tories, and was by his execution made, in the heat of passion, to suffer for all. In private life there is not a blot on record against his character as a man, or his integrity as a gentleman. In his efforts to repel the Indians in 1776, who were aroused against the whites by the British Agents, Stewart and Cameron, he appears at first to have sided with the patriots.

His descendants are among the ablest and most respectable citizens in the South and Southwest. Allaire in his diary says, in referring to the executions at Bickerstaff's, that "Mills, Chitwood and Wilson died like Romans."

CHAPTER XXVIII.

CORNWALLIS GROWS ALARMED FOR HIS SAFETY AFTER THE OVERTHROW AT KING'S MOUNTAIN.—ABANDONS WHILE AT CHARLOTTE FURTHER INVASION OF NORTH CAROLINA.—RETURNS TO SOUTH CAROLINA AND ESTABLISHES CAMP AT WINNSBORO.—BATTLE OF FISH DAM ON BROAD RIVER.

THE victory and final overthrow of Ferguson at King's Mountain was a great blow to the British interests in the Carolinas. We have already stated that before and during the engagement at that place, Cornwallis was stationed with his army at Charlotte, North Carolina, having marched to that place after his victory over General Gates at Camden, on the 16th of August, 1780. Before leaving the latter place, he left behind him a small force, detachments from which were constantly annoyed by a considerable body of militia from North and South Carolina, under the command of Generals Davidson and Sumter, who took post in the vicinity. Among those who were most successful in intercepting the enemy's foraging parties and convoys, was Major Davie, whose command had been greatly recruited by volunteers from the lower country. It is recorded that notwithstanding the enemy's recent victory in that locality, their position was still one of uneasiness and exposure. The American riflemen would frequently penetrate the British camp and make sure of their object from behind trees. They dared not leave their encampment, even for a few hundred yards.

These deeds of daring and this harrassing of the enemy's forces, as well as the recent victory at King's Mountain, caused Cornwallis to grow alarmed for his safety. Believing he had already subjugated South Carolina to British authoirty, he had commenced the invasion of North Carolina to accomplish the same end. The sudden and unexpected turn of events, however, made him apprehensive lest he might share the fate of his subordinate, Ferguson. His position became the more critical by reason of the fact, that the Loyalists no longer manifested the same zeal to join his standard, and he found himself with a feeble army in the midst of a hostile and a sterile country. Seeing that a forward movement would but further increase the embarrassments that were surrounding him, he resolved to relinquish further invasion of North Carolina, where the public mind was growing more decidedly in favor of the patriot cause, and return to South Carolina. Accordingly he abandoned Charlotte, repassed the Catawba River and took post at Winnsboro, South Carolina. On his way to this place he was annoyed by the Whig forces, who took several of his wagons loaded with stores. It is said that the Whig troopers would ride up singly, within gunshot of his army, and discharge their pieces and make good their escape.

The panic which had been caused by the reduction of the Continental army at Charleston under Lincoln and the defeat of Gates at Camden, began to wear off. The overthrow of Ferguson and the retreat of Cornwallis from Charlotte placed the American situation in a different light. The Whigs hastened in great multitudes to place themselves under the standards of their most daring chiefs, Marion and Sumter. The former scoured the lower, while the latter scoured the upper, portion of South Carolina.

Cornwallis, having taken a stand at Winnsboro, a chain of British posts were established, consisting of Georgetown, Camden, Winnsboro, Ninety-six and Augusta. Within this circle was an interior chain consisting of Fort Watson, on the road to Camden, Mott's House and Granby on the Congaree. Inside of these were Dorchester and Orangeburg, which were fortified as posts of rest and deposit on the lines of communication between the points mentioned. These posts were all judiciously chosen by the British commander, both for covering the country and obtaining supplies from the confiscated and sequestered estates of the Whigs in the vicinity. The total numbers occupying these different points amounted to about five thousand.

Let us go back a few months and examine the state of affairs, just before the changes which we have mentioned. After the battle of Camden, Marion performed the brilliant exploit of recapturing the prisoners taken at Gates' defeat. After this, he was obliged to dismiss a large portion of his followers and retire to his secret hiding place in the almost impenetrable swamps. Sumter also, after the surprise and dispersion of his command at Fishing Creek (in Sumter county), fell back with the wreck of that fatal day, to secure regions in the mountains. But no sooner had Cornwallis turned his face to South Carolina and the American army put in motion, than these brave leaders emerged from their several retreats and renewed their bold and harrassing enter prises against the British forces and their Tory adherents.

To counteract these and and to save his army from ultimate defeat was a matter which doubtless occupied the attention of Cornwallis. Tarleton's former successes against Sumter pointed him out as the proper officer to ferret out and destroy Marion. In this undertaking, however, he was doomed to disappointment. Indeed it may be observed here, that after the affair at Fishing Creek the star of Tarleton began to decline. He never afterwards performed any important services in South Carolina. Marion eluded and baffled all his plans and maneuvers to bring him into action, and remained in possession of the disputed country.

Cornwallis, finding that Tarleton could make no headway against Marion, recalled him to confront his old adversary, now within twenty-eight miles of the British camp at

Winnsboro.* Sumter's forces had considerably increased in numbers, having formed a junction with the commands under Colonels Taylor, Winn, Middleton, Lacy, Bratton, Thomas, Hill and a number of Whigs from Georgia under Colonels Clarke and Twiggs. Being now at the head of an imposing command, he, it appears, lay encamped too long at Fish Dam on Broad River. The daring measure of Sumter in approaching so near the British encampment suggested the enterprise to Cornwallis of surprising him in his camp before the arrival of Tarleton. Such was the importance of securing Sumter in person, that an officer and five dragoons were specially charged to force their way to his tent and take him dead or alive.

The expedition was placed under the command of Colonel Wemyss, who obtained for his guide a young Loyalist whose name was Sealey, who had been discharged from confinement in Sumter's camp the day before and who knew exactly the position of Sumter's tent, which stood beside the main road crossing the encampment. Fortunately, General Sumter was on the alert, having remained in camp so long at this place he was anticipating a surprise. He had given unusual strength to his advance guard, which was placed under the command of Col. Thomas Taylor. In order that he might be able to see the approach of the enemy, Colonel Taylor caused a number of fires to be lighted in his front. At a short distance behind these, his men were arranged and concealed. Sure enough, as expected, the enemy approached. The videttes and pickets did their duty and by the time the enemy's forces had reached the fire-lights, Taylor's men were under arms ready to receive them. They instantly poured a well-directed and murderous fire into their ranks, which prostrated twenty-three of them, including Colonel Wemyss, their commander. The rest immediately recoiled and retreated one hundred yards—in front of the fires—before they

*See Johnson's Life of Greene, Vol. I, page 315.

could be rallied. Here the infantry dismounted and advanced again with fixed bayonets on Taylor's men, who had no bayonets. The latter were ordered to retire and form under the cover of a rail fence in the rear The order was executed with precision. A well directed fire from this position caused the enemy to stagger and draw off. The fact is recorded, singular as it may appear, that at the instant the enemy retreated, Taylor's men that had repelled them, broke and fled also, their flight being concealed by the darkness of the night. But had this been known to the enemy, it would have been of no avail to them, as Sumter's army was already under arms awaiting their approach.

On the morning after this affair, the fact was revealed that the enemy had fled precipitately after the last encounter with Taylor's men. Colonel Wemyss was found next morning shot through both thighs. He had recently returned from an expedition against the Whigs on Black River and the Pee Dee, where he had acted under the orders of Cornwallis. Though it was believed that he had superintended the execution of Mr. Adam Cusack (who was hung) and had in his pocket a memorandum of several houses burned by his command, still he received every consideration as a prisoner of war at the hands of Sumter.

A singular fate happened to Sealey, who guided the British to Sumter's camp at night. He died of a sabre wound inflicted by his own men. It occurred in this way · After conducting the small party that had been selected to penetrate Sumter's tent, he forgot that the presence of the party whom he accompanied was necessary to prevent his being mistaken by his homespun clothing for an American. He thus met the fate that he deserved.

The soldierly conduct of Colonel Taylor was the decisive cause of the repulse of the British in this engagement. Had it not been for the obscurity of the night which rendered it impossible for Sumter's whole command to become engaged, this affair would have been fatal to the British party. Not more than one hundred and fiftv of the Americans were engaged.

The battle at Fish Dam on Broad River, which occurred in the night time, was on the 12th of November, 1780, only one week before the battle of Blackstock's an account of which will be given in the next chapter.

CHAPTER XXIX.

BATTLE OF BLACKSTOCK'S, NOVEMBER 20, 1780.

AT the time of the battle at Fish Dam, which we have just related, and for several days afterwards, Sumter was entirely ignorant of the near approach of Tarleton from the lower country, where the latter had gone in pur suit of Marion. He had. it seems, no apprehension what ever for his own safety, notwithstanding Cornwallis' superiority in infantry. Being unencumbered with bag gage he knew that at any moment he could retreat with superior swiftness. Says a writer,* "his men wanted no covering but the heavens and were satisfied to subsist on the coarsest diet. Provided with their own horses and intimately acquainted with all the roads, streams and recesses of the country, they could move with the speed of the Arab; and when pressed, disperse and retire to to meet again at some place of rendezvous assigned by their commander."

Sumter received information that a large quantitv of provisions for the British army were deposited at Sum mer's Mill, under a small guard, and also that a party of British militia or Tories, were stationed at Captain Faust's, on the waters of (probably) the Enoree. To break up that station and to capture the stores at Summer's Mill was a matter of great importance with Sumter, inasmuch as his men were poorly supplied, not only with food but with every comfort. He detached Col. Thomas Taylor, of South Carolina, and Colonel Candler, of Georgia, with wagons and a small force to proceed at once down the country to Summer's Mill, with orders to get possession of and bring away or destroy the prison-

* See Johnson's Life of Greene, Vol. I, page 317.

ers, as circumstances might require. "At the same time," says Colonel Hammond, "Lieutenant-Colonel Williamson, of Clarke's regiment of Georgia, and Major S. Hammond were detached towards Captain Faust's to attack and if possible break up that station."

It appears that these detachments were ordered, after they had performed the duties assigned them, to rejoin Sumter at Blackstock's, to which point he had decided to move his army. While the detachments were absent and Sumter was on his march from Fish Dam to Blackstock's he received the first intelligence of the near approach of Tarleton. This, it is said, was communicated to him by a Mrs. Dilliard,* who lived on the south side of Enoree River, (now) in Laurens County, and on the route of Tarleton's march to Blackstock's. Tarleton, in his "Campaigns," states that "A woman on horseback had viewed the line of march from a wood near, and by a nearer road had given intelligence" to Sumter. It seems that the latter up to this time had been falling back very leisurely, intending as much as possible, to hang upon the skirts of Cornwallis and hold him in check.

In the biography of Colonel Taylor† it is stated that Taylor discovered the approach of Tarleton about fifteen miles from Blackstock's and sent expresses to inform Sumter of his approach. The latter had, however, already gained intelligence, whether from Mrs. Dilliard or otherwise we are not informed. He halted before he reached Blackstock's, not only to refresh his men but to give Taylor's detachment time to rejoin him. His delay, however, had to be short. It was necessary that he should make as hasty a retreat as possible, in order to throw

*See foot note, Draper's "King's Mountain," page 74. It has been claimed that it was Mrs. Dillard instead of Mrs. Thomas that gave the timely warning of the British advance on Cedar Spring. (See Johnson's Tradition's, page 518). This is a mistake, however, according to the testimony of Major McJunkin (son-in-law of Mrs. Thomas) and others.

†See Johnson's Traditions, page 536.

the rapid Tyger between himself and his adversary. He learned that Tarleton, who was hurrying forward to overtake him, had both cavalry and artillery, and being destitute of both, and having only a short time before been defeated by that officer at Fishing Creek, he fully appreciated the critical situation.

Williamson, who with Colonel Hammond had been sent to surprise and capture the enemy at Captain Faust's, failed in the enterprise in consequence of their hasty removal from that place. He, with his little command, rejoined Sumter the day before the battle at Blackstock's. Sumter, however, was unwilling to beat a hasty retreat across the Tyger before his missing detachment under Taylor and Candler might have time to rejoin him. He was now within a half mile of Blackstock's house and was anxiously awaiting the arrival of this detachment. His suspense was happily removed. Says Colonel Hammond. "the horses and men were fed hastily, the line of march was resumed and when Blackstock's house was in view, our rear videttes fired at the advancing cavalry of the enemy. Colonels Taylor and Candler at this moment, drove in with their wagons loaded with flour, &c., passed our rear guard and entered the open field at Blackstock's.* At the next moment Tarleton's legion charged our rear guard, but Taylor and his escort were safe."

This was indeed a trying hour for Sumter. Tarleton's

*Among the parties who composed Colonel Taylor's detachment was William White, husband of one of the heroines of Mrs. Ellett's "Women of the Revolution," (see vol. iii, page 290). White on this occasion drove a wagon loaded with flour. It appears that the understanding between Taylor and Sumter was for the latter to remain at the place where they parted until Taylor's return. Sumter, hearing that Tarleton was rapidly advancing to attack him, fell back to Blackstock's in order to secure a more advantageous position. Taylor knew nothing of Tarleton's approach and when he returned to the place where he was to rejoin Sumter, not finding him he was not a little displeased. His men being very hungry he allowed two or three hogs to be cleaned and some of the flour made into bread. They were en-

unexpected return had exposed his command to imminent danger. It was impossible for him to make a successful retreat across the river. He must now fight with a vengeance and determination, or suffer his army to be totally destroyed. But the "Game Cock" of the Revolution was not the man to be cowed by the dangers which were about to surround him. Tarleton was in his rear and the river was in his front. He lost not a moment in getting his men in line for action. In the performance of this hurried task, he was ably and actively assisted by Maj. James Jackson, of Georgia, who acted as a volunteer aid and brigade major for his army. In the biographical sketch of Col. Thomas Taylor, already referred to, it is stated that Taylor sent two detachments of his men to watch and retard the approach of Tarleton. The first was ordered to fire on the enemy as soon as they came within gunshot; then to retreat and occupy another hill on Tarleton's route. The second was to do the same, and thus to continue their fire alternately, from one hill top to another. By this means Tarleton was checked at every elevation in the road and Sumter notified of his position and strength. The two detachments sustained each other in their alternate movements. Thus

---

gaged in baking bread, "Johnny Cake" fashion, on a piece of pine bark at the moment when Sergeants Ben Rowan and Ben Hannah, who had been sent out by Sumter to reconoitre, rode up in great haste and informed them that Tarleton was approaching near by. There was a general hurly-burly. The hogs and dough were thrown into the wagon uncooked, and William White drove the wagon at a full gallop until he reached Sumter at Blackstock's. As he turned the corner of a little stable the firing commenced and a ball passed through the sleeve of his hunting shirt. White, as soon as he carried his wagon to the rear, returned with James Wylie to the fight, with three balls in his mouth, to have them ready. While the battle was going on, Wylie partially parried a blow dealt upon a Whig by one of Tartleton's dragoons. A friend near him shot the dragoon and Wylie seized his sword, which he took home with him. Afterwards he presented it to his son Peter, who, when a captain in command of a company, wore it, and years afterwards carried it with him to the Florida war.

was Sumter enabled to choose his position and get his men into line before Tarleton could come up. The men were admonished to keep cool and ordered to reserve their fire until it could be effectual on their foes.

Blackstock's house stood on the southwest bank of Tyger (or Tiger as it is called in some of the old books) River, and near the ford of the same name—the crossing of the old Blackstock road, the location of which has been described in a former chapter. It was with reference to the favorable crossing at this place that Sumter had decided to move with his army. There were at that time no bridges and but few safe fordings on the Tyger. The ground about the Blackstock buildings afforded a position highly favorable for drawing up a small force in order of battle. Botta says that "the position of the Americans was formidably strong; it was covered in front by the river, log houses and palisades, and upon the two flanks by inaccessible mountains or narrow and difficult defiles." * Colonel Hammond, who participated in the battle, states that "in front of the buildings a small branch of the Tyger River passed through the field, margined by small bushes, but not obstructing the view of the British movements from the hill. This water course formed a half moon with its concavity toward the enemy and the ridge corresponded with this shape of the branch. Sumter had the houses filled with his troops, and these with a strong, new fence on each side of the road, afforded a tolerable cover for his men. The rest were posted on the ridge from one hundred to one hundred and fifty yards west of the branch or ravine. In this position the British commander found Sumter when ready to advance upon him. †

In "Johnson's Life of Greene," (page 318), it is stated that Tarleton's command consisted of his legion, a battalion of the 71st and a detachment of the 63d regiments;

* See Botta's "American War," Vol. II, page 311.

† See Johnson's Traditions, page 524.

with a lieutenant's command of Royal artillery and one field piece. Of this force about four hundred were mounted. With these he pressed forward to overtake and retard Sumter before he should have time to cross the river and escape.

Sumter intended only to make a temporary stand. Not doubting but that the whole force of the enemy was upon him, he resolved, as the day was fast declining, to maintain his ground during the day and escape under cover of the night across the Tyger and disperse. It was not long, however, before he discovered that only a part of the British force had come up. He, therefore, very judiciously resolved to commence the attack at once and cut up his enemy in detail. Tarleton, supposing that he had his game bagged, immediately on his arriving secured an elevated piece of ground in front of Sumter's position and across the stream referred to. Here he dismounted his men to rest themselves and horses, and to await the arrival of his artillery and infantry, in order that he might commence the attack with better advantage. Sumter seized this critical moment and began the attack at once. His men descended from the heights and poured in a well-directed fire upon Tarleton's men, who were now compelled to take to their arms at once. Sumter's men were met by the bayonet, and being armed only with rifles were forced to retire. The British advanced, but were met by a reserve of rifles, which brought many of them to the ground and threw the rest in confusion. Tarleton, seeing his danger, made a desperate effort to change the situation by ordering his men to charge directly up the hill. This brought them within close rifle shot of Sumter's men, who stood firm. The British ranks were thinned by the deadly rifle. During this encounter the Blackstock buildings were about one-fourth of a mile or less to the right of the British position and northeast of the same. Tarleton decided to attack this point. Says Johnson, "drawing off his whole corps he then wheeled upon the American left towards Blackstock's house, where the ground was not so precipitious, and a better footing was afforded for the horses. Here the Georgians were posted under Clarke* and Twiggs, and their little corps of about one hundred and fifty men displayed the courage of veterans, but the pressure of Tarleton's whole force was too much for them to withstand, and at this point was gained the only semblance of advantage on the side of the enemy. The left gave way, but the timely interposition of the reserve under Col. Richard Winn, and the enfilading fire from the house in which a company had been posted, soon restored the fortunes of the day, and the officer who in the face of the world had boasted of a victory, actually ran away and was pursued, and as the Americans say, was saved by the darkness of the night." †

Just before this last encounter on the American left, the approach of the British infantry was observed from the American position. General Sumter, says Colonel Hammond, ordered Colonel Clarke to take one hundred good men, pass the enemy's right, then forming in the field and in cover of the woods, attack and cut off, if practicable, the horses there piqueted, and further to attack an armory of the enemy in the rear and divert their attention as much as possible. This order was promptly obeyed by Colonel Clarke and Col. Candler, of Georgia, who just coming in with Colonel Taylor from the Summer's Mill expedition, volunteered on that service, as did also Major Hammond with his command. When the British retreat was finally ordered from before the Blackstock houses, Clarke and Hammond attacked the infantry in the rear and took a part of their horses, but the whole retreating British force coming up they, were com-

*According to Colonel Hammond's account Colonel Clarke was not personally engaged in the last encounter, but had already, in compliance with his orders moved around the enemy's left, to attack the British infantry in the rear.

† See Johnson's Life of Greene, page 319.

pelled to retire, and only carried off a few infantry horses and cut others loose. It was now dark, and Clarke being in doubt as to Sumter's situation, retreated before the British until next morning.* William Gilmore Simms says that "Tarleton fled, leaving two hundred men upon the field of battle."†

Tarleton, in his "Campaigns," asserts that "from the time the left yielded, the Americans began to disperse, and nothing but the approach of night prevented the pursuit." This could not have been, since it is proven beyond a question of doubt, that the Americans possessed themselves of all his wounded and many of his horses. The fact is proven that Tarleton, after his retreat, never halted until he joined the residue of his corps two miles distant. Here he encamped for the night.

The Americans accomplished all they fought for. Being destitute of cavalry and artillery they could not venture from their heights, but they made a safe crossing over the river, after which they, according to a previous understanding, dispersed for security among their friends in different sections. General Sumter was severely wounded in the breast and was taken from the field. The command of his army was then assumed by Colonel Twiggs, of Georgia,‡ who after taking possession of the battlefield and having the rolls called and collecting and caring for the wounded, ordered the little army to take up its line of march and cross over the Tyger River. Here it encamped for the night, to resume its march the following day up (what is now) the old Blackstock road.

Tarleton, who has already been quoted, virtually acknowledges his abandonment of the battlefield by the statement "that before they (the Americans) left the

---

* See Johnson's Traditions, page 525.

† See Simms' "History of South Carolina," page 195.

‡ See Johnson's Traditions, page 525.

ground they paid the most humane attention to the wounded of the enemy."

We have already stated that Clarke, who was plying in Tarleton's rear during the engagement, retreated before his forces until next morning. According to Colonel Hammond's statement he did not extricate himself from this retreat in the dark until he came in sight of the camp fires of an advancing reinforcement to Tarleton. Here he wheeled from the main road, crossed the Tyger River, and rejoined Sumter about noon the next day.

According to the most authentic information the British forces amounted to about four hundred, with three hundred more in the rear with their artillery.* The American forces amounted to about four hundred and twenty, certainly not exceeding five hundred. Colonel Hammond states, however, that Sumter had about five hundred and sixty men in this action, exclusive of the main and horse guards. About forty of this number are reported to have run away and were over the Tyger River before the battle ended.†

The American account of the British loss in this engagement is killed ninety-two, and wounded one hundred. Tarleton, however, only acknowledges a loss of about fifty. Among the prominent killed on the British side were Major Money and Lieutenants Gibson and Cope.‡ Ramsay states "that the British loss was considerable." They never reached the American lines with the bayonet on account of the elevated position of the latter. The British soldiers fired over the heads of their enemy. The American loss was very slight, only three killed and three wounded. Among the latter was Colonel Sumter, as already noticed. Colonel Clarke with his isolated force,

---

* See Johnson's Life of Greene, page 320.

† See Johnson's Traditions, page 526.

‡ See Ramsey's History of South Carolina, page 221.

had only two men killed and a few wounded, but not badly—they were taken off in safety.

Colonel Tarleton in his narrative states, that he cut up the American rear-guard and carried off fifty prisoners. This is explained in Johnson's "Life of Greene" as follows: Colonel Thomas Taylor, in the expedition already referred to, "having made prisoners of a few maimed men and boys driving carriages and supposed to have passed through the enemy's camp, or to be able otherwise to convey intelligence, he had them loaded with provisions (doubtless, those captured at Summer's Mill) and was proceeding with them to rejoin Sumter when he found himself pursued by a party of dragoons. Taylor's party escaped easily by the fleetness of their horses, but the prisoners were left behind, and as the British dragoons passed these unhappy wretches in pursuit of Taylor, they amused themselves with hewing them down from their horses. This was the rear-guard that was 'cut to pieces.' As to the fifty prisoners, the high-minded colonel had read of the triumphs of a Roman Emperor over the ocean, and had gathered on his return a few unarmed rustics, many of them Loyalists, to grace his entry into camp."

Sumter's wound was very severe, the ball passing through the right breast near the shoulder. He was carried on an uncomfortable litter, continuing with his troops until the latter passed Burwick's Iron Works. Here the command was divided. Sumter, suspended between two horses and guarded by one hundred faithful followers, was conveyed to the mountains of North Carolina. Twiggs, Clarke, Candler and their persevering Georgians turned westward, taking their course along the foot of the mountains to annoy the enemy in another quarter. The rest of Sumter's force separating into small parties retired to places of security, ready to reassemble whenever their country's service required it.

The writer is informed by Capt. Charles A. Barry that Sumter's principal scout at Blackstock's and other places was Robin Hanna, of York County, who married a daughter of Charles Moore, of Spartanburg County.

The battle of Blackstock's was fought while General Gates was still commanding the Department of the South, his headquarters being at this time at Charlotte, North Carolina. He was relieved only a few days afterwards by General Greene. Sumter appears to have acted entirely independent of the orders of Gates, and history gives the latter no credit whatever, for the brilliant achievements of the former.

GENERAL THOMAS SUMTER,

the "hero of Blackstocks" and other hard fought contests, was born in 1734. History does not state where he was born, but a native of Sumter County informed the writer that he was born in Caldwell County, North Carolina, near the foot of the Blue Ridge Mountains. Nothing can now be obtained of his family connections, early training or education. His name is spelled *Sumpter* by Judge Johnson and other older writers of Revolutionary history.

Governor Perry, in his sketch of General Sumter, says that he was a farmer and planter, and that his early education was limited.

Before the Revolutionary war he was colonel of a military regiment. As the population of the country was rather sparse in his day, the military districts covered a considerable space of country. It was in this way that Sumter first acquired his military reputation. The Provincial Congress of South Carolina appointed him, in 1776, lieutenant-colonel of the second regiment of riflemen. He does not figure prominently in the State, however, until after the fall of Charleston, in 1780, when the State was overrun by the British troops. It was then that Sumter, Marion and a few other brave partisans took the field, while others equally as patriotic, seeing at that time no hope for the recovery of South Carolina from the royal grasp, sought British protection. Colonel Sumter, being compelled to leave the State, fled to North Carolina, where he raised a regiment of rebels and returned to South Carolina. Soon after his return, he destroyed Captain Huck, who commanded a large body of Loyalists, and seventy or eighty British regulars. For this gallant service he was made, by Governor Rutledge, a brigadier general. His command amounted to about six hundred men. With this force he made a daring attack on the British post, at Rocky Mount, but, having no artillery, failed to capture the fort. His next daring exploit was on the enemy's position at Hanging Rock, in the present county of Lancaster. The British garrison there consisted of five or six hundred regulars, a part of Tarleton's legion, Brown's regiment, and Bryan's corps of North Carolina Tories. He succeeded at first in driving the enemy back, but his men became demoralized by reason of the plunder and spirits they had found in the British camp. The enemy took advantage of this and attacked Sumter. He made a successful retreat. The enemy did not pursue him. His loss was very small, while that of his enemy was considerable.

We have already explained that Camden and Ninety-Six were among the most important of the British's outposts during the Revolution. General Sumter, hearing that a detachment of the British forces were on their march from Ninety-Six to Camden, fell upon a convoy and captured forty-four wagons with a large number of prisoners.

Men of military renown, however, mav not always expect their efforts to be crowned with success. The most vigilant are now and then caught "napping." Sumter was surprised at Fishing Creek and defeated. After this defeat he retired to the upper country, where he recruited his command. His next engagement was at Fish Dam, on Broad River, which was followed in a few days by the battle of Blackstock's. Both of these engagements are recorded in this and the preceding chapter.

After the Revolution, General Sumter served in the Legislature of South Carolina, and voted against the call of a convention to ratify the Federal Constitution. Being elected to the convention he voted against the adoption of the Constitution.

When the Federal Government was first organized he was elected a member of Congress. In a speech of some mark he urged that the Federal Government be established on the banks of the Potomac. He was opposed to the granting of power to the President to remove members of his cabinet. Said that it was "a detestable principle, destructive to the Constitution and to liberty." In 1792, he made a strong speech against the reflections cast on the militia of South Carolina by General Greene, and in 1793 he made another speech on the same subject, being very severe on his colleague, Mr. Robert Goodloe.

In 1801, General Sumter succeeded Governor Charles Pinckney in the United States Senate, who had resigned. He was re-elected in 1805, and served that body until 1810, when he was succeeded by Governor John Taylor. This was the last service he rendered to his country. He died in 1832, at the advanced age of ninety-eight years. His biographer says that "he was tall and robust, with a bold and open countenance, expressive at once of energy and decision."

General Sumter was a bold and determined man. During the Revolution he did not scruple to do whatever he thought the emergency of the times demanded. He pressed for his destitute army, horses, provision, clothing and whatever they needed, wherever and whenever he could find them. It is charged that he paid off his officers and men with negroes, horses and cattle, taken from the Tories. By his boldness he acquired the sobriquet of "the Game Cock of Carolina."

General Sumter had two sons, both of whom were members of Congress. One it is said had some foreign mission and married a French lady. The other commanded a company in the regiment of General Butler, in Mexico. One of his grandsons was also a member of

Congress about 1832, and was a great "fire-eater."

General Sumter, it is stated, lies in a neglected and forgotten grave. His memory and noble deeds will, however, live in spite of this.

COLONEL RICHARD WINN.

In referring to the prominent heroes of the battle of Blackstock's it would be unfair to fail to notice the services of Colonel (afterwards General) Winn. Richard Winn, who resided in Fairfield County, South Carolina, was a native of Virginia. He was commissioned first lieutenant of the South Rangers in June, 1775, and served in Thompson's campaign, in the winter of this year against the Insurgents or Tories, an account of which is given elsewhere. He was one of the party who captured Colonel Fletchall in the hollow tree, on the banks of Fair Forest, in the present County of Spartanburg.* He was with Thompson on Sullivan's Island and performed distinguished services in the battle of Fort Sullivan (afterwards Fort Moultrie). He afterwards defended Fort McIntosh, on the north side of Satilla, but after gallantly defending this post for three days against Major-General Duval, he was compelled to capitulate.

Returning to his home in Fairfield he raised a regiment of refugees and was very soon in the field. At the battle of Hanging Rock the British regulars under Colonel Fraser were defeated, which was largely due to his conduct and courage. In this battle he was severely wounded and borne from the field.

Upon his recovery, Colonel Winn continued to render valuable aid to General Sumter, participating, as we have already said, in the battle of Blackstock's.

We are unable to state in full his valuable services to the State during the Revolution. He acted in concert with such immortal heroes as William Butler, Col. William Bratton, of York County, Captain McClure, of Chester,

---

* See Johnson's Traditions, page 334; also Drayton's Memoirs.

and many others during that time. After peace he was elected Brigadier-General by the Legislature and subsequently Major-General. He filled various civil offices in the State, and was for several years a member of Congress. In 1812 he removed to Tennessee and died shortly afterwards. The present town of Winnsboro was named in honor of his memory.

He was an uncle of the late Dr. John Winsmith and Elihu Smith, of Spartanburg County.

CHAPTER XXX.

GENERAL GREENE RELIEVES GENERAL GATES AND ASSUMES COMMAND OF THE SOUTHERN DEPARTMENT. CONDITION, NUMBERS, &c., OF THE SOUTHERN ARMY.—THE ARMY IS DIVIDED.—GENERAL DANIEL MORGAN ASSUMES COMMAND OF ALL FORCES IN UPPER SOUTH CAROLINA.—GENERAL GATES RETURNS HOME.

ON the 5th day of October, 1780, Congress passed a resolution, authorizing General Washington to appoint an officer to the command of the Southern army, in place of General Gates, until a Court of Inquiry could be held as to the conduct of the latter. In compliance with this order, General Washington appointed Gen. Nathaniel Greene, on the 22d of the month referred to. Soon after this, General Greene repaired to Philadelphia to inform himself of the force and condition of the Southern army, and to make such arrangements for its present and future wants as were necessary.

The information thus gained by General Greene was anything but encouraging. To General Knox, he wrote that the Southern armv was "rather a shadow than a substance, having only an imaginary existence."* On the fatal day of Gates' recent defeat, horses, baggage, stores and everything had gone by the board. General Greene received but little aid from Congress. The only support was the annexing of Delaware and Maryland to his department. He was barely furnished with enough money to bear the expenses of the journey. Governor Reed, of Pennsylvania, however, supplied him with arms from the depot of that State, and even with wagons to convey them. Liberal promises were made him from the depart-

* See original order, "Johnson's Life of Greene."

ments of each of the several States. The same power was conferred on him by Congress as on General Gates to draw from the States in his department men and money and to make impressments for the subsistence of the troops whenever necessity required it.

On the 23d of November, General Greene set out upon his journey to the South, accompanied by Baron Steuben and two of his aids, Colonel Morris and Major Burnet. His journey was only interrupted by a short halt at the seat of government of each State for the purpose of investigating their resources. On his way he arranged to have established, at different points, magazines and depots of stores and arms.

On the 4th dav of December, General Greene reached the headquarters of General Gates at Charlotte, and took command of the army. He conducted himself with great delicacy toward his unfortunate predecessor, using every effort to console his feelings and preserve respect for him in the minds of the army. It was impossible at this time, to hold the Court of Inquiry into the conduct of General Gates at Camden, as ordered by Congress, because there were not enough Generals and field officers in the army, not present at the battle of Camden, to constitute the court. Those who were in that battle would have been needed as witnesses and if not, would, perhaps, from their personal knowledge of the facts, have been one-sided in their verdict. Besides, General Gates had recently lost an only son, and the present state of his feelings disqualified him from entering upon the task of defense. It was rather regarded as a case of misfortune than otherwise. The order of Congress was subsequently revoked.

The first cheering event that took place, after Greene assumed command, was the capture of Rugley's command at Clermont, by Col. William Washington. Nearly everv school boy, in ante-bellum days, has read the story and seen the picture of a pine log mounted on wagon wheels in imitation of a field piece. A number of prisoners, a good supply of refreshments and munitions of war was the result of this successful enterprise.

The army, when General Greene assumed command, did not amount to more than eleven hundred regulars in all, and they were so ragged that not more than eight hundred could be mustered for duty. Such was the naked condition of Colonel Washington's command, that it was ordered, for a time, to Virginia. General Greene at once devoted himself to the duty of obtaining every means of subsistence for the army. The country around him was so poor that supplies could not be obtained for more than a week longer, and subsistence could not be brought from a distance for want of transportation. It was necessary, therefore, that he move his army to another section of the country. The region selected was on the Pee Dee River. This was at the head of boat navigation. It was a very fertile country and had never been visited by an army of any size. General Kosciusko was dispatched with a single guide to examine the country and select a position. Greene, in the meanwhile, gave attention to a plan for combining the commissariat and quartermaster generals' departments throughout the country. At the head of these was placed Major Davie, who entered at once upon the duties of his office.

While these arrangements were being made, General Greene received the intelligence of the departure of the British General, Leslie, from the Chesapeake Bay, and also of a large embarkation of troops from New York. The destination of these were not known, but it was believed to be either for Charleston or Norfolk. Greene fully realized the situation. If the destination was Charleston, he was in danger of the torrent that would press from this place northwardly. If from Norfolk, he was still in danger of being cut off from his resources in Virginia, and possibly of being hemmed and crushed between this army and the force under Cornwallis, at this time at Winnsboro, S. C. In any event, it was evident that North Carolina was to become the scene of future hostilities in the South, and it was absolutely necessary that General Greene should combine all the resources within his reach, so as to act with a full knowledge of the means of subsistence and transportation which every section could furnish him.

On the 20th of December, General Greene's army left their huts at Charlotte, for their destination on the Pee Dee. On the march they were commanded by General Isaac Huger. The main army reached their encampment on the 26th of the same month, and were soon afterwards joined by their commander.

But as our narrative is only intended to be confined to the military operations in the upper portion of South Carolina, we must now leave General Greene, to direct our attention to other qarters.

We now introduce to our readers, General Daniel Morgan, who was destined to control military operations of the American forces in the upper part of South Carolina. It has been stated in "Botta's American War," (vol. ii, page 312) that General Greene was accompanied by Colonel Morgan when he came South. This is a mistake.* General Morgan reached the camp of General Gates, then at Hillsborough, N. C., more than two months earlier than General Greene. General Morgan had reaped a rich harvest of laurels at Quebec and Saratoga. He brought a few young men with him, emulous to serve under him. Although General Gates had neglected to officially notice the distinguished services of Arnold and Morgan in his report of the battle of Saratoga, he now, in the hour of his misfortune, paid to General Morgan every attention due to him. Immediateiy on his arrival, Gates ordered four companies to be drafted from the different regiments composing his army, and to be equipped as light infantry. These were to form a partisan corps to serve under Morgan. Colonel Washington's cavalry,

---

* See "Johnson's Life of Greene," Vol. I.

composed of about seventy men, was also added to Morgan's command, to which was also added a small corps of riflemen, about sixty in number, under the leadership of Major Rose. General Gates was also enabled to furnish Morgan's command with a good supply of clothing which had been recently provided by the Government of North Carolina.

When General Greene reached the army of General Gates at Charlotte, the latter had only recently advanced from Hillsborough. Morgan, with his command, had marched a day ahead of the main army and passing onward, had taken post in the neighborhood of Camden, S. C., and occupied the ground which was the scene of General Gates' disaster, on the 16th of August. He was here when General Greene assumed command of the Southern department and in due time received from the new commander, the following letter: *

General Morgan, soon after the receipt of this letter from General Greene, set out upon his mission. The route he pursued led him across the Catawba at Biggins' Ferry, below the mouth of Little Catawba, and across the Broad River above the mouth of Pacolet. On the banks of the Pacolet he took position, on the 25th of December, and was soon after joined by 220 mounted militia from North and South Carolina.

In Bottas' "American War" it is stated that General Greene was blamed by many military critics for dividing his army into two military forces so far apart; that had

---

* "CAMP CHARLOTTE, Dec. 16, 1780.

"You are hereby appointed to the command of a corps of light infantry of three hundred and twenty men detached from the Maryland line, a detachment of Virginia militia of two hundred men and Colonel Washington's regiment of light horse, amounting to from sixty to one hundred men. With these troops you will proceed to the west side of the Catawba River, where you will be joined by a body of volunteer militia, under the command of General Davidson of this State, and by the militia lately under the command of General Sumter. This force and such others as may join you from Georgia, you will employ against the enemy on the west side of the Catawba, either

the British pushed rapidly forward, they might have thrown themselves between the corps of Greene and Morgan and crushed both without difficulty.

In explanation of this, we quote the following summary, which was gathered from General Greene's correspondence as communicated to friends from time to time: "I am here," said the General, "in my camp of repose, improving the discipline and spirits of my men, and the opportunity for looking about me. I am well satisfied with the movement, for it has answered thus far, all the purposes for which I intended it. It makes the most of my inferior force, for it compels my adversary to divide his and holds him in doubt as to his own line of conduct. He cannot leave Morgan behind him to come at me, or his posts at Ninety-Six or Augusta would be exposed. And he cannot chase Morgan far, or prosecute his views upon Virginia while I am here with the whole country open before me. I am as near Charleston as he is, and as near Hillsborough as I was at Charlotte, so that I am in no danger of being cut off from my reinforcements while an uncertainty as to my future designs has made it necessary to leave a large detachment of the enemy's late reinforcements in Charleston," &c.

General Gates, as soon as he was relieved by General Greene, turned his steps northward. It is due to him to state that while encamped at Charlotte, he applied himself with zeal in reorganizing, re-equipping and reinforcing his army for the coming campaign.

The season at that time was too bad, in his judgment,

---

offensively or defensively as your own prudence and discretion may direct—acting with caution and avoiding surprises by every possible precaution. For the present I give you entire command of that quarter, and do hereby require all officers and soldiers engaged in the American cause to be subject to your orders and command.

"The object of this department is to give protection to that part of the country and spirit up the people, to annoy the enemy in that quarter, to collect the provisions and forage out of their way, which you will have formed into a number of small magazines in the rear of the position you may think proper to take. You will prevent plunder-

to renew hostilities, although it will be noticed that General Greene began military operations within fifteen days after his arrival. It appeared from the renewed energies of General Gates, that fortune was about to smile upon him anew, when General Greene arrived at camp. "He evinced," says a writer, "in this conjuncture, that country was dearer to him than power or glory. He supported so unpleasant an incident with such constancy that he did not betray a single mark of discontent." When he passed through Richmond on returning to his own province, the Assembly of Virginia sent a deputation to compliment him. It gave him assurance that the remembrance of his glorious achievements could not be effaced by any misfortune; praying him to be persuaded that the Virginians in particular, would never neglect any occasion to manifest the gratitude they bore him, as members of the American Union.

The military career of Gen. Horatio Gates, however, was ended. A biographical sketch of him appears in one of the volumes of "Washington and his Generals," prepared by the eminent writer, J. T. Headley. His traits of character are very unfavorably commented upon by this writer. In a short time after his success at Saratoga, he was associated with Conway and Mifflin in a miserable conspiracy to have General Washington superceded by himself as Commander-in-Chief of the American armies. He neglected, as we have said, to notice Arnold and

---

ing as much as possible, and be as careful of your provisions and forage as may be, and giving receipts for whatever you take, to all such as are friends to the Independence of America.

"Should the enemy move in force towards the Pee Dee, where the army will take a position, you will move in such a direction as to enable you to join me if necessary, or fall upon the flank or into the rear of the enemy, as occasion may require. You will spare no pains to get intelligence of the enemy's situation, and keep me constantly advised of both your and their movements. You will appoint for the time being, a commissary, a quarter master and a forage master, who will follow your instructions in their respective lines. Confiding in your abilities and activity, I entrust you with this command, persuaded, &c."

Morgan in his official report of the capture of Burgoyne and his army.

His military glory and renown were of short duration, being overshadowed by his Southern misfortunes. To use the phrase as expressed by another, his "Northern laurels were turned into southern willows."

CHAPTER XXXI

THE WHIGS IN SOUTH CAROLINA THROW OFF BRITISH PROTECTION AND RALLY UNDER COLONEL ANDREW PICKENS.—COLONEL WASHINGTON ATTACKS AND REPULSES A BODY OF LOYALISTS AT HAMMOND'S STORE.—MORGAN'S PERMANENT STAND ON THE PACOLET ALARMS CORNWALLIS FOR THE SAFETY OF NINETY-SIX.—HE DETACHES TARLETON TO PUSH HIS ADVERSARY TO THE UTMOST.—MORGAN'S REASONS FOR FIGHTING.—TARLETON AND CORNWALLIS AGREE TO MARCH PARALLEL TO EACH OTHER, THE FORMER ON THE WEST SIDE, THE LATTER ON THE EAST SIDE OF BROAD RIVER.—CORNWALLIS' FAILURE TO MOVE AND REASONS THEREFOR.

IN the preceding chapter we left General Morgan on the banks of the Pacolet, where as already stated, he took post on the 25th of December, 1780. The state of affairs in upper South Carolina at this time were such as made the entrance of General Morgan and his army into this section highly favorable to the success of the American cause. It will be remembered that after the fall of Charleston, the Whigs had been obliged to submit and give their paroles to remain inactive in South Carolina by the official proclamation of the British authorities, they having been declared subjugated. The Whigs became convinced by the oppression and arbitrary conduct of the enemy that the promised protection to themselves, their families and property, already disregarded would not be longer afforded. There was a general inclination to resume arms once more. A leader was all that was necessary to arouse them to action. That person proved to be Gen. Andrew Pickens, who, among the rest of the Whigs in South Carolina, had been compelled to submit.

But now the time had come when submission and forbearance "ceased to be a virtue." Buckling on the sword, General Pickens resolved to lead the way in exciting the well affected to the American cause to hazard all and rally once more in defense of Liberty. His boldness and determination to resist British oppression and outrage, soon brought to his side Colonels Clarke and Twiggs, who after the battle of Blackstock's had kept together a small body of their followers, and moving in rear of the Whig settlements towards Georgia, present l a favorable opportunity to the inhabitants to unite with their commands.

General Pickens and Colonel McCall were soon at the head of about one hundred faithful followers. Sending their families and slaves over the mountains for security, to they proceeded at once to join Morgan. Hundreds of others were ready to follow their example and had only been waiting a favorable opportunity to effect their purpose. The Whigs of Mecklenburg, North Carolina, had also begun to assemble and General Davidson, having collected about one hundred and twenty men, marched them to Morgan's camp. Returning to hasten on five hundred more who were collecting, this gallant officer lost the opportunity of participating in the battle of Cowpens.

On the second day after Morgan's arrival on the Pacolet, an opportunity for an enterprise against the enemy presented itself, which was promptly embraced. A body of Loyalists sent to check the feeling of disaffection which was growing everywhere, had advanced from the banks of the Savannah to Fair Forest Creek, and had commenced their depredations upon the inhabitants along that stream. Their number was reported to be about two hundred and fifty, and their distance from Morgan's camp was twenty-five miles, and in the direction of Ninety-Six. Says a writer, "Colonel Washington with his cavalry, seventy-five in number, but of very superior quality, and two hundred mounted militia under

Colonel McCall, were dispatched to dislodge this body of Loyalists. The latter receiving intelligence of the approach of Washington, retreated about twenty-five miles to a place called Hammond's Store, where, being covered as they supposed on their right by Cornwallis at Winnsborough, and on their left by the post at Ninety-Six, they halted in mistaken security. Washington pressed the pursuit with such diligence that he overtook them early the next day after a march of forty miles and instantly ordered a charge. It was a flight and not a conflict that ensued, and we regret to state that the killed and wounded were reported at one hundred and fifty and the prisoners at forty.

Such were the bloody sacrifices at that time offered upon the shrine of civil discord. Posterity will never conceive an adequate idea of the dreadful state of society then prevailing in that unhappy country. Yet let not unmerited censure fall on the officers. Men who had been in the habit of giving no quarters expected none, and in their flight the unerring rifle brought many to the ground.

Colonel Washington was now in great danger, having advanced very far between the enemy's posts, yet he could not let a favorable opportunity which was at hand escape him, though it brought him still nearer the enemy. At a place called Williams, General Cunningham was at this time posted with about one hundred and fifty men in a stockade fort, which without the aid of artillery, could only be carried by surprise. To this place Colonel Hayes, at the head of a detachment of infantry, and Cornet Simmons, at the head of a body of cavalry, were sent. Cunningham got wind of their approach, however, and made a precipitate retreat as the Americans came in view of the fort. A few of the British party were killed, others captured and the fort destroyed.

General Morgan, hearing that Colonel Washington had penetrated so far between the enemy's posts, became somewhat excited for his safety. He advanced his whole force for some miles to cover and protect him on his return to camp. Colonel Washington's detachment reached the main army, however, in safety. General Morgan resumed his post on the north bank of the Pacolet, in the neighborhood of Grindel Shoals, in Union County,* shifting his camp every night to guard against surprise.

Morgan's advance and Washington's daring enterprise and their effects upon popular sentiment soon began to be sensibly felt by Lord Cornwallis and the British authorities. It has been suggested that the reason for not adopting at once stringent measures to drive back Morgan, or destroy him, was for the purpose, as the sequel proved, of entrapping him. As soon, however, as it appeared that he had permanently established himself on the banks of the Pacolet with a view of embodying the neighboring Whigs preparatory to important movements in the future, Lieutenant-Colonel Tarleton was dispatched by Cornwallis with orders, as he expressed himself, "to push Morgan to the utmost."

At the time General Greene divided his army on his advance into South Carolina, Cornwallis had been for sometime preparing to prosecute his designs upon Virgina. This officer, who had recently arrived at Charleston with his army, was now on his way to Camden, at which point his Lordship informs us he intended to hold Greene in check and observe his future movements. Cornwallis, however, was expecting reinforcements from Leslie upon the arrival of which depended his getting ready to march upon Virginia. But the unexpected arrival of Morgan on the banks of the Pacolet and upon his flank caused him to change his plans. His future movements now depended upon those of his adversary. The posts at Ninety-Six and Camden were the British strongholds and had kept South Carolina in awe, and while Morgan's movements threatened the former the

* The precise place of Morgan's camp is said to be where the present residence of Mrs. Dr. Thomas Littlejohn now stands.

position of Greene was looking towards the latter. This being the case, Cornwallis became uneasy for his safety. He had intended to leave these places to their own protection and to the Loyalists of the surrounding country. These places were well supplied with munitions, provisions, &c.

Lord Cornwallis therefore determined to divide his force, one detachment under Tarleton to press forward and destroy Morgan, or drive him out of the State, while he with the remainder of his force was to move forward and cut off his retreat. Leslie, who had not yet united with him, was directed to march up the east side of the Catawba River to effectuallv prevent Greene from going in case of necessity to Morgan's support. We will see further on that all this well arranged plan was interrupted by the unexpected battle of Cowpens. Cornwallis' army at this time amounted to between three and four thousand, some of whom were well trained and disciplined. It lay between the Broad and Catawba Rivers, the main body with Cornwallis being at Winnsborough while Tarleton was posted a short distance in advance, having lately returned from the pursuit of Sumter to Blackstock's.

Morgan's advance to the Pacolet, as already stated, greatly excited the fears of Cornwallis for the safety of Ninety-Six. He had already heard that the Whigs in that and other sections, who had taken British protection, were rallying under Pickens and others to take the field against him. On the first of January, Tarleton received orders from the British commander to strike across the country and throw himself between Morgan and the post at Ninety-Six. Here he remained for a day or two, when he was joined by his baggage and reinforcements. His whole force now amounted to about eleven hundred men, five hundred and fifty of whom were a strong legion, who had met with unvarying success in every part of the State, triumphing over all bodies of troops they had encountered. He had two field pieces, which were supported by a detachment of Royal artillery. The residue of his army was composed of the seventh regiment of two hundred men, the first battalion and the light infantry of the seventy-first, the dragoons of the seventeenth, and some Loyalists.

With this force he was now prepared to obey the orders of his commander, "to push his adversary to the utmost." It had been concerted between Cornwallis and Tarleton that the former was to move northwardly on the east side of Broad River, (through the present County of York), as far as King's Mountain, in order to cut off the retreat of Morgan, who, it was believed, would be compelled to surrender or retreat hastily across the mountains. Morgan's bold stand and resolution to fight does not seem to have entered the minds of either Cornwallis or Tarleton.

On the 12th of January Tarleton marched to attack Morgan. The latter, hearing that he had already crossed the Enoree, at Musgrove's Mill, fell back to Burr's Mills on Thickety Creek, where he wrote to Greene, the letter bearing the date January 15th.* It was at this time, as we will show further on, entirely within the power of Morgan to have evaded an engagement with Tarleton. Lee, in his Memoirs, states that Morgan's decision to fight him "grew out of irritation of temper." This was not the case, however. The letter referred to furnished ample reasons which induced him to fight. Sumter, refusing to recognize his authority, had interfered with his collecting his magazines in the rear, which would have been indis-

---

*See copy of original letter, Johnson's "Life of Greene," vol. 2, page 371. The writer has been at a loss to know just where stood the old site of Burr's Mills on Thickety Creek. Some of the older citizens think it was the old Boise or Bise Mill, which stood on Little Thickety, a short distance above the Air Line Railroad, at the crossing of the Green River road. It was afterwards known as Otterson's Mill. Later as the Garrison or "Apple Jack" Turner Mill. Others think Burr's Mill stood on Big Thickety, near the site of the Dawkin's Mill, in upper Union County.

spensable to a rapid retreat to the mountains. The vast consumption of forage, necessary for the militia horses, made it impossible for him to maintain his present position; to return without a battle before the enemy would be injurious to the American cause, and especially so since Tarleton's forces were numerically speaking very little superior to his own. On account of Colonel Washington's recent success against the Loyalists at Hammond's Store, Morgan's men were clamorous to be led against Tarleton. Morgan accordingly marched with his army from Burr's Mills on the afternoon of the 15th, and reached the banks of the Pacolet at Grindel Shoals. in Union County, about the same hour that Tarleton arrived from the opposite side. The latter did not leave Morgan long to deliberate. The Pacolet is a small stream and fordable in many places. On the same evening Tarleton put his army in motion up the stream,* thus indicating an intention of crossing above Morgan's position and placing the latter between himself and Cornwallis. Morgan, for fear of being entrapped, made a corresponding movement up the stream. Tarleton detecting this, silently decamped in the night, descended to a crossing at Easterling's Ford, a few miles below, and made good the passage of the river before daylight on the morning of the sixteenth. Morgan had in the meanwhile moved off precipitately, regaining before night his former position on Thickety Creek, and by nightfall his position at Cowpens. Tarleton halted and encamped for the night on the ground that the Americans had abandoned, resuming his march at three o'clock on the morning of the seventeenth, intending to overtake Morgan and embarrass his progress by hanging upon his rear until he could form a junction with the main army under Cornwallis. Tarleton had been on the march five hours when

---

* Morgan in his official account states that his scouts followed close behind Tarleton in his movements and kept him well posted.

he came in sight of Morgan drawn up in line of battle at the Cowpens, at eight o'clock in the morning.

Up to this time Tarleton had been laboring under the impression that Cornwallis was making a parallel movement to his on the east side of Broad River. It had been concerted, as already intimated, between these officers that Cornwallis should commence his march a few days before Tarleton; that by marching on the east side of Broad as far as King's Mountain, Morgan would be cut off from retreat and compelled to fight or surrender, or, as we have said, to flee across the mountains for safety.

It turned out, however, that Cornwallis failed to make the contemplated corresponding movement, without having notified Tarleton of his change of plans. The reasons assigned for what appeared to be a neglect of duty on the part of Cornwallis may be summed up as follows: The force remaining with him did not, according to his account, much exceed that detached under Tarleton; and second, the expected reinforcements under Leslie, which were ordered to cross from the east side of the Catawba River and join him on his route to King's Mountain had not yet arrived. Had General Leslie with his cammand marched directly from Charleston via the Congaree, he would have been up with Cornwallis. Instead of this, however, his route lay by Camden, where he was expected to counteract any movement that General Greene might make from the Pee Dee. In his march to Cornwallis, Leslie consumed several days in the swamps and on the 16th (the day before the battle of Cowpens) Cornwallis had advanced no further than Turkey Creek, (in York County). twenty-five miles southeast of Morgan's position at Cowpens. Had he pressed as many miles northeast he might have prevented the junction of Greene and Morgan, which took place a few days later.

But may there not have been other reasons why Cornwallis did not boldly advance to cover Morgan's flank, and, if possible, to cut off his retreat. We have stated that his route lay by the ominous King's Mountain.

Did he not have some reason to fear that the same over-mountain warriors that had overtaken and destroyed Ferguson at this place, only a few months before, might, like a fire burst from earth as it were, fall upon and destroy him. The truth about it is that Cornwallis was not rash but deliberate. He knew the dangers that were about to entrap him. He knew that the reinforcements which were constantly flocking in upon Morgan, might cause him to have the audacity to strike at the army before Leslie's reinforcements should come up, and he knew further, that the Whigs of Mecklenburg were embodying under Colonel Davidson and that he might be confronted by these, which would make his position perilous, as General Greene and his army were only about one hundred miles on his right. His conclusion was wisely made, for the official correspondence of the day proves that Greene contemplated striking at both Cornwallis and Leslie's corps in their detached and divided situations.

With these observations, let us, in the succeeding chapter present the details of the battle which was the begin ning of series of events which culminated in the surrender of Cornwallis at Yorktown.

CHAPTER XXXII.

BATTLE OF COWPENS, JANUARY 17, 1781.

DURING the trying times of the Revolution in Upper South Carolina and at the particular period which we have just mentioned, no military event took place which appeared to be more peculiarly the subject of a special Providence than the battle and victory at Cowpens. Had religion, poetry, oratory and all the sacred and refined influences combined and concurred in addressing the Supreme Being as the God of battles, for a victory for the American arms, a more satisfactory answer and result could not have been brought about. Certain it is, that it must have been the interposition of Providence, since General Morgan has been severely censured for his choice of ground and for risking a battle under what appeared to be the most adverse circumstances. At that time an open woodland, possessing nothing to recommend it but a trifling elevation, and Broad River winding around his left and parallel to his rear at a distance of about five miles, so as to cut off all retreat in case of misfortune, the ground selected by Morgan to meet his adversary presented little or no advantages in his favor. Charged with irritation of temper, extraordinary indiscretion and imprudence in leaving his wings exposed to a superior cavalry and a more numerous infantry, we find the following paragraph on record as written by Morgan himself, which is but a brief justification of the extraordinary boldness and originality of design which he displayed in his determination to engage his adversary: "I would not," said the General, "have had a swamp in the view of my militia for any consideration. They would have made for it, and nothing could have detained them from it. As to covering my wings, I knew my adversary and was perfectly sure I should have nothing but downright fighting. As to retreat, it was the very thing I wished to cut off all hope of. I would have thanked Tarleton had he surrounded me with his cavalry. It would have been better than placing my own men in the rear to shoot down all those who broke from the ranks. When men are forced to fight, they will sell their lives dearly, and I knew that the dread of Tarleton's cavalry would give due weight to the protection of my bayonets and keep my troops from breaking, as Buford's regiment did. Had I crossed the river, one-half of the militia would immediately have abandoned me."

If we will inquire into all the facts, we will see that there was an imperative necessity for Morgan to fight at Cowpens. It has already been stated that Tarleton occupied the ground abandoned by Morgan on the morning of the 16th. This made the distance between them only about twelve or fifteen miles. Further, the British dragoons had been hanging upon Morgan's rear during the day of the 16th, for the purpose of impeding his march, and Morgan knew that the moment he decamped at Cowpens, intelligence would at once be communicated to the British commander, and the forces of the latter would at once be set in motion to overtake him. This, probably, would have been done before he was clearly over the river, and his troops, fatigued and dispirited by retreat and desertions, under the disadvantages of forming in the face of a superior enemy on ground chosen by the latter, might have behaved very differently from what they did under other circumstances, on the immortal field of Cowpens.

The battle of Cowpens was fought within the limits of the present County of Spartanburg, about eight miles north of Cowpens Station, on the Southern Railroad, and near, and rather between, the junction of the main road from Spartanburg City via Cherokee Springs and the Green River Road, just below J. H. Ezell's store. It will be remembered that we stated in the beginning of this narrative, that there were two classes of persons who first moved into our up-country in advance of civilization One were the traders with the Indians, and the other the Cowpens' men, who were engaged in following and grazing herds of cattle, which when necessary were penned or enclosed here and there, in what was then a vast and uninterrupted wilderness. In referring to the battle field of Cowpens, Johnson says: "The place of this memorable event has now lost its name, but no American will reflect with indifference on the possibility of its identity ever becoming doubtful. The following remarks may direct the researches of some future traveler or historian. At the first settlement of the country, it was a place of considerable notoriety from a trading path with the Cherokees which passed by it. In the early grants of land in that neighborhood, it was distinguished by the epithet of "Hannah's Cowpens," being the grazing establishment of a man by the name of Hannah."

The writer has often traveled over the main road through the old battle ground and has taken some pains to inspect it. What has been described by several writers as eminences on the battle field, where the different lines were formed, are nothing more than ridges scarcely noticeable. The main road leading to Gaffney City, between Ezell's store, half a mile above the old monument and the Bobby Scruggs place, about the same distance below, between which points the battle was fought, is in fact so level that if ties were properly placed and rails spiked down, a train of cars could run over them with scarcely any grading. The only rising ground of any note on the whole field is a little eminence a short distance in the rear of the ridge, where the main line was formed. This is of sufficient height to cover a man on horseback placed in the rear of it. Behind this, as we will presently show, is the place where Colonel Washington remained concealed for a time with his cavalry.

We have examined several accounts of this remarkable battle and victory, as presented by different writers, and while some of them are conflicting, we have found none which we think more reliable than that given in Johnson's "Life of Greene," and this we have adopted as the ground-work of our present narrative. Unfortunately for us, at present, all the accounts of the battle of Cow pens which we find only deal in general facts, whilst the little interesting particulars and incidents, such as we find preserved in connection with the battle of King's Mountain, are lost in tradition.

In order that the reader may better understand the disposition of Morgan's forces, we will state that the forests at that time were more open, and the elevations and depressions were more easily seen, than at present, as the old battle ground is now covered with a thick, scrubby growth of blackjack and other timber, with here and there an occasional tall pine or oak of ancient appearance. Morgan selected his ground on a ridge gently ascending for about three hundred and fifty yards. On the crest of this ridge were posted his best disciplined troops, composed of two hundred and ninety Maryland regulars, and in line on their right, two companies of Virginia militia under Triplet and Tate, and a company of Georgians, about one hundred and forty in number, making his rear line consist of about 430 men. This was commanded by Lieutenant-Colonel Howard, of Maryland. One hundred and fifty yards in front of this line the main body of the militia were posted in open order under Col. Andrew Pickens. These were composed of North and South Carolinians, and the number, as given by Judge Johnson, is 270. Judge Schenck, however, in his recent work, states that the number was greater than this, because the Mecklenburg militia numbered 150, and perhaps only one-half or 95 of McDowell's men were detailed as sharpshooters in the front. Judge Schenck puts down the number at 315, which he says is approximately correct. We have already stated that the South Carolinians who had recently enlisted under the banner of Colonel Pickens were, for the most part, citizens, who, after the State had been overrun and overawed by British authority, had taken British protection, but could now no longer bear the oppression that was being heaped upon them and see their country backed up, as it was, by British bayonets, run over by a Tory mob. Determined no longer to submit to this indignation, they resolved once more to enlist in the cause of freedom. They fought figuratively, says Judge Johnson, at the battle of Cowpens with "halters around their necks.'

In advance of Colonel Pickens' line, about one hundred and fifty yards, were posted 150 picked men, extending in loose order along the whole front; the right being in command of Colonel Cunningham, while the left was commanded by Major McDowell,* both excellent appointments. General Morgan in his account states that Brannon and Thomas† were posted on McDowell's right, while Hayes and McCall were on Cunningham's left. These commands were, therefore, near together. It is also stated that Hops and Buchannon, of the Augusta riflemen, supported the right of this line. The front line of riflemen were instructed to "mark the epaulette men" as the British approached. Behind the eminence referred to, in rear of main line was posted the American reserve, which consisted of Washington's and McCall's cavalry, 125 in number, a position highly advantageous, as they were near enough to render the most prompt assistance, yet secure at the same time from the enemy's artillery.

---

*Judge Johnson speaks of Major McDowell as being from South Carolina. Judge Schenck, in his recent work, severely criticises this statement and says that the person referred to, was Major Joseph McDowell, of Burke County, N. C. It should be remembered by the reader that Judge Johnson published his two volumes, "Life of Greene," in 1822, while Judge Schenck published his work, "North Carolina," in 1889, sixty-seven years later. While a typographical error may have crept into Judge Johnson's narrative, it is absurd to insinuate that this eminent writer did not know what State each prominent officer represented on that memorable occasion. Says Judge Schenck: "It is the fault of history to give too much prominence to commanders and ignore the men who died or fought to make

The orders given to the front line of sharpshooters were to protect themselves, as much as possible, by trees, to fire from a rest and not to deliver their fire until the enemy was within fifty yards; after the first fire they were to fall back, loading and firing until they came to the second line under Pickens, when they were to fall in with the line of militiamen which would consist, when these orders were executed, of about 450 men.

The order to the militia, or second line, was to deliver two deliberate charges at the distance of fifty yards, and then retire and take their post on the left of the regulars, which was the first or main line. If charged by cavalry every third man was to fire and two remain in reserve—lest the cavalry should continue to advance after the first fire—to be used if they wheeled to retire.

The orders extended to the main line under Howard were to fire low and deliberately and not to be alarmed by the retreat of the militia—the orders as given to the latter being detailed to them. They were admonished not to break on any account and if forced to retire, to rally on the eminence in their rear, where they were assured the enemy could not injure them.

Early in the morning the baggage of the American army was sent several miles to the rear under a suitable escort, where they were ordered to halt. The horses of the volunteer militiamen were secured to the boughs of trees at a convenient distance in rear of the reserves. Every

---

them great, and in that way the truth is confounded. Col. Andrew Pickens, by mere accident, outranked Major McDowell, and being in command and from South Carolina, her historians are ever ready to ascribe all the glory of Cowpens to that State, etc." This is an unfair accusation and reflects unjustly on the memory of Judge Johnson.

† Colonels Brannon and Thomas were from the Spartanburg section of South Carolina. Col. John Thomas, Jr , the person referred to here, succeeded his father about the year 1780, as colonel of the famous Spartan regiment. Brannon did not probably rank higher than a captain. A notice of him will appear in another place. The commands of these officers, if any at all, were necessarily small.

arrangement being completed, the men were ordered to "ease their joints," that is, they were to assume a comfortable attitude, without quitting their ranks, until the enemy came in sight. All were in good spirits and full of confidence.

General Morgan, in his account, states that one of his scouts informed him about an hour before day, that the enemy had advanced within five miles of his encampment and that on this information he had made the necessary dispositions. When these had been made, it is said that he went along the lines encouraging his men and exhorting them to stand firm, as they were about to gain a great victory.

We have already stated that Tarleton left his place of encampment at three o'clock, a. m., and did not come up with Morgan until eight a. m., having been five hours on the way. He simply followed the route Morgan had taken, which is now known as the old Green river road, which runs via the Big Sam Littlejohn place, Thickety station and Macedonia church

The American army looked calmly on while the enemy formed his line of battle at a distance of about 400 yards.

The position of the British line may be better under stood by the account which Tarleton gives, as follows: "The light infantry were ordered to file to the right until they were equal to the flank of the American front line· the Legion infantry were added to their left, and, under the fire of a three-pounder, this part of the British troops were instructed to advance within three hundred yards of the enemy. This situation being acquired, the 7th regiment was commanded to form on the left of the Legion infantry and the other three-pounder was given to the right division of the 7th; a captain with fifty dragoons was placed on each flank of the corps which formed the British front line to protect their own and threaten the flanks of the enemy; the first battalion of the 71st was desired to extend a little to the left of the second regiment and to remain a hundred and fifty yards in the rear.

This body of infantry, and near to one hundred cavalry composed the reserve."

It will be seen therefore that the British line was co-extensive and parallel with that of the American, and further, that the position of the two pieces of artillerv were equally distant from each other and from the extremity of each wing, dividing the line into thirds. Tarleton states that his reserve consisted of the seventy-first, and two hundred dragoons. It is further stated that the residue of the dragoons covered the two wings, giving a squadron of fifty-two each.

The attack was made by Tarleton sooner than he intended, and he has been charged with impatience in commencing the attack. This is a mistake, however, as has been shown. It happened in this way: Advancing to reconnoitre the line of skirmishers under McDowell and Cunningham, and to distinguish satisfactorilv the American order of battle, he approached too near the former, who resisted his further advance with a few rifle cracks. Seeing he could advance no further he ordered the cavalry to advance and drive them in. Savs Johnson, "on the advance of the cavalry the American parties retreated and fell into the first line* and were thus precluded from performing the service for which they were most probably assigned to this advanced position. But they performed another which, in the sequel, answered a purpose nearly as beneficial. They gave the cavalry a few discharges, which made them tremble, for at least that day, at the deadly aim of the American riflemen." The disposition of the enemy being complete he marched steadily forward to encounter the line of the militia under Pickens. The latter maintained perfect coolness until he arrived at the distance which had been assigned for them to discharge their pieces. The account says that they

---

* In the arrangement of the order of the battle which we have given this was the second line; the skirmish line under McDowell and Cunningham consisting of the first line.

did it with unerring aim. It was, says a writer, "the magnanimous confession of a gallant officer of the Maryland line who fought on that day, that here the battle was gained." The killed and wounded of the commissioned and non-commissioned officers who lay on the field of battle where the fire of the riflemen was delivered, and the high proportion which the killed and wounded of this description bore to the whole number, sufficiently justified the assertion.

As soon as the militia had delivered their fire thev broke from the line. The enemy rent the air with their shouts and quickened their advance forward. The want of officers, however, was soon discovered by the confusion which ensued in their ranks.

Immediately after the militia had cleared away from before the main line of regulars under Howard, the latter commenced their fire and for half an hour or more kept it up with coolness and constancy. The British in their advance halted frequently to restore order. Their advance was attended with so much hesitation that Tarleton ordered up the seventy-first regiment into line on his left, while a portion of his cavalry made a sweep on the American right. Howard, seeing this movement, realized the necessity of at once covering his flank· He naturally cast his eyes to his reserve under Washington as the most natural means of counteracting it. Washington was at this time, however, actively engaged on the American left, where duty had called him. It appears that as the right of the line of militia had to traverse the whole front of the main line of regulars they were much exposed, and their retreat was closely followed by Tarleton's cavalry. It was at this moment that Washington flew to their assistance, and repulsing the enemy, enabled the militia to regain the tranquility necessary for returning to a state of order.

Apprehensive that the reserve could not be brought up in time to defend his exposed flank, Morgan dispatched an order to the militia, which had already formed on the right of the main line, to fall back from their right so as to form at right angles with his main line and repel the enemy's advance upon his right flank.* To excute this order with precision and dispatch, he at the same time. ordered his main line to face the right about and wheel on their left. The first part of the order (to face about sim ply) was executed with coolness and precision. Says Jonhson: "At this point of time it was that fortune ever hovering over fields of battle, played off that celebrated freak, which at first threatened destruction to the American arms, but in a moment after crowned them with the most signal success. Seeing the movement of the right of their line, and supposing that this was a state of things which required a retreat to the eminence in their rear, the whole American line faced about and began to move rather in a quickening step, but in perfect order, towards their intended second position. Howard, presuming that the order must have emanated from the commander, made no opposition, but gave his whole attention to the preservation of discipline and the encouragement of his men. Morgan, also, under the impression that the movement was made under the order of Howard, and thinking favorably of it under existing circumstances, rode along the rear of the line, reminding the officers to halt and face as soon as they reached their ground. But just at this crisis they were accosted by another officer and their attention was drawn to some facts which produced an immediate change of measures. This officer was a messenger from Colonel Washington, who having been carried

---

*In the sketch of *John Eager Howard*, published in the "National Portrait Gallery," it was stated that it was *Howard* and not Morgan who gave the order to the right company to change its front and protect his flank; and it was Howard who afterwards ordered the charge with the bayonets upon his own responsibility. We give his own language: "Seeing my right flank exposed to the enemy, I attempted to charge the front of Wallace's company (Virginia Regulars); and in doing so, some confusion ensued, and first a part and then the whole of the company commenced a retreat. The officers along the line seeing this, supposing that orders had been given for a retreat, faced their

in pursuing the enemy's cavalry some distance in advance of the American line, found the right flank wholly exposed to him and had a fair view of the confusion existing in their ranks.

This message was received by Morgan while the American line was falling back to the eminence in the rear. "They are coming like a mob, give them a fire and I'll charge them," was the message delivered. The messenger instantly galloped back to regain his command. At this instant Pickens, who had rallied and restored order among his men, appeared at the top of the ridge, or eminence as it is called, to which the main line was approaching. As soon as the American regulars reached the objective point the order flew from right to left. "Face about, give them one fire and the victory will be ours." This order was promptly obeyed. Pickens' militia had by this time united with the main line. The enemy were now within thirty yards, tumultuously shouting and rapidly advancing. Says a writer: "Scarcely a man of the Americans raised his gun to his shoulder; when their fire was delivered they were in an attitude for using the bayonet and the terrible *pas de charge* in a few steps brought them to that crisis which ever terminates in victory or defeat. The bayonets of the two armies were interlocked. The enemy threw down their arms and fell upon their faces. Happy was it for the honor of the American arms that the soldiers found before them only a prostrate enemy. These were the men, and this the commander (Tarleton),

---

men about and moved off. Morgan, who mostly had been with the militia, quickly rode up to me and expressed apprehension of the event; but I soon removed his fears by pointing to the line and observing that men were not beaten who retreated in that order. He then ordered me to keep with the men until we came to the rising ground, near Washington's horse; and he rode forward to fix the proper place for us to halt and face about. In a minute we had a perfect line. The enemy were now very near us. Our own men commenced a very destructive fire, which they little expected, and a few rounds occasioned great disorder in their ranks. When in this confusion I ordered a charge with the bayonet, which order was obeyed with great alacricy."

who had massacred the troops under Buford and "Tarleton's quarter" had already run from right to left. But Howard (and humanity seems identified with the name), anxiously exclaiming, "Give them quarters," soon had the pleasure to see that an American soldier could not shed the blood of a conquered enemv

The work on the battlefield was not yet completed. The seventy-first regiment had got on Howard's right and the British dragoons were also approaching the same point. Washington had his hands full with the artillery in front and the cavalry of the enemy's wing. Morgan was prompt in the execution of his orders. Sending one company forward to assist Washington, and leaving these in charge of the prisoners, he wheeled the right battalion upon the seventy-first. The affair here became animated. In vain did Tarleton urge his men forward. They could not resist the effective shots of Pickens' marksmen who were now upon him. Those who were not killed or wounded on the ground, soon broke and fled. The British artillery stood by their pieces with a commendable devotion. Having been thrown in the rear by the advance of the British line, and at last abandoned by the British dragoons, they resolved to surrender their guns only with their lives.*

They were mostly killed or wounded by the time that Tarleton and a number of mounted officers and all that remained to him of his cavalry, amounting in all to about fifty, had arrived to support them. It was here that the memorable conflict occurred in which Washing-

*Says Howard further: "As their line advanced, I observed their artillery a short distance in front and called to Captain Ewing, who was near me, to take it. Captain Anderson (now General Anderson of Montgomery county, Maryland) hearing the order, also pushed for the same object; and both being emulous for the prize kept pace until near the first piece, where Anderson, by putting the end of his spontoon forward into the ground made a long leap, which brought him upon the gun and gave him the honor of the prize. My attention was now drawn to an altercation of some of the men with an artilleryman who appeared to make it a point of honor not to surrender his match."

ton so narrowly escaped and has been briefly described thus: "Whilst Washington was engaged with the artillerists Colonel Tarleton, at the head of all the cavalry who could follow him, hastened to their relief. Washington perceiving his approach ordered his men to charge and dashed forward himself.* Tarleton prudently commanded a retreat. Being of course in the rear of his men and looking behind he could see that Washington was very near him, full thirty yards ahead of his troops. Attended by two of his offiers he advanced to meet Washington. One of his officers led; parrying a blow aimed at him by Washington, the sword of the latter proved of inferior temper and broke midway. The next effort must have brought Washington to the ground. But a little henchman, not fourteen years old, who was devoted to his master and carried no other weapon but a pistol at his saddle bow, had pressed forward to share or avert the danger that threatened his beloved colonel, and arrived in time to discharge the contents of his pistol into the shoulder that brandished the sword over Washington's head. It fell powerless, but the other officer had already raised his sword to inflict the wound when Sergeant-Major Perry reached the side of his commander, just in time to receive the sword arm of the officer upon his extended weapon. The weapon also broke this blow, but Colonel Tarleton in the meantime was securely aiming another from his pistol. The noble ani-

---

*Dr. James H. Carlisle, President of Wofford College, S. C., in a letter to the writer, Feb. 28, 1893, transmits a passage from Dr. G. G. Smith's "History of Methodism in Georgia," which is as follows:

"Rev. Samuel Cowls came from Virginia to Georgia in 1796. He had been a dragoon with Washington's Light Horse. In the battle of Cowpens, he swept down, with uplifted sabre, upon a British trooper, whom he disarmed and was about to cut down. The trooper gave him the Masonic sign of distress and he spared his life. Years after he met his old foe, in Thomas Dorley, a brother in arms, in the South Carolina Conference."

Smith's History, page 71.

mal that bore Washington was destined to receive the ball that had rather discourteously been aimed at his rider. Poor Perry's destiny was bound up with that of his commander, for at the battle of Eutaw when the latter was made prisoner, Perry by the same discharge fell under five wounds. We believe he never recovered from them.

It is said that during the hottest part of the engagement at Cowpens, the troops were greatly inspired by General Morgan, who rode in front of the militia as they were returning to action, and said: "Boys, form; old Morgan never was beaten in his life."

The bloody scenes were now ended. The engagement with the seventy-first, on the extreme right of the Americans, was spirited but of short duration. Be it said to the credit of the soldiers belonging to this command, that they exhibited a firm countenance and order to the last. Resistance was in vain with them, however, when the calvary had abandoned them and the whole weight of the American army was upon them. They laid down their arms and their commander, McArthur, surrendered his sword to Colonel Pickens.*

Colonel Tarleton takes credit upon himself for performing two gallant feats upon this occasion. One was for repulsing Washington's whole command with fifty of his dragoons and fourteen mounted officers, the circumstance just related. The other for dispersing an American party which had seized upon his baggage.

This was a ludricous incident. It is related by Tarle-

---

* Says Howard further, in his account of this stage of the action: "In the pursuit, I was led to the right, in among the 71st, who were broken into squads; and as I called to them to surrender, they laid down their arms and the officers delivered up their swords. Captain Duncanson, of the 71st grenadiers, gave me his sword and stood by me. Upon getting on my horse, I found him pulling at my saddle, and he nearly unhorsed me. I expressed my displeasure and asked what he was about. The explanation was that they had orders to give no quarter, and they did not expect any, and as my men were coming up he was

ton that an American party preceded the flight of the enemy and took possession of his baggage. This is a mistake. Colonel Tarleton had in his train a party of about fifty Loyalists, good woodsmen and excellent workmen, but great plunderers and scoundrels. So says a writer. They had been employed by the British commander as spies and expresses. Having moved off at a convenient distance during the battle, and finding the baggage of the British army abandoned during the action, they very laudably entered upon the work of saving what they could of the officers' effects for their own use. Hearing the tramping of Tarleton's horses returning, they became alarmed and took to the woods. This movement, as the British came up, caused the latter to believe that they were a part of Morgan's army. As soon as they discovered the mistake, however, the indignant dragoons let loose their wrath upon all who were not fortunate enough to make good their retreat. Some of this party secured themselves from the sword by the body of a wagon.

We have already given in a former chapter the relative strength of the two armies. The British loss amounted to about one hundred and fifty killed, and two hundred wounded, and about five hundred prisoners,* according to the account published at the time. These numbers may, however, be some what overdrawn. In the official correspondence between Clinton and Cornwallis, the latter admits of a loss of seven hundred and eighty-four men

---

afraid they would use him ill. I admitted his excuse, and put him under the care of the sergeant. I had messages from him years afterwards expressing his obligation for having saved his life."

It is further stated, that "at one time Howard had in his hands seven swords of officers, who had surrendered to him personally whilst he was in amongst the 71st."

* A number of negro slaves were also captured which were returned to their original owners.

between January 15th and February 1st. The American loss as reported was only eleven killed and sixty-one wounded. Never was a victory more complete. Says a writer· "Not a corps retired from the field under command except a few cavalry who accompanied Tarleton. "These did not amount to more than one hundred and seventy-five all told. Washington pursued the flying enemy," says a writer, "until the declining sun and his panting horses warned him to retrace his steps and join his commander. On his return he drove before him near one hundred straggling prisoners collected on his route."

As a result of the victory, two field pieces (four pounders), eight hundred muskets, two stand of colors, thirty-five baggage wagons and one hundred dragoon horses, fell into the hands of the Americans. The two pieces captured, called the "grasshoppers," had a special history. They were first captured at Saratoga. Afterwards they were recaptured on the same field, falling into the hands of General Greene after the battle of Cowpens. They were retaken by Cornwallis at the battle of Guilford C. H. They were finally surrendered at Yorktown.

Like the battle of King's Mountain, the engagement at Cowpens lasted about fifty minutes. Of the killed and wounded on the British side at least one-tenth were officers. Ten officers were found in the front of the ground where the militia had been formed in line. They were the "epaulette men," who had been specially marked in the beginning of the battle. It was the fall of these which produced such confusion in the British ranks, the men as they advanced receiving no orders—every man advancing at his own will.

The battle of Cowpens was one of the most extraordinary battles of the whole Revolution. Ramsay states "that the glory and importance of this battle resounded from one end of the nation to the other."

For the victory at Cowpens the Congress of the United States voted public thanks to General Morgan and presented him with a medal of gold. Colonels Washington and Howard received medals of silver, and Colonel Pickens a sword.*

The history of the battle of Cowpens would not be complete without a brief notice of the prominent heroes who participated in that engagement. We are sorry that we are unable to present a register of the entire forces of General Morgan's army. Their names and memories deserve to be perpetuated in the annals of our country's history.

GENERAL DANIEL MORGAN,

was born in Buck's County, Pennsylvania, during the year 1775. We know little of his birth, or education, or early training. He is said to have been a wagoner in General Braddock's army, and shared in his defeat in 1754. He emigrated to Virginia in 1755, and was employed as an overseer by Daniel Burrel, Esq., then in Shenendoah, now Clarke County, Virginia. At the beginning of the Revolution he enlisted in his country's cause. He was with General Montgomery at Quebec, and with General Gates at Saratoga. He was commissioned a Brigadier-General and joined the army of the South only a short time before General Gates was relieved by General Greene. After Greene took command, Morgan was detached, as we have already shown, to raise troops in the western portions of North and South Carolina. After various maneuverings he met Colonel Tarleton at Cowpens, January 17, 1781, and gained the brilliant victory just narrated, for which Congress presented him with a gold medal. Being compelled to continue his retreat he

* At the one hundredth anniversary of the battle of Cowpens, and the unveiling of the Morgan statue, "at Spartanburg on the 11th of May, 1881, Col. S. V. Pickens, of Charleston, a descendant of Col Andrew Pickens, wore in the street parade the sword of his illustrious ancestor referred to above. The writer had the pleasure of examining it. It has a silver hilt and is highly ornamented. The scabbard is leather. It is now, so we are informed, in the hands of Mrs. Francis W. Pickens, Edgefield, S. C."

united his army with the advance forces of General Greene, on the east bank of the Catawba. After his army had united with the main division of General Greene's army at Greensborough, he was seized with a severe attack of rheumatism, which compelled him to retire from the service. He returned to his farm in Virginia, where he remained until the war was over.

During the whiskey troubles in 1794, in Pennsylvania, he was appointed by President Washington to raise troops and put down the Insurgents. He remained among them for several months. After the difficulty was settled, he was ordered to withdraw his troops and return to his home, and soon after became an aspirant for political honors. He was defeated in his first race for Congress, but after a second trial, was elected and served as a member of Congress from 1797 to 1799. His health failing he declined re-election. He died at Winchester, Virginia, July 6, 1802.

First and last he was a brave and chivalric gentleman and soldier. In early life he is represented as being wild and reckless, but in the end he died a Christian.

The following is a copy from his tombstone in the Baptist churchyard, Winchester, Virginia. The words are placed thus on tombstone:

"MAJOR GENERAL DANIAL MORGAN
Departed this life
On July 6th 1802
In the 67th year of his age.
Patriotism & valor were the prominent
Features of his character
And
The Honorable services he rendered
To his Country
During the Revolutionary War
Crown him with glory & will remain
In the hearts of his
Countrymen
A perpetual Monument
To his
Memory"

JOHN EAGER HOWARD

was born in Baltimore County, Maryland, June 4th, 1752, and died there October 12th, 1827. He was well connected and educated; joined the American army at the beginning of the Revolution; was at the battles of White Plains, Monmouth and Germantown. In 1780 he was made lieutenant of the regiment of Maryland Regulars which belonged to the army of the South. Lieutenant-Colonel Howard fought at the battle of Camden under General Gates, and in 1780 was assigned by General Greene to Morgan's command. The gallantry which he displayed at Cowpens has already been narrated. It is claimed that the bayonet charge of his regiment secured the victory on that memorable occasion. At one time he held seven swords in his hands which were surrendered to him.* He greatly aided General Greene in his retreat from Guilford C. H., March 15th, 1781. At Hobkirk's Hill he succeeded to the command of the second Maryland regiment. At Eutaw Springs, where his command was reduced to thirty, he was the only surviving officer and made a final charge and was wounded. This was the end of his military career during the Revolution.

From 1789 to 1792 he was Governor of Maryland, and from 1796 to 1803, he was United States Senator from that State. In 1796 he was offered a seat in Washington's Cabinet but declined. In 1798, he was appointed a Major-General by President Washington in anticipation of a war with France.

In 1814, during the panic in Baltimore and subsequent to the capture of Washington by the British forces, he prepared to take the field and was opposed to any capitulation. In 1816, he was the candidate of the Federal party for Vice-President. His wife, Margaret, was a daughter of Chief Justice Benjamin Chew.

He entertained LaFayette at his beautiful mansion, "Bellevedere," near Baltimore, in 1824, only three years prior to his death.

---

* See Sketch of J. E. Howard, Appleton's Cyclopedia.

COLONEL WILLIAM WASHINGTON,

a kinsman of George Washington, was born in Stafford County, Virginia, February 28th, 1752. He was a son of Barley Washington. But little is known of his early life. It is said that he was educated for the Christian ministry, but at the springing of the Revolution he espoused the Patriot cause, and received a captain's commission early in the war and belonged to the third regiment of the Virginia line. While in this capacity he acquitted himself with great credit, and was severely wounded at the battle of Long Island. At Trenton (December, 1776) he led a charge on the enemy's batteries, capturing the enemy's guns. He was again wounded on this occasion. In 1778 he was transferred to the dragoons and assigned to the regiment of Lieutenant-Colonel George Baylor. In 1779 he joined the Southern army under Gen. Benjamin Lincoln, was promoted to the command of the regiment, with rank of Lieutenant-Colonel 23d March, 1780. Soon after this he defeated Colonel Tarleton at Rantowl's. He with Colonel White were surprised a few weeks afterwards at Monk's Corner and Dennard's Ferry.

It was in 1780 that Washington, then attached to Morgan's command, resorted to the stratagem of the painted pine log—"The Quaker Gun"—reducing as he did the post of Colonel Rudgeley and receiving the surrender of the latter with one hundred men.

We have already narrated the successful charge which Colonel Washington made at Cowpens at a very critical moment. For this conduct Congress presented him with a handsome sword. In this battle he had a personal encounter with Tarleton, the circumstances of which we have already given. With Howard and Lee he was chosen by General Greene to harrass the enemy on his memorable retreat. He took a very active part in the battle at Guilford Court House.

At the battle of Hobkirk's Hill he charged the enemy, secured many prisoners and saved the artillery from capture. At the close of the engagement he succeeded in drawing Major Coffin, the commander of the British cavalry, in ambush and he dispersed them and caused a number to be captured.

At Eutaw Springs, after the most heroic efforts, he was unhorsed, and while attempting to disengage himself, was wounded and captured. This ended his military career.

In 1782 he married a Mrs. Elliott, of Charleston, and moved to his residence near the city. He was afterwards elected to the South Carolina Legislature, and was strongly solicited to run for Governor, but declined "because he could not make a speech."

In 1798, when hostilities were threatened between France and the United States, General Washington recommended the appointment of his kinsman for Brigadier-General, which was made on the 19th of July, 1798. General Washington, in a letter to the Secretary of War, suggested that General William Washington be assigned as military director of the affairs of Georgia and South Carolina.

William Washington lived in retired life until 1810. He died at his residence near Charleston on March 10th of this year, his wife, a son and daughter surviving him. His biographer says that "he was modest without timidity, generous without extravagance, brave without rashness, disinterested without austerity."

COLONEL (afterwards General) ANDREW PICKENS was born in Buck's County, Pennsylvania, September 19th, 1737. His parents were of Huguenot descent, and removed in 1752 to the Waxhaw settlement, in Lancaster County, South Carolina. Colonel Pickens' first public service was in Grant's expedition against the Cherokees, in 1761. After this he moved to Long Cane settlement, in the present County of Anderson.

At the beginning of the Revolution Andrew Pickens was made Captain in the militia, and rose, by promotion, until he was made Brigadier-General. He kept the field at the head of a partisan corps, after the State had been overrun by the British, and in February, 1779, with four hundred men, he defeated a party of seven hundred men under Colonel Boyd, at Kettle Creek. At Stono, June 20th of the same year, whilst he was covering the retreat of the American forces, his horse was killed from under him. During the same year he inflicted a severe defeat on the Cherokees at Tanasee.

At the battle of Cowpens his conduct should never be forgotten. He commanded the militia, as we have already shown. These he rallied and brought into action a second time after his ranks had been broken and compelled to retreat. For this service Congress gave him a sword. He next invested the British forts at Augusta, Georgia (an account of which is given in this work), which surrendered after a two week's seige.

After participating in an unsuccessful seige at Ninety-Six, under General Greene, he followed the retreating army towards the coast and participated in the battle of Eutaw Springs. In this engagement he was struck by a bullet, which, but for the buckle of his sword-belt, would have inflicted a mortal wound.

In 1782 he made a successful campaign against the Cherokees in Georgia, and for this service he obtained a valuable cession of territory in that State.

In 1765 Andrew Pickens married Miss Rebecca Calhoun, in the present region of Abbeville County. In Mrs. Ellet's "Women of the Revolution" we learn that this wedding was an epoch in the social history of that section. The bride was specially noted for her beauty and accomplishments. The happy pair settled on the Keowee River, in what was afterwards known as the old Pendleton District, now Pickens County. From the close of the war till 1793 General Pickens was a member of the South Carolina Legislature. He was the first person from his district elected to the United States Congress, and served in that body from the 2d of December, 1793, till the 3d of March, 1795.*

General Pickens was a member of the first South Carolina Constitutional Convention after the Revolution, and was made Major-General of the South Carolina militia in 1795. He served again in the State Legislature from 1801 to 1812.

In several instances he was a commissioner to form treaties with the Indians. By the treaty of Hopewell he obtained from the Cherokees a part of the northwestern territory of South Carolina.

General Andrew Pickens died at Pendleton, South Carolina, on the 17th of August, 1817.

He is said to have been remarkable for his simplicity, decision and prudence. He was scrupulous in the performance of every duty.

He was a self-denying and a brave soldier and a pure patriot. He left behind him a highly respectable posterity. Governor Francis Wilkerson Pickens, who died in Edgefield, South Carolina, in 1869, and whose history is well known to the people of South Carolina, was a grandson.

---

*The late Rev. John G. Landrum once informed the writer that General Pickens, on his way to Congress, passed through the present County of Spartanburg. He traveled on horseback, in full military uniform, with his servant in livery also on horseback, about ten paces behind him. This fact was related to Mr. Landrum by the older citizens of the country, who saw General Pickens on his way to Congress, then in session in Philadelphia or New York.

CHAPTER XXXIII.

MORGAN RESOLVES TO RESUME HIS MARCH IMMEDIATELY AFTER THE BATTLE OF COWPENS.—LEAVES PICKENS TO CARE FOR THE WOUNDED.—PRISONERS SENT TO CHARLOTTESVILLE, VA.—MOVEMENTS OF THE ARMY OF CORNWALLIS.—MORGAN CROSSES SHERRILL'S FORD ON CATAWBA RIVER.—CORNWALLIS FOLLOWS.—RAPID RISE OF THE STREAM PREVENTS HIS CROSSING.—GENERAL GREENE LEAVES HIS ARMY ON THE PEE DEE AND JOINS MORGAN ON THE CATAWBA AND ASSUMES COMMAND.—MORGAN RETREATS TO THE YADKIN.—GENERAL GREENE REMAINS BEHIND TO COLLECT MILITIA.—CORNWALLIS CROSSES THE CATAWBA.—FALL OF DAVIDSON. TWO WINGS OF AMERICANS UNITE AT GUILFORD C. H.—RETREAT ACROSS THE DAN.—CORNWALLIS OUTSTRIPPED IN THE RACE.

THE brilliant success of General Morgan on the field of Cowpens did not lull or dazzle him into an imagined security. He knew that when Cornwallis received intelligence of Tarleton's annihilation, he would attempt to head off his retreat. The camp of this officer on Turkey Creek (in York County) being only twenty-five or thirty miles away, Morgan knew that it would require only five or six hours for Tarleton and his flying cavalry to reach it. Morgan knew, too, that the army of Cornwallis was under marching orders and to elude his grasp was a matter of great importance to him in the circumstances.

It was not yet noon when the battle ended. Morgan resolved, after refreshing his men and prisoners, to put his army in motion at once. Colonel Pickens, with a detachment of mounted militia, was left upon the field to bury the dead and provide for the comfort of the wounded of both armies. It is said that this brave and benevolent man performed this duty faithfully and humanely. Sufficient tents were procured from the enemy's wagons which had been captured. The Americans had none. Other comforts were drawn from the same source.

Those of the enemy's wagons which could not be carried away were burned. Colonel Pickens, after performing the duty assigned him, and placing a safe guard and a yellow flag over the wounded, departed and rejoined his commander on the following day.

Morgan's army crossed the lower Island Ford* the same afternoon and encamped several miles beyond the river. Early on the morning of the 18th he resumed his march, going north, towards Gilberttown, pursuing the same line of retreat as had been formerly traveled by the King's Mountain men. Scouts were sent out in the morning in the direction in which Cornwallis was expected to approach. Morgan was delighted on the return of those to learn that not only had Cornwallis not yet moved, but that there were no signs of his moving. At Gilberttown, three miles from Rutherfordton, Morgan detached the greater portion of his militia and a part of Colonel Washington's cavalry as a guard to the prisoners. This detachment took the Cane Creek road, towards Morganton, crossing the Catawba at Island Ford. Here Washington's cavalry turned the prisoners over to Colonel Pickens and rejoined General Morgan's army, which crossed the Catawba at Sherrill's Ford, eight or nine miles lower down the stream.

On the east bank of Island Ford, Major Hyrne, the commissary of prisoners, receved six hundred prisoners from Colonel Pickens. These were carried by an upper route to Charlottesville, Virginia, where prisoners were usually kept at that time.

Let us now return to the movements of the British army. Cornwallis was resting quietly in his camp on Turkey Creek, waiting, as his lordship informs us, for Leslie to reach him. Says a writer: "When the night

* In the present plantation of old Mr. John Camp.

gathered around his camp, the sound of the cavalry approaching at rapid gait was heard, the weary sentinel challenged the advance, the countersign was exchanged and then the news was broken: 'Tarleton is defeated and his corps is destroyed'" It is said that the revelry of the camp ended. Grief and dismay were written on every countenance. Guards were doubled and parties were sent to gather more tidings of the battle. So dumbfounded was Cornwallis, that he scarcely knew what course to pursue. Reason would have dictated to him to move at once to cut off, if possible, Morgan's junction with Greene, but he did nothing for a whole day, and that day Morgan and his prisoners were out of reach. Had he pressed forward at once with one thousand infantry and a few pieces of artillery, with orders for his scattered cavalry to follow, "it is," says Johnson, "unquestionable that he must have overtaken General Morgan at Ramsour's Mill, where their roads united and crossed the south fork of the Catawba." His baggage was in no danger, as he could have left a sufficient guard behind to take care of it, while the army of General Leslie was only a short distance away. In war, days are years. The loss of the 18th. the precious and irretrievable day to Cornwallis, was forever gone to him, and Morgan made good use of the advantage he had thus gained. Cornwallis did not leave his encampment until the 19th—two days after the battle. He moved north, taking all his cumberous baggage with him, with orders to his cavalry to return to his camp every night. He marched up the east bank of Broad River, crossing Buffalo and King's creeks to the second or Little Broad River, where, hearing that Morgan had gone east, he turned to the north-east until he came to the old Flint Hill road, which Morgan had traveled, and thence down said road to Ramsour's Mill, on the 25th of January, 1781. Morgan, at this time, was on the north bank of the Catawba, at Sherrill's Ford, twenty-five miles away. It is a common error in the histories of our country to attribute the escape of Morgan to the sudden rise of the Catawba River, for though the rain did descend in torrents on the 26th, still Morgan had the advantage of a whole day's march. Morgan, hearing that Cornwallis had reached Ramsour's Mill, took advantage of the sudden rise of the Catawba in order to give his men a day's rest and enable the American guard in charge of the prisoners to get out of reach, for Morgan was anxious to secure every one of them to exchange for the troops of the Continental line, taken at the surrender of Lincoln at Charleston, then languishing in the prison ships at that place.

Cornwallis, having lost the 17th and 18th, was six days in reaching Ramsour's Mill. By a direct route he could have reached that place in two days, and thus intercepted the retreat of Morgan. At Ramsour's Mill he remained two days, thus giving further advantage to his adversary to outstrip him in the race.

"On the 25th of January, the day that Cornwallis reached Ramsour's Mill, the news of Morgan's victory reached General Greene at his camp on the Pee Dee. His little army was immediately ordered to prepare to march to the assistance of Morgan. The troops were poorly clad and the winter was cold, but they received the orders of their commander with cheerfulness and confidence. The 25th, 26th and 27th of January were spent in energetic preparations for the march, and the most minute orders were given as to every detail before General Greene would consent to leave."

Having made every necessary arrangement for the retreat of his army, General Greene did what has been deemed by Johnson and others one of the most imprudent acts of his life. "With only a guide, an aide and a sergeant's guard of cavalry he struck across the country to join Morgan and aid him in his arduous operations." He traveled from Hicks' Ford, on the Pee Dee, to Beaty's Ford, on the Catawba, a distance of about one hundred and twenty-five miles, in two days.* He reached

*See Johnson's Life of Greene, vol. i, page 403.

Morgan at Sherrill's Ford on the 30th, and assumed command of his forces. Cornwallis' forces were at this time on the other side of the Catawba, and about eighteen miles below that point. All the fords of the river below, as far down as Charlotte, were guarded by the militia under General Davidson. Cornwallis was only waiting for an opportunity to force a passage. The river was at this time very high, and the two armies lay in perfect security from each other, though not many miles distant. By the 31st the waters of the swollen stream began to recede.

Notwithstanding the fords of the Catawba were numerous, Davidson kept a vigilant watch. He had under him only about five hundred volunteers and three hundred mounted riflemen, which served as a corps of oberservation along the eastern bank of the stream. The British commander had so masked his intentions, that it was impossible to know just where he would attempt his first crossing. As soon as it was ascertained, however, that the Catawba was falling, and that Cornwallis was making his dispositions to cross, Morgan began his retreat. He moved off in silence on the evening of the 31st, and pressing his retreat that night and all of the next day, he gained a full day's march on his adversary.

Before we proceed further, let us take special notice of some of the dispositions which Cornwallis made prior to his crossing the Catawba, and his pursuit of his adversary. An error has crept into history that this officer, before leaving his camp on Turkey Creek, set fire to and burnt up all of his heavy baggage, first setting the example by burning his own. This has been furnished as an excuse for his loss of the 18th, a day which he never regained. It is, however, a mistake. It was at Ramsour's Mill that he destroyed his baggage six days after the commencement of his march. He spent two whole days in this work and the collection of provisions and did not resume his march until the 28th.* It was during the march of Cornwallis

*See Johnson's vol. i, page 389.

from Ramsour's Mill that the swell of the waters of the great Catawba took place, and not *on the night of the day* that Morgan crossed that river. The swell of the stream occurred on the night of the 29th.

But to return to the progress of events. When General Greene left his army on the Pee Dee, their orders were to cross that river, then to proceed up the stream, and with all possible dispatch reach Salisbury in order to form a junction with the army of General Morgan. Having placed himself at the head of Morgan's troops, he lingered behind after the departure of the latter from the banks of the Catawba, with a view of collecting and bringing off the militia of General Davidson as soon as the enemy had effected the passage of the river; and for this purpose he issued orders for them to repair, as soon as that event should take place, to a place six miles in advance of Tarrant's Tavern, and about sixteen miles in advance on the road to Salisbury. To this place he repaired in person to await their arrival, and at this place, as we will presently show, he came very near terminating his military career.

The British army crossed the Catawba at two points. With his main army Cornwallis crossed at McGowen's (called Cowen's by some writers) Ford. It was fortunate for him that he attempted this passage at night. Says a writer: "The appalling prospect of a stream five hundred yards in width, foaming among the rocks, and frequently overturning men and horses in its course, might have shaken the stoutest heart. Nor would the aim of the riflemen then have been distracted by the shades of the night, or the men themselves been directed by nothing but the voices of the British officers, the increased noise of the current, or the mutual exhortation of the British soldiers. Placed among the trees and bushes that lined the banks, secure must have been the aim of the militiamen against a body of men plunged up to their waists, moving slowly, and supporting themselves against the swift waters of the stream, endeavoring to preserve their arms from the spray. A singular instance of good fortune attended the British commander. In the midst of the stream the guide, who had been employed to pilot him across, got alarmed and fled away. The advance of Cornwallis' forces took the wrong course, and escaped the danger that awaited them."

Says Johnson, "Davidson had posted his men so as to receive the enemy at the point where they well knew the course of the ford would lead them to the eastern bank. Upon losing their guide, the enemy deviated from the ford, waded through water somewhat deeper, but approached a point where they were not expected. The darkness of the night and the noise of the waters prevented this deviation from being discovered until the enemy approached the margin of the river; and as Davidson led off his men to take a position in their front, it brought him between the light of the fires and the advancing column. A well directed volley from them put an end to his existence as he mounted his horse."

Thus fell a noble, brave and tried patriot. His loss was universally deplored. His men soon dispersed after his fall, though not without inflicting a severe injury to the enemy. A number of them were killed, including Colonel Hall, of the British guards, whose loss was much regretted by his companions in arms.

We have already stated that the enemy effected a crossing of the Catawba at two different points. At Beaty's Ford, higher up the stream, Colonels Tarleton and Webster crossed with a strong detachment. Finding that ford unguarded, it was passed without loss or delay. At Tarrant Tavern, ten miles distant from McGowen's Ford, the roads from the different fords come together. While many of the militiamen, after the fall of their commander, were making their way to their homes, others were moving forward to join General Greene at the appointed place of rendezvous, which was six miles from Tarrant's, and in the same direction the American army were moving. When the militiamen reached Tarrant's, thinking themselves secure, they halted to take refreshments. Tarleton, soon after he crossed the stream, got wind that the party had assembled at Tarrant's. He resolved at once to strike at it. The militiamen numbered only about one hundred, and the officer in command of the same did not take the proper precaution to put out videttes to guard against surprise. Tarleton's attack was unlooked for. The militia, mounting their horses, quickly fled to the woods, after delivering one fire. Says a writer: 'A few victims remained to greet the English broadsword. There were a small number of old men and boys, either not mounted, or badly mounted, who sought security in imploring mercy on the strength of their gray hairs or their youth. Seven of them were wantonly sacrificed, and that number is boastingly swelled in 'Tarleton's Campaigns' to the number of fifty. Dearly did the Loyalists afterward pay for the blood of these men."

After this exploit Colonel Tarleton leisurely retired to the main army, little dreaming that a coveted prize, General Greene and his suite, were only a few miles ahead of him and unguarded. Twenty horsemen could easily have captured him. General Greene, learning of the fall of Davidson and the dispersion of the militia, proceeded to Salisbury. On his arrival at Steel's tavern, in that town, he exhibited signs of hunger and exposure. His dress was deranged and his limbs were stiffened. To the enquiries of Dr. Read, who received him on his alighting, he could not refrain from answering: "Yes, fatigued, hungry, alone and penniless." This reply was overheard by Mrs. Read. When seated to a comfortable breakfast, she presented herself in the room, closed the door behind her and exhibited a small bag of specie in each hand. "Take these," said she, "for you will want them, and I can do without them." This favor was too delicate and touching to be declined and was afterwards amply repaid.

General Greene had not more than finished his meal when he was admonished to hasten away on account of the numbers and hostility of the Loyalists who surrounded him. He hastened at once to rejoin his army, then crossing the Yadkin River.

But we are admonished that we are getting too far away from the scenes of our narrative. We can only give an outline of General Greene's further movements.

General Morgan, after leaving the Catawba, made directly to Trading Ford, on the Yadkin, reaching that place by the 3d of February. Lord Cornwallis now made a desperate effort to retrieve what he had lost by a previous want of decision. A second conflagration of wagons and baggage announced his intention to resume his march. This enabled him to double his teams and mount more infantry. Leaving the Catawba about the 1st of February, he attempted to overtake Morgan before he crossed the Yadkin. The incessant rains which drenched the army of General Morgan all through the first, only quickened his movements. General Greene knew that in two days the river would rise past fording.

Cornwallis made but little progress on the first, owing to a narrow and bad road which he traveled from McGowen's (or Cowen's) Ford. Adding General O'Hara with his mounted infantry to his cavalry, he ordered them to push forward and overtake Morgan before he crossed Trading Ford. The latter, however, was too sagacious for him. Only a few wagons were left behind stuck in the mud. These were guarded by some American militia who skirmished with the approaching cavalry of O'Hara. Two militiamen were killed, while twelve or more of the enemy were slain on the ground.

Morgan transferred his army across the river on boats which had been previously collected, while his cavalry forded the stream. It was General Greene's foresight on his way South that caused these boats to be in place. As soon as the army was safely over, all the boats for miles up and down the river were secured. Morgan now viewed complacently the swelling stream between him and Cornwallis and gave his troops a much needed rest.

So chagrined was O'Hara that Morgan had eluded his

grasp, that he opened up a furious cannonade on the American troops across the river. Morgan had none to reply. The two little three-pounders, "grasshoppers," captured at Cowpens, had been sent back with the prisoners. During this cannonade General Greene established his headquarters in a cabin not far from the river. Here, while issuing his orders and conducting his letters of correspondence, a cannon ball struck the roof of his cabin and shattered it to pieces. It is said that the General wrote on and seemed to notice nothing but his dispatches. O'Hara, after cannonading across the stream, returned to Salisbury, where General Cornwallis was awaiting him. Cornwallis discovered that he could cross at Shallow Ford, a few miles above Trading Ford. He put his army in motion on the fifth, and crossed at that point on the evening of the sixth.

General Greene moved from Trading Ford on the evening of the fourth, and marched directly to Guilford C. H., where he formed a junction with his army under General Huger, on the 10th of February. It will be remembered that General Huger had marched from the Pee Dee section by order of General Greene. It is an error in history to state that it was "a race" between Greene and Cornwallis to this place. The former was master of his own movements and it was at that time that he selected the celebrated position (Guilford C. H.) as a fighting ground for a battle, which took place a month later. After calling a council of war it was unanimously decided that the army should retreat across the Dan River. The returns of General Greene's army show that he had at this time, rank and file of all arms, only 2,036 men; of these 1,426 were regulars. The force of Cornwallis amounted to about three thousand.

General Greene, having decided upon a further retreat, put his army in motion about the 12th. Cornwallis' army at this time was at or near Salem. It was unfortunate for General Greene that General Morgan at this time became disabled. He was stricken down with a severe attack of rheumatism, contracted in his recent retreat by exposure to wet and cold. He had in former years suffered from this painful malady. With the assistance of a few friends he was carried to his home in western Virginia.

General Greene's objective point was Irwin's Ferry, on the Dan River, seventy miles from Guilford C. H. Colonel Carrington was sent forward to secure all the boats and make every necessary preparation for the army to cross. General Greene formed a light corps consisting of some of his best infantry, under Lieutenant-Colonel Howard, who were to take post between the retreating and advancing army, to hover on the skirts of the latter and retard in every way the enemy's progress, while Greene with the main army hastened towards the Dan, which stream he successfully crossed with his entire forces by the 15th of February.

Thus ended the memorable retreat of General Greene, which not only met with the appreciation of the friends of the Revolution, but has at all times commanded the admiration of the entire civilized world. Here was displayed military tact, genius and strategy, under the most trying self-sacrifices, hunger, and deprivation ever recorded in the pages of American history.

Following the battle of Cowpens, and being so intimately blended with the same, an account of the one in this work would not be complete without a brief narrative of the other.

CHAPTER XXXIV.

GENERAL REVIEW OF MILITARY OPERATIONS IN NORTH AND SOUTH CAROLINA.—CORNWALLIS REPAIRS TO HILLSBOROUGH AND ERECTS A ROYAL STANDARD.—INVITES THE INHABITANTS TO JOIN HIM—GENERAL GREENE RECROSSES THE DAN AND MARCHES TO GUILFORD C. H.—BATTLE OF GUILFORD.—ITS EFFECTS.—GENERAL GREENE RETIRES TO SPEEDWELL'S IRON WORKS.—CORNWALLIS RETREATS TO WILMINGTON.—GREENE PURSUES TO RAMSEY'S MILL.—THE TWO ARMIES TURN BACK TO BACK.—CORNWALLIS MARCHES TO VIRGINIA.—GREENE RETURNS TO SOUTH CAROLINA.—CAPTURE OF FORT WATSON.—BATTLE OF HOBKIRK.—RETREAT OF LORD RAWDEN.—FALL OF ORANGEBURG, FORTE MOTTE AND GRANBY.—SEIGE AND FALL OF AUGUSTA.

IN order to give the reader a proper chain of the important military events following those which we have alreadv narrated, and those which we propose to present in the succeeding chapters as happening in the upper part of our State, it will be necessary to review briefly, some of the important military operations both in North and South Carolina, which occurred during the remainder of the year 1781. These, for the most part, ended the inter esting Revolutionary events in the States referred to.

Before we proceed further, let us return to South Caro lina and view the state of affairs during the memorable retreat of General Greene, an account of which is given in the preceding chapter. During this time the distinguished partisans, Generals Marion and Sumter, were at work in their daring enterprises, maintaining, as they did, a show of American authority in the State. Since Cornwallis had left the State the Whigs were gathering everywhere. Surrounded as they were by enemies, they kept the field to animate the Whig inhabitants to deeds of valor. Sumter, though not yet recovered from his wound received at Blackstock's, assumed authority in the western portion of the State. He was ably assisted by Colonel Pickens with his brigade, which had recently returned from North Carolina and operated between Ninety-Six and Augusta. Sumter was also ably supported by Colonels Neil, Lacy, Hill, Winn, Bratton, Brandon and others.

Marion's field of operations was confined to the eastern portion of South Carolina and does not belong properly to this narrative, which is intended only to record the military events in upper South Carolina. We will further add that Marion was ably supported by Colonels Peter and Hugh Horry, and James Postel, Lieutenant-Colonel John Baxter and Majors John Postel and James.

During the time that Marion and Sumter were at work in South Carolina, the scenes in North Carolina were no less stirring. Cornwallis being compelled to relinquish further pursuit of General Greene, after the latter's retreat across the Dan, now meditated upon the course he was to pursue. Being master of North Carolina, he decided to remain in that State and work to enlist the Loyalists in the name of the King. With this intent he quitted the banks of the Dan and repaired to Hillsborough; where, having erected the Royal standard, he issued a flaming proclamation, inviting the inhabitants to form themselves into regular companies. These efforts, however, did not meet with the success he had hoped for. The long domination of the Whig elements and the horrible enormities committed by the Royal troops in different parts of the American continent, had given birth to a sentiment of another cast.

Towards the middle of March, General Greene, having received reinforcements, resolved to march at once on his enemy. Accordingly, he recrossed the Dan and pushed forward with all his troops and took post at Guilford Court House. His army amounted to about 5,668 men,*

* See Schneck's "North Carolina," page 312.

the greater part of which were militia from Virginia and North Carolina; while the remainder were regulars from Virginia, Maryland and Delaware. The English, including the Hessians, amounted to 2,400 soldiers.* After various maneuverings the two armies confronted each other on the great road which leads from Salisbury to Guilford. This was on the 15th of March. We cannot give the details of the battle here. The ground was chosen by General Greene. The forces of General Greene were superior in numbers and those of Cornwallis superior in discipline. As soon as the action opened up, which was about 1 o'clock and lasted about two hours, the American militia did not stand firm, otherwise the result would not have been doubtful. A large per cent. of the militia organizations, however, had been enlisted only a short time, perhaps less than a month. The raw recruits behaved badly, broke line and fled. This caused a confusion. Those of Greene's forces, who had been well drilled and trained, fought hard, but they were eventually driven from the field, and forced to retreat for several miles. The British loss, in killed, wounded and missing, according to Cornwallis' official report, was 1,059,† while the American loss, in killed and wounded, was only about three hundred. Although the battle of Guilford Court House cannot be claimed as an American victory, yet the reader will pardon the deviation here when we present a paragraph of Senator Benton's eulogy on the character of Nathaniel Bacon, who was a soldier under General Greene. In commenting upon the battle of Guilford, this eminent statesman said: "The philosophy of history has not yet laid hold of the battle of Guilford, its consequences and effects. *That battle made the capture of Yorktown.* * * * * It broke up the plan of Cornwallis in the South and changed the plan of Washington in the North. Cornwallis was to subdue the Southern States and was doing

* See Botta's "American War," Page 323.

† See Schneck's "North Carolina," page 380.

it until Greene turned upon him at Guilford. Washington was occupied with Sir Henry Clinton, then in New York, with 12,000 British troops. He had formed the heroic design to capture Clinton and his army, the French fleet co-operating in that city, and thereby putting an end to the war. All his preparations were going on to that grand consummation, when he got the news of the battle of Guilford, the retreat of Cornwallis to Wilmington, his inability to keep the field in the South. and his return northward through the lower part of Virginia. He saw his advantage, an easy prey, and the same result, if successful. Cornwallis or Clinton, either of them captured, would put an end to the war. Washington changed his plan, deceived Clinton, moved rapidly upon the weaker General, captured him and his 7,000 men and ended the Revolutionary War. The battle of Guilford put that capture into Washington's hands; and thus Guilford and Yorktown became connected. * * * The lesser event was father to the greater.*

General Greene's camp was at "Speedwell's Iron Works," to which place he retired on the morning of the 16th of March, 1781. Here he remained until the 20th of the same month, endeavoring to repair the disorder and derangement always incident to a fierce and sanguinary battle. In a letter to Colonel Lee at this time he says: "I mean to fight the enemy again, and wish you to have your Legion and riflemen ready at the shortest notice. Lord Cornwallis must be soundly beaten before he will release his stronghold." No one understood the temper and resolution of General Greene better than Cornwallis. He therefore determined not to risk another engagement, but to retreat. Leaving the American wounded at Guilford Court House and those of his own, who could not be transported at New Garden Meeting House, he took up his line of retreat, using every artifice to avoid any

* See "Thirty Years View," United States Senate, by Thomas Benton, page 115.

further engagement. Profiting from the unpleasant experience he had realized in his pursuit of General Greene to the Dan, he now determined to keep *a stream* between him and his pursuer.

As soon as Lord Cornwallis began his retreat, General Greene put his army in motion to overtake him. After leaving his camp at Speedwell's Iron Works, on Troublesome Creek, he crossed Cross Creek and Buffalo Creek and continued the pursuit as far as Ramsey's Mill, some sixty miles from his starting point. He had expected to overtake and engage his adversary at Buffalo Creek. Says Johnson, "Such was the eagerness with which the pursuit was pressed that many of the American troops exerted themselves beyond their strength and fainted on the road."

General Greene, for various reasons, was compelled to abandon the further pursuit of Cornwallis. The term of enlistment of many of the militia, both from North Carolina and Virginia, had already expired, and these now turned their faces homeward, thus lessening the numbers of Greene's army. The further pursuit was through a region of Tories, who would have kept Cornwallis thoroughly posted as to Greene's strength and movements. Besides this, an inspection of his army revealed the fact that he was growing short of ammunition. The irregular troops had recklessly traded powder and shot, which were the best articles for procuring meat and bread.

There were still other reasons why Greene did not pursue Cornwallis. His route to overtake him lay through a dreary region, which had been already traversed by the army of Cornwallis, and could afford no supplies. Such being the case he wisely determined, as the sequel proved, to cast his eves in another direction, and to decide on the next course to be pursued.

On the day after the battle of Guilford, Colonel Wade Hampton* arrived in the American camp, and gave intel-

*Grandfather of present ex Senator Wade Hampton.

ligence that could be relied upon respecting the positions and strength of the enemy's forces in South Carolina. This intelligence, it is said, caused General Greene to decide at once on his future movements.

But before entering upon another campaign, General Greene deemed it proper to give a short rest to his army, preparatory to a new movement, and also to recruit and collect supplies, as his march lay for the most part through a barren and swampy country.

On the 6th day of April, the day before Cornwallis reached Wilmington, General Greene renewed his march, but now in a different direction. The two armies were now back to back. The face of General Greene was turned to South Carolina, where, in less than one year, he was to end a military career that was to make his name for all time glorious, while that of Cornwallis was turned to Virginia, where, in a few months, he was to end a course less glorious at Yorktown.

Continuing his march General Greene crossed at Mark's Ferry, on the Yadkin; then south, crossing Rocky River and Lynch's Creek, to Camden, South Carolina. General Greene's advance into South Carolina was preceded by Lieutenant-Colonel Lee,* who penetrated through the country, and in eight days effected a junction with General Marion, on the Santee. This not only surprised, but alarmed the British. To secure the provisions that grew on the fertile banks of the Santee and Congaree, the British had erected a chain of posts in their vicinity, reaching back in the direction of Georgetown. One of the most important of these was Fort Watson, near Wright's Bluff. This was a stockade fort, built on an eminence thirty or forty feet high, said to have been originally an Indian mound. This was closely invested on the 15th of April by about eighty men under General Marion and a number of mounted Continentals under Lieutenant-Colonel Lee. The garrison consisted of about one hundred and four-

*Lieutenant-Colonel Henry Lee, father of General Robert E. Lee, Confederate States army.

teen men, under Lieutenant McKay of the British regular troops.

Had Marion possessed even one piece of artillery, the task of capturing the fort would have been small. As it was, neither side had any other means of attack or defense but muskets. The steep side of the fort and palisades in front forbade an attempt at storming it. The Americans cut off the garrison from Scott's Lake, which supplied it with water. This was overcome on the part of the garrison, however, by sinking a well inside of the fort. Another stratagem was resorted to. A short distance from the fort there grew wood in abundance. This was cut down, and through the night the men carried the heavy timbers on their shoulders and placed them cross-wise. When morning came the besieged men were astonished. The fatal effect of a shower of balls announced to them that their stronghold was commanded by a superior work. Nothing now remained but to surrender, and a capitulation was at once concluded

Camden, during the Revolution, was a little village, located, as now, on a plain, covered on the south and east sides by the Wateree and a creek which enters into that river. It was here that Lord Rawdon was posted during the spring of 1781. The position was a strong one. It was defended on the north and west by six strong redoubts. Greene, upon his arrival at Camden, finding the post impregnable, took a strong position at Hobkirk's Hill, about one mile and a half north of Camden, intending, if possible, to allure the garrison out of their lines. In this he succeeded.

We have not time or space to give the details of the battle of Hobkirk. Lord Rawdon armed his musicians, drummers, and everything that could carry a firearm, and with great spirit sallied out to attack Greene on the 25th of April. An engagement ensued. It is stated by Botta and others, that Greene was surprised, while it is firmly denied by Johnson and others. At first victory seemed to incline to the Americans, but in the progress of the battle the tide turned. It is said that Greene had placed in his center the Maryland regulars, which had stood so firm at Cowpens and Guilford. For some reason unexplained, this veteran organization gave way at the beginning of the action. Lieutenant-Colonel Washington was ordered to turn the right of the British flank, and to charge their rear. So confident was he of Greene's success that he divided his command into small parties and placed them in secret positions which he thought most favorable for attacking the retreating fugitives of Rawdon's army. At one time he had captured nearly two hundred, but released the greatest part of them on seeing the American Army retreat.

The American forces, as we have said, consisted of about seven hundred; the British of about eight hundred. The American loss in killed, wounded and missing, was about two hundred. The British loss was smaller. General Greene retreated in good order with his baggage, artillery, &c., to Sanders' Creek, about four miles distant. In the evening after the battle Lieutenant-Colonel Washington, with fifty mounted cavalry advanced within a mile of the British camp. It appears that Lord Rawdon left Captain Coffin on the battlefield with his cavalry and some mounted infantry. Washington receiving this intelligence resolved to gain some advantage from it. Retiring with his cavalry into a thicket on the roadside, he pushed forward a small detachment, with orders to approach within a short distance of the enemy's position. The stratagem took effect. Coffin's whole command pursued, and having reached the hiding place of Washington's men, the whole command was attacked. Those who were not cut to pieces were compelled to fly for safety. The consequence was that the day actually terminated with the field of Hobkirk in the hands of the Americans.

Very soon after the action of the 25th at Hobkirk, General Greene, knowing that the garrison at Camden could not subsist very long without fresh supplies from Charleston, detached a reinforcement to General Marion on the Nelson's Ferry road.

General Greene remained at his camp the whole of the 26th and until the afternoon of the 27th, hoping that Rawdon, emboldened by his success, would make another attack. But the latter had been too severely used up to venture another experiment so far from his stronghold. The American commander retired five miles further, to Rugley's Mill, on the 27th, the depot of his baggage and stores. After this, on the 3d of May, he crossed the Wateree and took occasionally such positions as would prevent succor going into the town of Camden. On the 7th of May Rawdon received reinforcement by the arrival of a detachment under Colonel Watson. With this addition to his force he sallied out for several miles in the direction of General Greene's encampment, for the purpose of drawing him into an engagement, but finding this impossible, he decided after three days to break up his encampment and evacuate the town of Camden. On the 10th, after burning the jail, mills and many private dwellings, he retired with his whole army south of the Santee, leaving about thirty of his wounded and as many Americans, who had been captured by him after the action at Hobkirk on the 25th.

The evacuation of Camden was a necessary step for Lord Rawdon The position of General Greene at Rugley's Mill prevented succor from reaching him from that quarter, and the capture of Fort Watson had cut off his line of communication with Charleston.

Many of the Loyalist families accompanied Lord Rawdon on his departure. They chose this course rather than remain to fall into the hands of their exasperated countrymen. These families, it is said, were cruelly neglected after they reached Charleston. Having no houses provided for them they constructed a lot of huts outside of the works. This was called *Rawdontown.* Many women and children who had lived in comfort at their homes perished in these huts which were a reproach to British authorities.

In the fall of Camden Lord Rawdon lost not only this post, but the country and the confidence of the Tories. The Whigs everywhere were animated and the British alarmed. General Greene's ranks began to swell. On the day after the evacuation of Camden the post at Orangeburg, consisting of seventy British militia and twelve regulars, surrendered to General Sumter. The next day Fort Motte, on the Congaree, capitulated under circumstances peculiarly interesting. After the fall of Fort Watson, General Marion and Lieutenant-Colonel Lee crossed the Santee and moved up to this post, where they arrived on the 8th of May. The old site of this fort is south of the Congaree River, and only a short distance west of the South Carolina railroad. The garrison consisted of one hundred and sixty-five men, commanded by Lieutenant McPherson. The residence of Mrs. Motte stood in the center of the fort. It seems that the firing of this was necessary to bring about the capitulation of the fort. Mrs. Motte was consulted. When informed of what was necessary for the reduction of the fort, she presented the besiegers with a quiver of African arrows to be employed for that purpose. Skewers, armed with combustible materials, were also used with more effect. The experiment proved successful. Mrs Motte was overjoyed to witness the reduction of the post, though her private property was sacrificed.

Lord Rawdon, upon his arrival at Nelson's Ferry, on the Santee, hearing that all these posts had capitulated, marched directly to Eutaw Springs, after blowing up his fortifications and destroying many of his stores at Nelson's Ferry.

A few days later the British garrison at Granby, about twenty-five miles higher up the Congaree, and only a few miles from the present city of Columbia, capitulated. This post was commanded by an officer named Maxwell, who is represented as having been a notorious plunderer.

He surrendered on the first summons by Lee, who already had him in a measure within his grasp.

Only two important British posts now remained commanding the upper part of South Carolina, viz: Augusta and Ninety-Six. Let us first give our attention to the former place. The defenses immediately around Augusta consisted of two forts, Cornwallis and Grierson. The former was commanded by Colonel Brown, and the latter, Colonel Grierson. Lower down the Savannah River a few miles was Fort ~~Gilpin~~. Galphin

Pickens, who had been recently created a Brigadier, was ordered by General Greene to collect and enlist in his command the Whig elements in upper Carolina, concentrate before Augusta, looking to the reduction of that post, and to cut off all communication between Augusta and Ninety-Six. Lieutenant-Colonel Lee with his legion was also ordered, after the fall of Granby, to join Pickens at Augusta. The distance between those points was about one hundred miles. Lee's legion had been recently recruited by the addition of Colonel Eaton's command of two hundred North Carolina militia.

Says Johnson: "Among those who hastened into action upon the approach of the American army (into South Carolina) was Colonel Clarke of Georgia. His followers immediately gathered around him and he found himself at the head of a party sufficient to invest Augusta, as soon as Pickens was able to hold in check the garrison at Ninety-Six."

Clarke's approach to Augusta was sudden and unexpected. It was the custom of the British authorities to send annually presents to the Cherokee Indians. Several boats loaded with these annual presents were on their way up the Savannah River. Clarke heard of these boats and before they could make good their retreat he waylaid them. The stream, though deep, is narrow and Clarke's riflemen among the trees along the banks would soon have swept the deck of any boat not provided against attack. Unable to ascend or descend, these boats took shelter under Fort Gilpin; and Colonel Clarke was carefully guarding this invaluable prize when he was joined some days afterwards by Lee.

Immediately upon Lee's arrival he was complimented with the task of capturing Fort Gilpin. This was on the 21st of May. Lee captured the post by stratagem as it were. Appearing before it with a small force, the garrison sallied out to engage it, when Captain Rudolph, of Lee's legion, who was concealed with a larger force, rushed into the fort and captured it. All those outside were taken prisoners.

By the fall of this fort there were captured one hundred and twenty-six prisoners of all descriptions, including seventy commissioned officers and privates in the regular service, besides the boats on the stream with their loaded cargoes. The American casualties were small, only twelve wounded. The capture of these boats was a valuable acquisition to the American cause. They were loaded with a quantity of clothing, blankets, small arms, rum, salt, and other useful and much-needed articles of which the American army had long been deprived. There was also a good supply of ammunition and some articles of military equipment.

Notwithstanding, the command of General Pickens, representing the States of Georgia and South Carolina, were in a naked and destitute condition, yet the distribution of these articles exhibited the characters of Pickens and Greene transformed in a light that was honorable to both. Pickens, with modesty, begged of General Greene that his men be allowed to share, in their destitute condition, a part of the booty captured. Greene, in reply, authorized him to divide the same according to his sense of justice and the good of the service. Pickens set aside the military stores for public service, and loaded thirteen wagons with rum, salt, sugar, medicines, &c., for the main army. He divided the clothing into three equal parts, assigning one lot to Georgia, another to South Carolina and the third to the Continental troops. The fowling pieces were distributed among the militia on condition that they would remain in the army for specific service.

Fort Gilpin being captured, two forts still remained in the hands of the British, viz: Grierson and Cornwallis. General Pickens decided to attack Grierson first and carry it by storm. The plan was for General Pickens to make the attack on the north and west, while Major Eaton and his battalion and Colonel Clarke at the head of the militia, were to pass down the north side of the lagoon and approach the fort from the south. Lieutenant-Colonel Lee was to march down the lagoon parallel with Eaton and be ready to support the attack if necessary, and at the same time to hold Brown in check and prevent him from rendering any assistance to Grierson. The cavalry of Eggleston were ordered to draw near Fort Cornwallis, but to keep concealed in the wood, ready to fall upon the rear of Colonel Brown should he attempt to march to the assistance of Grierson.

The orders were promptly carried out. The garrison at Fort Grierson were soon overpowered. Colonel Grierson, galled by the fire from the American batteries, decided to evacuate the fort and retreat to Fort Cornwallis. He suddenly issued from the rear of the fort and attempted to retreat under cover of the river bank. The North Carolina troops and Colonel Clarke's men, perceiving the motive of Grierson, pressed forward to the river bank to intercept him. A lively action ensued. The British party with the exception of a very few, were either killed, wounded, or captured. It has been asserted by Lee that Grierson was killed in cold blood by some of his personal enemies among the Georgians. Besides Grierson, a major and thirty odd men were killed, while a lieutenant-colonel and over forty men were made prisoners.

By the capture of Fort Grierson the Americans had the good fortune to take two field pieces and some small arms.

Colonel Brown perceiving the fall of Fort Grierson,

withdrew within the walls of his fort and at once set to work to strengthen in every way his position.

In the attack on Fort Grierson the American loss was small, only a few killed and wounded, but among the former was a life valuable to the American cause. This was Major Pinketham of North Carolina. He had only been a few weeks with the light corps and fell gallantly at the head of his battalion in the moment of victory.

Pickens now directed his attention to Fort Cornwallis and pressed the seige with diligence and activity. Strong earthworks were erected on the south side until the parallels were very near the fort. Brown left nothing undone to protect his position. He was brave and obstinate and for two nights made reckless sallies on the besiegers, but was driven back by the accuracy of the American marksmen.

General Pickens, under the advice of Lieutenant-Colonel Lee, erected what is known as the Maham Tower. This was made by collecting logs and notching them together in a penshape and filling in them with stone and earth. Being built behind a house it was not discovered by Brown until it was nearly completed, which was late on the second day. Brown at once mounted two of his best pieces and endeavored to knock it down, but his efforts were unavailing. An American six-pounder was placed on the lofty top of the tower and soon made sad havoc with everthing inside the fort, even uncovering the magazine. Although the situation was now almost hopeless for Brown, still he determined to continue a stubborn resistance. On the night of the 25th he made another desperate assault, which was bravely met by the militia and Rudolph's company of the legion.

Pickens still pressed the siege with energy and determination. The troops were in the highest of spirits and eager for the assault. In another part of this work we have referred to Brown in the beginning of the Revolution as being of "tar and feather memory." In another place we have also mentioned his cruelties in putting to death American prisoners. The Georgia militia were intending to have a bloody revenge as soon as Brown was captured. He had hanged thirteen of their number with remorseless cruelty.

General Pickens, wishing to avoid a scene of slaughter, sent a final demand to Brown to surrender.* Negotiations followed, which resulted in the capitulation of the fort and garrison, the 5th of June, 1781. The terms were as follows: The officers and soldiers who were surrendered were to be conducted to such places the commander-in-chief of the Americans might designate. The officers were to be indulged on paroles.

At the appointed time the garrison, which consisted of between three and four hundred, marched out. It was necessary to take special precaution to prevent Brown from being mobbed by the infuriated Georgians. He was kept at Lieutenant-Colonel Lee's headquarters until the next day, when he was sent down the river to Savannah as a paroled prisoner, under the care of Captain Armstrong.

On the 6th of June, Lee recrossed the Savannah River, with a valuable accession of artillery, and hastened to join Greene, who was then laying siege to Ninety-Six. He reached him on the 8th. General Pickens, after securing the baggage, followed on the same day—the 8th.

Lord Rawdon, who was in Charleston, heard with consternation of the fall of Augusta. He was at that time impatiently waiting for reinforcements to march to the assistance of Ninety-Six. These reinforcements landed on the 3d of June and on the 7th His Lordship set out for Ninety-Six, with three Irish regiments just arrived. On his way he was joined by some other troops from Monk's Corner, giving him a total of 2,000 men. We will see the result in the next chapter

*See letters of correspondence. Gibb's Documentary History of South Carolina, 1780-82, pages 82 to 86.

CHAPTER XXXV.

SIEGE OF NINETY-SIX.—ADVANCE OF RAWDON.—RETREAT OF GENERAL GREENE TO TIM'S ORDINARY.—RAWDON ABANDONS THE POST AT NINETY-SIX AND RETREATS TO GRANBY, ON THE CONGAREE.—STEWART MARCHES FROM ORANGEBURG TO MEET HIM.—GENERAL GREENE ADVANCES TO GRANBY.—RAWDON RETREATS.—EXECUTION OF HAYNE.—RAWDON LEAVES SOUTH CAROLINA. EUTAW SPRINGS NOTICED.—OTHER INCIDENTS, &c.

AFTER the fall of Augusta the British had only two strongholds in South Carolina, viz: Ninety-Six and Charleston. The fall of the posts of Camden, Orangeburg, Fort Motte and Granby occurred in rapid succession, on the 10th, 11th, 12th and 15th of May, 1781. General Greene's attention after this was turned to the reduction of Ninety-Six. Accordingly, on the 17th (the day after Colonel Lee was dispatched to Augusta) he took up his line of March for Ninety-Six, moving up the north side of the Saluda, reaching that place on the 22d. By the fall of the four forts referred to, he had acquired a respectable amount of ammunition, provisions and small arms.

General Sumter was left in command of all the country recently recovered from the enemy. He was enjoined especially to watch the movements of the enemy, to keep General Greene posted as to the same, and to prevent, if possible, any relief being sent from Charleston to Ninety-Six. He was to continue to recruit his command, and collect stores for the maintenance of the army.

To General Marion was committed the care of reducing and holding in subjection the post of Georgetown and the Tory settlements to the North of it.

The village of Cambridge, or as it was called in that day, the post of Ninety-Six, was the district site where courts were held for Ninety-Six District, which comprised, as we have before stated, the present counties of Edgefield, Abbeville, Newberry, Laurens, Union and Spartanburg. The proper name of the place was Cambridge—the metropolis or county town of Ninety-Six District.

There are several traditions with regard to the origin of the name *Ninety-Six*. One is that it is just ninety-six miles each way from this point to Charleston and the site of old Prince George, in Oconee County, and that this fact was first discovered bv an Indian woman who had been charged with the delivery of an important message from the English troops at Fort Prince George to the official authorities in Charleston.

Johnson says that the name "Ninety-Six" was adopted by the ancient inhabitants of that section, who intended it "as a fanciful allusion to the uniform excellence of the soil" in that neighborhood. The two numbers (9 and 6) which compose its name, viewed on any side, will express the same quantity.

We have shown clearly in the beginning chapters of our Revolutionary history, in this brief narrative, that this place derives some celebrity in the annals of our country's history, from its having been the scene of the first conflict in the South during the Revolution. By reference to former chapters, it will be noticed that at this place commenced, in 1775, that dreadful conflict between Whig and Tory, called then *Patriot* and *Insurgent*, which well nigh ruined that country.

One reason why the hostile parties had been invited to this place was that it had been surrounded with a stockade, built vears before as a defence against the Indians, whose country was then not far off. This stockade was still remaining, and very soon after the British got possession of Charleston they placed a garrison there, and made it a principal point in their outer military posts. It enabled them to keep up a communication with the Cherokees, with whom they remained friendly, and to hold the Whigs west and north of the place somewhat in check, while, as we will see, it afforded great protection to the Loyalists in that immediate section.

At the time that General Greene sat down against Ninety-Six this post was commanded by Colonel Cruger, with a garrison of five hundred and fifty men, all of whom were Americans by birth, and mostly from New York and New Jersey. Some of them, however, had been enlisted and organized in the neighborhood by a Colonel King. These are all represented as being desperate men, and marksmen of the first order.

Cruger is represented as a man of talents, and his correspondence proves him to be a gentleman in deportment.

The siege of Ninety-Six was one of the most animated of the American war. It proved, from accidental circumstances, to be an unfortunate one for General Greene. Lord Rawdon had given orders to Cruger, before leaving Camden, to evacuate that post in order to concentrate his strength below, sufficient to assume aggressive operations and maintain his ascendancy on the coast. This order was communicated in two ways, first by Charleston and Savannah, and second, directly across the country. Both dispatches were intercepted, and consequently Cruger failed to receive them. Otherwise, Greene would have been saved the necessity of his western march to Ninety-Six, and would have found himself, without a struggle, master of all upper South Carolina.

It is probable too that Cruger, after leaving Ninety-Six and attempting to unite with Brown at Augusta (for such were his orders), would have been captured or routed by the combined forces of Pickens, Lee and Clark. Having no cavalry and in an open country he would have been placed at a very great disadvantage.

On the approach of Greene to Ninety-Six, Cruger lost no time in preparing for self-defense. Pressing into service all the able-bodied slaves in the surrounding neighborhood, he soon completed a ditch around his stockade, throwing the earth upon it and making it of parapet heighth. This he secured within by transverses and coverts in order to facilitate a safe communication between all his points of defense. The main ditch was secured by an abbatis in front. Block-houses of notched logs were also constructed at convenient points within the stockade. Besides this, Cruger constructed a respectable batterv of star shape* with sixteen salient and returning angles, which communicated with the stockade. This battery was defended by three pieces of artillery on wheel carriages, which could be moved from one point to another. On the north of the village is a small stream from which the garrison was supplied with water. The county goal built of brick (the same that was defended against the Insurgents in 1775) stood inside of the stockade and commanded the vallev next to the old village of Cambridge. [See accompanying map.] On the opposite side of the valley, and within reach of the fire from the jail, was a strong stockade with two block-houses. This was intended to cover communications from that quarter. A covert way led from the town to the stream.

It is said that when Greene first examined these defenses he apprehended the failure of the enterprise. He determined, however, not to let this doubt deter him from undertaking the design. He broke ground on the 23d of May and by the 3d of June he had completed his third parallel. The engineer of the American army was the celebrated Polish exile, Kosciusko, who on a dark and rainy night, the 22d, accompanied by General Greene and Captain Pendleton, his aide, made an entire circuit around the enemv's fortifications and planned the work which the besiegers attempted to execute. By the time the parallel was completed a mine directed against the star battery was commenced. This work was protected by a few pieces of artillery near by and was pursued by the besiegers both day and night without intermission. In spite of occasional sallies from the fort to repel the besiegers, the American works steadily advanced.

*The old star shape fort of Ninety-Six is still distinctly recognized to the present day by all visitors to that place.

As soon as the American fortifications, parallel with the fort, were completed the garrison was summoned to surrender. This proposition was defiantly refused. The siege went on. A fierce strife followed every step of progress the Americans made. Not a night passed without the loss of life on both sides. With proper time to complete all the plans of Kosciusko, the capture of the fort was only a matter of time. General Greene's forces, however, were inadequate. He had been promised recruits from Virginia, which failed to arrive. Many of the Carolina troops were below actively engaged in holding Rawdon in check. Cruger was very much aided from without by a marauding force of Loyalists under Captain Cunningham, who were well mounted and had dispersed themselves in small bodies all over the country for the purpose of waylaying recruits or supplies that might be going to General Greene's camp.

The Americans succeeded in completing the third parallel and from wooden towers which had been erected, the British artillerists were driven away from their guns by the American marksmen. Various means were resorted to for reduction of the fort. The experiment of Fort Motte was tried. Burning arrows were thrown to fire the houses inside, but Cruger freed himself from this danger by tearing the roofs from his houses. The work of the besiegers was so near completion that it did not appear that the besieged could hold out more than four days longer.

Besides the towers referred to, one of which was within thirty yards of the enemy's ditch, the besiegers had several batteries of cannon within one hundred and forty yards. One of these so completely commanded the "star" that the garrison were compelled to shelter themselves behind bags of sand, which were thrown up for protection. Embrasures were left in these for the employment of cannon at night.

Thus it was for ten days the besieged and the besiegers watched each other. During this time not a man on

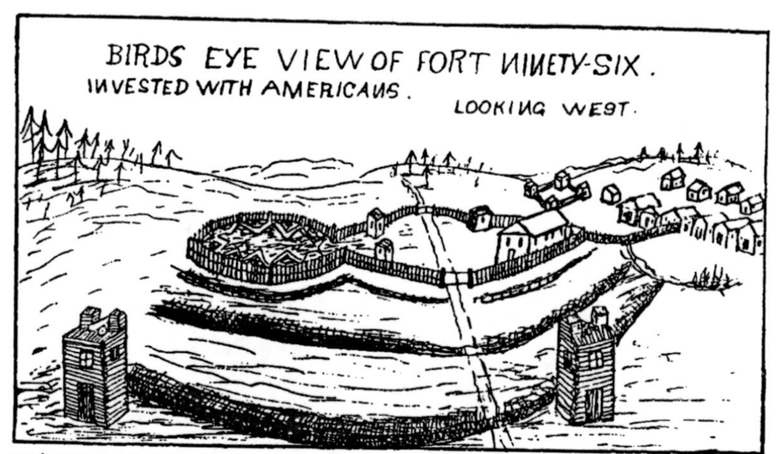

BIRDS EYE VIEW OF FORT NINETY-SIX.
INVESTED WITH AMERICANS.
LOOKING WEST.

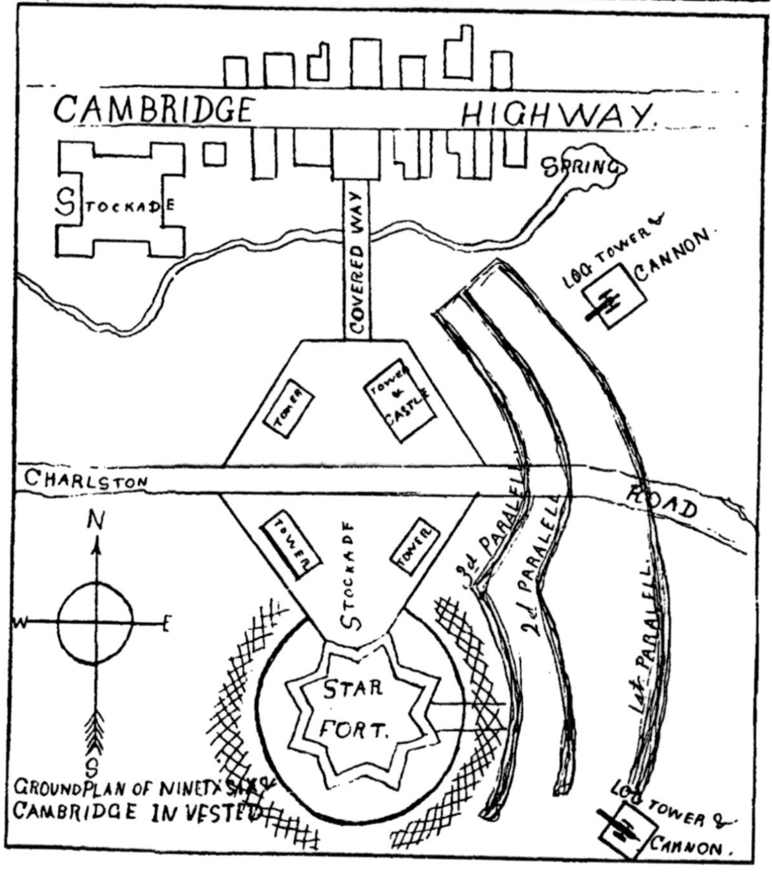

CAMBRIDGE HIGHWAY.
STOCKADE
SPRING
COVERED WAY
LOG TOWER & CANNON.
TOWER
TOWER & CASTLE
CHARLSTON ROAD
N
W
E
S
TOWER
STOCKADE
TOWER
3d PARALEL
2d PARALELL
1st PARALELL
STAR FORT.
GROUNDPLAN OF NINETY SIX & CAMBRIDGE INVESTED
LOG TOWER & CANNON.

either side could show his head without incurring the risk of being shot down. It is simply astonishing how the garrison stood the American fire, suffered so long, and maintained at the same time a defense, which, says a writer, "reflects the highest honor on its commander." His resolution, as we will see, was strengthened by advices which he had received from without; otherwise he might have surrendered.

Lord Rawdon, having received intelligence of the siege of Ninety-Six, determined to march at once to its relief. He had just been reinforced by three regiments from Ireland and with these, together with other troops which joined him at Monk's Corner on the way, he had under him a force of about two thousand.

But how was the intelligence of his march communicated to Cruger? It is said that a woman was the instrument employed. A daughter of a Whig patriot was residing in the neighborhood, and was allowed to visit the camp of General Greene under some trifling pretext. It turned out, however, that she was in love with a British officer and the ties of love proved stronger than relationship. In the opportunities that had thus been afforded her to visit the American camp, she artfully managed to apprise the garrison that she had a communication from Lord Rawdon. A young Loyalist received it from her lips at a farm house, and attiring himself as a farmer, he rode into the American camp, representing himself as a friend. After moving around among the troops and at last coming near the front line, he spurred his horse to a fearful speed and dashed through the fire of sentinels and pickets into the open space between the contending lines, when he took from his pocket a letter. This he held in view of the besieged. Rushing for the front gates, which were swung open to receive him, he was at the next moment inside the fort, where he was given a joyful welcome. In a few minutes more shouts of triumph went up inside the fort.

This circumstance made it necessary for General Greene

to abandon the siege or endeavor to carry the place at once by storm. On the 18th he set to work to execute the latter plan, and by midday the different detachments were all ready. Lieutenant Duval, with a command of Marylanders, and Lieutenant Selden, with a command of Virginians, were stationed in front of the star battery. Close by them followed a party furnished with hooks on the ends of staves. Near by were the first Maryland and first Virgina regiments. These were marched under cover of the approaches within a few yards of the enemy's ditch. General Greene, before he made the attack, ordered the sharpshooters from the rifle towers and advanced works to be manned so as to clear at once the parapets of the garrison. On the American right, against the stockade fort, was Major Randolph, of Lee's legion, and Kirkwood with the remains of the Delaware regiment, to lead the forlorn hope in that quarter. Duval and Selden were ordered to clear away the abbatis in their front, and drive off the enemy on the sides of the angle, and open the way for the men detailed to pull down the sandbags.

A discharge of a cannon at noon was the signal for the parties to begin the attack. Says Sims: "A blaze of artillery and small arms covered the forlorn hope in its smoke. Under its shade this gallant band leapt into the ditch and commenced the work assigned them; but the enemy was prepared for them and met the assault with valor and determination. Bayonets and pikes bristled above the parapet, and from the loopholes in the sandbags poured an incessant stream of fire, which swept the slender ranks of the assailants. The form of the redoubt gave the enemy complete command of the ditch, and their coolness and the comparative safety of their cover, enabled them to use it with complete success."

It is stated that the fire from opposite sections of the redoubt mowed down the brave Americans with a dreadful havoc. Duval and Selden both fell severely wounded, while their men lay bleeding and dead around them. But the strife was kept up for nearly three quarters of an hour.

The assailants seemed determined upon no other issue than victory or death. At last, General Greene seeing the utter failure of the attack, ordered a retreat. In the midst of a galling fire from the garrison, the assailants brought away many of their wounded.

On the left Colonel Lee's legion found no difficulty in getting into the stockade. It had been evacuated the night previous, but the movement was so silent that it was not discovered. Thus ended the bloody and spirited affair, which Johnson says for the number engaged, there was as much bravery displayed as was ever exhibited by man. The American loss was very serious. There were near forty killed and wounded, including some valuable officers. While no truce was proposed by General Greene for the purpose of burying the dead (this ceremonial by custom belonging to the victor), a proposal through the Adjutant-General was submitted for both parties to be mutually permitted to pass in security between the lines for the purpose of burying the dead. To this proposition Cruger made the following polite answer: "Major-General Greene may, with the fullest confidence, rely on every attention which humanity can dictate being paid to those men of the American army whom the fortune of war has thrown into our hands. The killed of your army yesterday, within our abbatis shall be immediately sent to you to be buried."

It has already been stated that it became indispensable with General Greene on the day of the assault to decide whether he would advance and fight Lord Rawdon, who was approaching at no great distance, or raise the siege and retreat. To be prepared for either alternative, he sent off his heavy baggage across the Saluda at Island Ford. This route led to his depots of supplies on the Catawba River.

Lord Rawdon, with his force of not less than two thous and, had been on the march since the 11th. He was pressing with all possible speed to relieve the garrison. Marion, Washington and Sumter had been instructed to watch and impede his movements in the lower part of the State, but his numbers were too large and compact for much headway to be made by these gallant officers. Of Rawdon's force, there were perhaps not less than four hundred mounted men.

Retreat now became indispensable for General Greene. Reluctantly, therefore, he resolved to raise the siege and on the night of the 19th, moved off across the Saluda on the track of his baggage. Lord Rawdon had already reached Little Saluda and would soon be united with Cruger. Sumter, with the cavalry of Washington and Lee, was moving up within the fork of Saluda and Broad to form a junction with Greene's army. The influence of the late misfortune and retreat, however, was bad on Sumter and Marion. Many were the desertions of the militia on this account.

General Greene's retreat from Ninety-Six was pushed without intermission to Bush River, a distance of about twenty-two miles. On the 22d he halted to inform himself of the movements of the enemy. He received intelligence that Lord Rawdon had entered Ninety-Six at 2 o'clock on the 21st. He immediately put his army in motion, crossed Enoree and Tyger Rivers, passing through the present County of Union, and after crossing Broad River, halted at Tim's Ordinary, eleven miles beyond Leslie's Ford, on Broad River.

In Mrs. Ellet's "Women of the Revolution"* the story is told that soon after the seige of Ninety-Six, and after General Greene had crossed Broad River, he was very anxious to send an order to General Sumter, then on the Wateree, to join him that they might attack Rawdon, who had divided his force. The country being filled with British and Tories, no one appeared willing to undertake this dangerous mission. At length a young girl, Emily Geigier, about eighteen years of age, appeared before General Greene and volunteered to convey this message.

---

*See vol. ii, page 295.

He accordingly wrote a letter to General Sumter and gave it to her, at the same time communicating to her verbally its contents. Mounting on a swift horse, upon a side-saddle, she performed a part of the journey in safety. On the second day she was intercepted by Rawdon's scouts, who suspected that she was coming from the direction of General Greene's army and was entrusted with some important message. Being shut up in a room, the officer in command sent for an old Tory matron to examine her. But, left alone for a moment, this heroic girl embraced the opportunity to tear up General Greene's letter and swallow the same piece by piece. Nothing suspicious being found on her person, she was allowed to depart whither she said she was bound. By taking a circuitous route to avoid further detection, she soon reached General Sumter's camp in safety, where she told of her adventure and delivered the message. This was to order Sumter to join the main army at Orangeburg.

This story is reproduced and illustrated in "Quackenbos' School History of the United States."* The writer has seen no account of it anywhere else. He has examined Ramsay, Johnson, Botta, Simms and others, and no mention is made of it whatever. It is stated by Miss Geiger's biographer, in Mrs. Ellet's works, that this adventurous young lady afterwards married a rich planter on the Congaree. She lived until about 1827.

Lord Rawdon remained at Ninety-Six until the 24th. Hearing from deserters that Greene's army was still at Bush River, he took with him troops of the garrison and the troops capable of sustaining fatigue—in all about two thousand—and made a vigorous effort to overtake the retreating American army. Greene, however, was out of his reach. Rawdon advanced no further than Duncan's Creek, a tributary of the Enoree River. He returned to Ninety-Six, knowing that as Greene was falling back in

---

*See page 290.

the direction of his reinforcements, he could accomplish nothing by pursuing him. It is a singular coincidence that General Greene lay at this time encamped at the very spot (Tims Ordinary) from which Lord Cornwallis commenced his career against Greene in South Carolina.

A distressing scene followed Lord Rawdon's return to Ninety-Six. This officer felt it to be his imperative duty to abandon that post and concentrate his forces at a point lower down the State. This resolution was a sad announcement to the Loyalists families in the surrounding country. A day of retribution had overtaken them. Ninety-Six had long been their market, their seat of power, their source of wealth and influence to the surrounding country. Lord Rawdon called together the heads of prominent families and explained to them the necessity of abandoning the post that protected them. These people rather than be left to the mercy of the infuriated Whigs, resolved to abandon their beautiful country in the height of its luxuriance, endeared to them by a thousand tender asssociations, and follow the fortunes of Rawdon's army. For some days, it is said, the roads to Ninety-Six were lined with unhappy calvacades of women and children, wagons, stock and slaves, collecting at that place, preparatory to a departure. With eyes streaming from grief, "how bitterly in their ears," says Sims, "at such a moment must have sounded the notes of that trumpet and drum, which had beguiled them from the banners of their country to those of the invader."

After the departure of Lord Rawdon from Ninety-Six, Cruger was left behind to cover the retreat of the Loyalist families. He commenced his march on the 8th of July, at the head of this large cavelcade of Tory families. Their journey is described as a distressing one, to every age, sex and condition. After reaching the tract of country in the lower part of the State to which they were ordered to retire—their "land of promise"—the rich estates of banished Whigs, they soon found that all the remuneration and protection that had been promised them ended in a delusion. At length, driven from their homes by the returning Whigs, they gathered in great numbers in the suburbs of the City of Charleston, and lodged in tents and formed a settlement, which, as we have already said in the spirit of burlesque and reproach, took the name of *Rawdon Town.* Here many perished miserably, while others moved to the British settlements on the islands. Others moved to Florida, at that time a part of the Spanish possessions, where their descendants still exist. Others resolved to return to their native homes. In Colonel Pickens, who commanded that section of country, they found a friend and protector, a man of kindness and benevolence.

Lord Rawdon, believing that by the retreat and direction General Greene had taken, he intended to abandon South Carolina, resolved to divide his army, with the intention of fixing a detachment at Granby, on the Congaree. He soon found, however, that his adversaries were not disposed to give up South Carolina, a prize for which they had so long contended. Greene, on hearing that Lord Rawdon had marched with a part of his force to Congaree, now faced about to give him battle. Lord Rawdon, before leaving Ninety-Six, had received intelligence from Colonel Stewart that his detachment was on its way from Orangeburg to meet him at Granby, and would reach that place by the 3d of July. The time was perfectly well calculated to form this junction before General Greene, from his position at Tims Ordinary, could march to prevent it.

General Greene, anticipating Rawdon's movement, marched a day's journey in the direction of Granby. This, in some measure, quieted the apprehensions of the country that it was his purpose to abandon the State. At the Big Spring on Rocky Creek, in the present County of Fairfield, the American General passed two days of rest to his army, but to him of anxious suspense. He had but little doubt that as soon as he advanced the enemy would retreat. In two days after reaching Granby, on the Congaree, hearing that Greene was advancing, Rawdon made an expeditious retreat to Orangeburg. This was a strong position. He had strong buildings on one side, little inferior to redoubts, and on the other side he was secured by the Edisto River. Greene pursued and encamped within five miles of Orangeburg. Lord Rawdon, feeling secure in his position, would not venture out; and General Greene was too weak to attack him in his stronghold with any prospect of success, notwithstanding he knew that Lord Rawdon's army was divided. Colonel Washington had intercepted a letter from Stewart to Lord Rawdon, informing His Lordship that he was on the march to join him, but that he could not reach Granby before the 3d of July. Lee, who had hovered on the heels of Colonel Cruger on his retreat from Ninety-Six, informed General Greene that Rawdon had marched from that place with less than half of his force.

In the course of Lee's movements in rear of Cruger, Captain Eggleston, of his legion, fell in with forty-nine British horsemen near Saluda, and took all but one of them prisoners. It was while the American army lay at Orangeburg that General Greene received advice that Cruger had evacuated Ninety-Six, and was then marching with the troops of that garrison, together with his calvacade of Loyalists, through the forks of the Edisto, to unite with Rawdon at Orangeburg. Knowing that the north fork of the Edisto was not passable by an army without boats for thirty miles above and below the British encampment, General Greene realized that he could not throw himself between the forces of Cruger and Rawdon with any prospect of preventing their junction, retired with his army to the high hills of the Santee.

With the ending of the siege at Ninety-Six and General Greene's retreat to Tims Ordinary and his subsequent advance to Orangeburg ended his military operations in upper South Carolina, and here we must leave him, as our narrative is only intended to give the history of events of the "up-country." There are some points, however, of general interest, which we will briefly touch upon. We hope the reader will continue, through other works, to follow General Greene to the end of his brilliant career in South Carolina. Nor are the military operations of Marion, Sumter, Lee, Hampton, Pickens and their subordinates any the less worthy of investigation. Their daring exploits to resist the British invasion, and their efforts to preserve the dignity of the State during the most trying period of her history, should never be forgotten by the rising generations of our country.

Lord Rawdon, driven from almost every post he had occupied, baffled in all his schemes and overwhelmed with vexation, became alarmed for the safety of his army. In the City of Charleston were quite a number of citizens who had taken the oath of allegiance to the king, with the understanding that they were to remain at their homes undisturbed. Upon this class Rawdon called to take up arms against their American brethren. Among the number was Colonel Isaac Hayne, whose capture and execution is recorded in the pages of the history of our State. Hayne, feeling that the British authorities had violated their part of the agreement, considered that he was, therefore, absolved from his part of the contract. Collecting a troop of horses he set out to enlist in the cause of his country. If he must fight at all he determined it must be for the cause he loved. He ranged the country, and after gaining some advantages, was defeated and captured. He was carried to Charleston, hurriedly tried, and sentenced to death. In vain did General Greene, representing the American authorities, the ladies of Charleston, the sister of the prisoner, and his children, implore the mercy of Rawdon. He was hanged on the 4th of August. He bore himself gallantly. Says Sims: "Ascending the fatal eminence of death he parted from his friends with the simple assurance that he would endeavor to show them "how an American should die." Sims further states, that, though it was not suffered to appear in the proceedings of his trial, Hayne was only a chosen sacrifice to the manes of Major Andre.

Very soon after the execution of Hayne, Lord Rawdon, leaving Colonel Stewart in command of the entire British army in South Carolina, set out for England. On his way he was captured by a French vessel and was made a prisoner. France having formed an alliance with the United States, he became virtually a prisoner of the latter. "He was," says Judge Schenck,* "a fit subject of retaliation for the execution of Colonel Isaac Hayne, but Colonel Fanning, the Tory leader, about this time made his celebrated incursion to Hillsboro, and carried off Governor Burke. This gave the British a hostage for the life of Rawdon, and perhaps saved His Lordship from the gibbet." At the surrender of Cornwallis, at Yorktown (Oct. 19, 1781), Rawdon being a captive on a vessel which formed a part of the French fleet at that place, was an unwilling witness to the scenes that transpired on that occasion.

Only one general engagement took place after this in South Carolina between the Brisish army under Stewart and the American army. This was the memorable battle of Eutaw Springs, fought on the 8th of September. It does not come within the scope of this work to present the details of this battle. Stewart, having taken position at Eutaw Springs, and General Greene's army having increased by reinforcements to 2,600 men, the latter resolved to march against and attack him. The battle was fought with desperate courage on both sides, but the British ranks were at length broken. Colonel Campbell, on the American side, fell mortally wounded on the field, while Colonel Washington received a bayonet wound and was captured by the enemy. Still the route of the British army was general, and the Americans, thinking the battle over, went to plundering. While they were thus scattered

---

*See Schenck's "North Carolina," page 445.

the enemy rallied and returned to the conflict. General Greene's vigilance saved his army from surprise, and with some loss he drew his men off, leaving the British masters of the field. The Americans, however, had gained decidedly the advantage. The British loss in killed, wounded and prisoners, was upwards of eleven hundred, while the American loss was about five hundred men, including about sixty officers. Stewart, having measured arms with Greene, knew the character of the man who was pressing him. The next day he destroyed his stores and retreated toward Charleston, leaving one thousand stand of arms and about seventy of his wounded behind him.

After the action at Eutaw Springs, the Americans retired to their former position on the high hills of Santee, while the British took position in the vicinity of Monk's Corner. The active partisans on the American side still kept alive their blows on the detached convoys of the enemy at different places. On one occasion, Colonel Maham, with a small party of American cavalry, took upwards of eighty prisoners within sight of the British camp. Says Ramsey: "The British no more acted with their usual vigor. On the slightest appearance of danger, they discovered a disposition to flee scarcely inferior to what was exhibited a year before by the American militia." By the end of October, the intelligence of the surrender of Yorktown reached Greene's army. The day was observed as a general jubilee in camp. The news gave new life and impulse to the ragged soldiers, who had so long followed Greene, their devoted leader. The latter determined to cross the river at once which separated him from his enemy and drive him to the sea.

The hopes of the American people were revived every where. Governor Rutledge had returned to South Carolina and was restoring the civil authority. He had issued a proclamation calling upon the people to elect representatives to the Legislature, to convene early in January at Jacksonborough, a little village on the Edisto River (at present a station on the Charleston and Savannah Railroad).

While the enemy were being forced back and reverses were attending their arms everywhere, and the people were rejoicing that the struggle for American freedom would soon be at an end, heartrendeng, bloody and unexpected scenes transpired in the up-country, the sad particulars of which we record in the succeeding and last chapter of this work.

CHAPTER XXXVI.

THE "BLOODY BILLS," CUNNINGHAM AND BATES.—EARLY YEARS OF WILLIAM CUNNINGHAM.—VOLUNTEERS IN CAPTAIN CALDWELL'S COMPANY.—DESERTS THE AMERICAN CAUSE AND BECOMES AN ACTIVE PARTISAN ON THE BRITISH SIDE.—MAKES A RAID TO THE UP-COUNTRY IN NOVEMBER, 1781.—UPRISING OF THE CHEROKEES.—EXPEDITION OF GENERAL PICKENS TO THEIR COUNTRY.—THE CHEROKEES SUE FOR PEACE.—CUNNINGHAM CONTINUES HIS BLOODY MARCH FROM ORANGEBURG THROUGH NEWBERRY, LAURENS, UNION, AND SPARTANBURG.—MASSACRE AT THE TURNER HOUSE.—MURDER OF CAPT. JOHN CALDWELL.—MASSACRE AT "HAYES' STATION."—ESCAPE OF MR. JOHN BOYCE.—CUNNINGHAM VISITS CHARLES MOORE'S PLACE.—KILLING OF CAPTAIN STEADMAN AND TWO OTHERS.—MURDER OF JOHN WOOD, EDWARD HAMPTON, JAMES WOOD, MR. LAWSON AND OTHERS.—CUNNINGHAM HASTILY RETREATS.—IS PURSUED BY CAPTAINS JOHN McCLURE, JOHN BARRY AND GENERAL PICKENS, AND HE RETREATS TO FLORIDA.—"BLOODY BILL" BATES APPEARS IN THE VICINITY OF GOWEN'S FORT, ACCOMPANIED BY INDIANS AND BAD MEN.—MASSACRE AT THOMSON'S FORT AND MILL'S STATION.—MURDER OF THE MOTLEY FAMILY.—BATES BECOMES A HORSE THIEF.—IS CAPTURED AFTER THE REVOLUTION AND CARRIED TO GREENVILLE.—IS SHOT BY YOUNG MOTLEY.

IN this, the closing chapter of our narrative on the Revolutionary events in upper South Carolina, we present to the reader a general review of the raids of "Bloody Bill" Cunningham and "Bloodv Bill" Bates, which we have gathered from time to time and which occurred during the month of November, 1781.

It is only after years of patient investigation into the scattered pages of history and anxions inquiry into the almost faded traditions of our country, that we are enabled to give as accurate an account as circumstances, at this late day, will allow, of the outrageous and bloodthirsty acts of these wicked and notorious men. In our researches we find nothing to disprove the fact, that the cruel and uncalled-for acts of these men did not meet with the sanction of Royal authority.

Some years ago the writer prepared for the county press (the Spartanburg Herald) a series of articles on Revolutionary events in Spartanburg County, the last of which was in reference to the subject-matter of this chapter. Fortunately, while he cared but little for them at that time, (having scribbled them as a matter of pastime), they were carefully preserved in a scrapbook by a loving daughter * and we have them at hand, for reference to facts which were then collected and recorded, and which might otherwise have been overlooked or forgotten. Much of the information which was then gathered, and which we here reproduce, was received from the lips of some of the oldest citizens of Spartanburg County, nearly or quite all of whom have passed away.

Of all the events that occurred during the Revolutionary War, the remembrance of the bloodv deeds and attrocities of "Bloody Bill" Cunningham have lived longest in tradition. In the outlines of the general history of our country this notorious character and his cruel acts have been overlooked in a large measure. We are indebted for the most part to Howe's "History of the Presbyterian Church of South Carolina, to O'Neal's "Annals of Newberry," and also the local traditions of Spartanburg County, to which we have already referred, for the information we here give.

From "O'Neal's Annals" we learn that Capt. William Cunningham was born not far from Ninety-Six, in the the present County of Abbeville. In early manhood he was promising and influential. At the beginning of the Revolution he enlisted in Capt. John Caldwell's company, which was composed of the most respectable young men

---

*Mrs. C. A. B. Jennings, Union, S. C.

in the region of Saluda, Little River and Mudlick Creek. This company participated in the captures made on the Savannah River, in Ninety-Six District, and also in Williamson's famous expedition against the Cherokees, in 1776, an account of which has already been given in this work. The company disbanded in October of the same year.

In "Curwin's Memoirs" it is stated that William Cunningham was promised the commission of a first lieutenant. Judge O'Neal observes that this could not have been true, as that commission had been filled when the officers of the regiment were appointed. The second lieutenants were appointed by the captains. Judge O'Neal further states that he has always understood when the difficulty occurred, which induced William Cunningham to abandon the service of his country, Captain Caldwell was about promoting him to the rank of lieutenant over his brother William Caldwell. It is further stated in "Curwin's Memoirs," that when William Cunningham recruited, he had stipulated that he was not to be carried to the lower country, and that when in the spring of '76 they were ordered to that section, he only agreed to go on condition that he be allowed to resign as soon as the company reached Charleston; that soon after reaching that city the company was ordered to James' or John's Island; that Cunningham at once tendered his resignation and claimed a fulfillment of the promises that had been made to him; that at last he was prevailed upon to go with his company to the island; that the moment he landed Captain Caldwell put him in irons; and, that he was subsequently tried by a court martial and acquitted, after which he left his company.

Judge O'Neal observes that while this information comes from too pure a source to be wilfully incorrect, yet it is true that if Cunningham had been a lieutenant, his captain, according to army regulations at that time, could not have put him in irons, since the most he could have done, would have been simply to have placed him under arrest and that for a very heinous offence, or to have placed him under the adjutant of the regiment, or else in the guard house or under a guard.

Be it as it may, Capt. William Cunningham deserted the American cause and became an active partisan leader on the British side. His service was, for the most part, directed against Marion. It is said that by his bold and agressive movements, he gained great favor with the British officers.

It is stated that after the battle of Eutaw Springs, Marion's command became very weak and suffered some reverses, in consequence of which the country between the Santee and Edisto Rivers was for a time left open. It is further stated that General Greene, who was at this time encamped on the high hills of the Santee, took immediate steps to close this opening space of country. His army about this time was reinforced by about five hundred men, under the command of Colonels Sevier and Shelby, of King's Mountain fame. These officers with their forces, together with the commands of Colonels Horry and Maham, were ordered to reinforce General Marion and to act in the country between the Santee and Charleston. The execution of this order was, however, too late to prevent Capt. William Cunningham and his command from passing through the opening referred to on his raid to the upper portion of the State, the circumstances of which we relate in this chapter. By the time that Marion had received this valuable recruit to his forces Cunningham had already taken post at Orangeburg, where he was busily strengthening his command from the numerous Loyalists in that vicinity.

It appears that about the time that Capt. William Cunningham had taken post temporarily at Orangeburg, General Sumter was ordered to occupy the same position, to cover the country from the inroads of the Loyalists from Charleston (Cunningham's command), who were making their pillaging excursions to the up-country. His advance forces fell in with Cunningham's Loyalists, from whom they sustained a repulse and some loss. It is stated in Johnson's "Life of Greene," (vol. ii, page 301), that William Cunningham was acting under the orders of *General Cunningham* who remained in the lower country to confront Marion. Whether or not this is true, it is certain that William Cunningham through his emissaries, had already arranged to co-operate with the Cherokee Indians in the bloody work which was ahead of him on the defenseless Whig families in the up-country.

By this concerted action between William Cunningham and the Cherokee Indians, the latter had already commenced their wholesale work of murder and desolation in the District of Ninety-Six, led as they were by unprincipled white men.

The reader will pardon a deviation in turning our attention to the Cherokees, who had again and for the last time arrayed themselves with hatchet and war paint against their white neighbors. It will be remembered that in the treaty which was concluded with these people in 1777, by Gen. Andrew Williamson, a large portion of the present territory of South Carolina was ceded to the State, including the present counties of Greenville, Anderson and Pickens. That portion which was reserved to them comprised for the most part the present County of Oconee.* General Pickens, who had command of all the scattered Whig militia during the latter part of the year 1781, was ordered to watch the Indians in that quarter for fear of an unexpected outbreak.

As soon as General Pickens discovered that the Cherokees had commenced their work of massacre on the white settlements he collected his militia at once. Placing himself at the head of three hundred and ninety-four horsemen, he invaded the Indian country, and after burning thirteen of their towns and villages and killing upwards of forty of them, and wounding and capturing as many more, the poor Indians sued for peace. The work of retaliation

*See map frontispiece, Ramsay's History of South Carolina, vol. i.

was complete. The Cherokees ever afterwards remained a friendly tribe of the great Indian family, being naturally the noblest of the aborigines of our country. In the expedition against them referred to, General Pickens introduced a new mode of warfare. Whenever his men encountered a party of Indians they would rush upon them with drawn swords and soon put them to flight. It is stated that he did not expend three pounds of ammunition, and yet but few Indians escaped after being seen.

But let us again turn our attention to the movements of William Cunningham. We have stated that Sumter's force was too weak to check his progress. It appears that in his efforts to form a junction with the Cherokees in the up-country, he "slipped away as it were," savs Johnson * "Joined by Hezekiah Williams and one Lawrence. enterprising leaders, General Cunningham detached a party of about three hundred well mounted men, to ascend the Saluda under the command of William Cunningham, familiarly known by the epithet "*Murdering Bill Cunningham.*" This movement, it appeared afterwards, was made in concert with the Cherokee Indians, who were once more sacrificed without remorse to the enemy's views; and was connected with a general movement which gave Wayne so much occupation soon after in Georgia."

It is further stated by Johnson that the movements of William Cunningham and his command to the up-country were rapid, lasting only a few weeks; but says this eminent writer, "they literallv left the country through which they passed in tears."

While General Pickens was engaged in the expedition referred to against the Cherokees, William Cunningham was putting in his bloody work in other quarters. Being foiled in his plans to unite with the Indians and fearing lest he might encounter Pickens, who was no very great

*See Johnson's "Life of Greene," vol. ii, page 301.

distance from him and in the same direction in which he was traveling, he changed to a northerly direction, passing through the Counties of Newberry, Laurens and ending his bloody career in the present County of Spartanburg.

It is impossible at this late period to know the extent of his atrocities. It is only here and there that we find recorded the most prominent of his acts of cruelty. The first that we notice is the "massacre at the Turner House," the particulars of which are recorded in Ramsay's History and also in "Johnson's Traditions."*

The unexpected appearance of Cunningham and the consternation which spread rapidly over the country on account of his cruelties, caused small parties here and there to get together and arm in self-defense. One of the parties was commanded by Capt. Sterling Turner, who had succeeded Capt. James Butler to the command of a company that had formed part of Leroy Hammond's regiment. Sterling Turner is represented as being a brave, intelligent and patriotic officer. Hearing that Cunningham and his Tories were in the neighborhood of Cloud's Creek, Captain Turner with twenty-three men, all or nearly all men of family, made an excursion into that neighborhood under General Pickens, who had directed him "to traverse the country between that and the waters of the Edisto and communicate from time to time such movements of the enemy as he might discover, &c."

It is stated in Johnson's Traditions that when William Cunningham made his bloody excursion to the up-country it was his aim to capture Colonel Hammond, who had been stationed at Anderson's Mills, on the Saluda. Missing his prey he appears in the section of Cloud's Creek. It is recorded that his march through that region was characterized by celerity and destruction. Burning houses, bloodstained homesteads indicated the course he

---

*See page 420.

had come, but, says a writer, "gave no advertisement of where he was going.'

Ramsay states* that Cunningham and his associates concealed themselves till they arrived in the back settlements far in the rear of the American army, and there began to plunder, burn and murder. "In an unsuspecting hour of sleep and domestic security," they entered the houses of solitary farmers and sacrificed to their revenge the obnoxious head of the family.

But let us return to the circumstances of the Turner House massacre. During the bloody march of Cunningham through the Cloud Creek section, Captain Turner and his twenty-two men who had volunteered their services, together with old Captain Butler, took refuge in a house, where they were attacked bv Cunningham. Turner and his brave men defended themselves until their ammunition was nearly exhausted. Cunningham's forces amounted to two hundred and fifty. While Turner and his men were making a sturdy defense the Tories set fire to a shed attached to the building. This led to a capitulation on the part of Turner and his men. Johnson says they were promised kind treatment, and were to be sent to the nearest British post and delivered to the commander, to be treated in all respects as prisoners of war. They were to march out with clubbed arms, and to ground them in front of the house. Captains Butler and Turner came out first. As soon as they passed the door of the house Cunningham drew his sword and said: "These fellows had better be paroled, and I will show you what kind of a parole they are to have. Do you follow my example?" With this he made a blow at Butler, but missed him, and Butler, with his clubbed rifle, struck one of them to the ground, and by a blow from another, he fell dead on the man he knocked down. In a few moments every man was thus murdered, except one who was saved, with difficulty, by the intercession of a relative belonging to Cunning-

*See Ramsay's "History of South Carolina," page 257.

ham's command. Thus fell the venerable Captain Butler and his worthy commanding officer, Captain Turner, together with twenty-three of their brave men. Captain Butler had been a very active and useful patriot in the early part of the war, and had resigned in favor of Captain Turner, by reason of infirmities of age. A writer, in referring to the Turner House massacre, states that by the fall of Turner's men twenty-three families were deprived of their husbands and fathers. Colonel S. Hammond, who furnished these particulars, was at the spot the next day. It was a heartrending scene to witness the women burying their dead.

The next victim of Cunningham's raid was his old commander, Major John Caldwell.* Different statements have been made as to the manner in which this noble patriot was killed. But the one as related by Mrs. Gillam, an eye witness, is accepted as correct. Cunningham, at the head of a partv, rode up to the gate of Major Caldwell and hailed him. The Major walked out, and when within a few paces of Cunningham, the latter drew a pistol and shot him dead in the presence of his wife, who fainted as she saw him fall. Major Caldwell was an uncle of John C. Calhoun, and a brother of William Caldwell.†

After the murder of Major Caldwell, which occured in the present County of Newberry, Cunningham and his command proceeded to *Hays' Station*, sometimes called "Edgehill," in the vicinity of Little River Church, in Laurens County. At this place there was a small block-house, inside of which was about twenty-three men, commanded by

*See O'Neal's "Annals of Newberry."

†Grandfather of Dr. John C. Caldwell, Gowensville, S. C. In Jenkins "Life of John Caldwell Calhoun" it is stated that "of the three Caldwells able to bear arms during the Revolutionary struggle, one was murdered by the Tories in his own yard after his house had been set on fire; another fell dead at the battle of Cowpens, being pierced by thirty wounds; and the third was taken prisoner by the enemy and confined for nine months in a loathsome dungeon at St. Augustine.

Colonel Joseph Hays. Cunningham reached this place unexpectedly to Hays' party. Two accounts of this affair are before us. One is that William Caldwell endeavored to reach this station before Cunningham, and inform Hays of his danger, but being compelled to take a circuitons route, Cunningham reached the place first. The house was set on fire by irons heated in a blacksmith shop near by, which were thrown into the roof. Colonel Hays, as the only alternative, surrendered, on condition that he and his men were to be treated as prisoners of war. Cunningham separated from the party some women, youths and children. and Reuben Golden, to whom he was indebted for some past favors. The rest he put to death. Colonel Hays and Captain Daniel Williams were hung on the pole of a fodder stack. Joseph Williams (a boy fourteen years old) cried to his eldest brother, as they were putting him to death: "O! Brother Daniel, what shall I tell mother?" Cunningham turned to him and replied: "You shall tell her nothing, you d——d Rebel suckling," and with his sword hewed him down. These were brothers of Colonel James Williams, the particulars of whose death, while leading his men into action at King's Mountain, we have recorded.

Ramsay* states that the fodder stack upon which Hays and Williams were hung broke. Says this writer: "Thus breaking, they both fell, on which Major William Cunningham cut them into pieces with his sword when, turning upon the others, he continued upon them the operations of his savage barbarity until the powers of nature being exhausted, and his enfeebled limbs refusing to administer any longer to his insatiate fury, he called upon his comrades to complete the dreadful work, by killing whichsoever of the prisoners they pleased. They instantly put to death such of them as they personally disliked. Only two fell in the action, but fourteen were deliberately cut to pieces after their surrender. Their names and

---

*See Ramsay's "History of South Carolina," *Miscellaneous*, page 257.

ranks were as follows: Colonel Joseph Hays, Captain Daniel Williams, Lieutenant Christopher Hardv, Lieutenant John Neil, Clement Hancock, Joseph Williams, Joseph Irby, Sr., Joseph Irby, Jr., John Milven, James Ferris, John Cook, Greaf Irby, Benjamin Goodman and Yancy Saxon."

After the massacre at Hays' Station, we next hear of Cunningham in the southern portion of Union County, at the house of Mr. John Boyce.* Mr. Boyce was a prominent Whig, having participated in the battles of King's Mountain, Cowpens and Eutaw, and his character was well known to Cunningham. He had just returned home to the bosom of his family. While seated at his table to partake of a cup of milk and a piece of bread he was startled by the sound of approaching horses. He sprang to the door and saw Cunningham and his party, including McCombs, a dreaded outlaw, immediately before him. He knew they intended to kill him, and that his only safety was in flight. Throwing his hat in the faces of the horses, which caused them to open right and left, he sprang through the opening, and was soon out of sight in a bodv of wood about seventy yards off. Before he could reach this, however, Cunningham was at his side, and made a blow at him, which struck his uplifted hand, nearly cutting off three of his fingers. Before the blow could be repeated bv Cunningham, he had reached the thick brush and impenetrable woods where it was impossible for cavalry to go, and made good his escape. From his cover he watched the retreat of his foe. Then hurrying to his house to have his fingers bound up, he mounted his horse and hurried to the home of his old commander, Captain Casey Before night, Casey, with a body of fifteen, were in pursuit of Cunningham. They captured a small number of his party, including McCombs, near the mouth of Duncan's Creek, on the Enoree River. They were conveyed to the

*Grandfather of the late Rev. James P. Boyce, D. D., of Southern Baptist Theological Seminary, Louisville, Kentucky.

place where the old Charlestown road crossed the main road to Ninety-Six, where speedy justice was administered to them under a stooping hickory. They were buried in a common grave at the foot of the tree.

Cunningham, continuing his march to the up-country, came within the present borders of Spartanburg County. The first place we notice on record is at the house of Mr. Charles Moore* on Middle Tyger. Here Captain Steadman, a young man of promise, was lying sick. He was killed in bed. Two other young men, knowing what their fate would be if captured, attempted to make their escape by running. They were shot down within a few hundred yards of the house, and were buried at the place where they fell, which was the beginning of the family burial ground of the Moores, Barrys and others, and which is only a short distance west of the old Moore residence. The tradition is that Captain Steadman was engaged to Mr. Moore's daughter.

Miss Rosa Duncan, who departed about forty years ago, and who had lived among the Moore family, stated to Captain Samuel C. Means, who informed the writer, that when the Tories reached the house of Charles Moore, each of them had a green pine top in his hat. One of them, it is stated, stuck his pine top in the ground, which grew to be a large tree, and is still standing to this day.

The next place we notice Cunningham, after leaving the house of Charles Moore, is at the house of Colonel John Wood, who had been a prominent Whig, and who resided on the waters of Lawson's Fork. After the killing of John Wood, his wife married Colonel John Earle, on North Pacolet. Mrs. Earle lived to an extreme old age, and the writer is indebted to Major John Earle Bomar, her grandson, for the particulars of the killing of John Wood, her first husband. We here insert Major Bomar's letter:

*This is the former residence of Capt. S. C. Means. The old building remodeled to some extent is now occupied by Mrs. Catherine Montgomery and family.

SPARTANBURG, S. C., March 18, 1894.

DR. J. B. O. LANDRUM, Guthrie, Oklahoma Ter.:

My Dear Sir:—Your kind letter asking me to give my recollections of the killing of John Wood by the band of Tories led by Capt. Bill Cunningham, the "Bloody Scout," and their infamous raid through upper South Carolina, as told me by my grandmother, has been received, and I take pleasure in complying with your request.

My grandmother died in 1837, at an advanced age, when I was only ten years old, but my remembrance of her is very vivid, and her graphical account of the murder of her husband, has left upon me a lasting impression. The facts of the killing, as she told them to me, are about these:

John Wood was a staunch Whig and a gallant soldier, greatly hated and feared by the Tories. He and my grandmother, whose maiden name was Rebecca Berry, were born and reared in Virginia, and were married when she was quite young. Soon after their marriage they emigrated to upper South Carolina, then a country sparsely settled, and located in what was afterwards Spartanburg District, upon Lawson's Fork of Pacolet River, about five miles north of what is now Spartanburg City, and not far from the spot where Jackson Tuck has for many years resided. From the beginning of the contest with the mother country, he took sides with the colonies, and was a commissioned officer, actively engaged in the service of his country, up to the time of his death. He would not have been found at home by Cunningham and his band when they made their raid but from the fact of his being there then on sick furlough. Nor would he have been found there had their coming been delayed a day or two longer, for he had nearly recovered from his sickness, and was preparing to return to his command He had no intimation of the approach of the Tories until they had completely surrounded his house. When he saw the condition of affairs he went out to confront his enemies, followed by his wife and little son, a lad of only a few summers. He saw at a glance that resistance was useless, and that there was no possible way of escape. Nothing was left therefore for him to do but to offer to surrender and throw himself upon the mercy of his enemy, which he did, saying that he surrendered himself as a prisoner of war. This was met by curses and cries from the Tories, "Shoot him, d——d him, shoot him!"

The intercessions and prayers of his wife to spare him were unheeded, as were the entreaties of his little son, who was cursed as a little rebel, and ordered back into the house. The command was given by Cunningham to shoot him down. A volley was fired into him and he fell a lifeless corpse into the arms of his wife, who caught him as he fell. His death was instantaneous, and she gently laid his body upon the ground.

Before leaving the murderous crew proceeded to pillage the house, taking with them such things of value as they could easily carry. Not far from John Woods', as they proceeded on their murderous and thieving expedition, they met on the road a brother of John, hung him to a tree and left his lifeless body swinging by the roadside. A young woman in the neighborhood who chanced on that fatal day to pay a friendly visit to the Wood family was a witness to this cowardly murder, overheard the Tories say that the next house they intended raiding was the house of a Mr. Ballenger, a neighbor living some miles distant. As soon as she heard this she stole quietly out and running with all her speed along the pathway through the woods, she reached Ballenger's before the Tories and gave the alarm so that he escaped. She was thus the means of saving Ballenger's life, but it came near costing her own. She was recognized by the Tories as being one that they had seen at Wood's house and they knew she must have run ahead of them and given notice of their approach. They cursed her and threatened her life and said that thev would surely kill her if they met her again.

Some years after the killing of John Wood, my grandmother was united in marriage to my grandfather, John Earle. He was also a true patriot. I have often seen and played when a little boy in the home where he lived. It was made of heavy hewn logs—there were no saw mills in those days—and was built as a fort with port holes near the roof. It was situated on what is now the plantation of LaFayette Prince, Esq., a lineal descendant of John Earle, in Polk County, North Carolina, near Earle's Ford, on North Pacolet River. It was located upon a high promontory, overlooking the country in all directions, so that an enemy approaching from any point of the compass could be seen at a long distance; but you are perfectly familiar with this locality and have often seen the place where the old house stood. This is the true story of the cowardly murder of John Wood, as related to me by my grandmother, who was an eye witness, and as I recall it after the lapse of nearlv fifty years.

Yours very truly, JOHN EARLE BOMAR.

The next victim of Cunningham's rage was Colonel Edward Hampton, whose name has already appeared in the pages of this work. Colonel Hampton had been to the settlement on the Congaree, where his family connections lived. He was returning to the house of his father-in-law, Mr. Baylis Earle, on North Pacolet. The Tories perchance got wind of his passing near them and pursued him. Colonel Hampton, after having ridden all night, stopped at a house to breakfast. Very soon after he entered the building, it was surrounded by the Tories.

He snatched his pistols from the table, thinking to defend himself, but it was no use. He fired his pistols in the air. The Tories shot him down* A truer patriot than Edward Hampton never lived. Reference will be made to him again.

Lieutenant-Governor James Wood, (brother of John Wood), resided on Lawson's Fork, near the Choice homestead. Being a staunch Whig and a prominent citizen, he was the special object of Cunningham's hatred and revenge. The accounts and the tradition as to the manner in which he was put to death are conflicting. The letter of Major Bomar states upon the authority of his grandmother that he was hung. Captain Tuck, who lives near by, stated to the writer years ago. that the old historical dogwood on which he was hung is still standing and has been pointed out. and the execution of Colonel Wood on the same has been kept in tradition in that neighborhood bv the generations that have come and gone since that time.

In Howe's history, it is stated that James Wood was shot and that his wife begged on her knees for the life of her husband, which request they denied, and further that she begged that she might see him die. "They took him out of sight and shot him."

Such is the record given in connection with history of Nazareth Church. The particulars as given here of the shooting of James Wood may have been confounded with those of the killing of John Wood.

Some fifty years after the burial of James Wood his nephew, Dr. Robert Young, of Spartanburg, caused his remains to be disinterred and carried to Greenville, S. C., for burial. Nothing was found except the undecayed bones, but these were identified by a fracture of one of the bones of the arm, which in the memory of some of the old inhabitants had happened to Colonel Wood in

*For an account of the killing of Edward Hampton see Howe's History.

his lifetime. These facts were related to the writer by the late Mr. Allen Thomason, who died at an advanced age only a short time ago, and to whom reference has heretofore been made.

Mr. Thomason says that Cunningham killed another man near a sassafras tree, at the Poole old place, now owned by the estate of John B. Archer, deceased. The name he had forgotten, but his father stated the fact to him. Mr. Archer afterwards, so he states to the writer, learning of the circumstances regretted that he had caused the tree to be cut down.

In Howe's history it is stated that John Snoddy was shot at Poole's Iron Works by "Bloody Bill" Cunningham. This may have been the same party referred to by Mr. Thomason as having been killed at the old Poole place.*

Mr. Thomason says that on the same day that the Tories killed James Wood, they visited the house of a Mr. Lawson, who lived where Hilliard Thomas now lives, near Zion Hill Church. It was near sunset when they reached his house. Mr. Lawson with another man was standing in his door. Mr. Lawson was shot down, while the other man made his escape through the back door.

Mr. Thomason says that Cunningham encamped the same night at Wofford's Iron Works, which were set fire to and reduced to ashes by his ruthless hands, which wicked act not only lives in tradition but is also recorded in the pages of history by Ramsay and others.†

But must we go further to recount the villianous acts of "Bloody Bill" Cunningham? It is needless to say that the general uprising of the Whigs in the up-country to arrest his further progress caused him, even before a successful resistance could be organized against him, to

---

*In Johnson's Traditions (page 344) it is stated that John Knox was among the wounded by Cunningham in Spartanburg County.

†See Ramsay's History of South Carolina, appendix, page 307.

retreat hastily to regain the British lines around Charleston. The information of his bloody acts in Spartanburg County and elsewhere, caused the Whigs in the present counties of Union and Chester to arm themselves for resistance. It is stated in "Johnson's Traditions," (page 344), that Capt. John McClure was sent after him. McClure came to the present County of Spartanburg with a company of determined men, but too late to prevent the bloody deeds which we have recorded, but in time to protect the distracted Whig families from extended and continued ravages. "The Tories heard of his coming," says Johnson, "and took to flight." McClure pursued them with his party from Spartanburg through Union towards Ninety-Six. He failed to overtake the main body but captured four of them, who could not keep up with the rest, either from failure of their horses or being overloaded with plunder, or from both causes united, and brought them into Sumter's camp."

It is further stated in "Johnson's Traditions," (page 454), that after the killing of Edward Hampton, Capt. John Barry raised a company of militia on the following day and started in pursuit of the "bloody scout," but did not overtake him. The pursuit was extended through Laurens County.*

It is also recorded in "Johnson's Traditions," (page 505), that Cunningham on his return to the lower country had with him about one hundred and fifty men, and while feeding on the right bank of the Little Saluda, Hammond came upon the opposite bank with about seventy men.

*In an extract from "Orion," vol. iii, page 218, is an amusing account of this pursuit given by Gov. B. F. Perry. While in pursuit of Cunningham, Captain Barry and his party reached the house of an old Tory whose name was Myer Franks. The Whigs were feeling very hungry, not having tasted food for twenty-four hours. The old Tory had a bountiful supply of bacon on hand. The Whigs concluded to help themselves. David Anderson acted as commissary and judged what would be a liberal supply for the company. It is said that Frank's smokehouse required neither lock nor key after the Whigs

The forces being unequal Hammond decided not to attack them, but to follow on and harass the footsteps of his retreating foe until reinforcements could arrive. While the two parties were within easy reach of each other on opposites sides of the river, Capt. Richard Johnson called for volunteers, saying that if thirty would follow him he would make the attack. The required number volunteered, but Colonel Hammond interfered and issued an order forbidding the movement, and to make the order more effectual he placed himself in the way and gave peremptory orders to halt. While there may have been prudential reasons for this order on the part of Hammond, yet Johnson always condemned it. On the following day, General Pickens came up with his men and commanded the pursuit of Cunningham, which was continned as far as Orangeburg. The pursuit, however, was to no purpose, as Cunningham was out of reach.

We have taken the pains to inquire what became of William Cunningham after the Revolution. The writer has been informed by Justice McGowan and Maj. J. K. Vance, of Abbeville County—the section of his nativity—that he never dared to show his face any more among the people with whom he had been associated in early life. A short notice of him is found in "Biographical Sketches of American Loyalists," by Lorenzo Sabine. It is stated here that in two instances he murdered thirty five persons. His property was confiscated in 1782. After peace with the mother country he retreated to Florida. then a part of the Spanish possessions. His name and character is heaped with so much infamy that

---

had left it Several years after the Revolution, when the circuit court was re-established in Ninety-Six District, one of the first cases for trial was *Myer Franks vs. David Anderson—trespassing*. The case was called. A number of witnesses were examined to prove that the bacon had been taken from the plaintiff. After getting through the testimony, His Honor, the presiding judge, ordered the case to be stricken from the docket, leaving Myer Franks to mourn over the fact that "his bacon" was not saved.

it is impossible to know what became of him finally. It is supposed he died in the country which he considered a safe retreat for himself at the time.

Having disposed of Cunningham, let us now turn our attention to examine into the history of another bloodthirsty character, whose name was William Bates, generally known as "Bloody Bill" Bates. His name it is true appears only in a few places in the pages of our written history, but the traditional memory of this bad man has lived longer in the section in which the writer resides, and which was the principal scene of his operations, than any other character who figured during the times which embraced the closing scenes of the Revolution.

In history we find a bare reference to Bates in Draper's "King's Mountain," (page 242), and also in "Johnson's Traditions," (pages 420 and 428). Gov. B. F. Perry wrote a series of articles concerning him for the press at Greenville, which were published some forty or fifty years ago.

The first revelation that the writer received, however, of the cruel acts of "Bloody Bill" Bates was from the lips of old Mr. O'Hara Barton, who lived in the northeastern (dark corner) portion of Greenville County. Mr. Barton passed away a few years ago (1888), at the advanced age of ninety years. Since that time he has interviewed Mr. Henry M. Earle, of Greenville County, now about eighty, and Mr. Theron R. Prince,* of Polk County, North Carolina, now about seventy-five years of age. As we have already intimated, the scene of the operations of "Bloody Bill" Bates was for the most part in the northern portions of the present counties of Spartanburg and Greenville, chiefly in the vicinity of Gowen's Fort. As the raid of Bates occurred about the same time as that of Cunningham, there is every reason to believe that he was sent out as an emis-

---

*Mr. Earle and Mr. Prince have since passed away.

sary by the British to co-operate with Cunningham. In his expedition he was accompanied by a number of Indians as well as unprincipled white men. Like that of Cunningham in other localities, the appearance of Bates was unexpected in the vicinity of Gowen's Fort. The people were scattered and without ammunition, and being so far from the American army under General Greene, with whom they might otherwise communicate, they were left in an unfortunate predicament. According to the neighborhood tradition, which we have gathered up, a portion of the people fled to Earle's Fort, near the present residence of Mr. W. LaFayette Prince, on North Pacolet, while others fled to Thomson's Fort, near the Jackey Dill old place, in Greenville County.

It is stated in "Johnson's Traditions" that "after repeated assaults by the Tories and British, gallantly and successfully repulsed, *Gowen's Fort* was at last surrendered to an overwhelming force of Indians and Tories under Bates. We believe from what we have gathered that this was *Thomson's* instead of Gowen's Fort. It is further stated that the fort was surrendered under a stipulation that the lives of the prisoners should be protected from the savages. But this stipulation for mercy was soon violated. Only one escaped alive of all the inmates of the fort. This was Mrs. Thomson, wife of Abner Thomson, Esq., who having been scalped and supposed to be dead, recovered from her wounds and lived in Greenville County about fifty years after the awful scene.

It is recorded that Bates divided his force while conducting his wicked operations in the vicinity of Gowen's Fort. He dispatched another party against a small fort called "Mill's Station," in North Carolina, and on the way they destroyed several families of the scattered settiers along the frontiers, amongst others that of Mr. Stillman. Not expecting an attack, the little garrison at Mill's Station were scattered in the neighborhood, in consequence of which the fort was captured by the Indians, assisted by their more savage white allies. Although no resistance was made, the unfortunate inhabitants shared the same fate as at other places—an indiscriminate massacre.

Among the cruel barbarities charged against Bates was that he visited the house of old Mr. Motley, on Motlow's Creek, in Spartanburg County, and killed him and several others. He also arrested young Motley, his son, whom he intended to kill. He ordered him to take off his clothes and knee breeches with silver buckles, remarking at the time that he did not want to bloodv them. While Bates was in a stopping position to unbuckle them, knowing that death certainly awaited him, Motley made a sudden spring and knocked down one or two, who encircled him, and pitched down the hill, out-running Bates and his whole party.

It is said that he concealed himself under the bank of a creek near by, while Bates and his party passed over in search of him. Tradition says that he not only saved his life, but that he fairly " won his shirt."

The general uprising of the people from the neighboring settlements caused Bates and his party to put off quickly It has been related to the writer that the party of Indians who accompanied Bates carried off a girl by the name of Pattie Gilley, a sister and a little brother. After these children were stolen, two propositions were made to the girls; one was marriage to one of their number or death. One of the girls accepted, the other refused. Her life was only spared by the generosity of one Indian, who pro posed to give five hats as a ransom for her life.

Among those who pursued Bates and his party was Major Buck Gowen. With a party of resolute men, he overtook the Indians in their camp, beyond the head waters of Tyger River, and killed and captuered some o them, and routed the rest. Unfortunately, he did not capture Bates, but recaptured the Gilley children, whom we have just mentioned. The particulars of this circumstance were related to the writer about ten years ago by Mr. Elias Dill (now deceased), of Greenville County, who was at that time in his eighty-second vear. Mr. Dill stated that his father-in-law, Mr. Howard, was a member of Major Gowen's command, and had often related the story to him. Mr. Dill further stated that at the time Major Gowen's command was approaching the camp of the Indians, the little Gilley boy was breaking sticks to make a fire. He recognized Major Gowen's men, and joyfully ran to meet them. Among the Indians killed in Bates' camp by Gowen's men, was a squaw with a babe in her arms. The little surviving pappoose was committed to the care of Edwin Hannon, a lad of about fifteen years, who belonged to Major Gowen's command, and whose parents were murdered by the Indians in 1776, the circumstances of which we have related elsewhere. It is said that after young Hannon had carried the Indian babe for some distance, he was about to throw it into the Tyger River and drown it. When his friends remonstrated against his proposed cruelty, his reply was that "nits breed lice," and he wanted to get rid of the d——d thing.* Major Buck Gowen was a true patriot, and but for his active exertions in getting together his militia, there is no telling to what extent Bates would have extended his bloody work on the innocent and defenseless people. His place of residence was on the present plantation of Mr. Baker Caldwell, on South Pacolet. Nothing remains to show the old house place except a sunken place in the ground, which was his cellar. The present village of Gowensville, but a short distance from where he resided, was named in honor of him.

But let us go back and inquire what became of Bates after the Revolution. It is said that after peace was declared, he became a noted horse thief. In the neighborhood of Sandy Plains, in Polk County, N. C., and in other sections also, at that time unsettled, there were a number

---

This circumstance was given to the writer some ten years ago, in a Mss. letter, by the venerable Henry M. Earle, of Greenville County, S. C. It was mentioned in connection with a series of articles published at that time.

of wild or branded horses running at large, which were being constantly stolen by the horse thieves of the country, among whom Bates was a conspicuous character. For this cause he was at last arrested and carried to Greenville, and lodged in the little log jail there. Young Motley, who had barely escaped losing his life when captured by Bates several years before, heard of this. He lived near the present village of Gowensville. At the time he received the intelligence of Bates' arrest, he was in the field plowing. Throwing his gearing back on the plow he summoned a few resolute men, and went to Greenville. He demanded of the sheriff the jail keys. His request was complied with, and he and his party took Bates out a short distance and shot him dead. Governor Perry, who first published this circumstance, stated in a letter to the writer some years ago, that Bates was buried in a lot on Main Street in Greenville, which afterwards belonged to the Hoke estate, and which was opposite his former residence in that city.

With the raids of the "Bloody Bills," Cunningham and Bates, the bloodthirsty cruelties of the up-country were over. They comprised the last effort on the part of the British Government to humble into submission the people of South Carolina, and the responsibility of the dark deeds of these bad men should rest as much on that Government as the execution of the poor, unfortunate Hayne.

It is rather remarkable how the cruel outrages of Cunningham and Bates have been kept out of the pages of general Revolutionary history. Perhaps the principal reason for this was that they were perpetrated so far away from military headquarters that they were never reported, as the war had about ended.

It should be borne in mind that the greatest suffering in South Carolina during the great Revolutionary struggle, was shared by the people of the up-country. Ramsay*

*See Ramsay's "History of South Carolina," page 258.

states (1808) that "in the struggle the District of Ninety-Six, has been computed by well-informed persons residing therein to contain within its limits fourteen hundred widows and orphans; made so by war," which was remarkable for the then existing population.

It should be remembered too, that the great suffering, sacrifice and bloodshed in South Carolina during the Revolution ended in Spartanburg County. Let us preserve our memories, our traditions and our history, not only for our own information and pride, but for the benefit of the generations that come after us.

THE END.

ERRATA.

On pages 62, 65 and 75 the name *Richard Paris* appears It should be *Richard Pearis*.

On page 203 the date in headlines of battle and victory of Kings Mountain is inadvertently given *Oct*. 7, 1781. It should be *Oct* 7, 1780.

On page 36 is a foot note with reference to the opening of the Hampto[n] Graves, near Duncans, S. C., by A. M Golden and others. This should ha[ve] been placed at the bottom of page 89, as it is a continuation of subject mat[ter] contained in Professor Morrison's letter.

CPSIA information can be obtained at www.ICGtesting.com
Printed in the USA
LVOW10s0829290915

456151LV00016B/223/P